BIG BOOK

OF

KNOWLEDGE

BIG BOOK
OF
KNOWLEDGE

BARNES
&NOBLE
BOOKS
NEW YORK

Originally published in France by Editions Philippe Auzou
Copyright © 1995 Editions Philippe Auzou

English translation copyright © 1998 by Barnes & Noble, Inc.

This edition published by Barnes & Noble, Inc.,
by arrangement with Editions Philippe Auzou

1998 Barnes & Noble Books

ISBN 0-7607-0706-5

Edited and typeset by Book Creation Services, London

Printed and bound in Spain

99 00 01 02 M 9 8 7 6 5 4 3 2

BP

Contents

Preface

Big Book of Knowledge is a thematic encyclopedia that widens our understanding of the world around us, and its place in the universe, as well as giving a history of the plants, animals, and peoples that live upon it. The question and answer format makes learning fun and challenging.

The volume is divided into chapters covering sixteen subjects. You can open to any page and immediately find fascinating questions and surprising answers. Or you can read chapter by chapter, since each starts with basic questions, then continues in a logical fashion to develop the specifics of the topic.

Big Book of Knowledge is unique in providing *two* answers to every question. The first, a short answer, is perfect for younger children or for a quick "quiz." The second, an encyclopedic mini-article, gives more detailed information about the subject to satisfy older children's curiosity, or for parents to use as a teaching guide.

Hundreds and hundreds of the best quality full-color photographs and drawings have been included to illustrate the entries and help readers understand the text. Each illustration also has a caption that gives additional information on the subject. A comprehensive index allows you to use the book as you would an alphabetical encyclopedia.

Packed with information, accessible in so many ways and on so many levels, *Big Book of Knowledge* will quickly become one of the most popular books in your family library.

Prehistoric Life

What are the most important periods in Earth's history?

By studying the remains of extinct plants and animals left in certain rocks, experts have reconstructed the history of the Earth. They have divided time into great eons and eras. Then they have subdivided them into shorter periods. Each division can be identified by its fossils.

The first many-celled, soft-bodied animals appeared toward the end of a long era known as the Precambrian, which lasted for nearly four billion years. Then the great Primary or Paleozoic Era began. These 345 million years are subdivided into six periods: Cambrian, Ordovician, Silurian, Devonian, Carboniferous, and Permian.

Next came the Secondary or Mesozoic Era, which is divided into three periods: Triassic, Jurassic, and Cretaceous. The Tertiary and Quaternary Periods both form the Cenozoic Era, our most recent age. The Tertiary Period is divided into five epochs, the Paleocene, Eocene, Oligocene, Miocene, and Pliocene. Finally, the Quaternary Period is divided into two epochs, Pleistocene and Holocene, the time we live in now. The Mesozoic Era lasted about 160 million years, and the Cenozoic Era has existed for 65 million years.

Where did life first appear?

Today life covers the whole of the Earth. It exists on all continents. However, the first living creatures did not appear on dry land but in water, in lakes and oceans.

When the Earth first formed, its atmosphere was made up of a poisonous mixture of methane, ammonia, and hydrogen. Solar energy and lightning caused the gases to react with each other, producing amino acids – the "building blocks" of life. These gradually fell into the oceans. Hundreds of millions of years passed before the first proteins or "drops of life" formed in this "primeval soup." So simple organisms appeared in the seas. More complex living organisms

The Apatosaurus (or Brontosaurus) was the biggest of the dinosaurs: it measured 65 feet (20 meters) and weighed 20 tons. Its brain weighed just 18 ounces (500 grams). It was an herbivore that fed on ferns.

then evolved a system of circulation that replicated the original conditions of the sea.

What are the oldest organisms?

Although the Earth is about four and a half billion years old, the first recognizable plants and animals did not appear until about 600 million years ago. Before this, there were only microscopic organisms.

Life appeared in the sea three and a half billion years ago. The first cells were blue-green algae, the ancestor of all plants; invertebrates are the oldest sea and land animals.

The oldest organisms of which traces have been found were tiny, hardly a thousandth of a millimeter long, and lived about three and a half billion years ago. The remains of these one-celled blue-green algae have been found below stretches of shallow water.

How are fossils made?

Sometimes the body of a dead animal will sink into the bottom of a lake. Then slowly, over millions of years, the mud and the bones of the skeleton turn into rock. These remains are known as fossils.

Generally, dead animals are eaten or decompose and disappear. But when an animal falls into the bottom of a lake or sinks into a marsh, mud covers its body and protects it. The flesh rots away while the bones, through a chemical process, turn into rock at the same time as the mud. The buried layer of rock may be exposed by geological movement or erosion, or discovered when a quarry or mine is being dug. In this way not only skeletons, but also traces of trees, leaves, footprints, larvae, eggs, and even fossilized dung have been found.

Did living organisms affect the atmosphere?

The atmosphere that surrounds the Earth is a mixture of gases. One of them, oxygen, allows us to breathe. When the Earth was formed, there was no oxygen, and the air was unbreathable. The first

plants were responsible for putting oxygen into the air.

The lightest gases, hydrogen and helium, which were the most abundant when our planet was formed, were not held by the Earth's gravity, and they escaped into space. The early atmosphere was then made up of methane, ammonia, water vapor, and some remaining hydrogen. Ultraviolet solar rays transformed these gases, producing nitrogen and carbon dioxide. When the first blue-green algae came into being, photosynthesis reactions gradually absorbed the carbon dioxide and produced oxygen, which later allowed animals to breathe.

Can we find blue-green algae today?

Yes, they live in water or damp places. Similar to their distant predecessors, they are extremely hardy; they thrive on warm sea-shores, in sewers, in hot water, or in ice! Unlike plants, which are made up of many cells, blue-green algae have only one cell.

The single-celled blue-green algae do not contain a nucleus. This primitive genetic make-up of a single cell makes them virtually unalterable in the course of time. That is why blue-green algae have hardly changed in the last three billion years. They can form structures made up of layers and are called stromatolites. Modern stromatolites are similar to those found in rocks dating from the Precambrian Era. These same life-forms brought oxygen into the atmosphere – today their offspring live in Australia.

Why did animals appear after plants?

Only plants are capable of using solar energy to grow. Animals cannot do this and must eat plants to live. So animals appeared on Earth after the plants.

The oldest life-forms, such as bacteria, were made of a single cell with no nucleus. These evolved into eukaryotes – single cells with a nucleus that controls reproduction and other functions. The first real animals were made up of several of these cells joined together to form a single organism. Little is known about these first animals. However, in Ediacara in Australia, paleontologists have found fossils of all sorts of jellyfish, worms, and coral more than 500 million years old. Today we can find their descendants in our seas.

What is the oldest true plant known on Earth?

Experts have called the first true land plant *Cooksonia*. The shoots, a fraction of

Stromatolites made by blue-green algae existed when our atmosphere was first made. They absorbed carbon dioxide dissolved in water and produced oxygen. Stromatolites still survive today in Australia.

some ancient families of plants have living descendants. Examples are the club mosses, also called *Lycopodium* or wolf's foot. In addition, there are ferns, horsetails, and seed-bearing plants.

In the Devonian Period of the Paleozoic Era, plants quickly diversified. Plant stems grew increasingly taller, stretching toward the light. Horsetails and ferns became giants of the boggy forests, and their descendants are with us today. On islands in the Indian Ocean, for example, there are ferns as tall as palm trees.

500 million years ago, primitive plants, such as the Boiophyton, *that lived on the edges of shallow seas, had started adapting to drier places.*

an inch in length, grew in damp soil more than 400 million years ago.

Over time, algae were left on banks by the sea, when the water level fell or when a marsh dried up. Evolution preserved the algae that could survive with little water. Lichens and mosses appeared. The oldest traces of vegetation, spores, date from 470 million years ago. Next, short green stalks evolved with tiny tubes inside that allowed water to circulate. Since then, plants have flourished. The most primitive land plant known,

Cooksonia from the Silurian Period, reproduced with a capsule containing spores. Today its descendants have become extinct.

Are there any plants that still exist from the Paleozoic Era?

Most of our existing plants have no direct ancestor from this time. However,

How did the first plants reproduce?

Single-celled algae simply divide into two. The first plants on Earth reproduced by tiny spores, with a complicated life cycle. Ferns, for example, have spores that produce a little shoot which, if it is fertile, will produce a true fern leaf in its turn.

The first club mosses produced spores of different shapes: thick parts protected female cells, smaller parts protected the male cells. Sometimes the large spores remained attached to the plant, which protected them. Gradually this system improved: pollen, which is like little spores, fertilizes female cells on the plant. The seeds produced are found either on cones (these plants are called gymnosperms, or conifers) or in the core of a fruit (these plants are called angiosperms, or flowering plants).

What animals were the most widespread at the start of the Paleozoic Era?

570 million years ago, soft-bodied animals such as worms and jellyfish already existed. At the bottom of the ocean, however, animals with body joints, similar to woodlice, also existed. They have been called trilobites because their bodies were divided into three parts.

During the Cambrian period, animals with hard, chalky shells and carapaces became abundant in the oceans, and the trilobites were the most widespread. They dug into the mud to get food. Beneath their body armor, the smallest of these invertebrates measured hardly ⅛ inch (3 millimeters). In the Burgess Shale in Canada, exceptionally well preserved Cambrian sea fauna has been found, including trilobites and an incredible variety of shell creatures, worms, and sponges.

What were the first giants of the ocean?

The biggest trilobites did not measure more than 30 inches (75 centimeters). But later, real monsters came to haunt the seas. They looked like scorpions with pincers, five pairs of claws, big heads with round eyes, and long tapering tails.

During the Ordovician Period new animals called eurypterids, known more simply as sea scorpions, appeared. The first were no bigger than 4 inches (10 centimeters), but certain types from the Silurian Period were close to 10 feet (3 meters) long. These formidable predators

500 million years ago, trilobites, cephalopods (mollusks), brachiopods (shellfish), and echinoderms filled the warm, shallow waters of the Silurian Period.

dominated the seas in the Paleozoic Era. They are distant relatives of today's scorpions.

What did the first sea urchins look like?

Sea urchins already lived in the sea during the Paleozoic Era, but there were not very many. Certain types had very big spikes that meant they could move around.

Sea urchins, starfish, and sea lilies are all echinoderms. Their distant ancestors appeared in the early part of the Paleozoic Era. Their skeleton is inside their bodies and made up of plates or chalky substances that are fixed and mobile. Their bodies have five parts. Many other types of echinoderms existed at this time, but little is known about them because they did not fossilize well. Certain types of sea lily, or crinoids, of the Paleozoic Era formed underwater "bouquets" that could measure up to 65 feet (20 meters) in height. Each "branch" of the bouquet contained more than two million joints.

Horsetails, club mosses, and ferns dominated the Devonian countryside 400 million years ago. They grew beside marshes and lakes.

Were ammonites the snails of the sea?

We must remember that just because an animal lives in a shell does not mean it is a snail! Snails belong to the phylum Mollusca, which includes octopuses and squid, shellfish like oysters and mussels, as well as creatures like snails. Ammonites, which lived about 200 million years ago, were cephalopods. **Squid are also cephalopods, so they are distant relatives of ammonites. Ammonites grew in shells that looked like a ram's horn.**

Nautiloids were cephalopods that appeared in the Ordovician Period. Their shell was cone-shaped and could grow up to 16 feet (5 meters) long. They gradually disappeared and were replaced in the Mesozoic Era by the round ammonites, the biggest of which could measure 8 feet (2.5 meters) in diameter. Ammonites died out at the same time as the dinosaurs, 65 million years ago. Today, creatures resembling ammonites live in the warm waters of the Pacific and Indian oceans.

What was the vegetation like in the Mesozoic Era?

In the forests 150 million years ago you would have seen the ancestors of conifers (pine, cypress, and yew) and giant ferns. At about this time, the first cycads and ginkgoes appeared, and they are still with us today.

But not a single flower existed.

Toward the end of the Paleozoic Era, the climate grew drier. The giant horsetails, for example *Calamites* which reached 60 feet (18 meters), and club mosses, like wolf's foot which reached up to 100 feet (30 meters) in height, became rarer, but the ferns continued to flourish. In the Jurassic countryside there were many conifers (gymnosperms), including ginkgoes and cycads, in particular Bennettites. The Bennettites disappeared in the Cretaceous Period. It was during the Cretaceous Period that plants with flowers, the angiosperms, came into being.

Where did the first fish come from?

In fossils of animals dating back 500 million years, fragments of fish may be found. However, these early "fish" must have had distant ancestors about which we know nothing.

Fish were the first animals with backbones, the first vertebrates. Their vertebrae or spinal column gave them such an advantage that it was not long before they took over from the invertebrates, which had been the dominant animals since the start of the Paleozoic Era. The most primitive type of fish had a simple, flexible rod, called a notochord, which later evolved into a backbone. However, not many remains of the earliest fish or their ancestors have been discovered – probably because they did not have hard skeletons – so their origins are uncertain.

What did the first fish look like?

They looked nothing like the fish of today. If it had not been for their tapering tails, they might have had trouble swimming. Their

The first fish had no jaws and were covered with bony plates. They existed at the same time as the last trilobites.

heads were covered by large bony plates, and they had only a hole for a mouth. The first fish had no teeth with which to chew their food.

The ostracoderms were the first animals we know of that looked like fish. They appeared at the start of the Ordovician Period and measured less than 20 inches (50 centimeters). They had bony heads but no jaw. The true age of the fish was the Devonian Period. During this time, there were many placoderms (bony-plated fish with jaws), fish with skeletons of cartilage, and fish with bony skeletons.

Are there still fish without jaws?

Yes, but they are rare. They are the lampreys and the hagfish. The lampreys have a mouth like a trumpet, which is covered with hooks that allows them to fasten onto their prey and drain it of blood.

Fish evolve rapidly. At the top right of the picture is an Osteolepis, *a freshwater fish with a bony skeleton. It belongs at the beginning of the long line of evolution that leads to humans.*

Fish that do not have jaws are called agnathans. There were two important groups of agnathans in the Ordovician Period, the ostracoderms and the conodonts. The ostracoderms have all died out, but conodont fish have survived as lampreys and hagfish.

What is the oldest type of fish alive today?

In 1938 some fishermen from the Comoro Islands hooked a fish out of the Indian Ocean that experts thought had been extinct for 65 million years. It was a coelacanth. If experts had thought the fish was extinct, the Comorians had not, because they had been eating it for years!

The coelacanth is a meaty fish; it has plump fins and a large tail in three sections. It lives at a depth of about 1,650 feet (500 meters). It does not have a true spinal column but a tubular cord; its nose is a strange-looking thing. The female coelacanth lays eggs as big as apples. The fossils of the first coelacanth date from the Devonian Period.

Are there fish with lungs?

In order to breathe while living in water, fish have to have gills, not lungs like animals that live in the open air. However, lungfish are fish, and they do have lungs!

During the Devonian and Carboniferous Periods, the lungfish inhabited lakes and streams. But they were not the only fish with lungs at this time. The rhipidistians also had them and used their lungs for breathing in the open air when their water was too dirty or did not have enough oxygen. Lungfish still exist in Africa, South America, and Australia.

How did fish leave the water?

It is thought that some fish with lungs started climbing up onto the banks when the pools of water in which they lived dried up. Other fish are thought to have left the water and ventured onto the shores of lagoons and estuaries.

Three placoderms of the Devonian Period. Their heads and bodies were covered with thick bony plates.

It was thought that lungfish were capable of heaving themselves onto river banks by using their fins and digging into the earth, and for a long time they were believed to be the ancestors of land animals with four legs. However, lungfish never adapted completely to the open air. The true ancestors of the four-legged animal, or tetrapods, are probably the rhipidistians. To prove this ancestry, there have been many studies of the skeletons of rhipidistians, focusing on the spinal column, the head, and the structure of the teeth. But there are still many unanswered questions concerning the early ancestors of the tetrapods and their evolution.

What was the first land animal on four legs?

The *Ichthyostega*. In ancient Greek, which is the language used for naming and describing various species, it means fish skull.

We still do not know in any great detail how certain rhipidistians became land animals. The first amphibian known lived in Greenland 350 million years ago, which at that time did not have its present polar climate. Amphibians live in water and on land. The *Ichthyostega* clearly had feet, the skeleton of a "walker," a solid thorax, and a tail that made it look like a giant salamander. It was about 3 feet (1 meter) long.

Did other animals leave the water?

The vertebrates were not the only animals to colonize the land. The invertebrates, for example insects, centipedes, and spiders, were the first to take to the river banks.

When plants started to grow on dry land, animals were tempted to live in the open air as well. The arthropods, a group that includes crustaceans and insects, gradually began to live on the wet river banks. It is not known when or how the arthropods moved from water to land. Giant dragonflies (with a wing span of 28 inches/ 70 centimeters), cockroaches, and grasshoppers lived in the forests of the Carboniferous Period, along with centipedes, spiders, and scorpions. To breathe, the insects had tubes inside their bodies connected to the outside, which carried oxygen around their bodies.

How were fins changed into feet?

The fins of most fish consist of a sort of soft skin between firm parts. But several types of primitive fish had fins that were fleshy and contained muscles and bone. By stretching themselves out, they formed feet that were capable of supporting their bodies.

When the early tetrapods began to appear 350 million years ago, a rhipidistian with fleshy fins existed,

Stegocephalians were probably the first land tetrapods. Here we can see two Ichthyostega, *amphibians that could grow to 3 feet (1 meter) in length.*

the *Eusthenopteron*. This may have been the ancestor of the tetrapods, and the bones of its fins may have evolved into the feet of amphibians.

What did the first amphibians look like?

Tens of millions of years after the first *Ichthyostega*, some amphibians lost their feet and looked like water snakes and newts. The *Diplocaulus*, which lived 250 million years ago, had a curious triangular-shaped head. This peculiarity made it difficult for the creature to be eaten.

Now that the atmosphere was rich in oxygen, the amphibians diversified and conquered the land. This happened 400 million years ago.

The amphibians did not reach the river banks and stay there like an army of invaders! Their evolution stretches over tens of millions of years. Some of the early species of amphibians spent most of their time in the water; for example, there was a sort of flat giant grub that trailed its gills, and there was another that was shaped like a crocodile. Other early amphibians lived on the dry land, but found their food in the water and laid their eggs there. Today,

amphibians have to spend the early stages of their lives in watery places.

How did the first reptiles come to exist?

Once again, we do not know exactly. There are many different types of reptile, including lizards, tortoises, crocodiles, and snakes. Their dry skin, conical teeth, and distinctive bodies make it easy for their fossils to be identified, but the oldest reptiles and amphibians looked very much like each other.

About 320 million years ago, reptiles started to look different from the early amphibians. Their skin was drier, they had lungs and a

The Sauroctonus *evolved from a group of mammallike reptiles. It was carnivorous and had powerful teeth.*

good breathing system, a skeleton, a skull, and claws, all of which made it easier to adapt to life on land. The first reptiles lived in the forest of the Carboniferous Period. Unfortunately they left few fossils. The *Hylonomus*, despite having certain characteristics of amphibians, is one of the first known reptiles. It was a sort of lizard, about 12 inches (30 centimeters) long.

What advantage did the eggs of the first reptiles have?

One of the main differences between amphibians and reptiles is found in their eggs. A reptile is able to lay its eggs on land, not just in water.

Toward the end of the Paleozoic Era, the reptile's egg became amniotic – the embryo developed within a fluid-filled membrane inside the egg. The fluid cushioned the embryo and provided it with food. On the outside, a hardy, porous shell protected the egg from damage and from drying out. This allowed reptiles to breed on land.

What is a mammalian reptile?

It is not a reptile with breasts or udders, but one that is capable of regulating its body temperature. It is able to breathe while eating and it can support itself on its feet.

The warm, humid climate of the Carboniferous Period was good for reptiles because their body temperature is affected by their environment. However, one particular family, the pelycosaurs, was able to control their body heat. On their backs was a sort of delicate sail covered by long bony spikes that allowed them to trap warmth and circulate it in the bloodstream. This allowed them to cope, for example, with the cold hours of night. The most well-known of the pelycosaurs is the *Dimetrodon*, which was about the size of a calf. The reptiles that were most like mammals were the therapsids. They evolved a body with upright limbs and a skull that contained jaws, teeth, and palate. The *Lystrosaurus* had very strong teeth, resembled a hippopotamus, and lived in Africa and Antarctica 230 million years ago.

How did the first flowering plants evolve?

The ginkgoes and the cycads are the oldest of all trees and have remained unchanged for 200 million years. They developed seeds instead of spores. Then the first conifers, similar to the yew, produced seeds in cones. Finally, other plants evolved that protect their seeds in the middle of their flowers.

Flowers are a complex arrangement of stamens, pistils, and petals, capable of producing fruit. We do not know how or when exactly the first flowers came into being, since leaves and flowers do not fossilize well. To demonstrate that a leaf came from a fruit-bearing plant, we must find a fossil with the leaf and fruit and flower in place.

What is the oldest flowering plant?

The oldest flower found in a fossil dates back 65 million years to the time of the dinosaurs. It came from a sort of palm tree that grew in what is now Colorado.

It is generally thought that the first flowers appeared about

The first seed-bearing plants, such as the cycads, appeared in the Mesozoic Era. They looked like palm trees.

260 million years ago. During the Cretaceous Period, however, flowering plants became incredibly varied and replaced other types of vegetation. The magnolia is, according to some botanists, one of the earliest flowering plants.

What was the Age of Reptiles?

Today, mammals seem to us the most important animals on Earth, perhaps because we, as mammals, dominate the world. Yet even today, there are more

birds, fish, and insects than mammals. For the whole of the Mesozoic Era, reptiles dominated the Earth, and this period is known as the Age of Reptiles.

Reptiles became really important at the start of the Triassic Period. Some species returned to the oceans — the ichthyosaurs, for example, were adapted for a completely marine way of life. Other reptiles took to the air, for example, the pterosaurs. On Earth, the dinosaurs became absolute masters until their extinction at the end of the Cretaceous Period. The age of the reptiles lasted more than 160 million years.

Why did certain reptiles return to the water?

Today, there are some mammals that have returned to the water and adapted perfectly. The most familiar examples are seals, dolphins, and whales. It is thought that some reptiles may also have returned to live in

Some reptiles adapted to living in the sea. This Mixosaurus *grew up to 40 feet (12 meters) in length. It was an ichthyosaur, and one of the best adapted to water. Despite its looks, it is not related to the dolphin.*

the oceans and seas during the Mesozoic Era.

Animals move into a new area if it offers protection, food, more space, or no predators. Reptiles that returned to the water after having mastered life on land probably went for those reasons. Their bodies adapted by becoming fishlike in shape with webbed feet, but they still needed to breathe air.

Why do we speak of the *Sphenodon* as a living fossil?

A "living fossil" is not a fossil that has come to life
or has been reincarnated. It is a plant (for example, ginkgoes or cycads) or an animal (for example, the coelacanth and the *Sphenodon*) that still exists today, but looks very much like its ancestors from millions of years ago.

The *Sphenodon,* or tuatara, looks like a lizard, but is in fact the last representative of a group of reptiles that lived at the beginning of the Mesozoic Era. The *Sphenodon* lives on a few little isolated islands around New Zealand and is known to the Maori as tuatara, the prickly one. The *Sphenodon* appears to have a very slow birth, its egg taking two years to hatch, but the reptile lives for nearly a century. It is a nocturnal animal and lives in a burrow that it often shares with birds.

How did the great sea reptiles live?

The first sea reptiles stayed close to shore and fed in shallow water. Later, others became virtual masters of the seas; they swam and hunted as efficiently as our fish today.

At the start of the Mesozoic Era, there were many different types of primitive sea reptiles, of all different shapes and sizes, and which ate a wide range of seafood. Placodonts ate shellfish; *Tanystropheus* possessed an extremely long neck that it used like a rod for catching fish. After several million years of evolution, pliosaurs and plesiosaurs, with their stocky bodies, paddlelike feet, and jaws full of teeth, lived in deep water, as tuna fish do today. At the end of the Mesozoic Era, turtles and crocodiles kept close to the shore, as did the mosasaurs, terrible carnivorous sea lizards that could grow to more than 33 feet (10 meters) in length.

What were the ancestors of crocodiles and turtles?

The oldest turtle known is the *Proganochelys*. The *Proterosuchus* is the crocodile's ancestor. Both lived 200 million years ago and measured 3 feet (1 meter) in length.

Unlike its descendants, the *Proganochelys* could not retreat beneath its shell. It was a turtle that probably lived partly on the land and partly in the sea, and its head and feet were equipped with pointed spikes.

Although they resembled crocodiles, the phytosaurs of the Triassic Period are not their ancestors, but were their competitors. The *Saltoposuchus*, a little two-legged reptile, had a head that looked like that of a crocodile. However, the most direct ancestor of the crocodile is probably the *Proterosuchus*. This animal had the beginnings of the adaptation that allows crocodiles to open their mouths in the water without drowning.

Were dinosaurs reptiles?

Yes, just as the ancestors of crocodiles, lizards, snakes, and tortoises were. But dinosaurs developed along different lines before they became extinct.

At the end of the Paleozoic Era, a group of reptiles, the thecodontians, appeared, whose teeth were fixed in their jaws. From these developed the crocodiles, the flying reptiles, and two other types of reptiles, which later evolved into giant lizards and dinosaurs. These two groups had different jaws, although their names stem from the location of their hip bones: Saurischia (reptile hips) and Ornithischia (bird hips). One of the most ancient dinosaurs was *Coelophysis* of the Triassic Period. It was a good runner and very agile.

How big were the largest dinosaurs?

Contrary to what most people believe, not all

A fight between a Triceratops *and a* Tyrannosaurus *must have been a really violent sight. The* Tyrannosaurus *was carnivorous and 40 feet (12 meters) tall. The* Triceratops *was the biggest dinosaur with horns.*

The Camptosaurus, *like most dinosaurs, was a peaceful herbivore. It measured more than 8 feet (2½ meters) and spent most of its time eating.*

dinosaurs were huge, but it is true that some were really enormous. The largest weighed tens of tons and were more than 100 feet (30 meters) long.

The sauropods are the most famous saurischian dinosaurs. They had enormous bodies, long necks balanced by massive tails, and heads that were ridiculously small. The size of these animals from the Jurassic Period is calculated from their skeletons and footprints. The *Diplodocus* and the *Apatosaurus* (or *Brontosaurus*) were more than 65 feet (20 meters) long, while the *Brachiosaurus* was 80 feet (25 meters) long. It is thought that another dinosaur existed that was close to 115 feet (35 meters) long, although very little is known about this animal. It would have been able to graze at the height of a six-story building and would have weighed more than a hundred tons.

Why were dinosaurs so big?

The bigger an animal is, the easier it is to keep warm. This meant that the great dinosaurs could survive the cold nights.

To protect them against the cold, birds have feathers and mammals have hair. Reptiles only have their bare skin. The ratio of body surface to volume is much less for a larger animal than for a smaller one. This means that large animals lose less heat, and that heat is lost more slowly. This has nothing to do with body fat, which also provides protection from the cold.

Were all dinosaurs carnivores?

No, the opposite is true. Most were peaceful herbivores. The largest of them were quadrupeds that probably spent most of their time grazing grass and trees to feed their enormous bodies.

To defend themselves against attacks by carnivores, herbivorous dinosaurs developed different techniques, for example, hiding in water and running away, just like today's animals. Some had bodies covered in hard scales, spikes, or horns, which made them very difficult to kill.

Did dinosaurs live next to the water?

Dinosaurs did not live in the water, but certain types, like the huge *Apatosaurus*, spent most of their time next to lakes or in

marshes. **There they were able to hide and cool their bodies in the water.**

For a long time it was thought that the biggest dinosaurs lived in the water but left their heads above the surface in order to breathe through their nostrils, which were on top of their skulls. But their chests, many feet under water, would have been crushed by the pressure of the water. These animals definitely lived on river banks, where they used their long necks like giraffes to forage for food. Their feet were more like those of the elephant than the hippopotamus.

Is it true that certain dinosaurs had several brains?

You might think that such big animals needed two brains! But, like all animals, the dinosaur had only one brain in its thick skull.

The *Stegosaurus* of the Jurassic Period was an herbivore, despite its looks. Its body was protected from attacks by carnivorous dinosaurs by tough scales like armor. This also helped it to keep warm.

Wicked spikes stuck out of its tail. It could not have been very intelligent because its brain was the size of a nut! A swelling of the spinal cord in the pelvis allowed the animal to operate its lower body and tail. This is what some people call its second brain. The ostriches of today possess a similar nervous system.

Did dinosaurs live in herds?

Like the buffalo today, the herbivorous dinosaurs sometimes formed herds. They did this to impress their enemies, especially the deadly *Tyrannosaurus.*

A group of about 20 *Iguanodon*, preserved in mud, has been found in Belgium. This shows that the clumsy sauropods lived in herds, as did the *Hadrosaurs*, dinosaurs with duckbills, and the armored ankylosaurs, dinosaurs with horns.

Is it true some dinosaurs were armor-plated?

In addition to the stegosaurs with their hard scales, there

Brachiosaurs *were giant sauropods that lived in marshes where they could hide in case of danger. These creatures were found all over the world in Jurassic and Cretaceous times.*

was also a group of dinosaurs, the ankylosaurs, that had the equivalent of armor.

The spiky armor of the ankylosaurs allowed them to fend off attacks by large carnivorous dinosaurs. Some also had a ball of bone at the end of their tails that they could use as a weapon. They were big and low on the ground, which made them seem even more massive. Some were over 16 feet (5 meters) long, between 3 and 6 feet (between 1 and 2 meters) broad, and weighed several tons.

The Chasmosaurus *looked a bit like the* Triceratops. *Its enormous collar, studded with teeth, its deadly horns, and its powerful mouth, made it a dangerous animal even though it was an herbivore.*

What were the continents like in the time of the dinosaurs?

The age of the dinosaurs (Mesozoic Era) lasted 160 million years. It was a time of great change: continents separated, the climate changed, and plants and animals were transformed.

In the Triassic Period, a supercontinent, Pangaea, appeared from the ocean. In the east, part of the sea, the Tethys, cut a deep trench.

In the Jurassic Period, the southern area, Gondwanaland, detached itself from the north, Laurasia, while small seas flooded low lands. During the Cretaceous Period, the North Atlantic was formed. Then the South Atlantic appeared while Gondwanaland divided into many parts, making Africa, South America, and Australia. New climates were created by new mountain ranges. These changes account for the distribution of species throughout the world.

What were the dinosaurs with duckbills like?

In the ornithischian group of dinosaurs were the ornithopods, which had various kinds of birdlike feet. Their feet had three claws at the front like birds today.

Some dinosaurs, such as the hadrosaurs, had a snout that was flat like a duck's. Inside this horned structure was a mouth with 2,000 pointed teeth set on several levels – the perfect tool for crushing vegetation and stripping trees. Their skull was often extended by a crest that might have made their cries louder. This cry would have frightened their enemies. Fossils of hadrosaurs have had the stomach contents analyzed and were found to contain pine needles and seeds.

What is the smallest dinosaur known?

No bigger than a rooster and running like an ostrich, upright on its back feet, it was called *Compsognathus*.

In the late Jurassic Period, about 150 million years ago, *Compsognathus*, or "big jaws," hunted lizards and little woodland animals. It was a skillful and fast hunter. Even smaller dinosaur fossils have been found, smaller than a pigeon, but these are of young *Psittacosaurus* and *Mussaurus*.

What was the largest lizard on two legs?

Forty feet (12 meters) long and 16 feet (5 meters) tall, it ran upright on its back feet and took strides of up to 16 feet (5 meters). It was equipped with teeth 6 inches (15 centimeters) long and sharp as daggers. This was the terror of all the dinosaurs, and so was called *Tyrannosaurus*, or lizard tyrant!

All the carnivorous dinosaurs were bipeds. Some were big; others small; some were hunters; others ate dead animals. Eighty million years ago, the *Tyrannosaurus* only ate meat. According to some, it only ate wounded or sick animals. Its front limbs were very short. Its head was enormous with jaws able to rip its prey apart.

What did the horned dinosaurs look like?

Our modern rhinoceros has a horn but is not a dinosaur, and horned dinosaurs are not the ancestors of the rhinoceros! They are both large herbivores that use their horns to defend themselves.

The head of certain herbivorous dinosaurs was spiked with horns. Some had one, two, three, or even more. The *Triceratops* weighed up to 8 tons and was 30 feet (9 meters) long. The *Styracosaurus*

The Compsognathus *was about the size of a chicken and probably lived on insects and berries. It ran swiftly through the foliage on powerful limbs.*

The Pteranodon *was the largest flying reptile of all time. It had a wing span of more than 25 feet (8 meters), a pointed beak, and a crest made of bone.*

Some reptiles learned to fly so they could feed and defend themselves. Others went back to the sea for the same reason.

By learning to fly, reptiles escaped the predators on the land. They built nests in hidden places, in trees and along rocky ledges. While they were in flight, they caught insects or dived into the sea for fish, just as birds do today. However, the first reptiles that took to the sky did not fly very well. Once they had scrambled up a tree by using their claws, they had to jump from branch to branch as a squirrel does today.

had a knifelike collar that extended its skull and protected its neck like a helmet. It had a horn on its nose like that of a rhinoceros, and its mouth was a giant beak like a parrot's.

Have dinosaur eggs been found?

Yes, they are frequently found, but are stone fossils. However, they show up every little detail.

In Mongolia, paleontologists have found the nests of *Protoceratops*. The eggs had been laid in a circle at the bottom of a hole dug in the sand. And the nests of the *Maiasaurus* form a perfect little mound about 6 feet (2 meters) square. These nests have helped us get a better idea of how dinosaurs grew up. The newborn were defenseless, and their parents had to protect them from predatory dinosaurs such as the *Oviraptor*, a great eater of eggs. We know that the hadrosaurs guarded their young fiercely. After hatching, some dinosaurs underwent amazing growth. For example, by the time a dinosaur such as a *Apatosaurus* reached adulthood, it had increased its weight 3,000 times! A whale, in contrast, increases its weight only 50 times.

What did the first flying reptiles look like?

Pterosaur means winged reptile. Pterosaurs were not in fact dinosaurs, but were their cousins. They looked like giant bats

with a wing span of several feet.

Flying reptiles appeared 200 million years ago. Their skeletons were like those of a bird, with hollow light bones. Their heads ended in a long beak, often with teeth, and were extended at the back by a sort of bony crest. This was not a rudder, but a counterbalance for their enormous beaks.

What were the wings of the pterosaurs like?

The wings of the pterosaurs were a fleshy membrane between their legs and arms, which were extended by a fourth, very long, finger. The wings could open out easily, but closing them was difficult.

The first flying reptiles, such as the *Rhamphorhynchus*, were fairly small in size, but those that existed at the end of the Mesozoic Era were much larger. *Pteranodon* reached 25 feet (8 meters), although its body weighed less than 45 pounds (20 kilograms). The *Quetzalcoatlus* had a wing span of 40 feet (12 meters).

Do we know what the ancestors of birds were?

During the Mesozoic Era, insects and flying reptiles were not the only ones who evolved in the air. Strange feathered reptiles also took to the skies. They were the first birds, even though they were pretty clumsy.

In 1861 a fossil from the Jurassic Period was discovered in Bavaria. This changed everything that was known about birds. This fossil was of a feathered animal about the size of a crow. It was called *Archaeopteryx*. It was similar to a pigeon, but with a reptilelike skeleton almost identical to the *Compsognathus*. It had teeth, a long beak, and clawed fingers.

What use were feathers?

For biologists, there is little difference between hair, scales, and feathers. They often have the same basic functions – to protect the body, to provide warmth, to act as a camouflage, or to attract a mate.

Some paleontologists believe that *Archaeopteryx* was descended

The Archaeopteryx, *the first known bird, was about the size of a crow. The mouth, the wings, and the tail show that it was a close relative of the reptiles.*

from earlier feathered dinosaurs. Feathers offer a number of advantages: they fold out easily and increase the surface of the wings, they can be turned, they are very light, and they grow again after an accident. It is also believed that feathers, which in the course of evolution developed from the scales of reptiles (the feet of birds have scales), were first used as protection against heat, before being used for flight.

When did the first sea birds appear?

More than 50 million years after the appearance of the *Archaeopteryx*, birds were perfected. Fossils reveal that they lived at the water's edge. Their beaks contained teeth, and this helped them catch fish.

The birds of the Cretaceous Period are only known through some fragments. The webbed feet of the *Hesperornis* looked like those of a cormorant, and it was made for the sea, even though its small wings, like those of the penguin, prevented it from flying. On banks, the little *Ichthyornis* was an excellent flier like the seagulls of today. At this time there were also types of flamingo. Land birds did exist away from river banks, but they have left few fossils and were probably quite rare.

The Ichthyornis *was a bird even though it possessed teeth. It lived on river banks and was about the size of a pigeon. It could fly well and was an adept fisher.*

What did the ancestors of the ostrich look like?

The African ostrich, the Australian emu, the South American rhea, and the New Zealand kiwi are all walking birds and unable to fly. Their ancestors evolved on the great southern continent at the end of the time of the dinosaurs.

Not much is known about the group of non-flying birds, the Ratitae, that lived on the continent of Gondwanaland in the Cretaceous Period. When the Earth broke up into various areas, these

The dinosaurs became extinct 65 million years ago. A huge meteorite may have struck Earth and changed the climate and was perhaps the cause of extinction.

birds became the species that now exist in the southern continents. They were giant birds that ran through the fields in the Tertiary Period and used nests left empty by the extinct dinosaurs. The *Diatryma* and the *Phororhacos* were also common, but are not related to the Ratitae. They grew to 10 feet (3 meters) tall, and the head of *Phororhacos*, with its huge parrot-like beak, was the size of a horse's.

What happened at the end of the Mesozoic Era?

We do not really know why, but a great many species suddenly disappeared 65 million years ago. This disaster marks the end of the Mesozoic Era and the beginning of the Tertiary Period.

At the end of the Cretaceous Period, ammonites and belemnites disappeared from the oceans. On the continents, most of the large reptiles and dinosaurs became extinct. Only a few lines were spared: crocodiles, turtles, snakes, and lizards. Although the reasons for this mass extinction still remain a mystery, paleontologists have a few theories. Maybe the climate changed too quickly, or an asteroid struck the earth, or there was a devastating volcanic eruption, or the sea levels fell.

What were trees in the forest like in the Tertiary Period?

More than 50 million years ago, when mammals and birds took the place of the giant reptiles, the first flowers appeared. The trees of the forest looked pretty much as they do today.

Fossilized leaves of plane trees and maples, aged about 100 million years, date back to the Cretaceous Period. After another 30 million years, all the great families of today's plants existed. No new types of species have appeared since. Toward the middle of the

When the dinosaurs disappeared, mammals, which were better adapted to the new climate, spread and quickly diversified. Soon they would dominate all the land available.

and possessed a diaphragm in their chest that enabled them to take in more oxygen than their fellow reptiles. The structure of their mouths allowed them to breathe even while they were eating. Reptiles swallowed their food without chewing, but mammals had good teeth, which helped them catch prey and break it into pieces before chewing. Finally, a mammal's brain was more developed than that of any kind of reptile.

Tertiary Period, great grasslands spread into empty spaces not occupied by tropical forest.

size of a mouse. They were so small that finding their remains is a painstaking operation.

When did the first mammals appear?

About 200 million years ago, when dinosaurs first appeared, the mammalian reptiles disappeared – but not before some had evolved into small hairy animals that breastfed their young. They were the first mammals.

The first mammals at the end of the Triassic Period, such as the *Megazostrodon*, were about the

What advantages did mammals have over reptiles?

The hair of mammals gave them an advantage because it protected them from the cold, while small reptiles had only scales or a shell.

In order not to freeze, small mammals were covered with hair, while their body heat was controlled by an internal system. They were very active creatures

How did the first mammals live?

At the time of the great dinosaurs, the first small mammals had spread over most of the continents. However, they were inconspicuous, shy creatures that did not compete with the dinosaurs and probably stayed out of their way.

The most ancient mammals laid their eggs in a similar way to the duckbilled platypus of modern Australia. At night, when the giant reptiles were sleeping, they foraged for their food: worms, insects, grubs, and sometimes eggs or even small reptiles. Some mammals eventually became rodents, while others became ruminants with molar teeth and a system of stomachs. In the Cretaceous Period, for example, after the appearance of flowering plants, some mammals discovered fruits and nuts, which were a source of protein that could replace meat.

Why did mammals take over from reptiles?

After the disappearance of dinosaurs and other reptiles, vast tracts of land opened up and were gradually filled by mammals. All this happened about 60 million years ago.

By the end of the Mesozoic Era, the major groups of mammals already existed. After the disappearance of the giant reptiles, which marks the beginning of the Tertiary Period, the continents were more broken up than at the time of the first dinosaurs. That is why the mammals in different parts of the world are different and have different ancestors, depending on climate, environment, competition, and isolation.

Did all the early mammals leave descendants?

While several families of mammals died out without leaving descendants, others evolved into the three groups of mammals, the monotremes, marsupials, and placentals, that survive today. Humans belong to the placentals.

In the Tertiary Period, the more adaptable mammals with pouches (marsupials) and mammals with placentas (placentals), which share a common ancestry, replaced the early egg-laying mammals (monotremes) of the Mesozoic Era. During the Paleocene Epoch, insectivore, herbivore, and carnivore placentals and marsupials grew larger. Dogs, cats, badgers, and bears are all descended from the same group of carnivorous mammals, called creodonts. However, some mammals did become extinct. *Dinocerase* of the Eocene Epoch, which weighed as much as a ton and whose head was covered with strange bulges, disappeared about 40 million years ago without leaving descendants.

The Andrewsarchus *was a large omnivorous mammal, possibly descended from an insect-eating animal from the end of the Cretaceous Period.*

What is a placental?

The majority of female mammals keep their young in their body long enough for them to be born perfectly formed and able to survive. These mammals are called placentals.

The placenta is attached to the wall of the uterus inside female placentals and feeds the fetus until birth. Newborn placentals are able to survive with breast milk and just a little help from their parents. Other mammals, such as kangaroos and koalas, are marsupials. Their young are born very soon after they are conceived, but they are too delicate to survive and therefore continue growing to a certain stage in a pouch on their mother's stomach.

What is an ungulate?

Ungulates are mammals with toes that end in big nails known as hooves. They are grazing animals that can grow large.

Modern ungulates descend from condylarths and include elephants, horses, and cows. Some ungulates have an odd number of toes, for example the rhinoceros, the tapir, and the horse. They are from the Perissodactyla order. Another group, the artiodactyls, have an even number of toes, for example pigs, deer, reindeer, giraffes, okapi, cattle, and sheep.

What did the ancestors of the horse look like?

The ancestors of the horse are well known because a great number of fossils have been found. The oldest is the *Hyracotherium*.

About 50 million years ago, the little *Hyracotherium* grazed the foliage and the wet forest land. It was about the size of a fox and had four toes on each foot. As the climate and the countryside changed, the descendants of the *Hyracotherium* grew larger. The *Mesohippus* was as big as a dog, and the *Pliohippus* was the size of a man. Over time the number of

The ancestor of the rhinoceros was possibly the Hyracadon. *This extremely agile ungulate was about the size of a pig, but as slim as a horse.*

toes decreased, the feet became extended, and the animal left the forest for wide open spaces. Today horses run on just a single toe. The teeth of modern-day horses also differ from those of their ancestors. They have evolved large molars that allow them to eat grass and foliage with tough stems.

When did the first ruminants appear?

Some mammals began to feed themselves in rather a strange way 40 million years ago. They did not just graze, then chew and swallow their food, but they could bring their food back up and continue to chew it, as cows do today.

When the ancestors of horses and pigs were grazing for food with their heads lowered, they could easily be attacked by carnivores. The ancestors of cows, gazelles, camels, and giraffes all "chewed the cud." Their stomach was arranged so that they could swallow a great deal of food and then bring it up later when they could eat in safety. This was a big advantage, and hoofed grazing animals spread over the land in the Miocene Epoch.

Why are all Australian animals marsupials?

After animals and plants start to live in an area, that area may be split up by the sea or the movement of mountains. This separates groups of animals and plants, and they become isolated from other animals and plants they used to live with. They then begin to evolve differently and have different descendants.

When marsupials were on Earth, they spread throughout the continents in the south. South America, Antarctica, and Australia were one long piece of land separated from Africa. Before the placental mammals had reached Australia, the continent was cut off from the rest of the land by the Indian Ocean. That is why only marsupials are native to this part of the world. Australia and its regions also contain marsupial wolves, bears, moles, and hedgehogs in addition to kangaroos.

Why are there not more marsupials in South America?

Some millions of years ago, the narrow strip of land of Panama appeared and joined the northern and southern territories. Northern mammals took

The Thylacosmilus *was a carnivorous marsupial that lived successfully in South America during the Miocene Epoch. It had long teeth like those of the saber-toothed tiger.*

advantage of this "bridge" and invaded the south. Most of the original animals were not able to defend themselves and were killed.

At the start of the Tertiary Period, the South American continent was isolated from Eurasia and Africa. At this time, South America was inhabited by placental mammals, which were herbivores, and some carnivorous marsupials, such as the fierce saber-toothed *Thylacosmilus*. During this same period, North America was inhabited by extremely hardy placental mammals that had survived earlier competition from animals that came from Eurasia, via the Bering Straits. When the northern animals invaded the south, the tougher northern animals could easily adapt to their new environment. However, the southern animals could not adapt to the increased competition for food or survive against new predators, and their numbers fell. Many southern groups disappeared, but the marsupial opossum has survived.

Where do elephants come from?

Elephants are the largest land animal today. A little more than 50 million years ago, however, their ancestor the *Moeritherium* was hardly bigger than a sheep. This animal, from the swampland of North Africa, had no trunk and no tusks.

The ancestors of the elephant conquered the land throughout the Tertiary Period. One group was the mastodons, which in ancient Greek means "breast teeth." Another group, including the *Platybelodon* of the Miocene Epoch, had lower tusks shaped like a shovel. The last mastodons died out only 8,000 years ago in North America. The true elephant spread all over Europe and Asia tens of millions of years ago. The *Deinotherium*, an elephant with bent-back tusks on the lower jaw, disappeared without leaving any descendants.

Where did the smallest elephant live?

Just 10,000 years ago, there was an elephant in Malta and Sicily, in the Mediterranean, which was no bigger than a pony.

Elephas falconeri was a dwarf elephant that was related to the

The Gomphotherium, *a little mastodon the size of a cow, was one of the elephant's ancestors. It disappeared at the start of the Pleistocene Epoch, 30 million years ago.*

original elephant, but had been separated from it during the Pleistocene Epoch on the little islands of the Mediterranean. There were other dwarf species there, too, including deer and hippopotamus. They probably became so small because they had become isolated and did not need the advantage of size to survive against other animals.

What was the biggest land animal?

It is called the *Indricotherium*. It was 18 feet (5.5 meters) in height and weighed 16 tons, the weight of three big elephants. It had no horn, but is from the same family as the modern rhinoceros.

Indricotherium lived in Central Asia about 30 million years ago, during the Oligocene Epoch. They were herbivores with hooves and a long neck like a giraffe or okapi.

The forefather of the rhinoceros, the Indricotherium, *was the biggest land mammal. It was 26 feet (8 meters) long and 18 feet (5.5 meters) tall.*

How did sea mammals evolve?

Seals, otters, dolphins, and whales, even though they live in the sea, are mammals because they breast-feed their young. Their ancestors, however, were land mammals.

The ancestors of seals are close to those of the otter. The cetaceans, dolphins, and whales are the descendants of a group of herbivores, the condylarths, which existed at the start of the Tertiary Period. 40 million years ago, the *Basilosaurus* was a huge toothed whale about 65 feet (20 meters) in length. Other mammals related to the elephant also went back to the sea. These are now sea-cows, the rare dugong and manatee.

When did the first primates appear?

Primates are mammals with four "hands." Their most distant ancestor was the size of a rat and lived at the time the dinosaurs were disappearing.

Primitive primates appeared at the end of the Cretaceous Period. The oldest known fossils of primates are teeth dating from 70 million years ago. The lemur, loris, and tarsier from Africa and Asia descend from these early

Humans are descended directly from Australopithecus. *It walked upright and roamed the savannas of East Africa.*

What do we know about the first monkeys?

The first monkeys were African, but soon spread to Europe and Asia, where they killed off other less intelligent primates.

About 55 million years ago, the ancestors of the monkey, the prosimians, lived in African forests. However, no fossils have yet been found of an animal to connect the monkey and the prosimians. The oldest fossils of monkeys date back 35 million years. Five million years later, two lines had appeared: monkeys, with four feet like hands, and hominids, with feet and hands shaped like ours.

primates. But none of them have been as successful as the monkeys, our nearest cousins. It is thought that African monkeys made use of natural rafts to reach South America about 35 million years ago, but they never reached Australia.

How did the first primates live?

Modern tarsiers have big, wide-open, round eyes and long fingers capable of grabbing hold of branches.

They live in trees and like to come out at night. This is how their ancestors, and the ancestors of humans, lived.

In the course of evolution, primates developed smaller noses and gained a sense of smell. Their eyes moved closer to the front. This change allowed them to see in three dimensions. This was a great advantage because they could measure distance and jump from branch to branch. Their life in the trees also made them adept with their arms and hands. The first primates lived on fruits and leaves.

When did humans and monkeys become different?

A few fossils of jaws from about 15 million years ago reveal that *Ramapithecus*, a monkey, lived in Africa. According to some, this is our most distant ancestor.

Some say that gibbons started a new line 13 million years ago, then came the orangutan, chimpanzees, and humans. But not all specialists agree! However, we do know that some monkeys of the savanna, such as the *Ramapithecus* of the Miocene Epoch, possessed teeth capable of chewing hard food, as human teeth can. In East Africa were found the remains of two-legged animals that were omnivores and about 5 feet (1.5 meters) tall. They were called *Australopithecus*, primates that lived about five million years ago and are distant relatives of humans.

What did *Australopithecus* look like?

Its body was not as upright as ours and was covered with hair. Its face was like a monkey's. *Australopithecus* was perfectly adapted for life on the African savannas.

The shape of the inside of the skull shows that *Australopithecus* possessed a weak but effective brain. Their foreheads and chins were receding, their mouths prominent, and their brows very pronounced. They could use their hands accurately, and traces of their footprints have been found fossilized in mud from 3½ million years ago. Several types of *Australopithecus* have been found.

When did *Homo habilis* live?

Specialists say *Homo habilis* dates back two million years. They lived at the beginning of the Pleistocene Epoch in eastern Africa in the savannas.

Homo habilis was descended from *Australopithecus*, and is called "man with skillful hands" because their intelligence was more human than animal. Proof of this is found in the stone and bone tools found with *Homo habilis* remains in Tanzania. *Homo habilis* represent the first humans because they walked upright and their body was similar to ours. They were able to make objects and use gestures. They were smaller than today's African pygmies, about 5 feet (1.5 meters) tall, and ate birds, rats, and fish.

Homo erectus *reached Europe about 700,000 years ago. They were more intelligent than the* Australopithecus, *and used simple tools.*

Java man was more evolved than Homo erectus. *Java man was able to make stone tools and used a club as a weapon.*

How far did Homo erectus travel?

Originally from Africa and Eurasia (a vast land mass formed by Asia and Europe), *Homo erectus* spread throughout Africa, Asia, and Europe. By about 800,000 years ago, they had reached the continent of Europe via Asia Minor.

Certain groups of *Homo erectus* arrived from North Africa, through the Straits of Gibraltar, which was narrower at that time. Their knowledge of fire meant they could cope with the colder climates. So about 280,000 years ago, *Homo erectus* conquered regions that were very different from their original savannas. They entered Europe, including England, since the English Channel did not then exist. They continued to evolve, and *Homo sapiens* appeared 250,000 years ago. Having invaded the whole of Europe and Asia, *Homo sapiens* finally reached the American continent about 40,000 years ago. They crossed over the Bering Strait, which was covered with ice at that time. *Homo sapiens* went from North America to the south about 30,000 years ago.

Did *Homo erectus* look like us?

The descendant of *Homo habilis* is *Homo erectus*.

Homo erectus walked upright and had a developed brain. The oldest remains of *Homo erectus* date back 1½ million years, and their bodies were similar to ours. Their upright posture has been confirmed by examining the hip and leg bones, in particular the femurs. From remains found in China, Java, Europe, and Africa, we know that the volume of the brain of "Peking man" was far more than that of the great apes. From this, we conclude that *Homo erectus* was "intelligent" and could speak. Although the skull of *Homo erectus* shows thick eyebrow arches and prominent jaws, their teeth were like ours. It is agreed that *Homo erectus* is the direct predecessor of *Homo sapiens*, the name of humans today. *Homo erectus* made tools out of stone and used them to hunt and carve up animals. They knew how to make fire by rubbing two dry sticks together.

How did mammals adapt to the cold?

The woolly mammoth and the woolly rhinoceros, as their names suggest, easily survived cold temperatures because of their thick coats. Other mammals were less well adapted to the cold and therefore less fortunate.

The larger animals had evolved favorably to new conditions and could cope with the cold. The hair of the mammoth and the wool of the rhinoceros consisted of a dense fur, which made a long-haired coat. Other herbivores grew smaller, which meant less meat for their predators, such as cheetahs and bears, to feed on. By comparing skeletons, we know that the bears of the Ice Age were 20 percent smaller than their predecessors.

What sort of climate did *Homo erectus* find in Europe?

***Homo erectus* found a relatively favorable climate in Europe and that is why they stayed.**

The climate was quite mild 700,000 years ago, and the ice cap only existed in the outer reaches of Greenland. But the climate for the next few thousand years was much more severe. At the time of Neanderthal man and *Homo sapiens*, 80,000 years ago, enormous masses of ice covered the entire north of Europe and America. This ice cap, which appeared during the Quaternary Period, stretched from the North Pole, over the continents, before it disappeared after four major ice ages. These ice ages were separated by warmer periods. The layer of ice affected sea and lake levels and changed the vegetation. Forests became steppes and tundra, and the habitat of animals altered. These climatic changes were so hard and cruel that *Homo erectus was* forced to evolve.

Who was Neanderthal man?

Neanderthal man was not very big, just over 5 feet (about 1.5 meters) tall, but was sturdy. They lived from

Neanderthal man is not our ancestor. They were certainly intelligent and buried their dead, but they disappeared without descendants 40,000 years ago.

The Smilodon neogaeus *was a saber-toothed tiger that lived in South America in the Pleistocene Epoch. It had already disappeared before the first human appeared.*

Did prehistoric humans encounter dinosaurs?

No, because more than 60 million years separates the disappearance of the dinosaurs and the appearance of humans. In fact, the earliest monkeys did not evolve until ten million years after the dinosaurs became extinct.

140,000 to 40,000 years ago in eastern Europe and Africa, in the middle of the Pleistocene Epoch.

Probably descended from a branch of *Homo sapiens* that had become isolated, the Neanderthals are named for the valley of Neander in Germany (*Tal* is German for valley) where their remains were first discovered. They are not strictly our ancestors because they disappeared some time after the appearance of modern humans. Neanderthal man had a flat skull, prominent forehead, and receding chin in a large head with powerful jaws, big nose, and withdrawn cheekbones. Neanderthals are thought to have been quite intelligent. They found ingenious methods of survival during the last ice age. The caves, which they had to fight bears for, protected them from icy winds and enabled them to light fires. They buried their dead with gifts on beds of flowers. They ate the meat from the large animals they hunted. They killed mammoths, woolly rhinoceros, hippopotamus, reindeer, ibex, and antelope. They knew how to skin an animal and use it for clothing. Some of their leather scrapings have been found.

The last dinosaurs died out 65 million years ago at the end of the Cretaceous Period, within the time of the Mesozoic Era, whereas prehistoric humans appeared a million years ago at the start of the Quaternary Period. The great apes also appeared a million years ago, so they did not exist at the same time as the dinosaurs. Only plants and small mammals such as the *Triconodon*, a sort of weasel 24 inches (60 centimeters) long, coexisted with the dinosaurs.

When did modern humans first appear?

Modern humans or *Homo sapiens* suddenly appeared

60,000 years ago. Their remains have been dug up in Europe and Palestine.

We still do not know how or where modern humans evolved. Cro-Magnon man, who had similar characteristics to modern humans, probably came from the Middle East. They shared a common ancestor with Neanderthal man, dating back to the Pleistocene Epoch, but were a different subspecies. Modern humans became the dominant species because they were the most intelligent. This intelligence, together with their hardy bodies, meant they were able to survive the cold and hot climates of the Pleistocene Epoch at the end of the Quaternary Period. Less than 12 million years had elapsed, a relatively short period in the history of time, for the little *Ramapithecus* to evolve into *Homo sapiens*.

Why did so many mammals disappear in the Ice Age?

Many animals found themselves trapped between the advancing ice from northern Europe and the Mediterranean Sea in the south, which they could not cross to reach warmer areas. They could not adapt to survive in the new climate.

With each new ice age (there were four ice ages and three inter-ice ages), animals with no protection against the cold and whose bodies needed to keep warm, died out. The new environment, with its lower temperatures, was hostile, and there was a terrible shortage of food. It was very difficult to adapt to these new, harsh conditions. So the climatic changes in the Pleistocene Epoch accounted for the extinction of many types of mammal.

Did humans know the saber-toothed tiger?

***Australopithecus* probably knew it but the saber-toothed tiger, which died out at the beginning of the Pleistocene Epoch, had already disappeared when *Homo erectus* arrived.**

Primitive humans were still ill-equipped to defend themselves because they had not learned how to use fire to keep predators such as tigers, lions, and bears at bay. The saber-toothed tiger of Europe, the *Machairodus*, had long, sharp

Homo sapiens *knew the cave-dwelling lion. It was the biggest cat that ever existed, and it lived in Europe.*

The Neanderthals disappeared about 35,000 years before our era. Perhaps it was because they were not as skilled in their everyday lives as the new types of humans coming from the southwest of Asia, who arrived as the European climate warmed up between the ice ages. These new humans may have had better hunting techniques, a more aggressive character, or could reproduce quicker. The Neanderthals lived side by side with *Homo sapiens* for thousands of years, sharing the same territory, and survived into the Ice Age. Were they massacred or peacefully colonized? As yet, nobody knows.

Woolly mammoths were larger than today's African elephant. Some of them were more than 15 feet (4.5 meters) tall. Humans were responsible for their extinction about 10,000 years ago. The mammoth was a typical inhabitant of the fauna of the Ice Age.

upper teeth, and it used these to tear its prey apart. Its cousin, the *Smilodon californicus*, lived in the same epoch in North and South America, where it was responsible for the extinction of several types of herbivore. The saber-toothed tiger also hunted large game such as horses, antelopes, and wild boar. This tiger disappeared soon after it had become specifically adapted, which shows that animals dependent for food on precise conditions cannot cope with change.

Why did Neanderthal man disappear?

Neanderthal man was either massacred by our ancestors, *Homo sapiens,* or disappeared by breeding with them. We cannot be sure, and it could have been both.

Where did the biggest mammoths live?

Measuring 16 feet (5 meters) in height up to their shoulders, the largest of the mammoths lived on the grassy steppes of Europe and Asia, to which they were ideally adapted.

The biggest European mammoth, in the time between ice ages in the Pleistocene Epoch, was the *Palaeoloxodon antiquus*. Covered

The cave-dwelling bear was the size of today's grizzly. Although sometimes hunted by humans, it usually died of natural causes. It is the best known of the animals of the Ice Age.

with more hair than any other mammoth, it had tusks that were as long as it was high. Excavations have discovered a pair of tusks 16 feet (5 meters) long. This creature is probably the direct ancestor of the North American mammoth, which lived in the great plains in the southern region of today's United States. The North American mammoth was 13 feet (4 meters) tall, so the little "grandson" of the great mammoths was still bigger than a modern African elephant.

What did the woolly mammoth eat?

The woolly mammoth was an herbivore. It fed on young tree shoots, such as from willows, alders, birches, and conifers. We know what mammoths ate because they have been found frozen solid in ice in Siberia. Their state of preservation was so perfect that the contents of their stomachs could be analyzed.

The wooly mammoth also ate different plants growing in the tundra, a vast region with few plants. The *Mammuthus primigenius* was very widespread in the cold environment that existed at the end of the Pleistocene Epoch. 25,000 skeletons have been found in Siberia. It used its gigantic tusks to shovel away the snow so it could feed on the vegetation underneath. If it was unable to do this, it could survive on reserves of fat in shoulder humps that it built up during the summer months. But to avoid these problems, it often migrated south to warmer regions.

When did the last mammoth die out?

About 10,000 years ago. Even though it had successfully survived the ice ages because of its thick coat, the last mammoth was probably hunted to death by humans in the Stone Age.

It is curious that this animal, which had survived the ice ages, was extinct by the last interglacial period. Other large animals also disappeared from some countries. However, in Madagascar and Australia, even the great, "running" birds managed to survive. This is why it is thought that the mammoth was hunted to extinction by humans using increasingly more advanced weapons.

When did the last woolly rhinoceros live?

The woolly rhinoceros, which existed at the same time as the woolly mammoth, died out 10,000 years ago. It was probably also **a victim of prehistoric humans, who would have prized this source of meat.**

The *Coelodonta antiquitatis* originated in Asia and reached Europe in the middle of the Pleistocene Epoch, during the third ice age. In the cold periods of the Quaternary Period, it was often found with the northern woolly mammoth. Like its companion, the woolly rhinoceros had been fortunate in adapting remarkably well to the new conditions. Its hairy coat certainly kept out the cold. Apart from its coat, it looked pretty much like our modern African rhinoceros, which has two horns (the modern Asian rhinoceros has only one). The woolly rhinoceros walked with its head and neck lowered down to the ground, possibly to help cope with the cold.

How did prehistoric humans kill a mammoth?

They had observed how the mammoth migrated twice a year, south in winter, north in summer. They

Prehistoric humans used to kill a mammoth by luring an isolated animal into a pit and attacking and killing it with rocks and sharpened stakes.

Cro-Magnon man is our closest ancestor. He was a skillful hunter with sophisticated weapons like the bow. Before a hunt Cro-Magnon man practiced magical rites.

Is Cro-Magnon man our direct ancestor?

Cro-Magnon man appeared between 40,000 and 25,000 years ago in Europe. He was solidly built and was 6 feet (1.8 meters) tall. He is our direct ancestor.

Cro-Magnon man originated in eastern Asia and spread throughout the world. They took over from the Neanderthals and lived in caves and rocky sheltered places in Europe. They were artists and drew cave paintings, made bone carvings, and modeled in clay. Cro-Magnon man was intelligent and used flint to make weapons and hunted deer with a bow and arrow. They sewed together animal hides for clothes and shelters. Their large skull, arched forehead, and open face are that of modern humans. They were strong and about 70 inches (170 centimeters) tall. Cro-Magnon man lived during the Stone Age and was followed by descendants that evolved quickly. Only a few thousand years after the Stone Age came the Neolithic Age, the discovery of agriculture, and the Iron Age.

located the path it would take and built a covered ditch. Once an animal had fallen in, there would be no means of escape.

The trapped animal could not escape and was killed with stakes and stones. Its body was a source of meat; its skin made warm clothing; its bones were used for building huts. Prehistoric humans prepared for the hunt by getting together in groups. There was safety in numbers, and these animals, 15 feet (4.5 meters) tall, were a real danger. Once the herd was spotted and scattered, they goaded an isolated animal toward a concealed pit. Another trick the humans used was setting fire to the grass and undergrowth, forcing the prey into the trap.

The Animal Kingdom

What is an animal?

The word animal comes from the Latin _anima_, meaning life or breath. Animals are living organisms, often belonging to a family or herd. They eat food, move about, and take care of themselves. However, the simplest animals can be very much like the simplest plants, and sometimes it may be difficult to distinguish between the two.

The difference between animals and plants is very clear when you look at the more highly developed animals. Plants make their own food. Animals eat plants or hunt down other animals, which of course means they have to be able to move around. Things are not so clear cut when you look at organisms that are made of only one cell. Sometimes it is hard to tell if they are animals or plants. Bacteria, for example, can have characteristics of both animals and plants.

What is a mammal?

The word mammal refers to a class of animals that have a backbone, breathe through their lungs, and feed their young with milk from the mother's breast.

Usually young mammals are born fully formed. The young grow in their mother's womb attached to an organ called the placenta. The placenta allows substances to pass between the mother's blood and the blood of her young. The placenta supplies the young with oxygen and food, and gets rid of any carbon dioxide or waste. But not all mammals are fully formed at birth. Marsupials, such as the kangaroo and koala, develop in a pouch on the outside of their mother's stomach. Some mammals even lay eggs, for example, the duckbilled platypus. These animals are also classed as mammals because once they are born, the young feed on their mother's milk.

Penguins and auks should not be confused. Penguins live in the southern hemisphere and do not fly, whereas the auks, which are shown in the picture, can fly and live in the Arctic.

Do all animals breathe?

All animals breathe, although it may be through different organs. Humans breathe through their lungs, which take in oxygen from the air and give out carbon dioxide. Fish breathe through their gills and take oxygen out of the water.

Tiny animals, like parasites inside other animals, or creatures living deep down in the earth, have other ways of exchanging substances between their body and the air or liquid they live in.

How do animals find their way around?

Animals know where they are by using landmarks and the position of the Sun.

Most animals have to move about a great deal to find their food. Some, like migratory birds, make huge journeys every year, and even then they do not get lost!

Honey-gathering bees sometimes fly up to 4 miles (6 kilometers) from their hives and still find their way back. A lost dog will find its way back to its master. Animals mainly use their senses of sight, hearing, and smell, to find their way. Their landmarks are often familiar smells or sounds. A dog puts its nose to the ground until it picks up its master's scent. But some animals are capable of using even more complex techniques for getting around. They can travel by using the stars or the Earth's magnetic fields. Bees are a good example. They use sunlight to guide them. They are even able to explain to other bees in the hive where the best flowers for honey are. They do this by dancing to show how far away the flowers are and in what direction. The direction is shown by the bee positioning itself in relation to the Sun. The speed of the dance indicates distance. Bees cannot fly at night, but they can fly when it is cloudy because they are sensitive to light waves.

Do all animals sleep?

All animals sleep. Rest is necessary for the nervous system, without which an animal could not live. However, some animals sleep much more than others, and not all animals sleep in the same position. A cow

The dormouse sleeps a lot. No wonder we say "as tired as a dormouse."

To move about, kangaroos do not walk, they jump! There are very few jumping mammals.

or a horse sleeps standing up. A whale sleeps in the water. Some birds even sleep in the air.

The larger an animal's brain, the more its nervous system is developed and the more it needs to sleep. All birds and mammals may sleep, but a sleeping fish is only in a state of rest and is just not as alert as usual. Social or herd animals sleep longer than solitary animals. Domestic animals sleep longer than wild animals.

How do animals move about?

Animals can move in different ways according to their environment: earth, air, or water. Some animals, such as ducks and swans, can swim, walk, and fly. Land animals can walk, crawl, run, or jump.

All these various ways of moving differ greatly from one species to another. There are all sorts of ways of walking, for example. Humans and two-legged creatures put one foot in front of the other. Rabbits have an up-and-down method, using the front legs first, then the back. Horses walk using their front and back legs in opposite motion, alternating the front-right and back-left legs with the front-left and back-right legs. Camels amble, raising both feet on the same side. There are also many different variations in the ways that animals run and jump.

Are there any mammals that do not walk?

Most land mammals walk, but others only move in the water or air.

Whales and bats do not walk. Even some land mammals use other ways of getting around rather than walking. As we all know, kangaroos jump!

Some mammals that live in water are not capable of moving about on the ground. A whale beached on a shore quickly dies. Other sea mammals, including seals and sea lions, are able to move about a bit on dry land.

What is hibernation?

Hibernation is the sleep-like state in which certain animals spend the winter. Some examples are the marmot, squirrel, bat, and snake. They can exist like this for four to six months. Throughout this period, the animal sleeps and does not eat or eats very little; the squirrel wakes up from time to time and eats something.

Hibernation and sleep are not the same. In sleep, only the nervous system relaxes. In hibernation, the whole body slows down, there is no need for digestion, the internal body temperature is low, and the breathing rhythm falls.

A hibernating animal cannot wake up instantly and could die if it did. Hibernation means an animal can save its energy and survive a harsh climate, usually a cold one. When a marmot comes out of hibernation, it has lost one-third of its body weight. Hibernation does not just mean that an animal is "getting through" winter.

Many bears sleep for four to five months during the winter. However, scientists do not agree whether this deep sleep is true hibernation.

Do animals look after each other?

Animals that live in highly organized social structures, such as wolves, monkeys, and dolphins, do look after each other, taking care of their sick and wounded, nurturing young who have lost parents, and bringing food to an animal unable to move.

Animals care for each other in other ways as well. Males defend their group from predators. They may share their food together as a group. However, as soon as food supplies run low, weaker animals will miss out and become prey to predators, and only the strong will survive.

What is mimicry?

Mimicry is a way of disguising yourself to deceive an enemy. An animal pretends to be something it is not, perhaps another living creature, a mineral, or a vegetable. Mimicry allows an animal to escape from its enemies or to hunt other animals.

Mimicry makes use of color and pattern. Chameleons can make themselves the same color as a leaf they are lying on. Some hares have fawn-colored fur in summer and white fur in winter. This allows them to blend in with a leafy summer or snowy winter background. The pattern on the wings of certain butterflies has the appearance of staring eyes, which frightens predators. Mimicry is also about shape. Some insects can make themselves look like a twig so they are not seen. Some grasshoppers and butterflies are shaped like leaves. Mimicry may be concerned with sound as well as appearance. Some insects send out ultrasonic noises that can trick a bat. Finally, mimicry uses smell. One type of insect can make itself smell like an ant so it can survive alongside true ants.

A chameleon is probably the best example of an animal blending in with its background. Its skin changes color to match its environment, making it almost invisible.

What is a

domestic animal?

The word domestic comes from the Latin word *domus*, which means house or home. Domestic animals are those that live either in our houses or next to them. They may be pets, such as cats and dogs, or animals that are kept to provide food, such as sheep, chickens, or cows.

Animals were first domesticated about 15,000 years ago. Dogs were the first to be adopted by humans. They were attracted by the humans' food, and they immediately became useful as both hunters and guard dogs.

Gradually humans realized it was a good idea to keep animals that would provide food such as meat, milk, and eggs. Other animals could provide fur or wool for clothing or, like horses and cattle, help with work that required moving or pulling objects. Today, more and more animals are being domesticated. People now keep as pets hamsters, guinea pigs, birds, fish, and sometimes even snakes, pigs, lizards, or monkeys, and of course cats and dogs.

Are any animals

cannibals?

A cannibal is a human who eats human flesh. Some societies, although they were rare, used to believe that if they ate the flesh of their enemies, they would gain the strength of their enemies. Cannibalism involved complex ceremonies. It was not just a case of people jumping on each other for food. Stories like that come out of silly books and unfounded rumor. When we speak of animals that are cannibals, we mean they eat the flesh of their own kind. In fact, few animals do this. Some carnivorous fish swallow

The praying mantis is a cannibal. The female insect eats the male after they have mated.

smaller fish of their own species. Bears sometimes eat cubs that belong to another family, if the mother is not there to defend them.

There are certain situations in the animal world that would lead an adult of the species to kill off its young. This is likely to happen for example if the offspring are deformed in any way, or if there is not enough food to go around when the population of the group has become too large. This should not be confused with human cannibalism: they are not the same. When animals kill in the ways described, it is to ensure the survival of the species. There is none of the ceremony or symbolic meaning present in human tribal cannibalism.

Are domestic animals weaker than their ancestors?

In general, domestic animals are weaker than their ancestors in the wild. If a domestic animal were to be released into the wild, it would not have much chance of surviving.

There are two reasons for this. Wild animals have to face up to harsh conditions and the weakest do not usually survive. This process is called natural selection. Also, when humans create new breeds of animals, they do not always choose the strongest animals to breed from – an animal is as likely to be chosen for its beauty and obedience as for its strength. So domestic animals become weaker. Cocker spaniels, for example, have very weak eyes and hearing, but are very attractive and friendly.

Can any animal be domesticated?

For an animal to become domesticated, it has to adjust to a smaller living space, live with another species, and obey certain rules. For some animals this is not a problem, but for others it is virtually impossible.

Some animals are much easier to keep in the house than others. Things you can teach a dog to do, a cat will find impossible. Solitary animals, with the exception of cats, are particularly difficult to domesticate. Rabbits are social creatures and easily domesticated, but hares are solitary and have to stay in the wild. They cannot be tamed.

Do animals we know actually communicate with us?

Animals do not have human language and could never learn it. An animal can try to communicate with a human and can understand a few words. This process takes time and effort.

Animals use various ways to communicate. They respond to touch, smell, gesture, and voice. But it is always a matter of signals. When an animal passes information to another animal, the response is in the behavior, not in another message. When we speak to an animal, the words it recognizes are taken as signals. For example, if we suggest a walk to our dog, it will not reply in words but instead looks for its leash or heads for the door.

Are domestic animals more intelligent?

Domestic animals do not live in the same conditions as wild ones. Humans took certain qualities they had and changed their lives. These animals are no longer as capable of adapting as their ancestors were, so on that level, they are less intelligent.

But intelligence may depend to a large extent on the way an animal is raised. Certain conditions may

Faithful to its master, a dog lives a domesticated life. All dogs are descended from wolves. Over the years, the dog has obviously changed a great deal.

develop a creature's intelligence. Chickens raised in cramped conditions so they cannot move around will lay more eggs, but they do not have to look for their own food. Consequently, they will not develop any intelligence. However, there are complex learning situations between humans and animals.

What is the best way to live with a domestic animal?

To live happily with any animal, we have to know and respect its needs, and recognize what the animal can and cannot be expected to do or achieve at different stages of its life. For example, an adult dog is a clean animal that will not normally use the house as a toilet. A puppy, however, does not have the same self control. Even an adult dog cannot control itself at all times. If the dog is not allowed outside regularly, it, too, may be forced to use the house as a toilet.

Cats are often very playful. The domestic cat probably came from ancient Egypt, where it was worshipped and mummified at death.

Humans do not always know and understand their animals well enough, which can lead to problems. You can teach a dog to use the gutter for its toilet, but you cannot prevent a male dog from cocking his leg. That is the way he instinctively marks his territory and indicates to other dogs that he has passed that way. It is unwise to own a big dog if you cannot take it for regular walks. An unexercised animal will quickly become restless, frustrated, and unhappy. Then it may use up its energy by becoming destructive and aggressive. There is no point in buying a dog if you have decided to stay up at night and sleep during the day! A dog needs to be out during the day in order to sleep at night.

How long do animals live?

Animals have different life spans. Some insects only live a day or two. In general, dogs live about 12 or 13 years. The elephant may live to be 60 years old, while a giant tortoise can live for 200 years.

There is a difference between the average age of an animal, the time it takes to die naturally, and the age reached by some individuals of a species. Long life varies depending on the conditions the animals live under. Domestic animals, which enjoy protection, usually live longer than their wild relations.

Can animals recognize poisonous plants?

Nobody knows how animals recognize a poisonous plant when they come across one, but they do because they do not get poisoned.

Plants that are poisonous to one sort of animal can be harmless to others. Koala bears live entirely off eucalyptus leaves. The oil from these leaves would be poisonous to other sorts of animals.

Is the wolfhound descended from the wolf?

The ancestors of dogs are either jackals or wolves. Sometimes a new breed appeared when a type of dog was crossed with a wolf. This is what happened with the wolfhound.

German and Belgian sheepdogs were crossed with wolves from the wild in the 17th and 18th centuries. This is why German shepherds look so much like wolves and their character is so temperamental. Some shepherds are difficult to train, others become difficult as they get older. However, when they are well trained they make excellent guard dogs and are used by the police. Wolves have been hunted in every country throughout history. They were killed by traps, weapons, and even poison.

There are no dogs living in the wild. German shepherds come from a cross between a dog and a wolf, which took place about two centuries ago. This explains why this particular dog looks so much like a wolf.

The last European wolf was killed 50 years ago.

Medieval farmers waged war on them and, in England in the 16th century, even burned down forests to get rid of wolves. These days, however, the wolf is a protected species. The gray wolf was reintroduced into Yellowstone National Park in the early 1990s. This program has been very successful. Today many wolves are thriving in this protected area.

What is a feline?

The word feline comes from the Latin word for cat. Therefore, a feline is an animal that looks like a cat. The cat belongs to the Felidae family, which is a group of carnivorous mammals. Cats, tigers, and panthers are all part of the same family.

All felids are excellent hunters. They are fast and muscular. Some felids have very long canine teeth with which they can tear their prey to pieces. Apart from the cheetah, all felids have retractable claws. Domestic cats are not descended from wild European cats, but come from Egypt. The Egyptians probably imported them from India 8,000 years ago.

What sort of hunters are lions?

Although some cats hunt just for the pleasure of killing, lions are not like this. They only kill for food or to protect their cubs. They are powerful predators and rightly known as "kings of the jungle."

A lion is an incredibly powerful animal. It is capable of killing a buffalo two or three times its own size. It can tear a giant python in two and will even attack adult hippopotamuses and crocodiles. It can carry prey bigger than itself over quite a distance. The lion is a subtle master of the hunt. Its fawn coat blends in with its background. It approaches its victim downwind so its scent cannot be detected. It is patient and prepared to wait for the best moment to attack its prey. Lions often hunt in groups. The lioness is a better hunter than the male. She will often go to hunt alone while the male looks after their territory; the lion will help the lioness if she needs it.

What is the biggest cat today?

The biggest type of cat alive today is the Siberian tiger, which weighs 660 pounds (300 kilograms).

The tiger is a majestic and solitary animal. It needs a lot of space. Most tigers come from India, Sumatra, China, and Siberia. This magnificent animal is dwindling in numbers.

The size of cats varies enormously. There are big cats, and there are very small ones. Among the smallest alive today are the Marguerite cat, which lives in the Sahara Desert, and the black-footed cat from South Africa. Cats of both these species do not weigh more than 2 pounds (1 kilogram) each.

Do white tigers

really exist?

No, there are no tigers that are completely white.

However, the Siberian tiger has thicker and whiter fur than that of the Bengal tiger.

Tigers live in the forest or savanna and survive equally well high up or on lowlands. They need a lot of territory in which to roam, something like 19 square miles (50 square kilometers), and do not take well to captivity. They are solitary by nature. The tiger is feared and has a reputation for being a man-eater. Their number has been severely reduced by hunters, and these days the tiger is a protected species.

Is the cheetah

a felid?

Yes, the cheetah does belong to the cat family, but it is different from the other big cats in one way: it does not have retractable claws.

The cheetah is a runner. The fastest animal on land, it is capable of going more than 60 miles an hour (100 kilometers an hour) when running short distances to take a prey by surprise. But it soon runs out of breath and will not chase its prey over long distances. Cheetahs have sometimes been trained by humans to hunt. This used to be the case in India, where cheetahs were raised to catch antelope. Other animals, though not as fast as cheetahs, can run longer distances.

Why do

cats purr?

Generally speaking, when a cat purrs it is because it is happy and contented. Perhaps it has eaten well, feels warm, and is enjoying being stroked.

There are times, however, when the purring means something quite different. It may purr to express how unhappy it is on the vet's table, for example. But it is not just the domestic cat that purrs, the big cats do it, too. Panthers and cheetahs purr, but it is not a good idea to put your hand into the cage to find out if they like being stroked! But not all the cat family purr. Tigers definitely do not.

What is the difference between a panther and a leopard?

The leopard and the panther are really the same species of animal but are known by these different names in different countries. Panthers are called leopards in Asia and Africa.

Panthers or leopards always have spots, but their coat can be fawn or black so the spots do not always show. Leopards can live in a wide range of habitats, including mountains, forests, and deserts. They are superb hunters. They are excellent climbers and will climb up vertical trees to drop down on their prey. Mothers usually have six cubs, and the young are born with their eyes closed, like ordinary domestic cats. Their eyes open after about a week.

Where do jaguars live?

Jaguars live on the plains and in the semitropical forests of Central and South America. They are the biggest cats found in the Americas.

Jaguars look like panthers, but they are less thickset and have a slighter build. Their spots spread across their bodies horizontally. They are nimble animals and capable of hunting birds and monkeys in the trees. They often hunt at night because they have good eyesight. They attack mammals much larger than themselves and have been known to eat humans.

What is the savanna?

Savanna is the name for the grasslands in tropical regions. They occur in the parts of the world that have rainy and dry seasons. The best-known savannas are in Africa.

The panther or leopard always has spots, but they are not always visible. This is the case for the black panther, a rare and beautiful animal.

Large numbers of animals, especially birds, live in the savanna.

They include insects that feed off herbivores, as well as many other parasites. There are also vultures that eat the bodies of dead animals. Some animals living in the savanna stick together in herds so they can defend themselves. Examples are gnus, antelopes, and zebras. There are also serious hunters in the savanna, such as the lion, leopard, and hyena.

What is a primate?

Primates are mammals. They typically have hands with five fingers capable of grasping objects and good eyesight. All primates have four types of teeth: incisors for cutting, canines for tearing and piercing, and premolars and molars for crushing and grinding. The young of primates are born fully formed. There are two large groups of primates. One group, which includes the lemur, has extended muzzles; the other is made up of monkeys, apes, and humans.

There are many different species of monkey. Some live in South and Central America, others in Asia and Africa. American monkeys live mainly in trees; Asian and African monkeys live mainly on the ground.

How do monkeys defend themselves?

Monkeys face different sorts of danger depending on how they live. Monkeys that live on the ground and in places where there is little ground cover have to defend themselves against predators like the lion, panther, and jackal. Monkeys that live in trees are threatened by birds of prey.

The baboon scares off its enemies by showing its mighty jaws. The baboon is a very dangerous animal.

Monkeys live in an organized society and use this to defend themselves. Lookouts will sound the alarm and warn the whole group of possible danger. The adult males are strongest and will go to the help of females and their young. Tree monkeys give a different type of warning cry depending on whether they are threatened by snakes or birds of prey, telling the group if danger is approaching from the air or the ground. Usually monkeys avoid actually fighting with an enemy and try to frighten it by standing upright and screeching, their hair on end. There are not many monkeys that are really able to fight off a predator. Baboons and macaques, however, have powerful jaws and can be very aggressive.

Are humans descended from monkeys?

Yes, we are. Humans are descended from monkeys. Humans, gorillas, and chimpanzees share a common ancestry, going back six to ten million years. The modern human is therefore a cousin of the great apes.

Anthropologists, people who study humans and our culture, have put forward various reasons to explain why primitive monkeys became humans. Their reasons are largely based on climate and the geography of Africa over several thousands of years. Monkeys developed in the forests where it was easy for them to fend for themselves and where there was plenty of food. On the other hand, humans developed in more difficult areas. But conditions change all the time, and the survival of humans and the development of human intelligence must have depended on finding the most favorable conditions. This is where many theories conflict.

What is a lemur?

Lemurs are primates. They are sometimes called monkeys, but although in some ways lemurs resemble monkeys, they belong to a different family. Lemurs have long muzzles, big eyes, and are covered with soft hair that is almost woolly.

Lemurs like to go out at night, and they are well adapted for this with their luminous eyes. There was a time when they were widespread throughout the world, but nowadays they can only be found in Madagascar, equatorial Africa, and Malaysia. They are usually quite small. Some species are only the size of mice. They live in trees. In Asia, certain species are called "flying lemurs." They do not actually fly, but swing from tree to tree.

With their long muzzles, soft fur, and staring eyes, lemurs belong to the order of primates. They are natural acrobats.

Are gorillas dangerous?

Gorillas are the largest primates alive today. An adult gorilla may be 6 feet (1.8 meters) tall and weigh as much as 450 pounds (200 kilograms). Although they look fierce, gorillas are not dangerous. They are vegetarians and live on bamboo shoots, wild celery, fruits, and buds. They only become violent if forced to defend themselves.

Gorillas live in East African countries, which have a humid climate and where vegetation is plentiful. They live in tribes made up of several families. Couples, once established, are faithful to each other until death. The female gorilla is a tender, loving mother. They are shy animals and stay away from humans. Sadly, even though they are a protected animal today, their numbers are falling. This is due to hunters and poachers.

What is the most intelligent ape?

The most intelligent ape is the chimpanzee. This is the animal that most resembles humans. Chimpanzees can make at least 20 different sounds, and they use these to communicate with each other. When brought up by humans, they are capable of understanding a large number of human words.

Chimpanzees have good visual memories. They understand how to make and use primitive tools. They live in trees in family groups, and eat fruit, leaves, insects, bird's eggs, and fish.

Male chimpanzees measure up to 5½ feet (1.7 meters) and weigh about 150 pounds (70 kilograms). The female looks after her young for two years. The young chimpanzee will not become an adult until it is seven or eight years old. Chimpanzees may live for about 40 years.

What is the monkey with the blue muzzle called?

The monkey with the blue muzzle is called a mandrill.

The mandrill is a baboon that lives in West Africa. Its impressive muzzle is bright blue and very long. Its body is covered with dark brown hair. Its buttocks are two bright red hard swellings. Mandrills have front and back limbs that are about the same size so the animal moves around on all four feet. The mandrill lives in groups made up

The mandrill, with its long blue muzzle, is a strange-looking baboon. In general, it will run away from humans, but it can be very aggressive.

An orangutan with its young. This species may be seen in the forests of Malaysia, but as more and more trees are cut down, the animal finds itself increasingly homeless and under threat.

If the forest disappears, so does the animal, since it has nowhere to live.

These days, the orangutan is found only in the forests of Sumatra and Borneo. In previous times, it occupied the whole of Southeast Asia. Orangutans live in trees, where they build nests from branches. Often these nests will be 65 feet (20 meters) off the ground. Orangutans live on berries and shoots. They move around on four feet on the ground. In trees they swing swiftly from branch to branch. Male adults generally live alone while the females raise their young in little groups. If an orangutan is threatened, it becomes a dangerous opponent.

What are the smallest monkeys in the world?

The smallest monkeys in the world are the marmosets.

The smallest of all is the pygmy marmoset, which lives in the Amazon basin near the equator, and is hardly bigger than a mouse. Another variety of marmoset,

of approximately 30 individuals. They usually prefer a humid climate. Mandrills will run away from people and always avoid developed areas. However, if they are attacked or threatened, mandrills will defend themselves fiercely. The mandrill can be heard from long distances away because of its extraordinary piercing cry.

Why are there so few orangutans?

The word orangutan means "man of the woods" in the Malaysian language. They are not the closest animals to humans and are only able to live in the forest.

found in Brazilian forests, measures about 8 inches (20 centimeters).

Which monkeys have tails?

Most monkeys from the South American continent have a tail that can be used for gripping things. The monkeys that come from Asia and Africa, however, have no tail or a tail that is not used. Humans and apes, which are close relatives of monkeys, have no tail at all.

Monkeys from Central and South America live almost entirely in trees. They use their tail to hang from branches. Asian and African monkeys live on the ground. This difference is due to the break-up of continental land masses. The ancestors of the monkey were cut off by the Atlantic Ocean 150 million years ago and so evolved differently.

Do wild horses still exist?

There is just one race of horses living in the wild

It is not entirely clear why zebras have stripes. However, each zebra's pattern of stripes is unique to that animal, so it may be that the stripes help zebras identify each other.

today. They are small horses found in central Asia and called Przewalski's horse. A few may still be seen in Mongolia, but this rare breed of horse is disappearing fast.

This little horse is so shy that if it met a human on the steppes of Mongolia, it would run a mile and not return to the same spot for a year. Horses like these can only exist in the wild, and they do not breed well in captivity.

However, there are many other animals that look like horses and that live in the wild. For example, there are two types of wild donkey in Asia and Africa. Perhaps best known of all are the zebras, which roam the savannas of Africa. Finally, the African and Asian rhinoceros and the Asian and South American tapir may not look like horses, but they do belong to the same family. They all continue to live in the wild.

Why do zebras have stripes?

It is not fully understood why zebras have stripes. They may be for camouflage or to dazzle a predator. Other suggestions are that the stripes help zebras recognize one another, or that they help regulate body temperature. One

theory suggests that they may even serve to repel flies.

There are three species of zebra: the plains zebra, the mountain zebra, and the Brevy's zebra. All three species have black and white stripes and inhabit the grasslands of Africa. Many striped animals, such as tigers, appear to blend into their background when they are in their natural habitat. However, zebras live on the open plains where their stripes have no value as camouflage. The benefit of stripes remains a mystery.

Why does a giraffe have such a long neck?

This is the tallest animal in the world. A giraffe's head can tower 20 feet (6 meters) above ground level. It may look odd, but the animal's height serves it well in two ways. First, it can eat leaves from trees that other animals could never hope to reach. Second, being so tall means it can see for miles around. If a lion, one of its worst enemies, is in the area, the giraffe has a very good chance of spotting it and making an early getaway.

The giraffe's height has its disadvantages, too. This animal has a terrible time going to bed! It is difficult for it to lie down and even more difficult for it to stand up. This is the time when it is most vulnerable to its enemies. Much of the time, the giraffe will sleep standing up: a lion will hesitate to attack a standing giraffe as its kick is so powerful it could break the lion's jaw. Giraffes are well-organized, sociable creatures. They live in herds, and the females take turns looking after the young.

The gazelle is noted for its graceful movements and soft eyes. It lives in herds in equatorial Africa and is a prey of lions.

Where does the gazelle live?

Gazelles belong to the antelope family. They can be found in equatorial and tropical Africa, from the Congo to Zimbabwe.

Gazelles and other types of antelope live in herds. Their only method of escaping a lion is to run away. They are fast runners and very sensitive to scent and sound. They scatter at the slightest hint of a predator in the area. Baby lions learn to hunt the antelope from a very early age. Antelopes, on the other hand, learn how to run as fast as possible and not to leave the herd if they are to have a chance of survival.

What is the difference between a reindeer and a caribou?

They are the same animal, but they have a different name depending on which country they come from. Caribou live in the North

One hump for the dromedary . . .   *. . . but two for the camel.*

That is the difference between these two animals, well known for their ability to keep going when the going is tough.

What is the difference between a camel and a dromedary?

A camel has two humps and lives in Asia; a dromedary has only one hump and lives in Africa. However, a dromedary is often called a one-humped camel.

Camels are found throughout central Asia. They have thick long hair and can survive in very cold climates. The dromedary is used in Arab countries as a beast of burden. People often refer to it as a "ship of the desert." Unlike the camel, the dromedary cannot stand the cold, but it has no problem with the heat and dryness of a desert. Its single hump contains reserve layers of fat that its body absorbs when food is scarce. The dromedary is able to cope with intense heat because it has the ability to raise or lower its body temperature. It can go long distances without water. Its feet are high and arched, allowing it to move easily through the sands of the desert. It can even deal with sandstorms by closing up its nasal passages.

American tundra (treeless regions), while reindeer live in similar terrain in Europe and Asia. Some are wild but others are partly tame.

The caribou is a very powerful animal and can weigh more than 310 pounds (140 kilograms). Males and females have antlers. They also have broad hooves, which means they can run very fast in snow. The animal cannot really be tamed, but Laplanders in the icy north often look after large herds of reindeer. They are raised for their skins, their meat, and to pull sleds.

Where are elks found?

Elks or moose are very big deer. They are found wild in the northern United States, in Canada, and in northern Europe.

Deer like wooded areas. They mate in autumn and the young, known as fawns, are born in spring. Then they are looked after by their mother throughout the summer. Deer lose their antlers every year, but the antlers grow again in the spring. This is called "shedding." Certain types of deer have huge antlers. The record is held by a deer that was killed in Hungary. This animal had antlers that measured 49½ inches (126 centimeters) long and weighed 32 pounds (14.5 kilograms). It also had 11 "branches" of antlers on either side of its head – quite a heavy load! Deer have lived in Europe and North America for centuries, and they have always been hunted by humans.

Why do llamas spit?

Llamas are said to spit when they are angry. They are moody animals and often bad-tempered.

Llamas have reddish-brown and white coats. They have big ears and look like little camels without a hump. They live in South America and have been raised there for more than 4,000 years by the Indian population. Llamas are used as beasts of burden and are quite capable of carrying heavy loads for up to 20 miles (30 kilometers) a day. They are also kept for meat, milk, and their wool.

Is it true that bison were almost extinct?

There used to be huge herds of bison in North America, but they were hunted almost to the point of extinction.

In the past, there were probably something like 50 million bison in North America. One of the first explorers records having seen a herd that stretched for 28 miles (45 kilometers), but by 1889 only 540 animals existed: pioneers slaughtered them; companies building railroads shot them because they damaged telegraph poles and got in the way of trains; farmers saw them as a danger to their fences and land. Those days have gone now. Today, the bison is a protected animal, and several thousand live in national parks. President Teddy Roosevelt was largely responsible for starting an association to save the bison in 1905.

Do wild cattle still exist?

Yes, they do. These days they can be found in Asia. There are several types of wild cattle, for example, the gaur, the gayal, and the banteng.

Wild cattle look very much like the domestic breeds except for a

For many years the bison was slaughtered. Today it is protected by law and lives on special reservations. A hundred years ago, just 540 animals remained; now there are 300,000.

lump of hairy flesh around their throats. European cattle are not descended from wild Asiatic cattle, but from a prehistoric animal that lived in Eurasia and North Africa. We know this from drawings found in caves. This particular animal, however, had died out by the end of the 16th century.

Elephants smell and pick up things with their trunks. The picture shows an African elephant, with its enormous ears.

What does an elephant use its trunk for?

An elephant's trunk has many uses. It is a nose, a hand, and an arm all in one. It uses it for smelling, feeling, and picking up things. The trunk is strong enough to uproot a tree and sensitive and gentle enough to pick up a nut.

An elephant uses its trunk to defend and feed itself. It picks up food and brings it to its mouth. It can also drink through it or hose its body down with water, which elephants love doing. Female elephants hug their young with their trunks, and in the mating season, male elephants will often put their trunk around their partners in a gesture of affection.

How many types of elephant are there?

There are two different types of elephants. One lives in Africa and the other in Asia.

Elephants are the biggest land animals alive today. The male African elephant is a mighty animal, 12 feet (4 meters) tall, 25 feet (8 meters) long, and weighing up to 7 tons. At birth the calf already weighs 200 pounds (90 kilograms). African elephants have a great bulging forehead and enormous ears. Males and females have tusks that they use against enemies but also to dig for water. Tusks are like canine teeth that have grown out of all proportion.

Tusks appear when the elephant is about two years old, and they are permanent, growing throughout the elephant's life. In the later stages of the elephant's life, tusks can weigh so much that the animal is no longer able to raise its head. Asian elephants are smaller than their African cousins, and only the male has tusks. Elephants need very little sleep, and much of their time is taken up with rooting around for food. Every day they need to eat something like 100 pounds (45 kilograms) of leaves and grass. Finding food and eating it may take up to 16 hours a day. They also drink a staggering 15–25 gallons (55–110 liters) of water a day. Elephants love water and are excellent swimmers. It is said that an elephant never forgets, but where this story came from, nobody seems to know.

The rhinoceros is hunted for its horn, which is claimed to contain powerful ingredients. It is now an endangered species.

Is the elephant a protected animal?

Yes, today they are.

For many years, elephants were hunted for their valuable ivory tusks. The hunting intensified with the invention of the gun and expansion of the ivory trade in the 17th century. Today they are a protected species, but the elephant is still not out of danger. The value of ivory has soared in recent decades, and as a result as many as 90,000 elephants are killed each year. Once a female has been killed, the young often cannot fend for themselves and fall victim to predators. Trading in ivory is now illegal in many countries, so perhaps the elephant has a chance of survival.

What group of animals does the hippopotamus belong to?

The word hippopotamus means "river horse." But this is misleading because the hippopotamus does not belong to the horse family, but is in fact related to pigs.

The hippopotamus is an enormous animal weighing between 2½ and 4 tons. The head alone can weigh up to a ton. They spend their days in the water, and when they come out in the evening to look for food, their skin secretes a sticky liquid to stop it from drying out. A baby hippopotamus at birth weighs between 55 and 65 pounds (25–30 kilograms) and is born in shallow water. It suckles its mother under water and every so often comes up to breathe in air. If there is danger around, perhaps a crocodile, the baby hippopotamus climbs onto its mother's back. These are social creatures that live in groups of 20 to 40.

Why is the rhinoceros hunted?

The rhinoceros is hunted for the horn that grows out of its forehead.

For a long time, people believed that the horn contained powerful medical ingredients. It was crushed into a powder and eaten. European kings thought the powdered horn was a cure against all poisons. Today, the horn is valued in Eastern countries, where it is believed to increase virility in men. The truth is that the rhinoceros' horn is nothing more than a weapon with which the rhinoceros protects itself. As with the elephant, this ancient-looking animal is officially protected by law, but this means nothing to a poacher. One method of saving the rhinoceros is to cut its horn off. This gives the animal some chance of survival as a poacher will almost certainly kill the animal only to get its horn.

How many bears are there in Europe?

The only bears in Europe today are in the zoos.

European bears were virtually wiped out by humans. This animal is incredibly strong. At the end of its giant paws, it has five sharp claws that can be used to tear a victim to pieces. The bear was relatively safe for a long time because it lived deep in the forest or up in the mountains. However, as soon as humans invaded its habitat, the bear's life was disturbed, and its numbers fell dramatically. For the bear to survive, its habitat must remain untouched and far away from humans.

What is a grizzly?

The grizzly is a very big brown bear that lives in North America. Standing up on its hind legs, it can be more than 10 feet (3 meters) tall.

The grizzly likes to live in the heart of the forest, where it knows how to get around. It does this by marking trees with its claws and using them as signposts. Although this ferocious animal usually eats small animals, it is quite capable of killing a deer with a single blow from its giant paw. The grizzly also likes to fish and will sometimes be seen on a river bank scooping out salmon. Today if you want to see a grizzly, you must go to an isolated mountainous region or a national park.

What is the biggest bear?

The white polar bear is the biggest bear and the biggest carnivore. It can weigh as much as 1,500 pounds (700 kilograms). It lives in the Arctic.

The polar bear lives in a sea of white. It hunts seals and is also an excellent fisher.

The polar bear is a great hunter. It prowls around ice floes, and when a seal comes up for air, the bear stuns it with a mighty blow and finishes it off with its teeth. It leaves a walrus alone, however, because this animal has two pointed tusks. Not only that, the walrus is a faster swimmer and capable of drowning a bear. Originally hunted for its white coat, the polar bear is today a protected species. Once, when polar bears went into a town in Alaska, no doubt attracted by the smell of cooking food, they were taken back to the ice floes by helicopter. Weighing as much as they do, it was one bear to one helicopter!

Why is the giant panda so rare?

Giant pandas are bearlike animals that live in the mountains in the west of China. They only eat bamboo, and they have to eat at least 26 pounds (12 kilograms) of it a day in order to survive. There are only about one thousand giant pandas left in China today because so much of this animal's habitat, the bamboo forest, has been destroyed.

Giant pandas have a black and white coat and a short tail. But there are other pandas. A species in Asia is smaller with a brownish coat and a long tail.

Why do kangaroos have pouches?

The kangaroo and the koala are both marsupials. At birth, the baby kangaroo is not fully formed and must develop in its mother's pouch.

The baby kangaroo stays hidden in the pouch for about four months, after which it can look out of the pouch. At the slightest sign of danger, it ducks back down in the pouch. At birth, a kangaroo measures just a fraction of an inch, and its body is translucent like that of an earthworm. Its paws are formed, however, and these are used to pull itself up in the pouch. Kangaroos are only found in Australia. They can weigh up to 200 pounds (90 kilograms) and are famous for their jumping ability. They can clear a 10-foot (3-meter) high fence and do a long jump of 26 feet (8 meters). Excellent skills if you are being chased! They live in groups of 20 to 50 and eat grass.

Are there any other animals that have a pouch?

All marsupials have pouches, but not always the same shape as the kangaroo's. It may be a simple fold of skin, a big open pouch like the kangaroo's, or it may even be closed. The marsupial otter carries its young deep down in a closed pouch.

All marsupials are mammals, but they look different because of where they have evolved. In the past there were even marsupial wolves, cats, moles, and anteaters.

Are there any mammals that lay eggs?

There are two species of mammals that lay eggs. They are the duckbilled platypus and the spiny anteater. They are defined as mammals because the young are raised on their mother's milk.

Duckbilled platypuses live in Australia. They weigh between 2 and 3 pounds (1 and 1.5 kilograms) and measure about 20 inches (50 centimeters) in length. In the daytime they fill themselves with enormous quantities of worms. They have excellent hearing but very poor eyesight. The female of the species lays between one and three eggs in a hole in the ground, which she then covers up. When the young are ready to hatch, she uncovers them and they suckle her milk.

Spiny anteaters resemble porcupines. The female only lays one egg. She keeps this egg in a pouch similar to that of the koala. The baby, when it hatches, suckles milk from its mother. Adult spiny anteaters live on ants and termites.

The koala may look like a little bear, but it is not a bear at all. It belongs to the marsupial family and lives in Australia.

Is the koala

a bear?

Its furry coat makes the koala look like a little bear, but in fact it is not. It belongs to the marsupial family.

Koalas live only in Australia. They live off the oil contained in the leaves of certain types of eucalyptus trees that only grow in Australia. To find their vital leaves, they cover large distances. They are gentle animals with soft fur and big noses. The young grow up in their mother's pouch.

What is the

smallest mammal?

The smallest mammal is the pygmy white-toothed shrew. This little insect-eating shrew is only about 1½ inches (4 centimeters) in length and weighs no more than $\frac{1}{10}$ of an ounce (3 grams).

Shrews are aggressive little animals that will attack and eat animals twice as big as they are. They have a huge appetite! They eat the equivalent of their weight every three hours. If they are

Because of its enormous size, the humpback whale has only one enemy and that is humans. Although it is a protected species, its future remains uncertain.

unable to find food, they die in less than a day. There is usually plenty of food around for them, including beetles, slugs, caterpillars, and grasshoppers. There are many different varieties of shrews. They look like small mice, with a slim body, a pointed snout, short legs, and a relatively long tail. Their fur is short and velvety and colored brown or gray. As far as humans are concerned, they are useful little creatures because they eat so many insects.

What is the

biggest animal?

The biggest animals known are found in the sea. The biggest mammal alive today is the blue whale, which may grow up to 100 feet (30 meters) in length and weigh more than 135 tons. They may live for up to 80 years, and they roam all the oceans of the world, from polar to tropical waters.

Sea animals are often much bigger than land animals. For example, the biggest land animals are elephants, and they only weigh up to 10 tons. Size and weight are not a problem for movement in water. A whale's size explains why it is not troubled by predators. However, whales have been hunted by humans so much that they are now protected species. There is still a season when certain countries are allowed to hunt whales, but they are only allowed to kill a specified number. Care must be taken with these mighty creatures as, like all large animals, they take a long time to breed and produce offspring.

Are dolphins

really intelligent?

From studies of the dolphin, we have to conclude it is an intelligent animal. They are social creatures that hunt together, and, if attacked, will help each other. They also look after their own wounded.

When dolphins hunt, they communicate by ultrasonic sound. Humans have studied their signals and tried to work out just how clever dolphins are in relation to other animals. Dolphins pose no threat to humans, and their playful character is much loved throughout the world.

Are there any

other sea

mammals?

There most certainly are. Manatees and dugongs are creatures that are probably responsible for all the stories about mermaids.

Dugongs grow to a length of about 10 feet (3 meters) and are mostly found in the Indian Ocean. Manatees like warm water and live close to the coast or in rivers. They can still be found off Florida and in South America, but the African species is in danger of extinction. They are about 10 feet (3 meters) long and, because they lie flat in the water and the females have breasts, they are probably responsible for all the stories we hear about mermaids.

What is the difference between a seal and a sea lion?

Seals do not have external ears, but sea lions do. The word otary describes the family of sea lions and comes from the ancient Greek language "otarion," which means "little ear."

Seals and sea lions are great swimmers. They live in Antarctica and the Arctic, but they are also found in warmer waters. They can dive to depths of more than 1,000 feet (300 meters) and can stay underwater for more than 40 minutes. They can swim under ice, and when they need to breathe, they break through it. However, when they surface, they are sometimes in danger from the polar bear.

Is the beaver a sea mammal?

No, not really, although they are excellent swimmers.

Beavers build dams to raise the level of a river's water. They do some damage to the environment when they build their dams. The dams are to protect the places where the beavers live. Once they have built their dam, beavers are largely protected from predators. These dams can be really huge; one is recorded as being 2,070 feet (630 meters) long. When beavers sense they are in danger,

The beaver is a builder and an engineer. It makes dams to protect its living quarters. Unfortunately, it causes considerable damage to plant life.

they beat their tails in the water. The sound is so loud it can be heard 1,000 feet (300 meters) away.

Do woodchucks sleep a lot?

Woodchucks spend the entire winter underground. They do not even wake up to eat. By the time their hibernation period has ended, they have lost a third of their body weight.

A woodchuck's winter home is marvelously cozy and well made. This animal is also an architect and builder. It builds its home with numerous passages, some of them as long as 30 feet (10 meters). These open out into a big chamber filled with grass and dry leaves. Safe and warm, a woodchuck family can sleep for six months without fear of being disturbed by predators.

Where do armadillos live?

Armadillos are mammals that have a shell around their bodies. They are found in North, Central, and South America.

Armadillos go out at night to look for food. They eat termites, ants, and insects. They are not in the least bit aggressive and if attacked will curl up into a ball rather than run away. This method of defense is extremely effective since their shells are hard and cover their entire body.

What is an insectivore?

An insectivore is simply an animal that eats invertebrates (animals without backbones) such as insects. Generally speaking, they tend to be small, but that does not stop them from being fierce, like the shrew.

Mammals that live mostly off insects are also referred to as insectivores. A hedgehog would come into this category, although strictly speaking it is an omnivore (eating a bit of everything). A hedgehog likes to eat insects, snails, slugs, worms, little snakes, eggs, and so on.

Woodchucks sleep all winter until spring. They are even lazier than the dormouse.

How do opossums defend themselves from their enemies?

They defend themselves by pretending to be dead.

This little animal has no defenses to speak of. It has no hard shell, sharp claws, vicious spikes, or a dreadful smell like the skunk. It cannot run fast and even lacks cunning. What it can do, however, is climb up a tree and pretend to be dead. It may even lie flat out on the ground in a deathlike posture. Fortunately for the opossum, this method of defense is very effective because a lot of carnivores like to actually kill the meat themselves before they eat it.

The opossum is a marsupial that lives in North America. They are about the size of a big cat, weigh a bit less than 11 pounds (5 kilograms), and have a fine coat of fur. The opossum's feet are extremely short, but they do have a long tail that allows them to hang from branches. Like the hedgehog, they are omnivores and live off seeds, fish, rodents, and anything else that is available to them.

Is there such a thing as a wild hamster?

There are wild hamsters living in central Europe. They build underground burrows or warrens in wooded areas.

A wild hamster's home is a marvelous place with many separate areas, rather like different "rooms." There is a main entrance and an emergency exit, a corridor, nest, room for food storage and even toilets. This little animal likes to keep plenty of food stored in its home. Best of all, it likes to eat seeds and fruits. The name "hamster" comes from a German word that refers to somebody who likes to store things up. Whenever this animal goes out, it always returns with food stuffed into its cheeks.

The hamster is nocturnal and sleeps safely during the day in its burrow. Baby hamsters are born 16 days after mating. To begin with, they are completely blind and hairless, but they do not take long to grow a warm, furry coat. Like many other animals, the female carries her young in her mouth.

The North American opossum pretends to be dead so it will not be attacked.

What is a flying squirrel?

There is a certain type of squirrel that is often described as "flying." However, this is not really true. The squirrel just gives the impression of flying. It glides between branches by means of winglike membranes that stretch between its front and back legs. These also act as parachutes.

All squirrels are great jumpers. They glide through the air at heights up to 165 feet (50 meters). Their tail plays a vital role in this, serving as a balance rather like the pole of a tightrope walker. Squirrels survive in a variety of environments, and their diets adapt to the changing of the seasons. They like to store food up in summer, ready for winter days when food is less plentiful.

Are there any mammals that fly?

There is only one mammal that can fly: the bat.

Bats are able to fly because they have flaps of skin between their enormously long fingers, and between their forelegs and smaller hind legs. They may be slower than most birds, but they are certainly more skillful than many. They can make quick sharp turns in the air and carry twice their body weight in flight. Bats are covered with hair and do not have feathers. They live for about 15 years and live mostly off insects.

How do bats know where they are going?

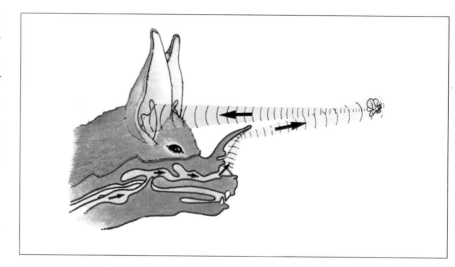

The remarkable bat sends out ultrasonic sounds from its nose. These sounds strike an obstacle and send back an echo. The bat hears this and knows from the echo how far away the obstacle is, its shape, and whether or not it is moving.

Bats do not use their eyes to fly, but their sense of hearing. They send ultrasonic sounds out of their mouth or nose. These sounds cannot be heard by a human, but they bounce off an object and send back an echo. The bat hears the echo and can tell from its quality whether the object is moving, its shape, and how far away it is.

The ultrasonic ability of the bat is a fascinating area of study. The animal must have extraordinary senses in order to fly accurately to a destination. For example, it has to distinguish between the echo from a tree branch and that of an insect so it can avoid crashing into the tree when trying to get its food. Then there is the question of sound interference. It manages to deal with this by cutting it out.

What animals build nests?

Most birds build nests, though some do not. The cuckoo, for example, lays its eggs in other birds' nests. Many other types of animals, for example some worms, and even certain types of fish, build nests.

For chicks that are very weak at birth, the nest must be sturdy enough to protect them for a period of time. Less vulnerable chicks can be raised in a fairly crude arrangement of sticks and leaves. Other building materials include animal hair, feathers, mud, stones, saliva, and mucus. Some nests are wonders of construction and cemented together in skillful ways. A silkworm's cocoon is a kind of nest and is used by humans to make silk.

What exactly is a bird?

All birds are vertebrates. They have warm blood, which means their body temperature is not affected by the outside temperature. They have feathers, and wings on both sides of their bodies. Their back legs end in claws. They have beaks but no teeth.

Even though all birds have wings, not all can fly, and we have already noted that even though the bat is not a bird, it can fly. Some birds are poor fliers, for example, chickens. Feathers are unique to birds – no other type of animal has them. The females lay eggs. There are about 9,000 species of bird in the world.

What is the biggest bird?

The biggest bird of all is the ostrich. Its egg may be up to 8 inches (20 centimeters) long and can weigh nearly 4 pounds (2 kilograms). A fully grown ostrich weighs about 220 pounds (100 kilograms).

Ostriches are very fast on their feet and can match a horse at the gallop. With each step they take, they can cover an incredible 13 feet (4 meters). Although they have little wings, they cannot fly.

Their legs end in great clawed feet, which they can use to defend or attack. It is said they can tear a dog in half with one blow. Ostriches lay their eggs in a hole dug in the sand. They may lay up to 30 eggs in their nest. The male bird helps the female cover up the eggs, which have a particularly tough shell. They need this to support the weight of a 220-pound (100-kilogram) bird sitting on them. Lots of stories are told about how an ostrich hides its head in the sand to defend itself. However, an ostrich is quite capable of defending itself and even going into attack. The only time an ostrich may lower its head onto the sand is when it is resting,

The ostrich is a great runner, which is just as well because it cannot fly. Ostriches live in the plains and deserts of Africa.

and this is an intelligent thing to do because, seen from a distance, the big bird will look like a rock, so it will probably not be troubled by an enemy.

Are there any other birds that cannot fly?

A small number of species of birds cannot fly. These birds use other means of getting around, such as running or swimming. Birds whose body weight is too much for their wings to carry include the emu, kiwi, cassowary, ostrich, penguin, and rhea. Other birds, for example, the tinamous in South America, are awkward fliers that spend most of their time on the ground and rarely take to the air.

The cassowary is a dangerous enemy. It has a sharp spur at the end of both feet that is capable of delivering a lethal blow. The emu belongs to the same family as the cassowary. They are extremely large birds that walk and run at great speed. Both live in Australia. The rhea, however, looks like a small ostrich but lives in South America. They are the biggest birds of that continent and are good runners and swimmers. Kiwis live in New Zealand. They have tiny wings buried in their feathers and like to go out at night. Unlike any other bird, they have nostrils in their beaks. They get their name from the sounds they make.

The cassowary is an example of a bird that has lost the use of its wings. It lives in Australia, home of many strange-looking creatures.

How much does the smallest bird weigh?

The smallest bird in the world is the hummingbird, which weighs 1/10 of an ounce (3 grams) at the most. Hummingbirds can be found all over the American continent.

Emperor penguins, the largest species of penguin, are found in Antarctica. Emperor penguins live in large groups and huddle together for protection from a blizzard.

Penguins and auks look so much alike they are often confused. But there are two differences between these birds. Penguins live only in the southern hemisphere. Their habitats range from Antarctica to the warmer Galapágos Islands and Peru. Auks, on the other hand, live in the northern hemisphere. Penguins have small wings that are not used for flying but for swimming; auks can just about fly above the water.

Penguins are very social animals and live together in groups of several thousands, known as rookeries. Living together as a group means they can survive the severe conditions of Antarctica. When a blizzard occurs, they huddle down together to survive. Penguins have a number of enemies, notably sea lions and seals. Young penguins also have to watch out for birds of prey. The wings of penguins have adapted to their marine life, becoming paddlelike flippers, which allow swift propulsion through the water. They have short, dense feathers that cover the body in an even waterproof layer that gives the penguins a streamlined shape. Of all the birds, they are the most agile swimmers.

Hummingbirds are great fliers. Their wings move 75 times a second, and they can reach speeds of 30 miles (50 kilometers) an hour. In a single flight they can cross the Gulf of Mexico, a distance of 465 miles (750 kilometers). Hummingbirds build tiny nests that they camouflage with moss. The female lays two white eggs about the size of a pea. Hummingbirds live off nectar from flowers, their favorites including sage and fuchsia. When they fly from plant to plant, these tiny birds pick up pollen on their feathers and so fertilize a great number of plants.

What is the difference between a penguin and an auk?

A few golden eagles may still be found in the Alps and the Pyrenees. In the past they were also found in the Highlands of Scotland. These days they are a protected species.

Are birds of prey hunters?

Most birds of prey are hunters or fishers, but there are some birds that fall into this category that actually live off fruit, for example the African vulture, which eats fruit and palm oil. Other birds of prey eat only carrion (dead animals that they have not killed themselves).

Birds of prey can be hunters or fishers. They may attack different sorts of animals. The kestrel, for example, swoops down on crickets and grasshoppers. In North America, there is a buzzard that lives entirely off snails. Other predatory birds only eat snakes or little birds, while certain owls only eat bats.

Where can you find golden eagles today?

The golden eagle is rare in Europe today, but a few may still be found in mountainous regions.

The golden eagle lives in Europe, Asia as far as the Himalayas, all of North Africa, and in certain areas of North America. Its wing span may be as much as 8 feet (2.5 meters). It is a great flier and can maintain speeds of 55 miles an hour (90 kilometers an hour) over a long period of time. In sweeping dives it may hit speeds of more than 90 miles an hour (150 kilometers an hour). The golden eagle does not drop straight down onto its victims, but skims about a foot (30 centimeters) above the ground and seizes its prey. Then it carries its food back to some hidden place where it can eat in peace. The golden eagle is a powerful bird (weighing 11–18 pounds/5–8 kilograms), and it can snatch an animal twice its weight, such as lambs or fawns.

What different flying techniques are there?

The three main techniques are hovering, flying, and gliding.

Insects hover, as do certain birds like the hummingbird. Their wings move so fast they are just a blur to the human eye. Most birds and bats, however, fly by beating their wings up and down in a regular movement. Birds and butterflies glide on currents of air above the earth and water. The fastest bird of all is the peregrine falcon. It can drop down on its prey at more than 100 miles an hour (160 kilometers an hour).

What is a hornbill?

This is a bird that lives in the forests of Malaysia. The hornbill has an enormous beak that looks like a rhinoceros' horn, hence its name.

These birds live off ripe fruits, insects, and little lizards. They often follow groups of monkeys around and eat the fruit that they knock out of the trees. The male hornbill stays in a tree with the female until brooding time. Then, when she has laid her eggs, he makes a nest around them out of mud, saliva, and plants. He leaves a little gap in the nest just big enough for the female to stick her beak through. She stays in this little fortress until the chicks are born and have got their feathers. This can take up to three months. During this time the male provides food for the whole family.

What is the biggest bird in Europe?

The biggest bird in Europe is the stork.

Storks are migratory birds. In winter they fly to Africa, and in spring they return to Europe. This used to be a very common bird throughout Europe, but these days they have disappeared from Italy, Greece, and England. Storks build very solid nests, which last from season to season and from generation to generation. Every year they repair any damage done to the nests. They are big birds, nearly 6½ feet (2 meters) tall. When young children ask their parents where babies come from, they are sometimes told they come from storks. This answer may have something to do with the fact that storks are devoted parents. On the other hand, mothers and fathers are sometimes shy about telling their children the facts of life!

Gray cranes are migratory birds. They fly south in winter and return to the north in spring. In this picture they are stopping off in Spain.

What are migratory birds?

Migratory birds breed in one country and then fly to another that has a warmer climate. Just before winter sets in, migratory northern birds fly south and return in spring when the weather is better.

Without migration some species of birds would not survive. In warmer countries they find the temperature and food they need. The distances they cover vary. Tits, for example, migrate tens or hundreds of miles. The arctic tern spends one season in the Arctic and the other in the Antarctic. Birds are not the only animals to migrate. One variety of aphid spends six months on apple trees and six months on blades of grass.

What is the difference between a seagull and a gull?

Seagull is the popular term for some varieties of gulls.

Not all parrots are good talkers. The American types with vivid colors are not very chatty.

Gulls are generally white with gray or black on the back and wings. Some species have a little "hood" of black feathers.

Seagulls and gulls are the most common bird found throughout the world. There are more than 43 types of gull. These birds live together in groups, and some of the birds are dominant. They follow rules and live in a highly structured society. Being in a group helps protect individuals from enemies. All gulls spend a great deal of their time preening their feathers. If their feathers are in good condition, they can stay in the air for long periods. They are tremendous fliers, capable of 50 miles (80 kilometers) an hour and covering 620 miles (1000 kilometers) in 24 hours.

Which bird is the best talker?

It is a popular belief that parrots can talk. The truth is they have no language, but are good at imitating human sounds. Other birds, such as crows, starlings, and jays, are also good mimics.

The best talking parrots come from Africa. One big parrot with silvery-gray plumage and a red tail, living in Gabon, western Africa, is so skillful it can imitate human speech. There are more than 400 different parrots, and they vary widely in size. Big South American macaws can be up to 3 feet (1 meter) in length, while their African cousins are much smaller.

How do you recognize a crow?

Crows are large birds that usually have black feathers with metallic sheens of purple, blue, or green. Most species of crows also have black feet and black beaks.

Crows are very sociable birds and build their nests close to one another. The young birds stay in the nest for about three weeks, and every day have to eat the equivalent of their body weight. They eat almost anything, and their diet can include fruit, vegetables, seeds, insects, eggs, fish, and even small rodents.

How do you tell the difference between a grass snake and an adder?

Telling a grass snake from an adder is very important when they both live in the same area. The grass snake is harmless, but the adder is

The viper or adder on the left differs from the grass snake on the right in a number of ways. The viper has vertical pupils, a turned-up nose, different coloring, and is deadly poisonous.

poisonous. Grass snakes can grow up to 5½ feet (1.7 meters) long, but the adder is much shorter. Grass snakes have rounded heads, whereas the adder's is triangular, and only the adder has poisonous fangs. The eyes of the grass snake are round, whereas those of the adder are vertical.

The adder's fangs are poisonous, and a bite may prove deadly if not treated immediately. Someone who has been bitten must be taken straight to a hospital.

What is the oldest snake known?

The oldest snake known is the tuatara, also known as the *Sphenodon*. This animal dates back to an era before the dinosaurs.

Tuatara live in New Zealand where they are now a protected species. They live on insects and look like large lizards. They are olive-green in color with white spots and have a little spiky crest. If their tail is damaged, it can grow back again in the same way that a lizard's can. The tuatara's way of life is very slow. Eggs take more than a year to hatch, and it is 20 years before a young snake becomes an adult. The tuatara breathes only once an hour. It has a cone-shaped gland on its head that is very much like a third eye.

Do sea reptiles still exist?

Yes, the saltwater, or estuarine, crocodile, the largest species of crocodile, is an example. It measures up to 25 feet (8 meters), and the largest known weighed over 4,400 pounds (2,000 kilograms).

The saltwater crocodile lives mostly along the coast of southern India, Indonesia, the Philippines, and other islands of the southwestern Pacific. They live both in brackish estuaries and in the sea. They are extremely dangerous and are known man-eaters.

What does *Crocodilia* mean?

This word refers to an order of reptiles that lives in warm climates. These animals have long powerful jaws and bodies like coats of armor. Alligators, caymans, and, of course, crocodiles are crocodilians.

There are about 20 different varieties of animal that can be called crocodilian. All these animals have cone-shaped teeth on the upper and lower jaw. When their jaw is closed, it is not watertight. However, crocodiles can eat underwater without drowning.

What is the difference between a crocodile, a cayman, and an alligator?

Many people will say they are all the same, but that is not quite true. Caymans and alligators are the same, but the crocodile is different. It does not live in the same areas, and it has different physical characteristics.

Crocodiles live in various parts of the world: central Africa, South Africa, southern regions of Asia,

Here, the jaws of the alligator are shut and its teeth hidden. The alligator is part of the crocodile family and lives in the southern United States. This one is enjoying life in the Mississippi River.

The crocodile has a pair of enlarged lower teeth. These teeth are still visible when the crocodile's mouth is closed.

Pacific islands, northern Australia, and South America. Alligators, however, live in North America in the southern United States. The most obvious difference between them is the shape of the jaw. An alligator's teeth are invisible when its mouth is closed. A crocodile has an enlarged pair of fourth teeth in its lower jaw that fit into a sort of notch in its upper jaw and remain visible. This gives the impression that the crocodile is smiling.

Is the crocodile a good hunter?

The crocodile is a born hunter. Its jaws are very powerful and its teeth are strong. As soon as one tooth breaks, another grows in its place. Its mighty tail is also a powerful weapon – one swipe can break an antelope's leg or overturn a boat.

The crocodile is a great swimmer and diver. It hunts at about surface level on the water and in this way remains almost invisible. Its eyes and nostrils are set at the top of its head so it can see and breathe while the rest of its body is submerged. When it attacks a big animal such as an antelope, it strikes it with its tail so the animal loses its balance. Then it drags it out into deep water to drown it. It is one of the few animals that will attack humans without provocation. The crocodile is also unusual because it is one of the only reptiles that makes a roaring sound.

Do crocodiles lay eggs?

Crocodiles lay eggs in the sand. The female covers them up and lets the warmth of the Sun hatch them. But she stays close by to protect her eggs from predators such as the mongoose, hyena, or monkey.

The crocodile eggs are buried beneath something like 20 inches (50 centimeters) of sand. Just as the baby is about to hatch, it calls out to its mother, who immediately digs it out. The young are about 10 inches (25 centimeters) long at birth, and immediately after hatching they head for the safety of the water. Storks and cranes love to eat newborn crocodiles, as do adult crocodiles. For every hundred eggs laid, only one crocodile will survive to become fully grown.

Crocodiles grow throughout their lives and can reach the grand old age of one hundred years. Because their skin is prized as a fine leather, crocodiles have been killed in large numbers. They are now protected on nature reserves or raised on farms.

Why are snakes cold to the touch?

Like fish, snakes are cold-blooded animals.

Warm-blooded animals keep their body temperature at the same level. Cold-blooded animals are different. Their body temperature varies, depending on the temperature of their surroundings. A snake may feel cold to us just because our hands are warm, but if we touch a snake that has been lying in the sun for some time, it will feel warm. Cold weather is bad for a snake. It can become almost paralyzed and so incapable of escaping from an enemy.

Why are people so afraid of snakes?

This is generally because people think all snakes are poisonous. Also, some people irrationally fear the snake's tongue. All snakes stick their tongues out to get the smell of an object and to touch it. The tongue itself is harmless.

A fear of snakes is not justified. Out of the 2,400 species known, only 200 are poisonous. But a bite from a poisonous snake is often fatal. In some cases the poison works so quickly that a human will die before he or she can be treated. Naturally, it is better to be cautious. Another false belief is that a snake is sticky or slimy. Quite the opposite is true. A snake has a dry, scaly, bright, shiny skin. Because it is shiny, it looks wet.

Do some snakes wear glasses?

Of course they do not, but the Indian cobra has sometimes been described as wearing glasses. This is because when it rears up, its head is covered with a sort of hood on which there is a pattern that looks like a pair of glasses.

Cobras are very poisonous snakes and a single bite from one can be fatal. The black-necked variety is common in Africa. This particular species can shoot its venom as far as 6½ feet (2 meters) into the eyes

We probably all know the rattlesnake from cowboy films. This highly dangerous snake lives in many areas of the southern United States.

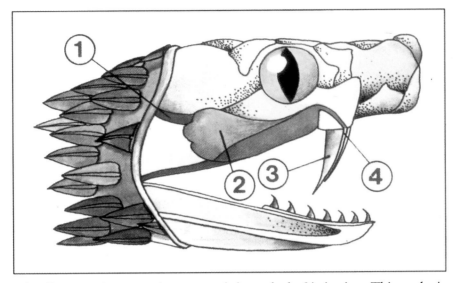

The diagram shows a poisonous snake's method of injection. This snake is from the genus to which the viper belongs. (1) Muscle injector. (2) Poison gland. (3) Movable fangs. (4) Channel.

Do all tortoises have a hard shell?

Almost all tortoises have hard shells. However, there are certain sorts of turtle and several types of fresh-water tortoise that have a relatively soft shell, a bit like thick leather.

The tortoises' ancestors probably had soft shells. However, most tortoises have a hard bony shell made up of hornlike sections. When frightened, they can withdraw their head, tail, and legs into their shell, which provides a good defense against predators.

of an opponent. The venom or poison is powerful enough to blind an enemy temporarily or permanently. Coral snakes, which live in South America, are also members of the cobra family. They are extremely poisonous. Their venom has the effect of paralyzing the nervous system of a victim. These snakes have a very distinctive appearance. Their shiny skin is colored by alternating bands of black, yellow, and red. Like many animals, coral snakes will not attack unless they are disturbed in some way.

What is a rattlesnake?

Rattlesnakes belong to the viper family of snakes. At the end of their tails are hard rings, shaped a bit like a horn. These rattle when they are shaken, hence the name.

Rattlesnakes are found in North and South America. They are deadly poisonous, and their venom can kill a fully grown human within an hour. Rattlesnakes slough or shed their skins on average about three times a year. Each time they do this a new ring appears. Rattlesnakes can go without food for a year before they die. We know this from zoological studies in which these snakes die after a year because they refuse to eat in captivity.

Where do green turtles lay their eggs?

The green turtle, like all turtles, lays its eggs on dry land. Every year they return to the same beach to do this.

Turtles have an uncanny sense of direction. Sometimes they travel as much as 1,200 miles (2,000 kilometers) to return to the beach they were born on. The female then crawls up the beach, lays her eggs, covers them with sand, and leaves them. Her job is done. She goes back into the sea and stays there for the rest of the year. The Sun takes care of the eggs, and they hatch about eight weeks later. The baby turtle has a powerful instinct for survival. It digs itself out of the sand and makes a dash for the area of brightest light – the sea. But this is a dangerous short journey. Their shells are still soft, and they are a delicacy for many predators. If they make it to the sea, the baby turtles still have many sea predators to deal with. Not an easy start to life!

Is the salamander a lizard?

The salamander may look like a lizard, but in fact it is an amphibian.

Lizards are reptiles, and there are about 3,000 species of them. They have a dry scaly skin, love to lie in the Sun, and in winter they hibernate in countries with mild temperatures. Some are oviparous (produce eggs), others are viviparous (produce living young). Salamanders live on land or in water. Those that live on land feed on earthworms and hibernate in holes made by moles. In the past, it was believed that these creatures could not be harmed by fire and that is why some buildings are decorated with them.

What is an amphibian?

An amphibian is an animal that lives both in the water and on dry land. A frog is a good example of an amphibian.

A frog starts its life in the water and them moves onto the land. A baby frog, known as a tadpole, is born in the water. It breathes through gills and has fins for swimming. Then, it gradually grows four legs and lungs, and becomes ready for a life on land. There is a point in its development when the tadpole has organs for living both in the water and on land. In other words, it has gills and lungs, and its tail acts as a fin. Its little feet are also already formed. The adult frog continues to live in the water, but now it breathes through its skin.

What is the difference between a toad and a frog?

The salamander shown here, a spotted batrachian, likes a wet environment. Its skin is covered with glands that secrete a harmful liquid.

Frogs and toads are both amphibians, but their bodies are different.

Toads generally have a rough skin and are dull brown in color. They usually have thickset bodies and short legs that are poorly adapted for jumping. Their skin contains a number of poison glands. When a predator seizes the toad, it secretes a fluid that burns the predator's mouth. Toads have no teeth. Frogs tend to be smaller, with a smoother skin, and they often do have teeth.

Do flying frogs exist?

In a manner of speaking, they do. There are some frogs that live in Southeast Asia that can launch themselves through the air for a distance of up to 50 feet (15 meters).

Flying frogs live in forests. They have very long webbed hands. In the water these could be used as flippers; in the air they serve as parachutes. At the end of their hands they have suction pads that allow them to hold onto a twig or branch. Fifty feet is no small jump!

The green frog, like all frogs, is an amphibian. This means it lives the first part of its life in the water as a tadpole. It then grows into a frog and lives on dry land.

Where does the biggest frog live?

The Goliath frog, which lives in western Africa, can weigh more than 7 pounds (3 kilograms) and grows up to 32 inches (81 centimeters) in length.

There are all sorts of frogs living in the United States. Perhaps the best known is the bullfrog. There are 150 different types of frog.

Some of them are so small they can fit into the smallest eggcup.

What exactly is a fish?

Fish are animals with backbones that live entirely in the water and have fins. Their bodies are protected by scales. They are cold-blooded so their body temperature is the same as the water in which they live.

The angel fish of the Caribbean shows off its dazzling colors. Tropical fish tend to be much more brightly colored than those living in temperate waters.

There are more than 22,000 known species of fish. They all have certain things in common, but they do differ widely. Some varieties of fish can only live in fresh water; others have to live in the sea. There are even eels that live in fresh water but reproduce in the sea. Fish come in many shapes and sizes, and their colors vary enormously. Generally speaking, the fish that inhabit temperate waters tend to be rather dull in color. Tropical fish, however, are often startlingly bright. Fast-swimming fish are usually smooth and streamlined. Other fish may be flat, spherical, disk-shaped, elongated, or ribbon-like; they may be adorned with spikes, barbels, crests, ridges, nodules, or enlarged fins. Fish breathe through gills, an organ that is the equivalent of a human's lungs. The gills enable the fish to extract oxygen from the water.

What is the oldest species of fish known?

It is called a coelacanth, and it looks the same today as it did millions of years ago.

For a long time, it was thought that this fish had died out 70 million years ago. However, it was rediscovered in 1938. The species was found living in the sea near the Comoro Islands, near Madagascar, off the southeastern coast of Africa. These fish are approximately 5 feet (1.5 meters) long and weigh between 100 and 140 pounds (45 and 65 kilograms). The fins of the coelacanth look like feet and are made of a mass of flesh held together by a jointed bone. The coelacanth could be one of the ancestors of those animals that evolved enough for them to leave the water and adapt to life on land. It is extremely rare to come across an animal that has not evolved for such a long period of time.

Are there fish that swim on their backs?

Fish swim on their bellies, and usually the only time you will see a fish belly up on the surface is when it is dead. However, there is a species of fish that swims on its back: the sydonont.

Sydononts are fish that inhabit African coasts. Their bladder is much bigger in the belly part of their bodies than the dorsal or back part. So it is natural for them to swim belly up. These fish only come out at night. During the day they hide under stones or in tangles of vegetation. They hunt insects on the surface of the water and breathe through an enormous mouth. When the sydonont is hungry, it makes sounds like the croaking of a frog.

Is it possible to farm fish?

Yes, there are fish farms.

These days, fish and even shellfish can be farmed. Bays or parts of the sea may be enclosed to keep the fish in, or fish may be raised in cages in the water. Little lakes are used for freshwater fish. When farming fish, it is important to be aware of the fishes' reproductive cycles and to create a favorable environment. Catfish, trout, and salmon are all farmed successfully. Scotland and Norway have led the way in farming salmon and have even succeeded in bringing down the price.

What is the biggest and what is the smallest fish?

The biggest fish is the whale shark. It usually measures 40 feet (12 meters), but can reach 60 feet (18 meters) and weigh up to 15 tons. Of course, whales can be much larger than this, but they are not fish but mammals. The smallest fish, the dwarf goby, is just ⅓ inch (9 millimeters) long.

The whale shark is an alarming sight to behold, but it is not dangerous to humans. It eats plants and small sea animals. Its appetite is quite incredible, and it spends most of its life looking for food and eating. Whale sharks can use their belly fins to stick to rocks.

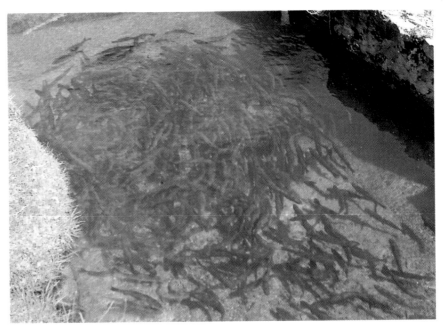

Trout farming has proved to be very successful and made this fish available to people without a high income.

Sharks are the great predators of the sea. They are found all over the world, in the English Channel, the Mediterranean, the Caribbean, and the Indian Ocean. Very few are really dangerous.

Is there life deep down in the oceans?

There is plenty of life in seas and oceans to a depth of 19,700 feet (6000 meters). Animals are able to survive because currents reach here and circulate food material.

Farther down toward the seabed, there are different types of animals. Predators, like the shark or squid, often dive deep in order to find food. They do not, however, live at great depths.

Worms and sea anemones on the seabed live on organic matter that has floated down from the water's surface, or on little animals. There are strange fish that live in the ocean depths. They are usually blind but have enormous eyes. Their bodies are slender and colorless, and they are always hungry. They do sometimes come up to the surface at night.

How fast can a fish swim?

The fastest fish in the world is the pilgrim fish. It can swim at more than 60 miles an hour (95 kilometers an hour).

However, there are very few fast fish. Generally, fish move about quite slowly, at 4 to 6 miles an hour (6 to 10 kilometers an hour). Tuna are very fast swimmers.

Where are sharks found?

Sharks are found in seas throughout the world. There are many different species of shark, including dogfish.

We do not need to be afraid of most sharks. Many are quite small with teeth that are not dangerous, and they will not attack humans. The great white shark is the most dangerous shark of all. These fish have an extraordinary sense of smell – if one pint of blood was diluted in 50 million pints of water, they would pick up the scent. They are attracted by sudden or jerky movements.

If you see a great white shark while you are in the water, you should get to shore with the least possible movement. This shark is one of the few animals that will attack humans without provocation.

What is the fiercest freshwater fish?

Without doubt, the answer is the piranha. It can be as lethal as a shark.

Piranhas are small fish that live in the Amazon and other rivers of South America. They have triangular, razor-sharp teeth that take precise bites — enough for one swallow at a time — out of their victim's flesh. They move about in schools of several thousand and attack as a single unit. Once they have spilled their prey's blood, they become increasingly frenzied in their feeding. The blood attracts other piranhas, which join the attack, and together the group can strip a big fish, animal, or human to the bone in just a matter of minutes.

What is an electric fish?

There are several sorts of electric fish. Probably the best known is the electric eel.

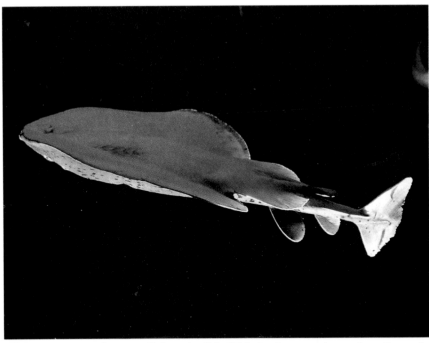

There are several types of electric fish. This is the torpedo variety from the Pacific Ocean. They are best avoided because, although they are not lethal, their electrical charge can be painful.

These fish use the electricity generated by their bodies as a form of defense or attack. They can use it to capture prey or scare enemies away. They send out an electric shock that stuns the animals within range and so provides a ready meal. In the breeding season, the role of the eel's electricity changes and is used to locate a partner. The male sends out electrical charges that are transmitted by rocks, little stones, and other fish. A female responds to the male by sending out her own electrical reply. This is not always a happy occurrence, because the female's charge may blind the male.

Do flying fish really exist?

Yes, they do exist.

Flying fish have highly developed pectoral or breast fins that they use to leap out of the water and glide. Perhaps a better name for them might be gliding fish because they cannot actually use their fins like wings. They live in large schools in warm seas and stay close to the water's surface. They jump out of the water to escape from their enemies. Sailors often find them beached in their boats.

What is the difference between an octopus and a squid?

The octopus and squid belong to the same family of cephalopods. Although both have tentacles, the octopus cannot hold onto the skin of its prey for very long. The squid, however, has suction pads that fasten onto its prey's skin. They can bring out a nasty rash on human skin.

The squid has the remains of a shell that looks something like a feather on its body. The octopus does not have this feature. Most octopuses do not span more than 3 feet (1 meter). Like the squid, they can discharge an inky liquid into the water to hide from an enemy. Their tentacles serve a dual purpose: to capture their prey and to open shells and get at the contents. They can move around on these rubbery limbs but usually they move forward by self-propulsion. They open their gills, suck in water, then shoot it out at the rear. Each intake of water can propel the animal about 6 to 10 feet (2 to 3 meters) forward.

Are there land crabs?

Yes, they do exist. There is, for example, the palm-tree crab.

Land crabs have gills and need a moist environment to breathe. But they cannot live in water and would drown if placed in it. There are other land crustaceans. The most common example is the woodlouse, a familiar sight in gardens and houses, especially in the countryside.

How can you tell a crayfish from a lobster?

Both are shellfish, but the crayfish does not have claws at the front, while those of the lobster are enormous. They also differ in color: lobsters are blue, black, or purple, crayfish are orange or red. The only time a lobster is red is when it is being cooked.

Crayfish and lobsters, like all crabs and crustaceans in general, live in a shell that does not grow in size. Their growth takes place in stages. The shell moves up into the middle of the back and splits. The animal's flesh forces its way

The palm-tree crab is a large land crab that lives in the Seychelle Islands in the Indian Ocean. It is becoming increasingly rare.

through the crack and grows extremely quickly, increasing in size by as much as a quarter. The old shell is then disposed of and a new one grows and hardens in two or three days. It does not grow again until its splits the next shell. As soon as a crustacean is without its shell, it is vulnerable. Its exposed flesh is soft and tender, a juicy dinner for a predator!

Are corals animals?

Corals certainly are animals. Just because they do not move around does not mean they are plants or minerals.

The hard fixed parts of the coral that we see are a sort of skeleton, made by the little animal that lives inside. The actual living part of the coral, the polyp or coral-insect, looks like a miniature sea anemone. Corals reproduce in two ways: either they bud, increasing the size of the colony, or they reproduce sexually, which leads to the formation of a new colony. The skeleton is chalky, and when it is first formed, it is a very pure white. The coral's color comes from the living polyps. They have microscopic algae in their cells that may be green, yellow, blue, or red. The structure of the

colony of coral does not move, but each polyp is crowned with little tentacles and it is these that capture floating or swimming food. Sponges are also animals and not plants. The horned kind are flexible, while the hard kind are chalky and contain silica or flint.

What is a pearl oyster?

A pearl oyster is simply an oyster that makes a pearl. There is also a pearl mussel.

A pearl is made naturally by the oyster. If a grain of sand or some kind of parasite gets into its shell, the oyster is in danger of being damaged because it is a soft creature. To protect itself, the oyster covers the invader with coatings of mother-of-pearl, a shiny substance secreted from inside the shell. Gradually the pearl forms and continues to grow steadily as time passes. There are, in fact, two types of pearls: natural pearls and cultured pearls. A natural pearl is made by the oyster itself without human interference. They are very rare and expensive to buy. Cultured

Australia has the most beautiful coral in the world. More and more sea-beds are plundered by souvenir hunters and fishermen. In the Philippines, hunting for the much-prized black coral has been made illegal.

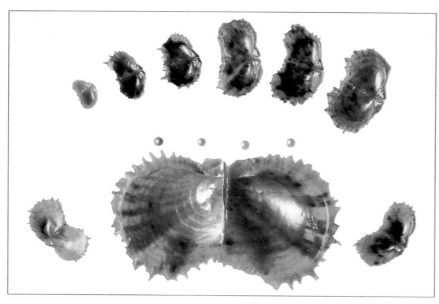

This photo shows the different stages in the growth of a pearl oyster for the first year of its life: from one to three months (top, from left to right), and up to one year (bottom). In the middle are four pearls of different colors produced by these oysters.

pearls are made by inserting a tiny piece of mother-of-pearl into the oyster's shell. This will eventually get bigger and become a pearl. Of course, larger pearls take longer to develop and are the most expensive.

Are sea urchins and starfish related?

Yes, they are, even though they do not look anything like each other. They are both members of the group called the Echinoderms.

Sea urchins, like starfish, live in the sea and have a neat little system of moving suction pads. The sea urchin's spikes form a very effective defense against predators and are also useful as crutches for getting around and hiding. Some tropical sea urchins have huge poisonous spikes that snap easily and remain in a wound. However, many sea urchins do not have spikes. Starfish are all star-shaped – hence their name – but vary from just over an inch (2.5 centimeters) to 3 feet (1 meter) across. Running the length of each arm are tiny tube feet that the starfish use for breathing, capturing food, and moving around.

What is a jellyfish?

A jellyfish, as its name suggests, looks a bit like a jelly. This animal has transparent tissues and is shaped like a bell. On its underside there are tentacles and a mouth. It is a very primitive form of life.

Jellyfish vary greatly in size. They have a sting with which they paralyze their prey. The cells that contain the sting are grouped around the tentacles and the lips. Unable to move, a victim is then the jellyfish's dinner. Fortunately, humans are too big to be eaten by this animal, but a sting can still be quite nasty and cause a serious rash. Certain species, the Portuguese man-of-war, for example, are capable of killing a human. Jellyfish move through the water by contracting their bell-shape and propelling themselves forward.

Are there mollusks without shells?

Yes there are mollusks, invertebrate animals with soft bodies, that do not have shells.

The word mollusk derives from the Latin word *mollis*, meaning soft, and primitive mollusks only had soft bodies. As time went by, they evolved shells as a means of protection. The shell also acted as a skeleton for their organs to be attached to. There are mollusks without external shells, and the slug and octopus are examples. The squid's shell is very thin and develops inside their bodies, acting as an internal skeleton. Cuttlefish also have internal shells, which are large, chalky, and shield-shaped.

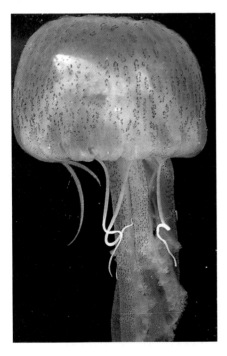

The jellyfish is an extremely primitive sea animal that has remained virtually unchanged since the Paleozoic Era. They should be avoided because they can give a nasty sting.

Are the octopus and snail similar animals?

They are both mollusks, but they are very different.

The octopus has eight tentacles and at the end of each is a suction pad. Its enormous head could easily be mistaken for its body if it were not for two magnificent eyes. The octopus is a carnivorous animal that lives in the sea and it is a predator. The octopus likes to eat crustaceans and always attacks them from behind to avoid their claws. The snail is quite different from the octopus. It is protected by a spiral shell, which it is able to withdraw into when it senses danger. It slides along the ground on a single muscular foot, leaving behind a trail of mucus. The snail has tiny eyes and a pair of slender movable tentacles on the top of its head. The tentacles contain tiny sensors with which the snail can detect food. The snail is a hermaphrodite, which means it is male and female at the same time. The ancestors of the octopus and snail probably had a similar shape and lived in the sea. Both probably had external shells and soft bodies.

What exactly is an insect?

Insects are little invertebrate animals with six legs and usually with wings. They have an external skeleton that is made of a substance known as chitin. This allows them to move freely through water and air. Their muscles are attached to their external skeletons.

An insect's body is divided into a head, thorax, and abdomen. Attached to the head are a pair of feelers, or antennae. The thorax bears three pairs of legs and usually two pairs of wings. An insect has a system of nerves and a digestive tract that is spread throughout its body. Its breathing apparatus is a series of tubes inside its body. Some insects are a problem for humans because they carry diseases, such as malaria, or eat crops. We are always trying to get rid of them, but it is a battle. Every time we invent an insecticide to kill pests off, they adapt and become more resistant. However, many insects are useful, and they form an important link in the world's food chains.

What is the biggest insect ever known?

The biggest insect ever known lived millions of years ago. This was a giant dragonfly, called *Meganeura*. Its body was nearly 16 inches (40 centimeters) long, and its wing span could be as much as 28 inches (70 centimeters).

The largest living insect today belongs to the family of stick insects, which look like twigs. Tropical stick insects live in Indonesia and can reach lengths of 12 inches (30 centimeters). There are stick insects in Europe, but they are smaller, perhaps 4 inches (10 centimeters) or so long. Apart from these animals, the biggest insects are beetles, such as the cockchafer or June bug. Beetles in the old forests of Guyana and the West Indies can grow to more than 6 inches (15 centimeters). Insects that have the biggest wings are butterflies. The female Queen Alexandra butterfly, for example, has a wing span of more than 11 inches (28 centimeters).

The cockchafer or June bug is a large flying insect, related to the ancient scarab beetles of Egypt. It is quite harmless.

How many sorts of insects are there?

There are more than a million and a half recorded insects on the Earth today, but the number changes every year as more are discovered.

Experts believe that there are probably two to three million types of insect living on the Earth today and that they only know about a half of them. Insects make up four-fifths of all animal life and, from a numerical point of view, are the largest class of animals. They outnumber all the other animals put together. It has been estimated that there are 200 million insects for every human being. Insects breed so much that as a group they are never in danger of becoming extinct, although individual species die out every year, owing to the destruction of the Earth's habitats. One of the reasons for the success of insects is that they adapt to the food sources of different environments. Insects have colonized practically every type of habitat on land and in the water, except for the deeper waters of the sea.

Do the wasp and bee belong to the same family?

Yes, bees and wasps both belong to an order of winged insects called Hymenoptera.

A bee society is highly organized. Every hive has a single queen bee, which is bigger than the rest. At birth, she is the same size as the drones or workers, but as a larva she is fed a special diet, which makes her grow to queen size. Her function is to reproduce, and every day she lays nearly 2,000 eggs. In each hive there are also about 200 male bees, or drones, whose main function is to mate with the queen. All the other bees are female workers with their own jobs. Some stay in the hive to look after the eggs or larvae; others scout out sources of food; yet others are gatherers that bring back the food.

The wasp, like the bee, is a hymenopteran, but unlike the bee, it does not make honey. When it stings, the wasp does not lose its sting and can use it again. The bee, however, dies once it has stung because it loses its sting.

Why must ladybugs be protected?

Ladybugs are very useful insects because they eat aphids that attack plants and trees. They are often encouraged by gardeners because they do the job of an insecticide naturally. Farmers even raise ladybugs for this purpose.

Ladybugs are beetles that have two pairs of wings and belong to the order Coleoptera. The front wings have been converted into hard sheaths that cover the other two wings when they are not in use. Ladybugs have characteristic black spots on a vivid red or yellow body. Coleopterans, or beetles, are found all over the world. There are at least 350,000 species, making up almost half of known insects. Beetles are found in almost every habitat and are able to survive even the harshest conditions.

What is a praying mantis?

This is a little green insect that gets its name from the position it is often seen in. It puts its front two legs together and looks like it is saying its prayers.

The praying mantis is well known because the female eats the male after they have finished mating. They are ferocious predators and feed mainly on other insects. This insect is also famous for its powers of camouflage. It blends perfectly into its habitat and so catches any approaching insects. The praying mantis is useful because it catches insects that damage plants or carry diseases.

Ladybugs are extremely good at getting rid of aphids. Many farmers raise them for that purpose.

How does a firefly make its light?

Fireflies, or lightning bugs, have small luminous organs that make light.

These luminous organs are made up of different layers of tissue. The upper layer is covered with grains that produce the light; the lower layer contains crystal cells that reflect the light. Air circulates through little veins in these grains. What probably happens is the firefly opens these veins, oxygen enters, and light appears. Male fireflies fly slowly over the ground, looking for females hidden in the grass. Every five seconds the light flashes, and if they are lucky, a female responds with her own light. This guides the male until at last he finds his partner. Some types of firefly only make light at the larva or grub stage of their development. They are known as glowworms, and their light has nothing to do with looking for a partner.

How are butterflies born?

Butterflies develop from caterpillars.

Butterflies lay eggs that grow into caterpillars. These are extremely greedy creatures, and for that reason the eggs are usually laid on the caterpillar's favorite plant so they can eat as much as they like. They grow fast and adopt various strategies to survive. They may be covered with prickly hair or just look like part of their background; they may even have a foul taste that a predator will avoid. When a caterpillar is big enough, it weaves a cocoon: it ejects a sticky substance that hardens in contact with air and becomes a sort of silky pocket. Within this cocoon, the caterpillar becomes a chrysalis. Then the animal changes completely, cuts a hole in the cocoon, and flies away as a butterfly.

Why do termites love wood so much?

Termites hollow out wood to build their structures

The hatching of a butterfly, like this two-tailed pasha, is a delicate moment in the life of the insect. It is an easy meal for any passing bird.

can be real pests. They are able to climb into narrow crevices, under floorboards, behind cupboards, and into drains and sewers. They raid human food supplies, spoiling the food and causing disease. These creatures are hard to get rid of. Insecticides are used, but then the cockroach adapts and once again survives to breed. The only real solution is to have nothing available for them to eat, which is not easy.

and because they eat the cellulose in dead wood.

Termites cannot actually digest cellulose, but little micro-organisms that live in their digestive tubes can. Termites are little insects, no bigger than half an inch (15 millimeters). They work together as a unit and are a formidable force. No house is safe once they have entered! Termites are cunning animals. They penetrate wood and then cover their tracks by blocking the hole through which they came. Termites also live on the ground and change the shape of the ground as they move earth to make their home, building towering structures. In the African Congo termite mounds have been found that weigh as much as 11,000 tons.

What exactly
are cockroaches?

Cockroaches were one of the first animals to appear on Earth and were here long before the dinosaur put in an appearance.

Cockroaches are great survivors and will eat virtually anything, including glue, plastic cables, and sometimes even other cock-roaches. In hard times they can live without food or water for up to a month. They also breed very often, and a female can have as many as 180 young in a year. Only about one percent of the three and a half thousand species of cockroach live in close contact with humans, but the ones that do

Termites are tiny insects that like to build. Structures several feet high may be constructed, such as the one shown above, involving millions of termites.

Do man-eating ants exist?

There are some ants that are capable of eating a human. This does not mean they will attack and kill someone. However, should a person be badly wounded and lying on the ground in their territory, he or she may end up being eaten by ants. These ants can be very hungry and very fierce.

There are 6,000 types of ants known today. They feed on many different things: seeds, fungi, sap, and even meat. Examples of carnivorous ants are found in South America and in Africa. Both species are capable of harming humans. They will attack and eat almost anything that gets in their way as they move in columns from place to place. Nothing is safe when these animals are on the march!

Do ants live in a kind of society?

Yes, all known species of ants do.

Ant societies vary greatly in the number of members they have. Some species of ants live in groups of just half a dozen, others live with a million individuals. In an ant hill, adults fall into two categories: workers and the queen. The division of labor is not as clear-cut as it is with bees. An ant worker can have a number of roles: scouting for food, digging the ant hill, protecting it against invaders, looking after the young, and so on. The queen's job is to lay eggs and nothing more. She can live as long as 15 years, while a worker generally lives no more than three or four months.

Why do ants have antennae?

Without antennae on their heads, ants would not be able to find their way around because they have very poor eyesight.

These antennae are sensory organs, highly sensitive to smell, taste, and touch. They are covered with very fine hair. Ants have their own smell and recognize each other by it. They can tell whether another ant is from their hill and will reject an ant that comes from somewhere else.

Is the spider an insect?

No, contrary to popular belief, spiders are not insects. They belong to a group known as arachnids.

There are many differences between spiders and insects. For a start, a spider has eight legs and an insect has six. An insect's body is divided into three parts: the head, thorax, and abdomen. A spider's body is made up of two parts: the head and the body. Insects have only two big eyes with lots of sides to them; spiders usually have eight eyes in two rows. Insects always have a pair of antennae; spiders do not, but their raised front legs are sometimes mistaken for antennae. Finally, all spiders are carnivorous. They have a little pouch of poison that they inject into their prey to kill it. The poison from most North American spiders could not harm a human.

Are there many types of spider?

More than 100,000 species have been recorded.

Contrary to popular belief, spiders are not insects but arachnids. They catch their prey in webs and are carnivorous (meat-eaters).

Spiders occur throughout the world, but the greatest number are found in the tropics. Their shapes, sizes, colors, and behavior vary tremendously. Some spiders have round abdomens; others are flattened, widened, or elongated. Some have hairy abdomens; others have spines and bumps. Some tropical spiders have smooth, brightly colored skin. Spiders may be identified according to their way of life. Sedentary or sitting spiders live on their webs and wait for their prey to come to them. Their web is both a house and a trap. Other spiders are the roving kind and run about the ground looking for their prey. Wolf-spiders hunt down their prey. Generally speaking, spiders are solitary animals, but there are some species that live in a large communal web. Spiders are land animals. There is one species, however, that spins its web between sea grasses. Once it has done that, it constructs a sort of diving-bell, fills it with air, and lives underwater.

Is the scorpion

like the spider?

Yes, the scorpion, like the spider, is an arachnid.

The scorpion has a flexible tail that can bend right over its body. At the end of this impressive tail is a poisonous sting. Scorpions are carnivorous. They seize their prey with two claws, situated at the front of the body. Then they

The scorpion belongs to the same family as the spider: Arachnida.

slowly. If they are disturbed by an enemy, many of them will curl up into a ball and secrete a toxic substance from their backs. This is a very effective method of protection.

Are earthworms harmful?

Quite the opposite, they are very useful animals. Earthworms are sometimes confused with white larvae of beetles.

inject their poison. The sting from most scorpions causes a physical reaction in humans, usually no worse than a bee sting. However, the sting of certain species can kill a human within a few hours.

How many legs does a centipede have?

Centipedes have a maximum of 300 to 400 legs. Centipedes and millipedes belong to a group of arthropods (animals with jointed feet) called myriapods.

The word *myriapoda* comes from Greek and means many-legged. The name indicates they have lots of legs, and certainly they have more than most other animals. Some centipedes have about 340 legs but some have only 30. Millipedes may have as many as 400 legs. Perhaps not surprising, centipedes are fast runners and chase their prey. They are carnivorous, predatory, and use a pair of poisonous fangs to paralyze their victims. They like to attack other arthropods, but some of the larger tropical species can catch small birds, lizards, or mice. Some centipedes can inflict a fairly painful bite on a human. Millipedes, on the other hand, are vegetarians and move around

Beetle larvae are a pest because they often eat plant roots. Earthworms, on the other hand, dig into the soil and feed on microorganisms in it. They frequently come to the surface and leave behind some of the earth they have swallowed. In this way, they break up the humus and allow air and water to get into the soil more easily. This not only contributes to the healthy growth of plants, but is also necessary for the wellbeing of microorganisms living in the soil. An earthworm's work is quite formidable. In a year, in 2½ acres of land (1 hectare), earthworms tunnel and aerate something like 30 tons of earth!

Are maggots worms?

Maggots are not worms. They are the larvae of flies.

There are several groups of worms. They fall basically into three categories: flat worms, tube worms, and earthworms. However, people mistakenly call certain animals a worm when in fact they are not at all. The most common mistakes are made with maggots and glowworms.

What is a hybrid?

Hybrids are the offspring of two different species or subspecies of animal or plant.

There are natural hybrids and hybrids created by humans. A natural hybrid is formed when two animals are genetically similar and live in the same environment. There are, for example, a great number of hybrids among birds and fish. Humans have created hybrids by breeding different species together. We have created domestic types of animal that no longer looked like their ancient

Tarantulas are big hairy spiders that live in warm climates. They are rarely dangerous.

ancestors. This is how the mule came into being. It is the offspring of a male donkey and a female horse. A hinny is the offspring of a male horse and a female donkey. Both are similar to horses, but they have their own character. Perhaps you have heard the phrase "as stubborn as a mule"? Hybrids cannot usually have offspring of their own, but there have been exceptions.

Are tarantulas dangerous?

Certain types are, but most are harmless. Tarantulas are often kept as pets.

Spiders are carnivores with poisonous fangs they use to paralyze their prey. But a spider's venom is usually so weak, and is ejected in such small quantities, that it is rarely a threat to a human. Scientists classify spiders as either true spiders or tarantulas, according to certain differences in their bodies. Tarantulas are large, hairy spiders that live in warm climates and throughout the tropics. The tarantulas found in the United States are quiet creatures that live in burrows. Their bite is no worse than a bee sting. They defend themselves by means of thousands of tiny body hairs, which they can fling in the air and which can cause a nasty rash. The bite of some South American tarantulas can be serious.

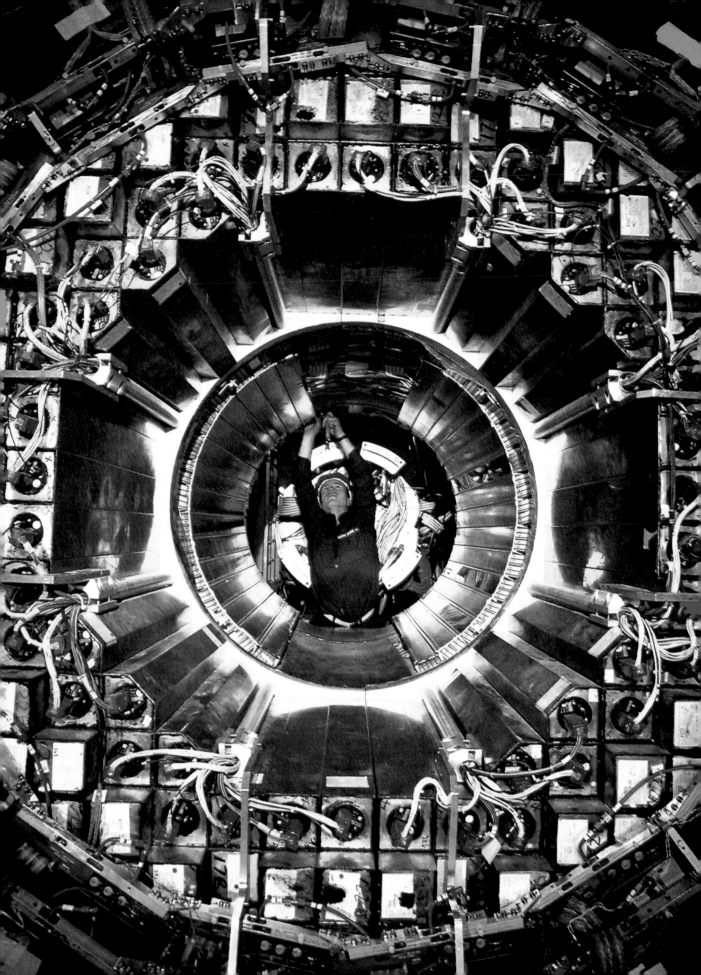

Science Basics

What is an atom?

All matter is made up of very small particles called atoms. The word "atom" comes from the Greek and means "that which cannot be divided."

The Greek philosopher Democritus deduced the existence of atoms as early as 400 B.C. John Dalton, an English chemist, first set out the atomic theory of matter in 1803. For a long time it was thought that atoms could not be divided. Hendrik Lorentz, a Dutchman, proposed that atoms could be split and contained negatively charged particles called electrons. Electrons were discovered in 1897 by J.J. Thomson, a British physicist. The electrons surround the central nucleus of the atom. The nucleus itself is made up of protons, which are positively charged particles, and neutrons, uncharged particles. In solids, the atoms are firmly linked to each other. In fluids (gases and liquids), the links are less rigid.

How big is an atom?

An atom is tiny (a hundred-millionth of a centimeter only) and is therefore invisible to the naked eye. However, individual atoms can be detected by modern electron microscopes.

An optical microscope can enlarge up to 2,500 times; an electron microscope can enlarge hundreds of millions of times. The nucleus of the atom is 10,000 times smaller than the atom itself. The protons and neutrons in the nucleus are made up of even smaller particles called quarks. To study these particles, scientists try to separate their constituents by bombarding them with beams of high-energy particles in machines called particle accelerators.

Are subatomic particles stable?

Subatomic particles cannot be divided, but can transform into other elementary particles. Therefore, in this sense they are unstable.

A particle accelerator like that at CERN is used for studying atoms and particles by making them hit each other at very high speeds.

A neutron can only exist outside the nucleus for about 15 minutes, after which it decays into a proton, an electron, and a neutrino. Neutrinos are not easy to detect and were only discovered in 1956. They are very small and have neither mass nor electrical charge. There are many other types of elementary particles that are unstable and can transform into other particles. These changes occur within a tiny fraction of a second.

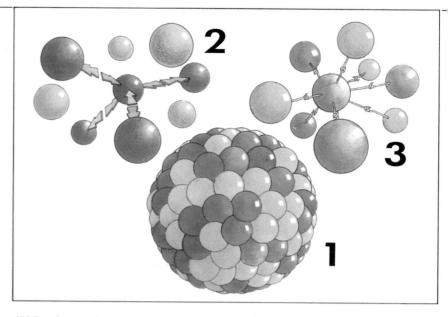

(1) In the nucleus of an atom, protons (shown red) and neutrons (shown green) are held together by the nuclear force. (2) Positively charged protons (red) repel each other just like any other electric charges with the same sign. This repulsive force acts against the nuclear force. (3) The nucleus has a spherical shape because of the tension at its surface.

What is nuclear energy?

It is the energy that comes from splitting the nucleus of an atom. This type of energy can be produced from a fuel called uranium, which is extracted from mines. The world's major uranium mines are found in the U.S., Canada, and South Africa.

The uranium fuel is shaped into rods and inserted into the center of a reactor, which is a kind of airtight box. The fuel is then bombarded with neutrons. The nuclei of the uranium atoms split into smaller nuclei, releasing energy and more neutrons. These neutrons strike other nuclei and produce an continuous chain of reactions that give out an enormous quantity of heat. One gram (0.035 ounce) of uranium produces the same energy as two and a half tons of coal. The scientist Albert Einstein (1879–1955) first described the energy contained inside the nucleus of an atom in 1905.

What is nuclear energy used for?

It has two different uses: one is for peaceful purposes and the other for military purposes.

The vast amount of heat produced in a nuclear plant can be used to boil water to produce steam at high pressure. This steam is used to turn turbines to make electricity. This causes less pollution and is safer than some other chemical industries. Nuclear energy is also used in nuclear arms. The atom bomb is the most devastating weapon ever created. By releasing all its nuclear energy at once, the atom bomb destroys its target through the blast of its explosion and the heat and radiation it gives out. The first atom bomb was exploded in Nevada on July 16, 1945. Two bombs were dropped by the Americans on Hiroshima and Nagasaki in Japan in August 1945.

No other atom bomb has been used in a conflict since.

Is a nuclear power plant dangerous?

When the uranium nucleus splits apart, it releases some of its nuclear energy as heat. The smaller nuclei left as waste products give off some dangerous emissions, called radiation. Anyone who is exposed to a large amount of radiation may die.

In order to avoid radioactive leakage, reactors in nuclear power plants are equipped with protective airtight devices. Highly sensitive machines close to the reactors monitor radioactivity levels continuously. Moreover, these power plants are designed to withstand violent shocks such as plane crashes and natural catastrophes such as earthquakes. Many people are opposed to nuclear power plants, in particular environmentalists who wish to protect nature. They emphasize the fact that the surveillance system cannot always prevent serious accidents, such as the fire in the Chernobyl plant in Russia in April 1986. Neither are they satisfied with the way nuclear waste (which is still radioactive) is disposed of. It is sometimes dumped on the seabed, which is dangerous for the environment.

What is radiation?

Unstable nuclei can change spontaneously into more stable nuclei. This process, radioactive decay, gives out radiation – alpha, beta, or gamma rays. The French physicist Henri Becquerel (1852–1908) began the study of radioactivity. He noticed that uranium salts could form a picture on a photographic plate and deduced that uranium emitted a kind of radiation.

A radioactive nucleus may emit a burst of radiation at any time. Alpha and beta radiation are particles, while gamma rays are short-wavelength electromagnetic waves. A Geiger-Muller tube is used for detecting these kinds of radiation. When a particle enters the tube, it produces a momentary electric current. By detecting the current, we can determine the number of particles passing through the tube. Radioactivity can be found in the atmosphere, in the

The radiation from the Sun consists of electromagnetic waves, which range from gamma rays to radio waves. The solar spectrum lies in between these two extremes: 55 percent infrared radiation (IR), 42 percent visible light (A), and 3 percent ultraviolet radiation (UV).

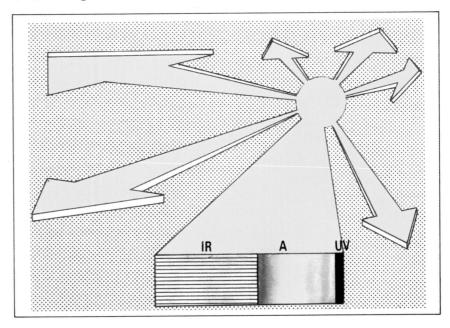

Earth, and even inside our bodies. Man can be exposed to different sorts of radiation: natural (for example, from rocks) and artificial (for example, medical X-rays).

What is a wavelength?

When you throw a stone into a pond, you see small, circular ripples that spread out farther and farther. These are waves. In the same way, light moves in a series of wavelike crests and troughs that travel in all directions in a straight line. The distance between two crests is fixed: this is the wavelength.

Wavelength can be very short (for X-rays) or quite long (for radio waves). Light waves travel very quickly in air (at about 190,000

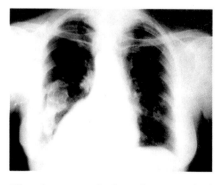

The human body photographed with X-rays.

miles per second/300,000 kilometers per second), but they travel more slowly in glass or water. The different wavelengths of the various types of electromagnetic radiation (visible light, radio waves, infrared rays, and X-rays) give them their characteristic properties.

What is an X-ray?

X-rays are invisible yet powerful rays. Like visible light, they travel in waves. Their wavelength is smaller than that of visible light.

X-rays were discovered by Wilhelm Roentgen (1845–1923). They may be produced in an X-ray tube when a narrow beam of electrons from a heated element strikes the surface of a massive heat-conducting target. The target is a small disk made of a heavy metal, usually tungsten. This metal is used because it does not melt at the high temperatures found in an X-ray tube. The electrons stop suddenly when they hit the target, giving out X-rays. Some electrons are traveling so fast when they hit the target that they knock electrons out from deep within the cloud of electrons around the atoms in the target metal. Other electrons take their

place, giving off high-energy X-rays as they do so.

Can you see inside someone's body?

You can take a picture of the inside of someone's body by placing that person between a weak source of X-rays and a sheet of film. This gives a picture of the person's skeleton because X-rays go through skin and flesh, but not through bones. X-rays allow doctors to see bone malformations and fractures.

The machines used to take medical X-rays send out beams of X-rays just as a flashgun sends out visible light. X-rays pass through the skin and flesh of a human body in the same way that light goes through glass. However, X-rays are unable to pass through bone. The X-rays produce an image on the film. X-ray pictures are also used by dentists to check how teeth are growing and to see if there are any cavities. Modern techniques such as computed tomography (CT scans) use X-rays and computers to produce images of the tissues and organs in the body, not just of the bones.

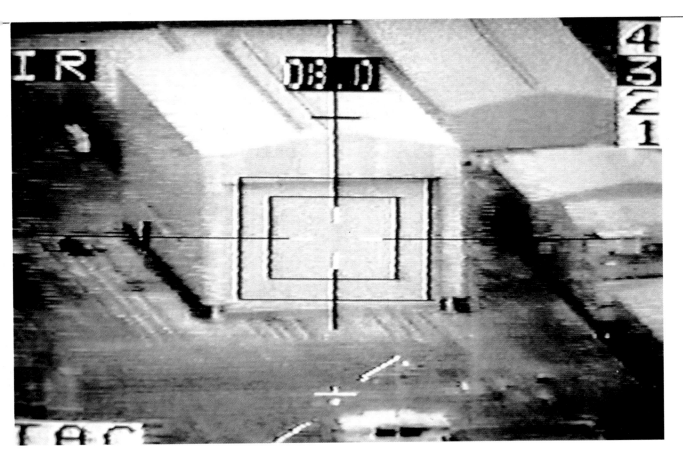

Even though infrared rays are invisible to the human eye, they can be detected by some photographic films and video cameras. Here you can see a target viewed with an infrared camera in a war plane during the Gulf War.

What is light?

Light is a form of energy that helps us see what is around us. There are many sources of light. Natural light comes from the Sun, the stars, and lightning. Burning wood, wax, oil, and all sorts of lamps (oil, gas, argon, and sodium) produce what we call artificial light.

The Sun is the most important source of light and heat for our planet. A large quantity of energy comes from the center of the Sun as hydrogen changes into helium through a series of nuclear reactions. Light from the Sun radiates into space in all directions. Without solar energy, the Earth would be dark and frozen. No animals could survive on it, and no plants could grow. Like the Sun, stars are luminous globes of burning gas producing their own heat and light. However, they are much farther away from us than the Sun and are so faint that they can only be seen at night when the sky is clear. The Moon is also a natural source of light. It does not give out light of its own because it is not a star, but it reflects the light of the Sun. Depending on its position in its orbit around the Earth, we can see a larger or smaller part of its surface that is lit by the Sun.

Are there rays that we cannot see?

Part of the Sun's energy is made up of invisible radiation (infrared and ultraviolet rays). These rays are invisible to the eye, but we can feel infrared radiation as heat, and ultraviolet rays cause our skin to tan.

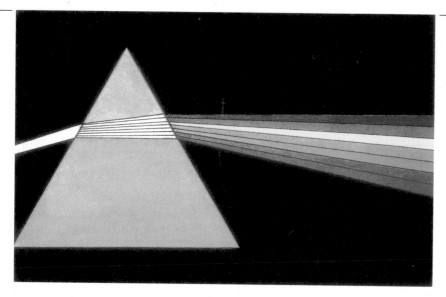

When a ray of light from the Sun passes through a prism, it is split into many colors.

The infrared rays keep the Earth and the atmosphere at a favorable temperature. Only small quantities of ultraviolet rays reach the surface of the Earth, since most are absorbed in the atmosphere. These small quantities are vital for life. The action of ultraviolet rays on our skin produces vitamin D, which is needed for bones, and causes the skin to tan, which protects us against the Sun's rays. However, too much exposure to ultraviolet radiation can cause skin cancer.

Why can we see colors?

Color is one of the most important aspects of light. Three hundred years ago Isaac Newton (1642–1727) experimented by shining a ray of pure white light through a glass prism. Seven colors appeared: red, orange, yellow, green, blue, indigo, and violet. These colors make up the visible spectrum.

These colors are seen in a rainbow because the raindrops act like tiny glass prisms, splitting the sunlight into the different colors. We see an object as a particular color because it reflects that color of light from its surface and absorbs the other colors. For instance, an apple looks red because it absorbs all the colors except red, which it reflects. An object that absorbs all the colors of the spectrum and reflects none looks black. Black is the absence of color and can only be seen in contrast to other colors.

What does "primary color" mean?

Primary colors are colors that cannot be made by mixing together other colors. When we mix light, the primary colors are blue, red, and green. These colors are used in a color television. When we mix paints or printing inks, as in the photographs in this book, the primary colors are magenta, cyan, and yellow.

By mixing together the primary colors used in printing inks, the printer can create all the other colors we can see. Mixing two primary colors together produces secondary colors: yellow and cyan make green, cyan and magenta make blue, and yellow and magenta make red. All of these colors together make black.

Can you make a rainbow at home?

You need a triangular-shaped piece of glass that

Laser beams lighting the sky at night during a music festival in Paris, France.

has no bubbles or defects in it. This is called a prism. Place it in sunlight: the light coming out of the prism will be split into the colors of the rainbow.

Each color of light has its own wavelength. When a beam of light passes through a prism, it is bent as it enters and as it leaves. The different wavelengths of light are bent by different amounts, which splits the beam of sunlight into the colors of the rainbow.

What is laser light?

It is an intense beam of light of a single wavelength, and therefore a single color. A laser beam is very narrow and can travel great distances without broadening. The machine that produces laser light is called a laser.

The word laser comes from the initial letters of Light Amplification by Stimulated Emission of Radiation. A laser beam is made up of light rays gathered in such a way that they oscillate together. As a result, these waves move together in a concentrated narrow beam, unlike light from the Sun or a light bulb, which travels in all directions. The process of stimulated emission was first described by Albert Einstein in 1917, but the first laser was not built until 1960, by the American scientist Theodore Maiman.

What are lasers used for?

More and more uses have been found for lasers in a wide variety of fields.

Lasers are used for making holes in metal, for soldering, or for cutting tiny objects. They can even be used for cutting diamonds. In the field of medicine, laser beams are used for surgery that requires a great deal of accuracy. Surgeons use them in delicate operations (on eyes or vocal cords). Engineers use lasers for measuring distances accurately. Using laser beams, it is possible to measure the distance between the Earth and the Moon to within a fraction of an inch. They are also used in optical fiber telecommunication systems, and low-power lasers are used in compact disk players.

What is a microwave?

It is an electromagnetic wave with a wavelength in the range of 300–300,000 megahertz (100 megahertz is the same as 100 million hertz). Microwaves are used to transmit signals in radio and television broadcasting, and also in cooking.

In the future, solar plants may be in orbit around the Earth. They will use microwaves to send solar energy to the Earth.

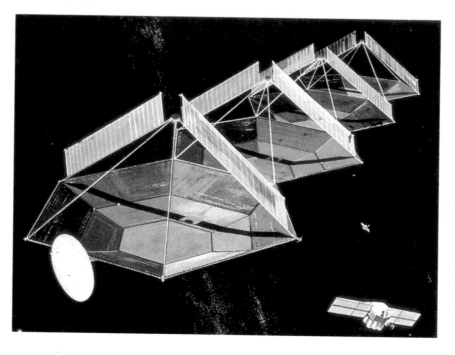

Percy Le Baron, an American scientist, noticed that the electromagnetic tubes used for producing radar also produced heat. He put some kernels of corn in a paper bag in the field of one of the tubes: the corn turned into popcorn. On October 8, 1945, he applied for a patent for what was to be the first microwave oven. This appliance had a power of about 1600 watts. At the time, microwave ovens were designed for hospitals and cafeterias, and they were very large and expensive. The first microwave ovens for home use only came on the market in 1967. Microwave ovens have three uses: defrosting, fast cooking, and pulsed heating.

How do we measure temperature?

Temperature can be measured with a thermo-meter. The most common thermometer is a glass tube containing a liquid (mercury or colored alcohol) that rises and falls according to the temperature.

Thermometers use the principle of the expansion of a liquid with heat. When the temperature rises, the liquid expands and its volume increases. It then needs more space and rises inside the tube. When the temperature drops, the liquid level falls. Along the tube are markings that divide the tube into small sections called degrees. The symbol for "degree" is a small circle placed next to the number of degrees (for example, 20°F). Thermometers can be used to measure the room temperature, the temperature outside (usually in a sheltered place), and the body's temperature. The first thermometers used for measuring the body's temperature were water thermometers, invented in 1626 by a doctor called Santorio.

The burner at the base of the hot-air balloon heats the air. This hot air fills the balloon, lifting it up into the sky and keeping it there.

What does the letter "F" next to the degrees mean?

It means that the temperature is measured on the Fahrenheit temperature scale, as so many degrees Fahrenheit. This scale is named after its inventor, the German scientist Gabriel Fahrenheit (1686–1736).

Another scale used for measuring temperature is the Celsius scale (°C), named after the Swedish scientist Ander Celsius (1701–74). This scale is commonly used in many countries around the world. The two fixed points in the Celsius scale, the temperature at which ice melts and the temperature at which water boils, are given the values 0°C and 100°C. The interval between the two is split into 100 equal degrees. In the Fahrenheit scale 32°F is the equivalent of 0°C and 212°F is the equivalent of 100°C. Both scales indicate the same thing; that is, the temperature where the thermometer is placed.

What is absolute zero?

It is the lowest possible temperature, at which all particles become motionless. Nothing can be colder than absolute zero. It is the zero of the Kelvin temperature scale and is equivalent to –459.67°F (–273.15°C).

Some scientists have managed to produce temperatures very close to absolute zero. The temperature in interstellar space is very close to absolute zero. At temperatures close to –459°F (–273°C), some metals lose their electrical resistance and become superconducting, which means that electrical current can flow through them without any resistance. The study of materials at temperatures close to absolute zero is called cryogenics.

Why does warm air rise?

Air is a mixture of invisible gases, mainly nitrogen, oxygen, and carbon dioxide. Warm air is lighter than colder air, so it rises.

This explains why winds blow. In the tropics, the air is warmed by the Sun and rises. Other masses of air come to replace it in the form of winds. This movement of the air creates circular currents all around the Earth. In a room, a radiator warms up the air that surrounds it. The warm air rises and cold air is pulled in from all over the room. This air warms up as it comes closer to the radiator and rises as well. This movement, called convection, is similar to the movement of the wind. It works like a light wind that spreads the heat of the radiator all over the room.

What produces heat?

Heat is the movement of the atoms that make up all matter. The more the atoms in an object move, the warmer the object is.

High-tension transmission lines carry electricity from power stations to the city. The lines are held above ground by pylons 165 feet (50 meters) high.

Objects can be heated in different ways. For instance, you can warm your hands by rubbing them together; this is friction. Or you can make a metal rod hot by hitting it hard; this is known as percussion. Heat is often released in chemical reactions. An example is the heat given off when an object burns in air, a process called combustion. Heat may also be given off when chemicals are mixed together, such as when sulfuric acid is mixed with water. A wire heats up when an electric current is flowing through it. Heat travels through solids from particle to particle in a process called conduction, and in fluids (liquids and gases) by a process called convection. Heat in the form of infrared radiation can also spread at a distance through air and even through certain materials.

What is electricity?

It is a form of energy produced by the movement of electrons. Electricity was discovered around 600 B.C. when the Greek philosopher Thales noticed that when amber was rubbed, it attracted light objects.

At the time it was not clear what released the electrical charge. It is easy to release and make electrons move in certain materials, in particular in metals where electrons are only lightly attached to the atoms. This is why metal wires are used to carry electrical currents; they are good conductors. There are two types of electricity: static and current. Static electricity can be found on objects or in clouds (which release their electric charge as lightning). The basic principle of static electricity is that opposite charges are attracted to each other and like charges repel each other. The French physicist Charles Coulomb (1738–1806) discovered the law of the forces of electric and magnetic attraction. Current electricity is created by the movement of electric charge in conductors. The Italian scientist Alessandro Volta (1745–1827) showed that electricity moves through conductors.

What is the difference between alternating current and direct current?

Everyday household current is alternating current (AC). The advantage of alternating current over direct current (DC), as obtained from a battery, is that its voltage can be raised or lowered economically by a transformer.

Alternating current is raised or lowered between zero and about 340 volts and then brought back to zero again. This cycle is called half-phase or half-period, and the frequency is the number of times the sequence is repeated in one second. In the U.S. there are 60 cycles a second (or 60 hertz, as one hertz is the equivalent of one cycle per second), while in Europe there are 50 cycles per second. Everyday household current (about 22,000 volts) is produced by power stations. It is raised to 400,000 volts and carried by high-tension transmission lines supported by steel pylons. These carry the current to substations where the voltage is reduced to about 132,000 volts. Underground or aerial cables take it (after the voltage has been lowered to 120 volts) to factories, offices, and homes.

How do electric cells work?

Electric cells change chemical energy into electrical energy. Chemicals inside the cell react together to make an electric current flow.

A cell usually consists of two electrodes separated by an electrolyte. The electrolyte reacts with both the electrodes. One of the electrodes ends up with an excess of electrons and therefore has a negative charge. The other electrode ends up with a deficit of electrons and therefore has a positive charge. When the electrodes are connected, for example through a light bulb, the potential difference between them causes a current to flow and the bulb lights. Most batteries are dry-cell batteries or primary cells; the chemicals inside them are eventually used up. Dry cells contain a chemical paste or gel and do not leak, which is why they are called dry cells. Car batteries are secondary cells, since they can be recharged. They contain liquid

chemicals and are called wet cells. In a laboratory in England, a battery has been working since 1840. It has been producing a low current for over 150 years.

What is the difference between a watt, a volt, and an ampere?

All of these are units used with electricity. The watt is the unit used for measuring the consumption of energy or power. The volt is the unit used for measuring electric potential difference. The ampere is the unit used for measuring electric current.

A 100-watt bulb will use up 100 power units in a second. This energy is turned into heat and

Modern batteries are more powerful and less damaging to the environment because they contain less mercury.

light. The watt is named after James Watt, the Scottish engineer who developed the steam engine. The Italian physicist Alessandro Volta gave his name to the volt. He invented the first electric cell. Operating voltages are quoted on all electrical appliances (bulbs, vacuum cleaners, heaters, and so on). Amperes are named after the French scientist André Ampère .

Why do magnets attract iron?

Over 2,500 years ago the Greeks discovered a rock, called magnetite, which attracted iron and steel objects and could mag-netize them. Today magnets are produced artificially.

Magnets are made from small bars of iron or steel (sometimes made in the shape of a horseshoe). The magnet is surrounded by a magnetic field, which attracts iron objects. The force of attraction is strongest at the ends of the magnet, called the north and south poles. Iron filings sprinkled around a magnet form into a pattern that shows the magnetic field lines. The north pole is so named because a freely suspended magnet will always turn so that this pole points toward the Earth's magnetic north pole. This property was used in the invention of the compass. Only certain materials are attracted by magnets: these include the metals iron, cobalt, and nickel.

What is an electromagnet?

When an electric current flows through a wire, it produces a magnetic field. A coil of wire carrying an electric current makes a stronger magnet. Magnets built in this way are called electromagnets.

Electromagnets are used for lifting heavy pieces of iron. When the current is switched on, the magnet can lift the iron. When the current is switched off, the piece of iron can be deposited in the desired place. They are also used for separating iron and steel waste from copper, glass, and aluminum. Many household appliances, such as electric bells and electric motors, contain electromagnets.

How does a wave propagate?

Sound waves are produced when an object vibrates. Sound waves reach our ears

Television transmissions travel only in straight lines. From the studio (1) the television transmission is sent via a small antenna (2) or sometimes along cables to the main transmitter (3); this transmitter sends out the signal into space where it can be picked up by private antennae (4). When there are mountains in the way (5), they act as screens and block the transmissions. Special relay transmitters are needed (6) to make sure that people who live on the other side of the mountains can also receive the television broadcasts. In some places, however, special antennae are required.

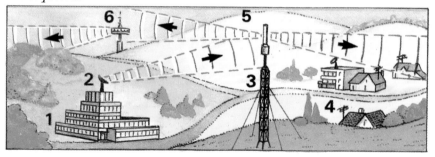

through the air; sound cannot travel in a vacuum. Sound waves travel in air with a speed of about 1,115 feet (340 meters) per second at normal temperatures. Light waves travel with a speed of 186,000 miles (300,000 kilometers) per second and can travel in air as well as in a vacuum.

These satellite dishes at a telecommunication station can receive television transmissions from all over the world.

Radio and television broadcasts are transmitted as electromagnetic waves. These waves are produced by the rapid oscillation of electric fields in the antennae of the transmitters. They are invisible and, like visible light, travel at 186,000 miles (300,000 kilometers) per second. Electromagnetic waves can propagate along cables or through space from an antenna, and can travel thousands of miles.

How is a radio

wave received?

It can be picked up through an antenna. The design of an antenna depends on the wavelength of the signal. Long waves may use long wire antennae, short waves may use rods and dipoles or reflectors; parabolic dish antennae can also be used.

A parabolic dish may measure up to 20 inches (50 centimeters) across and can pick up broadcasts as very weak signals from satellites in space.

When a radio wave reaches the antenna it produces a small electrical current. This current runs along a cable down to the receiver where it is converted into sound. The antenna captures signals that may come from many different transmitters. The signals do not get mixed up because each of them has a different frequency (number of vibrations per second). Radio signals are generally divided into the following categories: long wave, medium wave, short wave, and VHF (very high frequency). The radio can be tuned to receive

a particular signal. An antenna will receive as well as transmit. Radar antennae can receive and transmit at the same time.

How do we receive

a television

broadcast?

A television camera is made from a tube coated with a material that is sensitive to light. It converts the pattern of light it receives into a pattern of electrical charges. This is scanned line by line to produce an electrical signal, which is then amplified and broadcast as an electromagnetic wave.

The signal is received by the television set via its antenna or through a cable and appears on the screen in lines (the American standard is 525 lines; in Europe it is 625 lines).

The picture tube of a television is made of thick, transparent glass. All the air is removed from inside the tube. The inside of the screen is coated with dots of chemicals (phosphors) that glow when hit by a beam of electrons. A color television has dots that glow red, blue, and green. The beam of electrons comes from an electron gun at the end of the tube. The signal received causes this beam to scan across the screen in horizontal lines from the top to the bottom, mirroring the action of the gun in the television camera. Each second the screen is scanned 30 times (25 times in Europe), so we see a moving picture that is the same as the scene in front of the camera. John Logie Baird (1888–1946) is credited as being the inventor of the television.

Why can we hear sounds?

Sound travels as waves. A vibrating object makes the air around it vibrate, too. Vibrations travel through the air and make our eardrums vibrate. This sends messages to our brain, enabling us to hear sounds.

Sound can travel through water and hard materials such as glass and metal (sound waves need a substance to travel through). When you speak, the molecules in the air vibrate, creating sound waves. When sound waves reach someone's ears, their eardrums vibrate, and they can hear you.

What is the sound barrier?

Most planes fly at a speed that is below the speed of sound (1,115 feet per second/340 meters per second). Their speed is described as subsonic. Some planes can travel faster than the speed of sound, and they are described as supersonic.

The airliner Concorde, for example, can fly at a speed equal to twice that of sound (Mach 2). When a plane reaches the speed of sound, it comes across a resistance, called the sound barrier. When the plane flies through this barrier, a double boom can be heard, which is caused by the sound waves forming two shock waves, one at the front and one at the back of the aircraft. These are similar to bow waves from a fast-moving boat. American test pilot Chuck Yeager first flew through the "barrier" on October 14, 1947.

How is sound measured?

Instruments can measure the intensity (or loudness) of sound waves. The unit used is the decibel (dB).

The ear can bear sounds up to 120 decibels. Rustling paper has an intensity of about 10 decibels, and speech is between 20 and 50

The Concorde is the only airliner that travels faster than the speed of sound.

decibels; a train registers between 65 and 90 decibels, while the noise of a jet plane taking off has an intensity between 110 and 140 dB. Anything above 90 decibels can damage the ear. Our ears cannot hear very high- or low-pitched sounds. High-pitched sounds are called ultrasound. Bats find their way by sending out high-pitched "ultrasonic" sounds that bounce back to them as echoes.

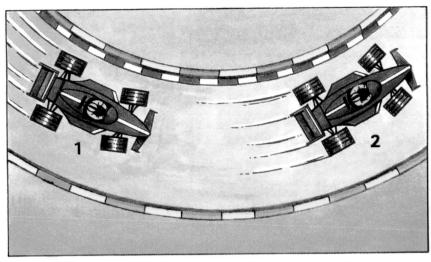

If the source of a sound is moving, the pitch of the sound will change. As a result, the sound you can hear when a car is coming toward you (1) will be higher-pitched than when it is moving away from you (2).

How can a low-pitched sound turn into a high-pitched one?

A sound has a high or low pitch depending on its frequency – the number of vibrations it makes per second (hertz, or Hz). A whistle produces rapid vibrations and a foghorn slow vibrations. The lowest note audible to the ear is about 20 Hz. The highest sound we can hear is 20,000 Hz.

The pitch of the sound produced by a stringed instrument, such as a violin, can be changed by tightening or loosening the string and also by holding down the string at different places so a shorter or longer length vibrates. In the case of wind instruments, the pitch of the sound is changed by blocking different holes with the fingers. The pitch of a sound can also change if the wave source moves relative to the observer. The pitch of a car engine as it approaches is higher than when it moves away. This phenomenon, the Doppler effect, is named after Christian Doppler, the scientist who discovered it.

Why can we see ourselves in a mirror?

A mirror is a plate of polished glass coated on the back with aluminum, silver, or pewter. This coating reflects the light waves back toward the eye.

Dull surfaces scatter light in all directions, but smooth surfaces reflect light in a regular way. When you look at your reflection, light travels from your face through the glass and bounces straight back again from the shiny metal coating, producing a sharp image.

Why do we look the wrong way around in a mirror?

The reflection produced by a flat mirror is exactly the

same size as the object and seems to be behind the mirror. The left side of the object appears on the left side of the image, which would be the right side of a real object. In the reflection right and left are reversed.

This is called lateral inversion. Our image is reversed, and we see ourselves "the wrong way around." A flat mirror produces a symmetrical image of the object in front of it. A spherical concave mirror can produce two kinds of image. If the object is near the mirror, the reflection is larger than the object, but if the object is far away, the image formed is small and upside down. A spherical convex mirror produces a smaller image, as in a car's rearview mirror. Whatever its size, the image is always the wrong way around.

Why do glasses help us see better?

People who do not have perfect eyesight can see better with glasses, which make corrections for their eyesight.

Light enters the eye through the cornea (the rounded part of the eye) and passes through the circular opening (pupil) in the iris (the colored part of the eye). The light is focused onto the retina at the back of the eye by the combined action of the curved cornea and the crystalline lens (the rounded transparent structure behind the iris). People need glasses or contact lenses if their eyes cannot focus the light on the retina to form a sharp image. The lenses in the glasses or contact lenses bend the light so that the eye's own lens can focus the image correctly.

Some very dry regions experience forest fires every summer.

Bright lights from advertising signs illuminate Las Vegas, the great gambling city in Nevada. Different gases in the lighting tubes (mercury, neon, and sodium) produce different colors when they are lit up.

What is fire?

Fire is the heat and light produced when something burns. A fuel burns when it combines with oxygen in the air. Fire needs a source of heat before it can start (such as the heat produced by rubbing a match head against the box or the spark from a lighter). Fire needs a supply of fuel and oxygen in order to continue burning.

Fire occurs naturally on the Earth and can be started by lightning hitting a tree or by molten lava from a volcanic eruption. We use fire for its heat, for its light, and to cook our food. It can be very dangerous if it gets out of control.

What color are flames?

Flames can be different colors: yellow, red and yellow, red and blue, and blue.

Substances that burn can be solids (for example, wood or charcoal), liquids (oil, gasoline, or alcohol), or gases (butane or methane). A flame glows brightly because the gases in the flame are hot. Coal burns with yellow and blue flames, while natural gas burns with light and darker blue flames. A yellow flame is not very hot; it contains products that have not burned, which are given off as smoke. The bluer a flame, the hotter it is. Some chemicals burn with characteristic colors: lithium burns red and sodium burns orange-yellow. Fireworks use chemical compounds to produce flashes of color.

What is a gas?

Matter can take the form of a solid, a liquid, or a gas, depending on temperature. When a solid is heated above its melting point, it becomes a liquid. As it boils, a liquid turns into gas.

Gas particles move freely because the bonds between them are very weak. Gas particles will completely fill any container into which they are put. The low density of gases makes it possible to compress and expand them. The space that a certain mass of gas takes up (its volume) depends on the temperature and pressure. Natural gas is extracted from deposits in the ground or under the seabed. Fuel gases can also be made from coal to produce coal gas. Gases can be liquefied by cooling and by compression. Butane and propane gas, made liquid under pressure, are sold as bottled gas.

What is air?

Air is a mixture of gases (nitrogen 78 percent, oxygen 21 percent, and argon 1 percent). Most of these gases are colorless and have no smell. There are also small amounts of water vapor, carbon dioxide, and other gases. The Earth is surrounded by a layer of air about 400 miles (640 kilometers) deep, called the atmosphere.

The atmosphere protects the Earth from the harmful rays of the Sun and keeps the Earth at a stable temperature. It exerts a pressure of about 1 ton over each square foot (approximately 10 tons over each square meter). The atmosphere fills all the space available.

What is water?

Water is a compound of hydrogen and oxygen. Its chemical formula is H_2O because each molecule

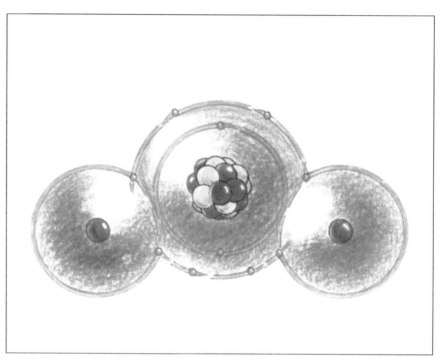

A water molecule is made of two different kinds of atoms: two hydrogen atoms for each oxygen atom. These bond by sharing their outer electrons.

consists of two hydrogen atoms and one oxygen atom.

Water is a liquid at room temperature. At 212°F (100°C) water starts to boil; its molecules move much more quickly and escape from the liquid to become vapor, which is a gas. At 32°F (0°C) water begins to freeze and form ice; its molecules move more slowly and become linked to each other, but still vibrate. On some planets there is ice so cold it is as hard as rock. On Earth water is constantly circulated in the water cycle. Water evaporates from the seas and is given out by plants and animals. Water vapor rises and condenses to form clouds. These release the water as rain, hail, or snow, and the cycle starts again.

What is a liquid?

In liquids, particles can move. A liquid can flow and has no fixed shape; this is why it spills.

Liquid particles are more loosely bound than solid particles. When they are heated, liquids expand. You can see this happen when the bulb of a thermometer is warmed. The liquid mercury slowly rises up the tube because the warmer mercury takes up more space. Ice is rather unusual. All liquids turn into a vapor when they reach a temperature that is high enough (the boiling point).

What is a solid?

A solid is a state of matter that holds its own shape. The atoms or molecules in a solid cannot move but merely vibrate about fixed positions.

In some metals it is possible to see the effect of expansion. When they are heated up, they take up more space. Power lines, for instance, hang more loosely when the weather is hot; the lines are stretched out longer. This phenomenon is used in thermostats.

What is gravity?

The force that attracts all objects to each other. The Earth's gravity holds you on the Earth's surface, pulling you toward its center.

Although gravity acts throughout the Universe, it is strongest near to large, heavy objects. Because the Moon is smaller than the Earth, if

you were on the Moon, the force of gravity would be only one-sixth that on the Earth. Gravity keeps the Moon in its orbit around the Earth, in the same way that the gravitational pull of the Sun keeps all the planets in their orbits.

What is the difference between mass and weight?

Mass is the amount of material in an object. Weight is the force of gravity pulling on that object.

Mass is consistent, but weight changes depending on where the object is. On top of a high mountain the force of gravity is weaker, so an object will weigh less although it has the same mass. An object's mass is determined by the material from which it is made. For example, a specific volume of iron has eight times the mass of the same volume of water.

Mountaineers use up a lot of energy climbing against the force of gravity.

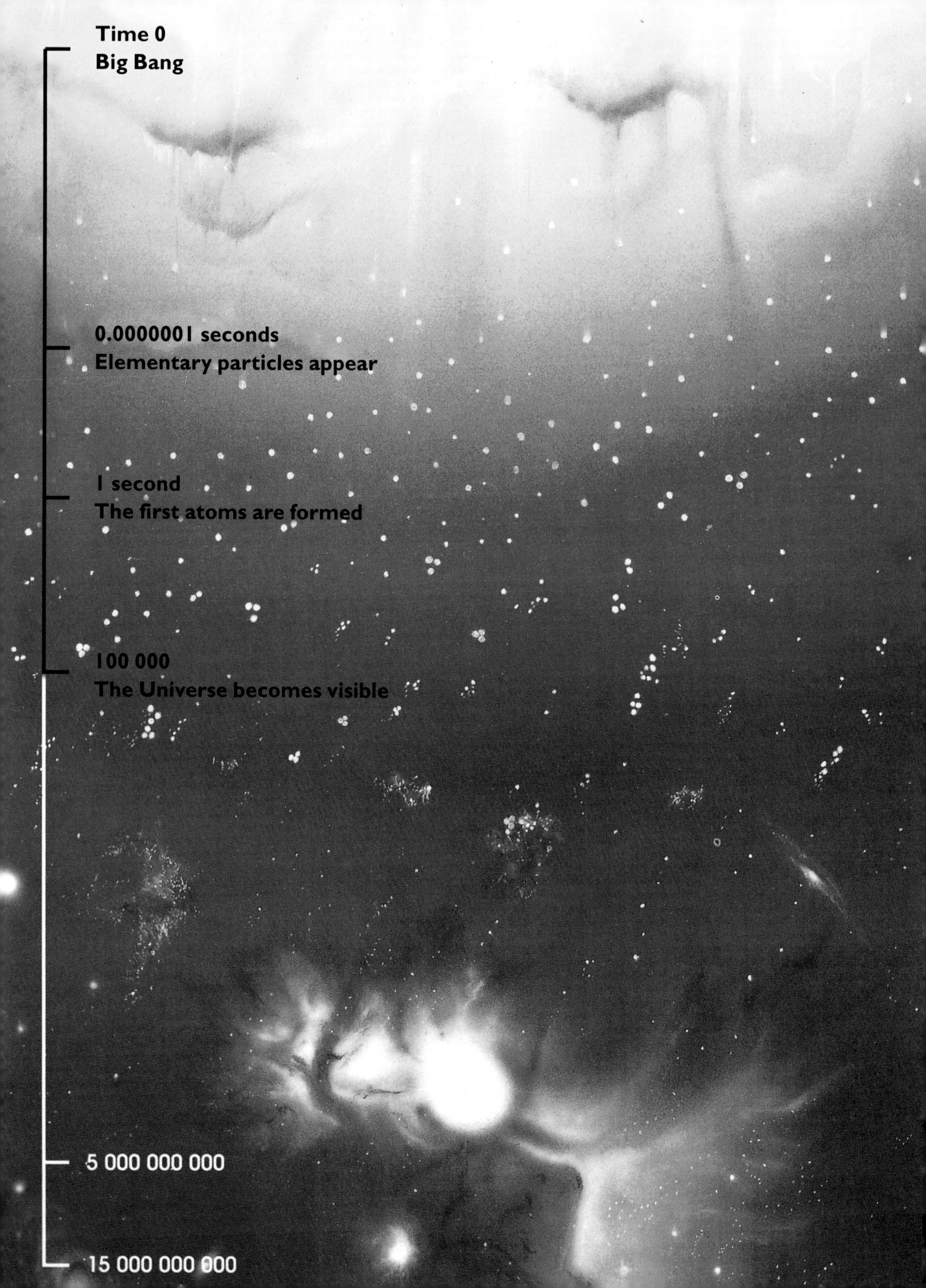

Time 0
Big Bang

0.0000001 seconds
Elementary particles appear

1 second
The first atoms are formed

100 000
The Universe becomes visible

5 000 000 000

15 000 000 000

The Mysterious Sky

What is the "Big Bang"?

Most scientists think the Universe was born in a huge explosion called the Big Bang, which took place in a fraction of a second. During the explosion the first atoms, originally crammed into a space the size of a pinhead, moved away from each other at a speed much faster than that of light. Time did not exist then.

The explosion marked the origin of the Universe as we know it. Before this, the entire Universe was squeezed into a hot, super-dense state. The Big Bang explosion threw this compacted material outward at immense speed, producing the expanding Universe. The elementary particles, the building blocks of all the components of the Universe, were all born at this time from the same gaseous cloud. Within minutes the first atomic nuclei formed. This cloud of matter has been expanding and cooling down ever since. In the first fraction of a second, the size of the Universe changed from that of the nucleus of an atom to several light years across (a light year is about 5900 billion miles/9500 billion kilometers). The cause of the Big Bang is unknown.

When did the Big Bang explosion take place?

Scientists think it took place about 15 billion years ago. This explosion marks the origin of the Universe, which has continued to expand at high speed ever since. Galaxies were formed from the matter created by the explosion.

The speed at which the galaxies are moving away from each other enables us to calculate approximately when they were all compressed together and deduce from this the age of the Universe. The Big Bang must have happened about 15 billion years ago, according to estimates based on

Quarks appeared one billionth of a second after the Big Bang and formed the first atomic nuclei only a fraction of a second later. The atoms gathered together into clouds, and the first galaxies were born. Ours was born 5 billion years ago. Today, the Universe is 15 billion years old.

The Universe is forever moving. Here we can see two galaxies colliding. Many stars will perish during this event, but many others will be born.

speed as the Universe expands. The most distant stellar systems are billions of light years away, and our most powerful equipment can only just see them. We do not know whether the Universe has boundaries, but we do know that it has developed throughout time and has not always had the same appearance. It has been through stages of expansion and may go through a stage of contraction.

the age of the oldest stars. We do not know whether the Universe will continue its expansion or whether it will contract and explode, creating a new Universe.

What is the Universe?

The Universe is everything that exists – stars, planets, and galaxies and all the space in between.

The Universe has no center, and its boundaries are unknown. It is sprinkled with billions of galaxies of differing sizes, each containing billions of stars ranging from supergiants to white dwarfs. In 1929 Edwin Hubble, an American astronomer, discovered that the galaxies are moving apart at high speeds, and the farther away a galaxy is, the faster it seems to be receding. It is as if the whole Universe is expanding like a balloon. The Universe is made up of stellar systems and clouds of matter made up of solid, liquid, and gaseous elements, separated by vast empty spaces.

How big is the Universe?

Even with the most powerful telescopes we cannot find an end to the Universe; there is always more beyond.

There is no such thing as top and bottom or left and right in the Universe. The galaxies are moving away from each other at a fantastic

Is the Universe motionless?

Everything in the Universe moves and changes. The Universe itself is constantly expanding. The billions of galaxies fly away from each other at enormously high speeds. The farther apart they are, the more quickly they recede from each other.

Within minutes of the birth of the Universe, the most common atomic nuclei, hydrogen and helium, appeared. These elements started cooling down and spreading out. Ever since, the matter that constitutes the stars has continued to spread out. This is what we call the expansion of the Universe. Imagine the Universe as a balloon with small pieces of paper stuck on it to represent the galaxies. As the balloon is blown up, the pieces of paper grow farther apart, although the pieces of paper (the galaxies) do not themselves get bigger. The Sun and all the other planets in our Solar System orbit the center of our galaxy at a speed of about 140 miles per second (230 kilometers per second).

What is a quasar?

It is a starlike object that emits more energy than 100 giant galaxies. Quasars are far beyond our galaxy. They are the brightest, fastest, and most distant objects in the Universe.

The word "quasar" is a contraction of the term "quasistellar object" (QSO). The first quasars were discovered in 1963. They are one of many mysterious celestial objects. The brightness of a quasar is similar to that of a starlike object. We know that they must emit huge amounts of energy. The energy they emit might come from a neighboring black hole, or quasars might be black holes in the making. They could even be stars and gas falling toward a black hole. On this point, as on many others, scientists can only speculate.

What is a galaxy?

A galaxy is a vast cluster of millions or billions of stars held together by gravity. Our galaxy is shaped like a flattened disk. We can see the bright arc of stars that make up this disk as the Milky Way.

Seen from a telescope, a galaxy looks like an island. There are billions of galaxies in the Universe. Scientists have categorized them depending on their shape. They can be spiral, elliptical, or irregular, and they move apart at high speed in the expanding space. Three galaxies are visible from the Earth to the naked eye: the Andromeda Galaxy in the northern hemisphere, which is the farthest away of the three, and the two Magellanic Clouds in the southern hemisphere, the Large and the Small, which are the galaxies closest to us.

Where does the name Milky Way come from?

Our galaxy, which looks like an arc of whitish light with a

Andromeda is our nearest spiral galaxy: it is more than two million light years away. The Milky Way is probably very similar to it.

The center of our galaxy is obscured by a huge dust cloud similar to the one which conceals the galaxy Centaurus A.

milky appearance, was so named by the Greeks. It is about 100,000 light years in diameter. For a long time the Sun was thought to be at its center, but this was later shown to be wrong. The Sun is about 30,000 light years away from the center of the Milky Way.

The Universe and the Milky Way were for a long time believed to be one and the same. People thought that the Milky Way had no boundaries. Our Sun is one of the billions of stars that make up the disk-shaped system known as the Milky Way. This huge spiral galaxy turns like a wheel. The Sun and all the other stars revolve around a globe-shaped nucleus, which contains a cluster of a billion stars much older than the Sun. In our galaxy, stars are continually renewed, but the spiral structure remains unchanged, held together by the force of gravity.

Is there anything at the center of our galaxy?

Nobody really knows. Recent evidence suggests there might be a grouping of about 20 supergiant blue stars, but scientists cannot rule out the existence of a black hole.

The center of our galaxy is about 30,000 light years away. Not even the most powerful telescopes can see this because it is obscured by thick interstellar clouds. Only radio waves and infrared rays are able to penetrate this barrier. For a long time it was believed that the center of our galaxy was occupied by a black hole. Modern instruments using infrared radiation have detected a radio source near the center of our galaxy called Sagittarius A. This source has been split into about 20 supergiant stars, all very close to each other. We do not know whether there might be a black hole hiding among these giant stars. Each is as bright as 100,000 suns and has a surface temperature of more than 54,000°F (30,000°C).

What is a star?

Stars are spheres of burning gas that produce their own heat and light, just like the Sun. Most of the bright dots that twinkle in the night sky are stars. The faintest are the most distant.

Each star is a sun – a vast ball of very dense, hot gas. In most stars hydrogen is the most abundant element. Many stars also contain helium, nitrogen, oxygen, and various metals including calcium and iron. Nuclear reactions in the core of the star convert hydrogen to helium, releasing enormous amounts of energy, which escape as light and heat. There is a constant battle between the star's own gravity pulling it in and the pressure of the heat and radiation it produces pushing it out. Stars are so far away that they seem to be still when in fact they are moving at very high speed. There are also thousands of binary stars. These are pairs of stars that revolve around each other. Mizar, one of the stars in the Big Dipper, is a binary star. Sharp-eyed observers can see its companion, Alcor. Stars are often found in larger clusters.

What is the largest known star?

At 9 billion miles (15 billion kilometers) in diameter, IRS5 is the largest known star, although there may be larger ones.

Interferometers are sophisticated pieces of equipment used for measuring the diameter of a star. Some stars are much larger than others. The diameter of the Sun is 100 times greater than that of the Earth, yet the Sun is just an average-sized star. A red supergiant star could have a diameter 1,000 times greater than that of the Sun.

What is a dwarf star?

In order to differentiate between stars, scientists put them into categories, depending on their size: supergiants, giants, and dwarfs.

Dwarf stars are called white dwarfs while they still shine or black dwarfs if they have become

It is common for a binary star to be made up of a red giant and a white dwarf. The size difference can be clearly seen.

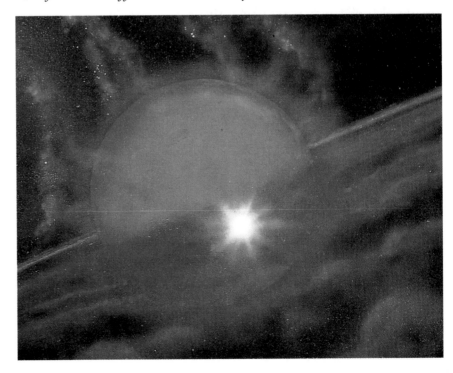

invisible. A white dwarf is a star near the end of its life that has used up all its fuel and shrunk until it is very tiny compared with its original size and very much denser. A white dwarf is about the same size as the Earth. This is what remains after the death of a giant star. There are no nuclear reactions in a dwarf star. The only remaining energy is that of the ongoing contraction process. The density of stellar matter may be a million times greater than that of the Earth: a spoonful of white dwarf has a mass of 1 ton.

How is a star born?

Stars are most probably born from nebulae, which are giant clouds of dust and gas. The most famous of these is the Orion Nebula. This is visible to the naked eye as a misty patch below the belt of Orion.

Stars begin to form when part of a cloud of gas collects into individual clumps, following a disturbance at the heart of the cloud. The clumps contract under their own gravity, becoming smaller and denser. The contraction makes the clump of matter rotate increasingly faster and the temperature and pressure at the center of the clump increase. Once the temperature has reached approximately 10 million degrees, nuclear reactions start occurring in the core, giving out vast amounts of energy. This energy finds its way to the surface, and the new star begins to shine.

Stars are often born in clusters from a single gas cloud. Most of them will turn into binary systems. The picture below shows some very young stars surrounded by gas and dust in the Pleiades cluster.

Can several stars be born at the same time?

Sometimes a dozen stars, or even several thousand, can be born at the same time. These are called clusters. Stars in a cluster are roughly the same age and in the same region of space. In time the cluster becomes more diffuse, and the stars become isolated. This is what happened to our Sun billions of years ago.

It is believed that the Orion Nebula contains enough matter to form a whole cluster of stars. The Pleiades cluster in the constellation Taurus was only recently born in a nebula. Our Sun may have been part of a similar type of cluster about 4.7 billion years ago. The stars would have separated a long time ago, and the stars of the Pleiades will one day do the same.

Are all the stars the same color?

At first glance, all stars appear white. They are

The Orion constellation is composed of stars of different colors: several blue ones, a red one, and a yellow one are clearly visible on the picture.

actually different colors: red, orange, blue, yellow, or white. A star's color depends on its temperature.

A star's color tells us about the temperature of its atmosphere. This is what enables scientists to put them into categories. However, the colors are not always very distinctive. Depending on whether the star is bright, light blue, or dark red, or even white, the temperature may vary from 3000 to 30,000°C. Red stars are the coolest ones and the light blue ones the hottest. Rigel is light blue, the Sun is yellow, Arcturus is orange, and Betelgeuse and Antares are red. Sirius, the brightest star in the sky, is white.

What is the nearest star?

The Sun is our nearest star. It is 90 million miles (150 million kilometers) from the Earth and halfway between the center of the

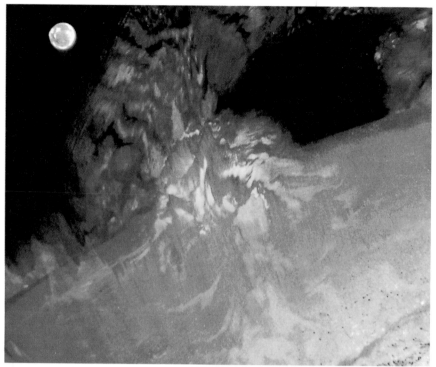

The surface of the Sun is constantly moving, and the eruptions from its surface are impressive: some spread over hundreds of thousands of miles. If they took place on Earth, burning gases would reach the Moon. This drawing depicts such an eruption on the surface of the Sun. The Earth, shown in the top left-hand corner, is drawn to the same scale to show the magnitude of the phenomenon.

The photosphere, the visible surface of the Sun that emits light and heat, is often marked by large dark spots and bright patches. Rising hot gases produce a mottling of the photosphere known as granulation. Tongues of gas called prominences extend from the chromosphere into the corona, a halo of hot, tenuous gas surrounding the Sun. Never look directly at the Sun. The intense light could damage your eyes.

Is there dangerous radiation in space?

Yes. The Sun and other objects in space give out streams of radiation and particles, including dangerous X-rays, gamma rays, and ultraviolet radiation.

Gamma rays, X-rays, cosmic rays, and intense ultraviolet radiation in space are a danger to astronauts. Space suits and spaceships protect them, but damage can occur to satellites that stay in space a long time. The two Van Allen radiation belts in the upper atmosphere, about 1,850 and 9,300 miles (3,000 and 15,000 kilometers) above the Earth, trap cosmic rays. The Earth's atmosphere helps protect us from dangerous radiation.

Milky Way and its edge. The next nearest star is Alpha Centauri, which is 4.3 light years away.

The Sun is the largest object in the Solar System, but it is quite a small star. It is 860,000 miles (1,390,000 kilometers) in diameter. If it were hollow, more than a million Earths would fit into it. If we were any closer to it, it would burn us, and if we were any farther away it would be so cold that there would be no life on Earth.

Why is the Sun so bright?

The Sun is a ball of glowing gas. Only a tiny part of the light this gigantic nuclear furnace emits falls on the Earth. It is brighter than other stars because it is so much closer to us. The Sun is the only star close enough for its surface to be studied in detail.

Which is the farthest star?

The farthest star will be found in the most remote galaxies of the Universe. These distant galaxies may be quasars.

Our galaxy is about 100,000 light years in diameter. A light year is the distance a light ray travels in a year. It is equivalent to 5,900 billion miles (9,500 billion kilometers). Although these distances are enormous, the most remote stars are far beyond the Milky Way. They are at the extreme edge of other galaxies and quasars, situated in the remotest regions of the Universe, about 15 billion light years away.

What is a constellation?

In the night sky, groups of stars seem to make patterns. In their minds, ancient peoples joined up the stars to form constellations. The Greeks named them after their gods and heroes. They made a map of the sky that can be used as a guide to the position of the stars.

Modern astronomers still use these names to divide up the sky. There are 88 constellations, and learning to recognize them is fascinating. Some constellations can only be seen from one hemisphere of the Earth and at certain times of the year. One of the best-known constellations is Ursa Major, the Great Bear. In the northern hemisphere it can be seen all year round above the horizon because it revolves around the Pole Star. The 12 constellations of the Zodiac are the same as the Sun signs in astrology.

How many stars are there in the Milky Way?

It has been estimated that there are 100 billion stars in the Milky Way. It is impossible to know for certain how many there are because there are so many of them, they are so far away, and because there is so much variation in the brightness of the sky.

In spite of this huge number of stars, the Milky Way is mostly made up of empty space. The distances between stars (the intersidereal distances) are vast. But in some places there are so many stars that they look like real stellar clouds, such as in the constellation Sagittarius. The center of our galaxy, called the galactic nucleus, can be found toward the Sagittarius constellation, where the Milky Way looks brightest. Our solar system is about 30,000 light years away from the center of the Milky Way.

The Big Dipper, or Great Bear, is one of the most easily recognized constellations. It helps to locate the Pole Star.

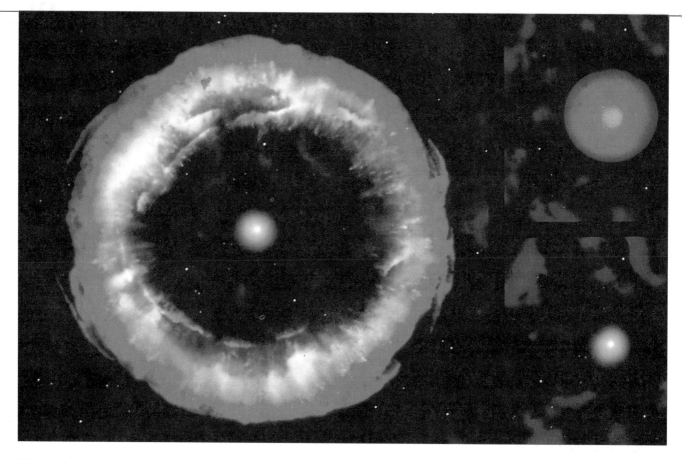

When you look at the sky, you are looking into the past. After changing into a red giant, this star exploded and turned into a supernova. The gases we can see today have probably already disappeared. It is likely that all that is left of it is the central star, which has turned into a white dwarf.

Do we see the sky as it really is?

Astronomers measure distances in light years. This is the distance traveled in one year by a beam of light, which travels at 190,000 miles (300,000 kilometers) per second. We do not see a star as it is now, but rather as it was long ago when the light set out on its journey through space. We are looking back in time.

Since the light of the Sun takes eight minutes to reach us, it means that we see the Sun as it was eight minutes earlier. When we look through a telescope at the Andromeda Galaxy, which is two million light years away, we see it as it was over two million years ago. In the same way, we can see stars now that have already ceased to exist.

How many stars are visible to the naked eye?

On a clear night with no Moon, about 3,000 stars are visible to the naked eye. When the Moon shines, it is so bright that we cannot see the fainter stars. Man-made light also interferes with our view of the stars.

In total, from both the northern and southern hemispheres, nearly 6,000 stars are visible to the naked eye at the same time. Different stars become visible through the course of a year. Most of the bright points in the sky are stars, but five out of the nine planets in our Solar System are also visible to the naked eye. Mercury, Venus, Mars, Jupiter, and Saturn seem to move very slowly in the sky. This is because of their revolving motion around the Sun and also because of the Earth's motion. More stars are of course visible through a telescope, and the largest telescopes make it possible to detect about 100 billion stars and galaxies.

Why can't stars be seen in broad daylight?

Even though they cannot be seen, they are still there. The Sun is so bright that we cannot see the much dimmer stars.

The planets Venus and Jupiter, as well as Sirius, the brightest star, sometimes manage to stand out on a bluish sky background, especially when the sky is very clear and its blue color is dark enough. If you use binoculars, you can find Venus, Jupiter, and Sirius if you know where to look. The Moon, our own satellite, is often visible in the daytime.

Where is the Pole Star?

In the northern hemisphere, the Pole Star lies above the North Pole. It never disappears below the horizon, and whenever you are facing it, you can be certain you are looking north. Then west will be on your left, east on your right, and south behind you. The Pole Star has long been used by seafarers to help them navigate.

To find the Pole Star in the sky, you must first find the Big Dipper, which is part of the constellation known as Ursa Major. The two stars that form the far side of the "bowl" of the Dipper are in line with the Pole Star. Follow from

If you focus your camera on the Pole Star for about two hours on a clear night, you will get a picture like this one.

these stars a distance about five times the distance between them to find the Pole Star. It is small and not very bright, but well separated from the other stars around it.

What is there

between stars?

There is a huge amount of space, mostly filled with large gaseous clouds and dust in suspension. Between these clouds and dust, there is emptiness. In space, there are no clouds of rain as above the Earth, and there is no air to breathe either.

In the space between stars, there is no water, and so clouds as we know them cannot form. Instead there is thick dust, gas (mostly hydrogen), particles of matter, and emptiness. In general, interstellar matter is very thinly scattered – a thimbleful of space would only contain one atom. In some places gas and dust concentrate in clouds, yet in these clouds there are only a couple of atoms per cubic inch (in our atmosphere, there are hundreds of billions of them in each cubic inch). These clouds almost completely mask the light of the stars, so they must be extremely large.

Is the Sun going

to shine forever?

Since its birth, over four billion years ago, the Sun has been gradually burning up its fuel. It has been estimated that it is halfway through its life cycle.

The Sun, which was probably born from the collapse of a nebula in the Milky Way, still has enough reserves to last another five billion years. It has now reached its stable middle age. When it runs out of hydrogen, the Sun will become hotter and will increase in size until it becomes a giant red star. Finally, when it reaches the stage where it only contains carbon, it will turn into a white dwarf. Stars do not last forever. They are born, they burn up their fuel, and finally, depending on their mass, they either explode or contract to a very dense cold mass.

How does a

star die?

Stars of average mass, like our Sun, first become red giants. Then they gradually contract, becoming fainter,

until they become cold and invisible dwarfs. However, stars with a much higher mass expand until they explode. Explosions of stars are called supernovas.

Once a star has converted all its hydrogen into helium (our Sun converts 600 million tons of hydrogen into helium every second), its center will collapse, and the temperature and pressure at the center begin to rise. At the same time, the exterior layers expand and the star inflates. Its surface temperature falls, and it becomes red. A star at this stage of its life is called a red giant. What happens after the red giant phase depends on the mass of the original star. In the case of an average-sized star, it contracts. This is the beginning of a series of contractions and expansions (the pulsation stage). The star will contract until it becomes a white dwarf, taking billions of years to lose its heat. A star with a mass greater than 1.4 times that of the Sun will experience a much more violent death. Becoming first a red giant and then a supergiant, it will continue expanding until the pressure of its mass causes a dazzling explosion. The supernova sends into space all the chemical elements formed during its lifetime. Some clouds of matter may form new stars and planets.

When the Sun becomes a red giant – in five billion years – it will also be the end of the Earth. The Sun will then turn into a white dwarf.

Why do we say that we are the children of stars?

Our bodies contain elements that were produced by stars that no longer exist. These elements are present in all living organisms on Earth and are therefore in our food. We are ourselves a part of the Universe.

How life appeared on Earth, from inanimate atoms produced at the heart of stars, remains a mystery. When a star bursts, multiple nuclear reactions take place, which give rise to the elements. These atoms are expelled into space and mix with gas clouds where they gather to make new stars. The atoms that make up the Earth were formed by supernova explosions before the Sun was born.

What is a black hole?

It is a region in space where the pull of gravity is so great that nothing can escape from it, not even light. Objects the size of a star can be sucked in. A black hole consumes anything that goes past it.

Black holes are thought to form when massive stars shrink at the end of their lives. This happens when a star can no longer withstand the pressure of its mass. The star then collapses; its center swallows up its own mass. If the Earth was compressed down to the size of a marble, it too would become a black hole. A black hole is a dynamic system; it is capable of

This is what you might see if you were close to a black hole: an invisible object swallowing a star in a blaze of blinding light.

interacting with other objects and of absorbing or giving out energy. In other words, a black hole can develop and change. It is thought that there are many black holes in the Universe, some of which may well be giant ones. In theory, black holes should increase in size forever. Black holes are invisible, but they can be detected because gas or stars falling toward them become so hot that they emit X-rays. Absolutely nothing can escape from a black hole. For scientists, black holes are one of the most intriguing mysteries of the Universe.

What is a planet?

Planets are moving celestial bodies that are in orbit around a star. They vary in size, color, and composition. The word planet comes from the Greek and means "wandering," because the astronomers in ancient times saw them as sky nomads that were always on the move.

Mercury is the planet closest to the Sun. Its surface temperature is over 900°F (500°C).

The planets in our Solar System are all satellites of the Sun. Venus, Mercury, the Earth, Mars, and Pluto are made of rock, while the four giant planets, Jupiter, Saturn, Uranus, and Neptune, are mostly gas. The different groups of planets have different types of atmosphere.

The birth of a planet is often very violent. Continually hit by asteroids, its surface heats up and melts.

What happens when a planet is born?

When our Solar System was formed, a huge cloud of dust, shaped like a pancake, started spinning faster and faster. The center became the Sun and the "lumps" that came off the edges became the nine planets.

Dust particles in the cloud that surrounded the newly formed Sun started clustering together to form clumps that gradually became larger and denser. This process continued for millions of years until the planets were formed, gases from the clouds becoming their early atmospheres. The rocky planets later lost their original atmospheres. In the case of Venus, the Earth, and Mars, these have been replaced by new atmospheres composed of gases expelled from the interior of the planets by volcanoes.

Why does a planet shine?

Saturn's moon Enceladus is made of ice. This is what gives it a shiny appearance.

The planets appear to shine because they reflect the light that reaches them from the Sun. Only one side at a time is lit, while the other side remains in darkness. All the planets rotate as they travel around the Sun, so they, too, have night and day. The lengths of night and day are different on different planets.

Stars give out their own light. The planets only shine because they receive and reflect light from the Sun. The way the light is reflected depends on the planet's surface and atmosphere. Six planets are visible without a telescope: Mercury, Venus, Mars, Jupiter, Saturn, and Uranus. Uranus is not very easy to see because it is so far away. Some planets shine more brightly than others: Venus is by far the brightest.

Do all planets look alike?

Even though planets have similarities, they are all different. They differ in size, brightness, and composition. They each have their own temperature, their own type of surface, a characteristic atmosphere, and a particular color.

The planets are usually divided into two groups: the terrestrial planets and the giant planets. The terrestrial planets are Mercury, Venus, Earth, and Mars. They are called terrestrial because they are roughly the same size and of the same rocky composition as our planet. In many ways they are part of the same family as the Earth. The giant planets are Jupiter, Saturn, Uranus, and Neptune. They are mostly composed of gas and ice. The giant planets are all very far from the Sun and have numerous satellites in orbit around them. Pluto, the most distant planet, is considered by many astronomers to be a very big asteroid. It has not been studied in as much detail as the others.

What is the Solar System?

The Solar System comprises the Sun and all the planets in orbit around it. It also includes the large number of comets in orbit around the Sun and the thousands of tiny planets called asteroids.

The Sun, with a diameter of 860,000 miles (1,390,000 million kilometers), is the largest object in the Solar System. Orbiting the Sun, and held by its gravity, are a large number of celestial bodies including the nine planets, most of which have one or more satellites, or moons. The Solar System also contains a gas called interplanetary gas. The planet closest to the Sun is Mercury, followed in order of increasing distance from the Sun by Venus, Earth, Mars, Jupiter, Saturn, Uranus, Neptune, and Pluto.

Jupiter is the largest planet in the Solar System. Four moons are visible with a good pair of binoculars. This picture shows Europa, which is as big as our Moon, flying above the atmosphere of Jupiter.

Which planet is the farthest away?

Pluto was discovered in 1930. It is the smallest planet in our Solar System, about the size of the Moon, and is not visible to the naked eye from the Earth. Light reflected from its surface (visible through a telescope) takes five hours and two minutes to reach us.

Pluto is so far from the Sun and so small that it gets very little sunlight. Its only satellite, Charon, was discovered in 1978. Pluto is a gigantic snowball made of icy gases. Might there be other planets beyond? Astronomers have not found anything. It is therefore possible that the Solar System ends with Neptune and Pluto.

Is there such a thing as a green planet?

The color of Uranus is mainly bluish green. It was first seen in 1690, the first planet to be discovered through a telescope. Initially, it was confused with a comet.

Uranus, which is between Neptune (which is also mostly green) and Saturn, is four times the size of the Earth. Its atmosphere is mostly composed of methane and steam, and its temperature varies between 320°F and −364°F (150°C and −220°C). In addition to its rings, Uranus also has 15 satellites, of which 10 were discovered in 1986 by the space probe Voyager 2. Uranus is almost Neptune's twin planet in size and composition. Their bluish-green color is produced by a large quantity of methane. Finally, Uranus has a unique characteristic in the whole Solar System: its axis is tilted so far that it nearly aligns with the plane of its orbit. Uranus is a planet that lies on its side.

The rings around the large planets are made of particles of rock and ice.

Which is the largest planet?

Jupiter is the giant of our Solar System. Its diameter is 11 times that of the Earth.

Jupiter is almost entirely made of gas. It is so big that its disk can be seen clearly with binoculars. Its four brightest moons are also visible: Ganymede, Callisto, Io, and Europa. Its cloud pattern seems to be constantly changing except for the Great Red Spot, which seems to be an anticyclone. Its surface is the most turbulent in the Solar System. The colors seen on its surface are mostly yellow, red, brown, and even purple. It would not be possible to land on Jupiter because the surface under its clouds is not solid, but a gaseous substance. Its gases are so dense that they liquefy under the great pressure of the atmosphere that surrounds the planet.

What are the rings around Saturn?

Saturn has several very thin rings that revolve around the planet above its equator and spread out over a great distance. The rings are made up of millions of dust particles encased in ice which orbit the planet.

Saturn, nine times the size of Earth, is composed of such low-density matter that it would float on water. After Jupiter, it is the second largest planet in the system. Saturn has characteristic flattened poles and bright rings. The particles that make up the rings are thought to be the remains of a shattered moon. These pieces are slowly falling back on the planet and will disappear within 100 million years unless another moon breaks up and forms new rings.

Do other planets have rings, too?

All the other giant planets – Jupiter, Uranus, and Neptune – also have rings, but they are not quite as spectacular as Saturn's.

In March 1977 it was discovered that Uranus, too, was encircled by rings. These are not bright or easily seen through a telescope. Nine of the rings were discovered when Uranus passed in front of a fairly bright star, and the tenth was discovered by the Voyager 2 space probe. They make a total of 10 dark rings about 6 miles (10 kilometers) wide. In 1989, the same Voyager 2 probe showed that Neptune is also encircled by a ring composed of debris and of two partial rings in the shape of an arc. Jupiter's only ring was discovered by Voyager 1.

Are the morning star and evening star really stars?

No. These are both names for Venus, the brightest of all the planets. At night, it is called the evening star, and when it is last to be seen before dawn, it is called the morning star.

The reason that Venus is even brighter than the star Sirius is because it is very close to the Earth and the Sun and its surface is covered by highly reflective clouds. Its atmosphere is very dense and is made up almost entirely of carbon dioxide. The atmospheric pressure is 90 times that at the surface of the Earth. The planet's surface temperature is 887°F (475°C). A detailed map of Venus was made by the Magellan space probe. Its radar pierced through the thick layer of clouds and sent back pictures of craters, mountains, and valleys, similar to those on Mars. There are also huge volcanoes, which may be active.

What color is the sky on other planets?

On Earth the sky is blue because of our atmosphere. On Venus, the sky is never clear: it must be very dark and look as if a storm is about to break. On Mars the sky is rosy orange.

Aboard a spaceship, whether one looks at the Moon, the Sun, or the stars, the sky always appears black. On Earth, our atmosphere scatters the light of the Sun, which makes the sky appear blue. If viewed from other planets, the color of the sky will be different, depending on the nature of the planet's atmosphere and the gases within it, which scatter the light of the Sun in different ways. The sky looks black on the Moon because there is no atmosphere there to scatter the light. The same applies to all planets that do not have an atmosphere.

Venus is surrounded by a thick layer of clouds. Only the radar of the Magellan probe has been able to see through it successfully. Computers have been used to recreate the landscape; this artist's impression looks realistic.

Do other planets have winds?

Winds have been detected on Venus, Mars, Jupiter, Saturn, Uranus, and Neptune.

On Venus there is almost no wind at the surface around the equator, but high above the planet's surface winds may be blowing at 190 miles an hour (300 kilometers an hour). On Mars, there are violent winds that can reach speeds of hundreds of miles per hour. When this happens, they carry dust and turn into sandstorms that can last for several days. Jupiter's fast rotation creates violent winds that blow continuously. Spiral cloud formations disturb the atmosphere. The Great Red Spot, a massive anticyclone, or vortex, is wide enough to fit two whole Earths across it. The colder the planet, the more violent the winds are. On Neptune wind speeds can reach up to 1,900 miles (3,000 kilometers) an hour.

What is the red planet?

Mars is the red planet. Ancient peoples associated

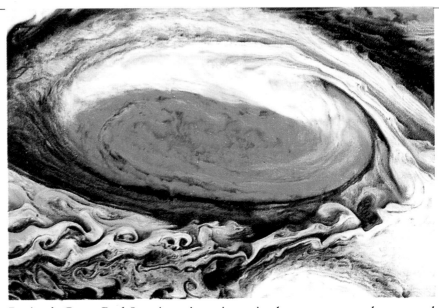

Jupiter's Great Red Spot is a gigantic anticyclone, or vortex, that started about 300 years ago. It is 17,400 miles (28,000 kilometers) long: the width of two Earths.

the planet with destruction, which is why scientists use the name that was given by the Romans to their god of war. The red color of Martian rocks might be linked to its high iron content.

Mars is the fourth planet from the Sun. It has two white polar caps and some dark patches on its surface. The landscape is arid and desolate, scattered with craters, canyons, and enormous volcanoes. The Viking probes have analyzed samples of the dusty soil but have been unable to identify any signs of insects or life. The conditions on Mars are much harsher than first expected. The atmosphere is extremely thin and 95 percent carbon dioxide. At the equator, during the summer, the temper-

ature just about reaches 50°F (10°C). Most of the time it is −58°F (−50°C).

Is there any water on Mars?

Pictures taken by the Mariner 9 probe revealed dried-out river beds that are several hundred miles long. It is believed that very long ago there may have been water on Mars.

Water that ran freely on Mars about four billion years ago has now evaporated, leaving channels of dried-out rivers. The Martian atmosphere contains less than 0.1 percent of water vapor. Today, most of the water can be found in

There are live volcanoes on several planets: on Earth and probably on Venus they eject lava; on Io they eject sulfur; on Callisto and Triton they eject water. Here you can see a geyser on Triton, which is one of Neptune's moons.

the form of permafrost beneath the surface and ice in the polar caps. Because there is little water vapor, clouds are rare on Mars.

Can we breathe on other planets?

We can only breathe in an atmosphere that contains enough oxygen. To breathe on planets where there is no air, humans need special breathing apparatus.

Mercury, which has neither water nor atmosphere, is heated to high temperatures by the Sun. Venus has a highly toxic atmosphere and is the hottest planet; we could not breathe there either. Mars is icy and has too little air. Jupiter and other planets are mostly composed of extremely cold gases. In the Solar System there is only one planet that can support life – planet Earth.

Are there volcanoes anywhere other than on Earth?

There are no volcanoes on the giant gas planets. Only planets with solid, rocky cores are likely to have had volcanoes. There are volcanic craters on Mercury, Venus, and Mars as well as on several moons in the Solar System.

Pictures sent by probes reveal that Mercury's surface is scattered with mountains, craters, and valleys, and it is believed that there has been some volcanic activity on this planet. Mars, too, has old volcanic craters, some of which are several hundred miles in diameter, and there are also some enormous chasms. Olympus Mons on Mars is one of the largest volcanoes in the Solar System: it is 370 miles (600 kilometers) in diameter, 18 miles (29 kilometers) high, and its crater measures 56 miles (90 kilometers) across. Like the other Martian volcanoes, it is no longer active.

Do extraterrestrial volcanoes also throw out lava?

Very few active volcanoes have been discovered other than on the Earth. Some have been found on Venus, on Io and Callisto (moons of Jupiter), and on Triton (a moon of Neptune).

In 1990, the Magellan space probe showed meteorite craters, volcanoes, and what seemed to be rivers of burning lava on Venus. Ten years earlier, the Voyager probes discovered that Io, a moon of Jupiter, had active volcanoes. It was the first time any had been found anywhere other than on the Earth. Io's volcanoes throw out sulfur and not lava (molten rock). The ground is yellow and orange with sulfur and salt. Callisto, another one of Jupiter's moons, is covered with craters. Some of Callisto's volcanoes may still be active and throwing out ice and water, which probably immediately freezes.

Have space probes been sent to all the planets?

A space probe is an un-crewed spacecraft that works automatically. Probes are sent beyond Earth to collect data from other parts of the Solar System and from deep space. The only planet not to have been visited by a space probe is Pluto.

The first probes were sent in 1959 to study the Moon, and in 1966 the first soft landing was made on the Moon. Probes were used to collect samples of lunar soil, and the same was later done on Mars. Since then, scientists have relied on probes in their study of other planets. The Mariner space probes were the first to fly past Venus, Mars, and Jupiter. The Viking probes flew past Mars. Several probes flew past Saturn in 1979, 1980, and 1981. Voyager 2 flew past Uranus in 1986, and after a 12-year journey finally reached Neptune in 1989. It has since left the Solar System.

Pluto and its moon, Charon, always face each other. They are less than 12,000 miles (20,000 kilometers) apart. The Sun, 4 billion miles (6 billion kilometers) away, looks tiny.

How fast is the Earth moving?

It has been estimated that the Earth's average speed is 66,600 miles per hour (about 107,000 kilometers per hour). By the time you have read this sentence, the Earth will have traveled 100 miles (160 kilometers) in space.

Even though its average speed is 19 miles (30 kilometers) per second, we are not aware of moving because its movement is continuous without any sudden accelerations or decelerations. The planets do not all move at the same speed around the Sun; the speed depends on their distance from the Sun.

Are there any planets around the other stars?

There is now evidence that there are planets around other stars that are similar to our Sun. So far planets have not been found outside our Solar System.

It could be that only single stars can have planets, as double stars have a different sort of system. One reason we cannot see any planets that might orbit a star is the extreme brightness of the star, which prevents anything else from being visible. It would not be possible to see Jupiter from our nearest star, Alpha Centauri, because the Sun is so bright. However, by monitoring the movement of the stars themselves and by analyzing the radiation they emit, it is possible to predict whether or not they have orbiting planets.

Is there life on other planets?

We have not seen any signs of life on any other planet. We do not know whether the conditions necessary for life exist anywhere else in the Universe. Some evidence suggests that there may have been water at one time on Mars. Two projects have been set up to try and find out more about extraterrestrial life. In one project, messages have been sent out into space, while in the other we are trying to pick up any signals coming in from space.

The first and only terrestrial message was sent in 1974 by the largest radio telescope, that in Arecibo in Puerto Rico, to the M13 star cluster, which has about 300,000 stars. A reply is expected in the next hundred years! In 1990 NASA decided to launch a "listening" program, called SETI (which stands for Search for Extra-Terrestrial Intelligence), and to use the radio telescope once again. The telescope, which is 1,001 feet (305 meters) in diameter, is the biggest "ear" on Earth. It can listen to 10 million channels at any time. It sweeps through the sky at random on several million frequencies, on the lookout for intelligible artificial signals that might be sent out by living beings. Given the huge distances and the very small chances of ever being able to pick up such signals, the likelihood of such projects ever being successful is extremely remote.

What is a satellite?

Anything that moves in space in orbit around another object is a satellite. Comets, planets, asteroids, and moons are natural satellites, and the space-craft sent around the Earth are artificial satellites.

The Earth and the other eight planets in the Solar System are all satellites of the Sun, while the Moon is a satellite of the Earth. Except for Venus and Mercury, all the other planets have at least one other satellite. Satellites launched into orbit from the Earth are called artificial satellites. Some of them are designed specifically for meteorological, telecommunication, military, or scientific purposes. Satellite pictures of space are clearer because they are not distorted by the Earth's turbulent atmosphere. The study of quasars and black holes is one of the most interesting areas of research done by these satellites.

Why doesn't the Moon fall on the Earth?

The Moon must be falling toward the Earth, because if it was not, it would continue in a straight line. Since its path is a circle, it is falling, but its orbital speed is so fast that it maintains its course at the same distance from the Earth.

The Moon is attracted to the Earth by the force of gravity. All planets, stars, and celestial bodies experience this force. The Earth attracts to its center anything that flies past it. However, the Moon's orbital speed prevents it from actually falling onto the Earth, although it is constantly pulled toward it. A transfer of energy between Earth and Moon means that every year the Moon moves away from the Earth by a few inches.

Why are there craters on the Moon?

The Moon is a ball of rock, about 2,160 miles (3,476 kilometers) in diameter, which is nearly a quarter of the size of the Earth. The craters that can be seen on its surface are mostly traces left by meteorites.

For centuries, the origin of the features of the Moon was a source of disagreement among astronomers. Some believed that the craters had been left by volcanoes while others claimed that they were scars left by meteorites. Astronauts and probes confirmed that most of the craters on the Moon had been caused by meteorites, up to four million years ago. Even today, meteorites leave craters and a constant showering of micrometeorites turns the surface of our satellite to dust.

Why does the Moon appear to change shape?

The Moon does not shine by itself, it merely reflects the light of the Sun. As it travels around the Earth, we see different aspects of it throughout the month. These changing aspects are called phases.

The first phase is called New Moon. Seen from the Earth, the Moon is completely in shadow even though its hidden side is completely lit up. This is the time when the Moon passes exactly between the Earth and the Sun. Seven days later, we see half the Moon, called the first quarter. Halfway through its course

Twelve men walked on the Moon between 1969 and 1974. On the left, Harrison Schmidt, a researcher, is collecting samples of stones in the Taurus-Littrow Valley during the Apollo 17 mission.

around the planet, the Moon appears as a bright circle, called Full Moon. The Earth is then situated between the Sun and the Moon, and the face of the Moon that we see is completely lit up. The fourth phase is the last quarter, when only the left half of the hemisphere is lit up. The cycle is complete on the return of the New Moon. This cycle lasts 29 days, 12 hours, and 44 minutes.

What did humans discover on the Moon?

The surface of the Moon is uneven and rocky. It is scattered with thousands of saucer-shaped cavities, called craters, gouged out by falling meteorites. The meteorites exploded as they hit the surface, and debris scattered everywhere.

The Moon's landscape is made of wide plains scarred by countless craters alternating with high mountains, deep crevices, and steep cliffs. The extreme old age of the lunar surface came as a big surprise. Samples have revealed that the rocks are volcanic in origin, that both the Moon and the

Earth are 4.6 billion years old, and that there has never been any water on our satellite.

Why are astronauts so light on the Moon?

Because the Moon is much smaller than the Earth, the force of gravity there is much less. A person who weighs 90 pounds on the Earth would only weigh 15 pounds on the Moon.

Gravity on the Moon is one-sixth that on the Earth. Astronauts cannot walk on the Moon as they do on the Earth – if they did, each time they took a step, they would rise several feet above the ground! Instead they have to drag their feet in order to keep their balance and remain on the ground.

How long has man been traveling in space?

Man ventured into space for the first time a little over 30 years ago. The cosmonaut

Jupiter's satellite Io will almost certainly receive visitors in the 21st century. It will then be possible to

Yuri Gagarin was the first person to fly into space, aboard Vostok 1, on April 12, 1961. Expeditions continue to this day.

While the Russians call the people they send into space cosmonauts, the Americans call them astronauts. In 1961, the U.S. began the Mercury program of manned flights and on February 20, 1962, John Glenn, the first astronaut, orbited the Earth three times. After people had traveled into space for the first time, the next great event was landing on the Moon. On July 21, 1969, Neil Armstrong became the first person to walk on the Moon. Eleven other people have walked there since.

study the sulfuric volcanoes, and even immortalize them in paintings using special paints, with Jupiter and the Sun in the background! Note the size of the Sun at a distance of about 500 million miles (800 million kilometers).

Scientists probably now have enough samples taken from the Moon for their studies so there is no need for another very costly trip just yet. However, it is possible that one day an astronomical base will be installed on the Moon that would allow observations of the sky away from the interference emitted by the Earth. The Moon could also be a useful stopping point on the way to a more remote destination.

How long does it take to get to the Moon?

The average distance between the Earth and the Moon is about 238,860 miles (384,400 kilometers). In astronomical terms, the Moon is a close neighbor. Many people have driven that sort of distance on the Earth, and many pilots have flown several times that distance.

If you were to draw an imaginary line between our planet and its satellite, the Earth would be able to fit in 30 times. A car traveling at 124 miles per hour (200 kilometers per hour) would take 80 days to get there. From the time it was launched to the time it went into orbit, Apollo's first journey lasted nearly four days. However, the return trip took less than three days.

When will we go back to the Moon?

The sensational phase of space exploration, which culminated in 1969 with the expedition to the Moon, has been suspended. However, people may one day return to the Moon.

Which planet will we go to next?

Plans are being made to go to Mars because it is the closest planet to Earth.

It is as hot on Venus as in an oven, and the atmospheric pressure is similar to that at the bottom of the sea. Before anyone can go there, we will have to find a way of protecting people from such extreme conditions. However, although on Mars it is much colder than on Earth, astronauts could keep warm by wearing specially designed spacesuits. Also, in about 10 years' time, the space station Freedom will make it possible for people to adjust to weightlessness and to launch missions to Mars and maybe even to other planets.

Are there any other moons in the Solar System?

In our Solar System seven planets, including the Earth, have moons. Mars has 2 moons, Jupiter has at least 16, Saturn 23, Uranus 15, Neptune 6, and Pluto 1. Each moon makes an orbit around its planet.

Only the inner planets, Mercury and Venus, have no moons. The moons of the other planets differ in size, surface, composition, and color. Titan, Saturn's largest moon, is bigger than Mercury. Triton, one of Neptune's moons, is the largest in the Solar System. Jupiter's four largest moons – Ganymede, Callisto, Io, and Europa – are remarkable for their diversity and beauty. Only three moons in the Solar System have a detectable atmosphere: Io, Titan, and Triton.

Why do the Sun and the Moon seem to be the same size?

A total eclipse of the Sun by the Moon is rare. It occurs when the Moon passes directly between the Earth and the Sun. When an eclipse occurs, scientists can study the corona and eruptions of the Sun, which then become visible.

It is coincidental that the Earth, the Sun, and the Moon appear to be the same size. If we were to move farther away or closer to one of these bodies, we would no longer get the same impression.

The similar appearance in size of the Sun and the Moon as seen from the Earth is unique in our Solar System. The relative distances between the Earth, the Sun, and the Moon make it possible for an eclipse to take place. These bodies conceal each other because they seem the same size.

What is an eclipse?

When an object is lit up, you can also see a shadow. When the Sun is shining on the Earth, the Earth casts a shadow on the other side. An eclipse occurs when one object passes through the shadow of another.

Eclipses of the Sun and Moon occur because the Moon orbits around the Earth, and because the Earth, Moon, and Sun look the same size. When these three bodies are lined up at Full Moon or New Moon, a lunar or solar eclipse occurs. Between two and five solar eclipses occur each year. There are eclipses on all planets whose moons pass between the Sun and the planet.

What is the difference between a solar and a lunar eclipse?

A solar eclipse occurs when the Earth passes through the Moon's shadow; the Moon is between the Sun and the Earth. A lunar eclipse occurs when the Earth's shadow passes across the face of the Moon; the Earth is between the Sun and the Moon. For each, the three bodies must be exactly in a straight line.

Occasionally, the Moon, the Earth, and the Sun line up in such a way that the Moon blots out the Sun's light to the Earth briefly. This is a total solar eclipse and can only be seen from a small area of the Earth, about 90 miles (150 kilometers) across, which is directly in line with the Sun and Moon at the same time. Except in

this small area, you can only see a partial eclipse.

Why do we only see one side of the Moon?

If you look carefully at the Moon, you will notice that we always see the same side. This is because the Moon takes the same time to make an orbit around Earth as it takes to spin around itself.

It takes the Moon 27 days and 7 hours to make an orbit of the Earth. It takes the same time to spin on its axis with one side permanently turned toward Earth. The other side is not visible from Earth. This also happens with the satellites of all the other planets. Pluto and its satellite Charon always show each other the same side.

A lunar eclipse occurs when the Earth passes exactly between the Sun and the Moon. The shadow of the Earth moves slowly across the face of the Moon.

An asteroid is an enormous stray rock that can be several hundred miles across. A comet is a ball of ice that evaporates to produce a long glowing tail as it passes near the Sun.

Why do we say that there are seas on the Moon?

On the surface of the Moon, dark areas alternate with some lighter ones. The dark patches are called seas, even though there is no water on the Moon.

The terrain in the dark patches is quite smooth. It was once thought that these lowland plains were seas, yet there is no water and no atmosphere on the Moon. In fact, the seas are made of dark lava. The dark and light patches form the Man-in-the-Moon impression.

Why do we have seasons?

Because the Earth is tilted on its axis, the position of the Sun in the sky at a particular place changes during the year, giving us seasons.

During winter, the Sun is low in the sky. It has less of a heating effect because of the oblique angle and because the sunlight has farther to travel through the atmosphere. In summer the Sun is higher in the sky, and sunlight reaches the Earth more directly. Its heating effect is greater, and the temperature rises. When it is summer in one hemisphere, it is winter in the other.

Are there seasons on other planets?

If the axis of a planet is tilted and sunlight reaches its surface, there will be a change in seasons.

Mars is tilted on its axis nearly as much as the Earth. This means that the Sun shines more strongly first in one hemisphere, and then in the other. Seasons on Mars are twice as long as on Earth because a Martian year is as long as two Earth-years; however, the seasons there vary in length. Jupiter's axis is nearly vertical, so there is little change in seasons. Uranus' spin axis is tilted at 98°, so that one pole points toward the Sun, giving it extreme seasons. There are no seasons on Mercury at all because its axis is vertical.

What is a comet?

A comet is a ball of ice and dust surrounded by a cloud of gas and dust. As it approaches the Sun, the heat from the Sun causes the ice in the comet's core to evaporate into gas. The gas and dust glow as they reflect the sunlight, forming a long tail. Comets are satellites of the Sun and have orbits in the shape of a long, narrow ellipse. They are the only objects able to travel as far as and even beyond Neptune and Pluto.

A comet looks like a star with a tail. This tail is made up of gas and dust, pushed away from the core by a stream of particles from the Sun. A tail may become forked at the end, and it can sometimes trail behind a comet for vast distances. Some comets are visible to the naked eye, but they can usually only be seen through a telescope. The famous Halley's Comet was seen in 1910 and then again in 1986. It will next appear in the sky in 2062. The comet Hale-Bopp in 1997 was one of the brightest in living memory. Some comets never return. Others gradually fade with age and lose their gases and dust particles, which produce flashing lights as they drop through the atmosphere: these are called shooting stars.

When can you see a shooting star?

A shooting star is a meteor – a piece of rock or a dust particle – that lights up as it travels through the atmosphere at high speed. As it collides with atoms in the atmosphere, the meteor becomes so hot that it burns up. The fire is the streak of light you can see.

The best place to look out for shooting stars is far from the light and pollution of large cities. Shooting stars are most frequently seen during summer nights, after midnight, and especially in August. Sometimes large numbers of them will appear in the sky as meteor showers, producing a marvelous display of light in complete silence.

Are asteroids dangerous for the Earth?

Asteroids are tiny planets that move around the Sun. The very large ones can be up to 600 miles (1,000 kilometers) in diameter, while the smallest ones are only 3,000 feet (1,000 meters) or even less. There must be hundreds of thousands of them, but they are too small and faint to be visible.

Hundreds of thousands of asteroids move between the orbits of Mars and Jupiter in what is called the asteroid belt. They are made of rock and metal, like the Earth and other terrestrial planets. Because of the elliptical orbits in which they move, asteroids can get dangerously close to the Earth. However, collisions occur, on average, only four times per million years. The atmosphere protects the Earth from most of the debris in space.

If the Earth collided with a huge asteroid, the consequences would be catastrophic: life could be completely wiped out.

Our Planet Earth

How old is the Earth?

The Earth was formed over 4.6 billion years ago, at the same time as the Sun and the other planets in our Solar System.

For a very long time, it was thought that the Earth was only about 4,500 years old. Christians arrived at this figure by adding together the ages of all the people mentioned in the Bible, from Adam and Eve to Jesus. It was not until the 19th century, when fossils of extinct animals were discovered, that it became apparent that the Earth must have been much older. At the end of the 19th century, it was still assumed that the Earth was between 40 and 90 million years old. Nowadays, it is thought that the Earth is a great deal older. The Solar System is believed to have formed 4.6 billion years ago. The galaxy in which it appeared had already been in existence for about 10 billion years.

How was the Earth born?

Before the Solar System was formed, matter was floating in a cloud of dust and gas. Part of the cloud contracted to form the Sun. The rest of the cloud substance contracted more to form large clumps of particles of ice and rock. These particles gradually fused together to form planets such as the Earth.

Rocks crashed together on the surface of the Earth while it was forming. This produced so much heat that the rocks melted and turned into a thick syrup. Rotation and gravity gave this soft matter its spherical shape. The heaviest elements, nickel and iron, accumulated at the center. The outside gradually cooled down to form the crust of the Earth. The lighter elements, silicon and aluminum, remained near the surface, where they now dominate the composition of the crust. We have learned about the formation of the Earth by studying the rocks beneath us.

Seen from space, the Earth is a very beautiful planet.

It only took one meteorite, with a diameter of 60 feet (18 meters), to create this vast crater in Arizona. So you can imagine how much more damage an asteroid with a diameter of 60,000 feet (18 kilometers) would cause!

What did the Earth look like in its early stages?

The surface must have been very bumpy because of the constant rain of meteorites. It must have looked like the Moon. Gradually, heavy rains softened its rough surface, wearing away the craters left by meteorites. The craters on the Moon have not disappeared since there is no rain there.

Before becoming a planet, the Earth was a swirl of dust and particles of rock. Over the years this free matter collected together and fused into a hot, rocky ball. When the Earth started cooling down, only its center remained molten. The crust became solid, turning to rock. At the beginning, the Earth was dry. There were no oceans or rivers. Owing to the unique gaseous composition of the planet, a primitive atmosphere soon appeared around the globe. This gas mixture was rich in water vapor, which condensed and started to fall as rain. The water flowed from the high ground down into the valleys, creating the first seas. Some water penetrated the ground to become springs. The heat of the Sun caused water to evaporate from the seas, and the water cycle began. Small rivulets cut beds in the ground that turned into streams and rivers. All this took millions of years.

How big is the Earth?

Our planet is about 8,000 miles (12,800 kilometers) in diameter and 25,000 miles (40,000 kilometers) in circumference. The distance from the equator to the center of the Earth is 3,963 miles (6,378 kilometers).

The diameter at the equator is 7,926 miles (12,756 kilometers). The polar diameter is slightly smaller at 7,900 miles (12,713 kilometers). This is because the Earth is flattened at the poles owing to gravity and rotation. The height of the highest mountain, 5 miles (8 kilometers), and the depth of the seas, 7 miles (11 kilometers) at the deepest, do not make much difference to the size. The Earth is ten times the size of Mercury, which is the smallest known planet (Pluto may be smaller). Jupiter, at 1,300 times the size of the Earth, is the most impressive planet in the Solar System – larger than all the other planets put together.

Are there any craters on Earth?

Meteorites that fall on Earth leave craters of various sizes, similar to those found on the Moon. The largest is the Chicxulub Basin, centered in Mexico's Yucatán Peninsula. It has a diameter of about 190 miles (300 kilometers).

One of the most famous craters is the Meteor Crater in Arizona. It was discovered in 1891 and may have been made 24,000 years ago. The meteorite is thought to have weighed at least 60,000 tons and had a diameter of over 60 feet (18 meters) for it to make such a hole; the crater is 39,370 feet (1,200 meters) in diameter and 590 feet (180 meters) deep. Meteorites themselves are not unusual, but they are usually much smaller. As they come through the atmosphere, they often explode, and smaller pieces fall on the Earth. In 1947, 20 tons of debris left by a meteorite was found in Siberia. The largest piece weighed 1.7 tons. Scars left by meteorites are not visible for very long on the surface of the Earth because they are soon worn away by the wind and rains.

What is the Earth's center made of?

The Earth's center, the core, is made of two hot layers of metals, one molten and one solid, encased in a mantle of lava about 1,740 miles (2,800 kilometers) thick. The continental crust above the mantle is quite thin.

The Earth's rocky surface is cold, but becomes hotter deeper in. At a depth of 5 miles (8 kilometers), it is burning hot. It is impossible to dig any deeper than 7½ miles (12 kilometers), but seismologists can calculate the density of the components of the Earth by studying the seismic vibrations. The Earth has several layers (crust, mantle, and core). The crust of the oceans, which is younger, is 6 miles (10 kilometers) thick, while the continental crust is 43 miles (70 kilometers) thick. The mantle goes 1,800 miles (2,900 kilometers) deep. The outer core, 1,240 miles (2,000 kilometers) thick, consists of molten iron at a temperature of about 3,990°F (2,200°C). The inner core is made of solid nickel and iron at about 8,100°F (4,500°C). This core is solid due to high pressure. The Earth's magnetic field is caused by the rotation of the inner core.

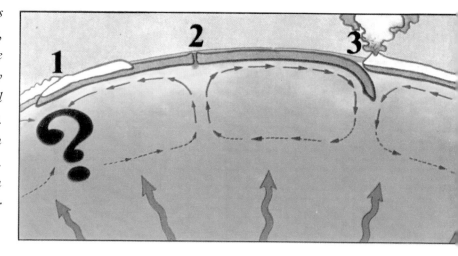

The heat inside the Earth creates currents in the mantle. As a result, the crust, which is solid and made of plates, is in a constant slow motion. (1) When two continental plates meet, a mountain appears. (2) Submarine volcanoes appear in the area between two plates. (3) Volcanoes appear when a heavier plate sinks below a lighter one.

Have the continents always been where they are now?

One hundred and fifty million years ago, there was only one huge continent in one enormous ocean. This vast island broke apart and the pieces drifted, gradually forming continents. These continents are still drifting very slowly.

One indication that the continents must have been moving was found by comparing the shapes of the coasts of West Africa and South America. The two fitted together like two pieces of a puzzle. Later, it was discovered that they contained the same rocks, and the same vegetable and animal fossils were found on both sides of the South Atlantic. This showed that the continents had once been one and had drifted apart. Convection currents within the Earth's mantle produce upwellings of new material along seamlines at the surface, forming ridges such as the Mid-Atlantic Ridge. The new material extends the plates, and these move away from the ridges. Where two plates collide, one overrides the other and the lower one is absorbed back into the mantle.

Why are the continents moving?

The continental crust is divided into 20 large plates, all of which are moving. They carry the oceans and continents. All these plates are made of hard rock floating on molten lava called magma. Scientists do not agree on the reasons why they move.

In some zones, the plates move apart, and the continents move away from each other. In other zones they collide. One of the plates then descends below the other into the magma, creating trenches. The plate that moves up forms mountains or volcanoes. This movement is called "plate tectonics." An example of this can be seen where the East Pacific plate is sinking under Japan, forming a large gap along the coast. Mountains and volcanoes are created at the same time. In other places, as the plates move past each other, they can become jammed and deformed, and earthquakes occur when they spring free. This is what happens in California along the San Andreas fault.

How are fossils formed?

They are the remains of animals or plants that have been turned to stone by being buried in the Earth for thousands of years.

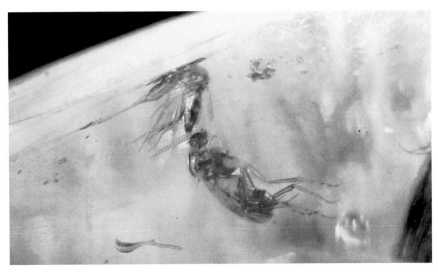

Today, insects that were trapped inside the sap of a tree tens of millions of years ago can be found preserved in amber.

The dead animal must be buried in sand or mud very quickly, before it decays, in order to become a fossil. This happens naturally in the mud at the bottom of the sea, which is why seabeds are so rich in fossils. Many fossils are found near volcanoes because lava petrifies the animal in a split second. Gradually, the plant or the animal will become mineralized (turned to stone). If the ground does not move too much, the fossil will remain intact. Only the skeletons of animals, shells, and scales turn to fossils. However, in some cases the bodies are preserved intact in ice, as in the case of mammoths that have been frozen for thousands of years. Plants turn into coal, so buried forests have turned into rich coal deposits. Resin becomes amber, and trees can be turned into silica. It is possible to come across insect antennae, and even whole flowers. Usually only imprints are found – not just those of plants and animal skeletons, but also footprints of animals that passed along the mud thousands of years ago. The first dinosaur fossils were discovered in the 19th century in the United States, when giant skeletons in perfect condition were excavated.

What do we learn from fossils?

We can learn about extinct animals and plants and about changes in climate. Fossils also tell us about the drift of the continents and the various geological ages.

When you find fossils of the same kind in two separate continents, it suggests that long ago these continents were one. An elephant fossil found in a temperate region indicates that long ago the climate was tropical. Certain shells enable us to find oil, which is a fossil mineral of the mud in which they used to live. Fossils help us piece together the wildlife and landscape that existed in prehistoric times. In the 17th century two scientists, Buffon and Linnaeus, established the first classification of plant and animal species. This classification, still used today, helped scientists to group similar types of fossils together. The study of soil rich in fossils enabled scientists to identify 27 distinct layers of fossils, telling us much about the different prehistoric ages. As a result, we know that life appeared on Earth some three and a half billion years ago and has evolved since.

What makes mountains rise?

The collision and welding together of two tectonic plates causes mountains to rise. This process distorts the rock and compresses the sediment between the two plates into mountain chains. It takes between 50 million and 100 million years for a mountain to rise.

The Earth's landscape results from millions of years of plate activity. Mountain chains are composed of faults, or cracks, and intrusions of many complex rocks. The Alps are the result of the collision of Europe and northern Italy with the African plate. Their formation took 40 million years, and they still grow a fraction of an inch every year due to the pressure of the African plate. The Himalayas were formed when the huge island that was then India collided with the land mass that is now China. The effect of frost, winds, and rain gives mountains their sharp peaks.

Classic volcanoes are the result of the collision of two tectonic plates. Their lava is viscous. Examples are Mount Fuji in Japan (1) and the Puy de Dôme in France (2). Other types of volcano appear when two plates move apart. Their lava is fluid. Examples are Hawaii (3) and the Deccan Plateau in India (4).

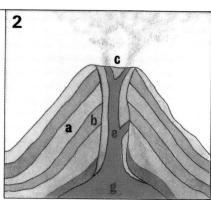
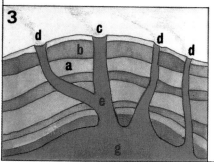
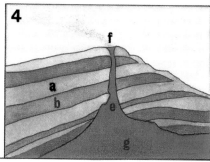

a = layers of ash; b = layers of old lava; c = main crater; d = secondary craters; e = lava; f = fissure; g = magma chamber.

Why are there fish fossils at the top of the Himalayas?

The Himalayan rocks are formed of different layers. One of those comes from the sea that separated India from Asia when India was still an island.

All mountains consist of layers of material: either sedimentary or volcanic. Clay, chalk, coal, and sandstone are sedimentary rocks. They appear when debris that accumulated at the bottom of the sea turns into minerals. Sedimentary rocks preserve the remains of fossilized animals and plants, and also retain an imprint of the movement of the sea where they formed. Some layers of rock have folds in them. This folding occurs when mountains are thrust upward as tectonic plates collide.

How are volcanoes formed?

Volcanoes appear where plates either move apart or collide and rub against each other.

As plates collide, small cracks appear and molten rock (magma) comes to the surface. This is the first eruption. When both plates are oceanic, an island appears in the sea. If one of the plates is oceanic and the other continental, the oceanic plate dives below the coast and volcanoes appear on dry land. They often come up along a line, as in the Andean Cordillera mountain range. The area where plates meet is called the destructive margin. The area between two plates that have moved apart is called the constructive margin. Most sea volcanoes are formed in the constructive margin. Iceland is situated right on top of a constructive margin. The shape of the volcano will depend on the eruption itself – the way lava comes out and hardens on its surface. Volcanoes are still appearing today. In Japan, a volcano suddenly appeared in the middle of a village, lifting it by about 330 feet (100 meters).

Before emerging in the open sea off Japan, this volcano was first a submarine volcano. It will soon become a new island.

Why are there not volcanoes everywhere?

Most volcanoes are near coasts and at the bottom of the sea; that is, on the edge of the continental plates.

This is because volcanoes are formed when tectonic plates come into contact. The chief volcanic regions are around the Pacific rim and southern Indonesia. They are all situated where plates have collided. Volcanoes in mid-ocean (Easter Island in the Pacific Ocean; Tristan da Cunha, the Azores, and the Canaries in the Atlantic Ocean) are situated where plates have moved apart. This is how Mount Kilimanjaro was formed in the middle of the African rift. A rift is formed when two plates move apart and the land collapses between them, forming a lake or even a sea. This may be how the Atlantic Ocean opened up. In a few thousand years, the African continent may split into two continents separated by a huge ocean.

Why do volcanoes often occur in lines?

There are hot spots below the ocean crust where magma rises to the surface. A hot spot becomes a volcano when magma erupts through the plate above it.

As the plate moves, new volcanoes appear and old ones become extinct.

This is how the Hawaiian, Marshall, and Tuamotu Islands in the Pacific Ocean were formed. There are other island chains in the Atlantic Ocean. The volcanoes are formed in sequence, from the oldest at one end of the chain to the youngest at the other. As each volcano moves away from the hot spot, it stops emitting lava. In a chain of volcanoes, usually only one is active and the others are extinct.

Can an extinct volcano become active again?

This is unlikely, but it could happen. A volcano is never completely dead.

A volcano that has been inactive for thousands of years may still produce hot springs and eject some gas. The bottom of the crater always remains in contact with magma. Such a volcano could suddenly become active again. The longer it has been dormant, the more violent the eruption. Molten rock from below the Earth rises into the crater of the volcano. The lava may solidify inside the crater as a plug until a build-up of gases causes the top of the volcano to explode. The volcano ejects ash and larger pieces of matter called bombs. Lava then flows over the rim and can cause damage over distances of several miles. The lava that remains inside forms a crater that can measure up to 60 miles (100 kilometers) in diameter.

Which was the most violent explosion?

Three thousand years ago, the eruption of Santorin in the middle of the Mediterranean was so violent that it completely destroyed the coast for hundreds of miles around, resulting in the end of Cretan civilization.

The eruption of Vesuvius in Italy A.D. 79 is the most famous. It totally destroyed the cities of Pompeii and Herculaneum. Two thousand people were killed by burning lava, and their bodies have been found fossilized. In 1980, Mount Saint Helens in Washington state erupted, destroying 370 miles (600 kilometers) of forest. In 1991, in the Philippines, the volcano Pinatubo exploded after lying dormant for 600 years. There are about 500 active volcanoes that could erupt at any time.

It is possible that volcanoes that appear to be dormant will unexpectedly become active again.

What can you see during an eruption?

First there is a loud noise, a mixture of whistling and rumbling sounds. Then a jet, the color of fire, rises from the crater and lava flows over the rim into the valley.

The noise a volcanic eruption makes really depends on the density of lava. The harder it is, the louder the noise, but it is also less dangerous. This is because only liquid lava can travel far and fast. However, if there are explosions, an eruption can be very dangerous. The volcano projects bombs of burning rock. Extremely fine ash can travel a long way around the Earth, and the eruption can last between a few minutes and several years. The volcano then calms down for a long time, sometimes for centuries. Others rumble for thousands of years like Stromboli in Italy, which has been spitting lava every day for about 3,000 years. When lava comes into contact with the air, it cools down and solidifies. What the volcano looks like depends on how quickly the lava cools down. If it cools rapidly, domes will form. If not, the lava can spread several miles. The landscape thus created can be extremely fascinating, as in the Giant's Causeway in Northern Ireland, where columns of basalt have formed in the shape of enormous steps.

Why is an eruption dangerous?

It can be dangerous because lava is so hot that it burns everything in its way in a split second. Volcanoes also project stones and may emit various toxic gases that can be lethal if inhaled.

Liquid lava flows out so quickly that there is no time to run away. When it is thicker, it flows much more slowly, but it destroys everything in its path. It burns houses and trees, or else it covers them up under a thick layer of molten rock. The smoke contains toxic acid gases that are heavier than air and form glowing clouds that move at a speed of up to 250 miles an hour (400 kilometers an hour). Such clouds can cover whole cities. Volcanic bombs are burning stones that can be thrown a great distance. One of the volcanoes in the Hawaiian Islands threw a rock that weighed several tons a distance of 2,600 feet (800 meters).

A volcanic eruption is always an unforgettable sight, but it is by night that it is most spectacular, as here in Hawaii.

Is it possible to predict an eruption?

It is impossible to tell exactly when a volcano is going to become active again. However, there are a few warning signs: the ground starts moving, and sometimes the side of the volcano swells up.

Nowadays it is possible to predict an earthquake by studying the waves coming from the Earth. This is very useful because earthquakes are often a sign that a volcano is going to erupt. A scale, called the Richter scale, is used to measure the force of an earthquake. Knowing the strength is essential, as a force 7 earthquake is 30 times more violent than a force 6 earthquake. Some scientists, called vulcanologists, specialize in the study of volcanoes. Sensitive machines are used to measure the swelling of the sides of a volcano. They look at rocks and gases in laboratories. Vulcanologists also look at craters from the sky using special planes; this lets them observe the glowing clouds emitted from the volcano from a very short distance. This is how they can forecast an eruption and warn the local population.

Why are there often hot springs near volcanoes?

Water circulates underneath the surface of the Earth. When this water comes close to very hot volcano rocks, it starts boiling.

Water does not always move in an orderly way under the ground. When it boils, it spurts out of the Earth in the form of jets, which can be anywhere from 4 inches to 30 feet (about 10 centimeters to 100 meters) high. These jets are called geysers. Old Faithful in Yellowstone National Park got its name because it spurts regularly every hour. Not all geysers are as punctual or so spectacular. Sometimes they are just a boiling puddle of mud. Some of these springs have beneficial effects for health, so thermal spas have been established nearby. You can also find hot springs near volcanoes under the sea. This is what makes the currents feel warm in those places. They can reach temperatures of more than 170°F (300°C).

Are there any volcanoes under the sea?

There are even more volcanoes under the sea than on dry land, and some rise up from the surface of the sea to form islands, such as Réunion Island in the Indian Ocean.

We know that there are around 10,000 volcanoes on the continents. There are even more under the sea, but we do not really know how many. New volcanoes are constantly forming. They can be extremely fragile, and submarine currents often cause them to collapse.

Which is the largest volcano in the world?

Mauna Loa in the Hawaiian archipelago in the Pacific Ocean. It is 30,185 feet (9,200 meters) high from the bottom of the sea to its peak. At the moment, it is not active.

Antarctica also has volcanoes: Mount Erebus is still active.

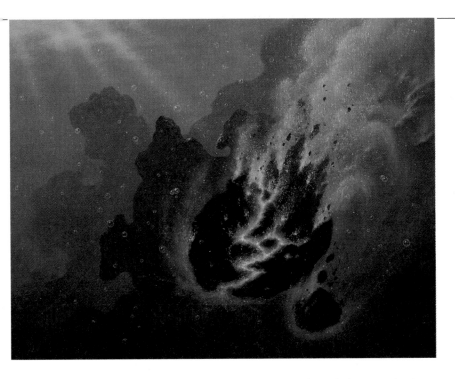

Under the sea, lava cools down very suddenly and explodes, producing some very small bubbles of superheated steam.

Volcanoes are many different shapes and sizes. It all depends on the type of ashes and lava. A volcano formed when two tectonic plates come into contact is cone-shaped, like Mount Fuji in Japan. This type of volcano is made of thick lava that cooled down very quickly and hardened in thick layers. If a volcano appeared because two tectonic plates moved apart, it is flat. These are called shield volcanoes. They sometimes have several craters, and their very thin lava spreads over great distances. Sometimes thick lava solidifies inside the crater. Gradually, the soft cone made of ash and lava is worn away by the rain. Only the very hard core remains. Sugar Loaf Mountain in Rio de Janeiro, Brazil, is one of these volcanoes.

What are islands?

An island is a piece of solid land entirely surrounded by water. The smallest islands in the sea are volcanoes. The largest ones are true continents. Islands on continents can occur in lakes or rivers.

Islands can form when the water level rises, or when land sinks. On the continents, islands can be made by rivers that erode the land around a piece of higher ground and end up encircling it. Islands can also result from deposition of sediment: when a river drops the earth and rocks (the sediment) it carries to form a platform in the middle of its waters. This type of island only lasts a few thousand years. In other places, rivers may form a bend where the current becomes weaker. An island can then form in the bend and grow until the course of the river changes. In the sea, islands can result from sediment deposits. The earth and other debris collects at the bottom and may end up rising above the surface of the sea or accumulating around a mussel bed, forming a reef. Movements of plates can produce a mountain on the seabed or can separate a piece of land from a continent. This is how Madagascar came to be detached from the African continent. The largest islands are Australia, Greenland, and New Guinea. These appeared when the sea filled the gap that separated them from the continent.

What is the difference between an island and an atoll?

An atoll is an old volcano in the middle of the sea. Its center has collapsed and left a circle of small coral islands on the surface.

Skeletons of small sea animals, called corals, make up the surface of these small islands. This is why atolls are also called coral reefs. There are two reasons for the collapse of a volcano. It either happens because the bottom of the sea drops or because the level of the water rises. Such an archipelago is not called an atoll until the volcano has completely disappeared under the sea. The islands that remain on the surface are made up of the corals that have accumulated around the volcano. The salt lake that remains in the center is called a lagoon. The Bahamas are a coral reef in the Caribbean. Tourists are attracted to atolls because of their mild climate and beautiful landscape.

Why do mountains disappear?

When the pressure that makes mountains rise disappears, they stop growing. Rain and winds gradually wear them to nothing more than a hill.

This wearing away of rocks by wind and rain is called weathering. Frost also plays its part in the disappearance of a mountain. Water gets into the rock through cracks, and when it freezes it expands, sometimes causing the rock to explode. The wind and the rain carry fragments of rock away. They are slowly turned into smaller stones or sand, and are washed or blown into the valley. Rivers then carry these rock fragments far from their place of origin. The effects of erosion vary with the density of the rock and can result in some very strange formations.

This is the Raiatea Atoll in French Polynesia. You can see the arcs of the coral reefs.

Can earthquakes be forecast?

Seismographs are machines used for monitoring movements below the Earth's surface. This information enables scientists to predict earthquakes and organize the evacuation of local people. In the 11th century, the Chinese had invented a machine for predicting earthquakes. It took the form of a large vase inside which a heavy pendulum was linked to some dragon heads. In each of their mouths was a marble. Below were some open-mouthed frogs. It was possible to tell which way the earthquake was coming from depending on which frog received the marble. Modern seismographs receive waves from the Earth. They

Seismographs are used to monitor the Earth's surface movements, and so predict earthquakes. This seismograph is at the bottom of the sea.

may be body waves, which travel through the center of the Earth, or surface waves: "primary" waves and "secondary" waves. Primary waves are the first sign of a quake. The majority of earthquakes occur on the seismic belts, which are all around the Pacific Ocean, in the Mediterranean, Samoa, the Azores, the Hawaiian Islands, Réunion Island, and Iceland. Local people must build houses that can withstand such tremors. In these areas, steel frames are essential and foundations must be dug in rock.

Why are earthquakes dangerous?

Earthquakes can destroy houses and mountains within minutes. They can also result in fires and open huge crevices in the ground.

Seismic waves make the ground shudder suddenly. Earthquakes are usually small, and some can only be sensed by seismographs. Other earthquakes give the impression that the ground is moving. Furniture shakes and objects fall. Glass shatters, fires start, and water pipes break, making it difficult to fight the fires.

The Richter scale is used to measure the intensity of quakes. Force 4 means that hanging objects oscillate. Force 6 means that windows break. Force 9 means that roads open up, and in a force 10, bridges collapse.

How many types of rock are there?

There are three: igneous rock, sedimentary rock, and metamorphic rock.

Igneous rock is formed from magma or lava brought to the surface through a volcano or solidified beneath the Earth's surface. Granite is an igneous rock made of three types of crystals. It has large crystals produced by slow cooling. Rapid cooling results in small crystals; basalt is a good example. Sedimentary rock is formed by the accumulation of deposits laid down by water, wind, or ice. These are compressed for centuries and turn into rock. Deposits of mud become clays, and clays become mudstone or shale. Mineral deposits become sandstone, while limestone is made of animal and plant remains. The word "metamorphic" means "changed." This type of rock was originally either igneous or sedimentary. Heat from the Earth caused it to change into hard, crystalline rock. Limestone turns into white marble and shale into slate.

What is the difference between a mineral and ore?

Ore is a rock that contains minerals, metals, such as gold or iron, copper, silver, zinc, or uranium, and non-metals such as salt and sulfur. There are thousands of such rocks.

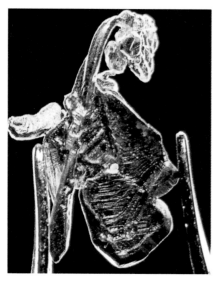

Gold is a very soft metal, which is why gold crystals are extremely rare. The nugget shown here reveals the cubic shape of some crystals that were deformed by pressure while under the surface of the Earth.

Ore comes from matter that has been transformed by various processes such as the putrefaction of plants or animals. Other ore deposits were buried so deeply in the ground that it took several million years for them to come up to the surface of the Earth again. All rocks are made of minerals with a grainy appearance: they are crystals. Depending on its nature, a rock may contain one or several minerals. Like all materials, minerals are made of chemical elements. The most common elements are silicon and oxygen, which make up 75 percent of the crust of the Earth. They combine to form silicates found in lava. Most rocks are made of silicates with only tiny amounts of other elements.

Is it possible to tell the age of rock?

You have to use very sophisticated methods to tell the age of a rock. However, if the rock contains a fossil, it is possible to compare it with another rock with a similar fossil whose age is known.

The age of a rock can be found by a technique known as radiometric dating. Scientists know the time it takes for certain radioactive elements to change into other elements. By finding out the proportions of elements present now, it is possible to find out when the process of disintegration started. Thus the oldest rock on Earth is at least 3.8 billion years old.

What is a crystal?

It is a very pure mineral. Its atoms are organized in a very regular manner.

Matter is made up of very small particles called atoms. In crystals, atoms are organized in a very orderly way. They follow geometrical shapes that are always the same for each material. The crystals in topaz are shaped like a brick; those in emerald are hexagon-shaped; and fluorite crystals are cube-shaped. Crystals are identified by their color, density, and brilliance. However, chemical elements in crystals can alter their color. Chromium gives a reddish color to ruby and a greenish color to emerald. Crystals are therefore not always pure. The only sure way of finding their composition is by carrying out laboratory tests using microscopes and X-rays. Precious stones are very rare crystals.

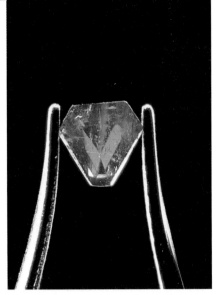

This is not a sapphire but an azurite, a typical semiprecious stone. Such crystals are popular with collectors, but they are not of much interest to jewelers as the crystals are too small and too fragile.

How many precious stones are there?

There are four: diamonds (usually colorless), ruby (red), sapphire (blue), and emerald (green). Others are semiprecious stones such as amethysts or hard stones such as jade.

Igneous rock contains pockets of gas called geodes. Precious stones grow inside these. They are minerals that have solidified in the cavities of the rock. Cut and used in jewelry, rare and beautiful precious stones have always been a symbol of wealth and prestige.

Diamonds are the hardest of all because they only contain one element: carbon. Diamonds can scratch anything, but they cannot be scratched themselves. They are used for cutting glass. Semiprecious stones like aquamarine, tourmaline, and topaz are more common. Hard stones such as jade and rock crystal are used mainly for making ornaments.

Is the shape of crystals natural?

Beryl comes in all sorts of colors: here it is green, very similar to an emerald. It can be cut or just used in its natural shape.

The geometrical shape of uncut crystals is natural. Precious stones must be cut before they can be used in jewelry.

Before an emerald has been cut, it looks like a green hard candy. Quartz looks like transparent sticks. When quartz is slightly purple, it is called amethyst, and when it is yellowish, it is called citrine. Gypsum looks like a sandstone. Salt is a crystal. When you look at salt crystals with a magnifying glass, you can see that they are cube-shaped.

Has the sea always existed?

Millions of years ago, it was so hot on Earth that it was completely dry. It is not known whether water came from rocks or clouds.

Water did not appear on Earth until the temperature dropped below 212°F (100°C). The air in prehistoric times was not the same as that we breathe today. It was saturated with steam and did not contain any oxygen. Volcanoes filled it with carbon dioxide, ammonia, and methane. When the temperature fell, this moisture was retained in the atmosphere. It condensed to a liquid that collected in the lowest areas of the Earth to form the seas. Chemical experiments have shown that, during the process of condensation, the atmosphere produced proteins, amino acids, and other molecules that are essential for life. It is thanks to these gases that seas and life have appeared on Earth.

What is the biggest ocean in the world?

At a depth of 5,900 feet (1,800 meters), where an oceanic plate dives under a continental plate, you can see "smokers." These are chimneylike structures that squirt out water, heated under pressure by magma to a temperature of 535°F (280°C) for white smokers, like here near Tonga, and 640°F (340°C) for black smokers.

Seventy percent of the Earth's surface is covered with water. The Pacific Ocean alone has a surface of 70 million square miles (180 million square kilometers) and accounts for half of this water.

The Pacific Ocean is bigger than all the continents put together. It was the first ocean to appear. The Atlantic Ocean, which covers an area of 41 million square miles (106 million square kilometers), appeared later when the continents moved apart. The Indian Ocean is even smaller, at 29 million square miles (74 million square kilometers). The oceans have all been given different names because they are separated by capes, but in fact they are all part of one single stretch of water. Oceans usually separate continents, whereas seas are included in them. Oceans are found mainly in the southern hemisphere, due to the movement of the tectonic plates. Oceans occupy 90 percent of the surface of this hemisphere. The Pacific is the biggest and also the deepest ocean. It conceals abysses up to 7 miles (11 kilometers) deep. The highest mountain could easily fit inside such an abyss.

How deep is the sea?

The depth of seas and oceans varies. On average the depth is 2 miles (3½ kilometers). The deepest submarine spot is 7 miles (11 kilometers).

The deepest spot is in the Pacific Ocean, near the island of Guam in the Marianas Trench. A unique marine animal life has developed in this abyss. Hollows in the sea are basin-shaped with steep edges and quickly become deep. The bottom

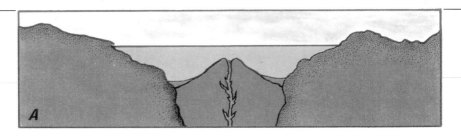

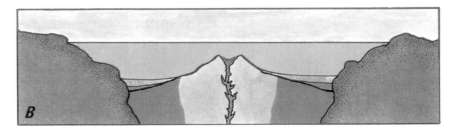

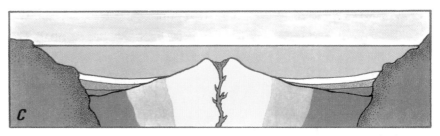

is usually rather flat. Without water, the submarine landscape would be similar to that on the continents. It is made of mountains, volcanoes, and large abysses, which can be between 4 and 6 miles (6 and 10 kilometers) deep. Sunlight cannot penetrate the depths – at 330 feet (100 meters) it is black – and the pressure increases quickly. It was once thought that there was no life in the ocean depths. Following the invention of the bathyscaph (a deep-sea apparatus used for exploration), a crablike creature was found that lives on the ocean floor and feeds on animal remains that fall from the surface. Sonar equipment is used to measure submarine depths. A sound is sent down into the sea; depending on how long it takes for the echo to come back up, it is possible to tell how deep it is.

An ocean is formed when a fracture appears in a continent. (A) Lava begins to rise up and the coasts start moving apart. (B) and (C) Fresh lava pushes the old lava back. The coasts move farther apart and the ocean grows.

Are oceans motionless?

Waves and currents on the ocean surfaces are caused by winds. At greater depths, it is the variations in temperature and saltiness that cause water to move.

Because of all these different influences, currents are complex.

They move clockwise in the northern hemisphere and counterclockwise in the southern hemisphere. This movement is due to the heat of the Sun, which can penetrate very deep into the sea. Water retains this warmth. Cold currents cool down the warm coasts, and warm currents warm up the coasts near the poles. This regulates temperatures and prevents water on some coasts from freezing. If it was not for the cold currents, life in oceans would not be possible and there would be no plankton. Warm currents can block off the cold ones and make it impossible for food to reach large numbers of animals.

What would happen if the polar ice caps melted?

The water from the melting ice would end up in the oceans. This would cause the level of the sea to rise by about 300 feet (about 100 meters).

Ten percent of the land on our planet is covered with ice. The ice caps are at the poles, covering Antarctica and Greenland. In places, the ice can be up to 13,000 feet (4,000 meters) thick. The ice is so heavy that the Antarctic continent has sunk below the level of the sea. Glaciers are rivers of slowly melting ice. When glaciers reach the sea, they break up and turn into icebergs, which float out into the sea. The melting process is quite moderate and does not threaten the level of the seas. The Earth may, however, be entering a period of global warming. In a few years' time, the ice at the poles may have partly melted. Coasts might be flooded, and some cities will probably be engulfed in water. Most of the land would remain dry. During periods of glaciation the opposite happens, and seas ice over. Sea level can drop by up to 300 feet (about 100 meters).

Why is the sea salty?

Sea salt comes from rocks on the continents. Over millions of years, the rain washes salts from the rocks into rivers, which carry the salt into the sea.

This is why the water in rivers is not salty; the salt they carry does not accumulate in them but only passes through. Salt is harvested from the sea by trapping seawater in large shallow pans called saltings. Sea salt is mostly a combination of chlorine and sodium called sodium chloride. Seawater is 3.3 to 3.7 percent salt. The saltier the water, the heavier it is. The water on the surface is not so salty and does not mix with water in the depths. Seawater not only contains salt; it also contains minerals and organic particles that allow aquatic plants and animals to live in it and feed.

Can seas dry out?

It is possible for the water in a sea to evaporate. This happened millions of years ago to the Mediterranean.

Seawater, heated by the Sun, is evaporating all the time. This evaporation cools the surface of the sea and increases the salt concentration. However, the lost water is replaced by rain and water from rivers. If this normal cycle is disturbed, the sea can dry out. This happened in prehistoric times in the Mediterranean Sea. The water in the sea evaporated until the Mediterranean was completely dried out, and then it filled up again. This happened 12 times over the course of a million years. During the dry periods, all that was left of the sea was a salt-covered valley and a few lakes. It is believed that movements of the Earth's crust opened and closed the Strait of Gibraltar, through which water from the Atlantic Ocean refilled the sea.

Where do waves come from?

The pressure of the wind against the surface of the sea creates hollows and bumps that seem to travel through the water. These are called waves.

The height of a wave depends on the speed of the wind and how long the wind blows. Even a gust of wind will raise some ripples. When the wind is stronger, the water rises and forms higher waves with more pronounced crests and hollows. The white foam is produced by air that escapes when the waves fall back. They break when their crests topple over, fringed with foam. Waves break when they reach the shore because the base of the wave meets the land and slows down, while the top part moves forward even faster. In the open sea, when the wind has died away, the waves seem to rise and fall very regularly and have a smooth,

When they reach the coast, the waves break, forming surf on the long, flat-bottomed beaches, or crash onto the rocks of the more rugged coastline.

with the cycle of the moon when Isaac Newton, in the 17th century, first explained how the Moon could influence the sea. He had already explained the laws of gravity and thought that they could be applied to planets. The Moon is closer than the Sun to the Earth, which is why the Moon's gravity has a greater effect.

What is a

tidal wave?

Also called a tsunami, it is a powerful wave generated by an earthquake or a volcanic eruption under the sea.

rounded shape. This is called the swell. In waves the water itself does not travel along – it just rises and falls as the wave motion travels.

Why are there

tides?

Tides are caused by the Moon, which attracts water from the Earth toward itself. The Moon's gravity pulls up the water directly below it, creating a bulge of water. At the same time, the Moon pulls the solid Earth away from the water on the opposite side of the Earth,

creating a second bulge. As the Moon moves around the Earth, these bulges of water follow the Moon and move from east to west.

If there were no continents, there would be two tides a day. Continents block the movement of the water. Only the Atlantic Ocean has two tides daily (depending on your location in the extremely large Pacific Ocean, there are either one or two tides a day). The effect of the Sun is not so strong, and it can only be felt at Full or New Moon: its gravity combined with that of the Moon produce what are called Spring tides. People had for a long time been aware of the correlation of the times of the tides

Earthquakes that generate tidal waves may be very remote from the place where the waves appear. Within a few hours, an earthquake in Australia could generate a tidal wave off the coast of Alaska. Shock waves traveling under the surface of the water at speeds of 620 miles per hour (1,000 kilometers per hour) produce tidal waves with speeds of up to 465 miles per hour (750 kilometers per hour). They often totally destroy coastal buildings. In the open sea the waves are not as noticeable, but may be up to 165 feet (50 meters) or more high near coasts. Most tidal waves occur in the Pacific.

Tsunami is the Japanese name for tidal wave. Japan is often hit by tidal waves because it is surrounded by submarine volcanoes.

What is an inland sea?

An inland sea is a sea that does not come into contact with an ocean. It is surrounded by land. Tides are so weak that they are hardly noticeable.

Inland seas are saltier than seas that open onto the oceans because the water in them never mixes with ocean water. Water may evaporate out of these seas faster than they are refilled by rain.

This is the case for the Dead Sea, which has evaporated so much that its water is very salty. Animals cannot survive in it, which is why it has been given this name. The landscape around it is strange, created by evaporation and winds. Most of the movements in inland seas are caused by the variations in the concentration of salt in their waters. Fresh water is brought in by rivers and streams. The Mediterranean, the Baltic, and the Aral seas are all inland seas.

What is a lake?

A lake is a pool of water contained in a natural basin.

Just like an inland sea, a lake is an enclosed stretch of water. There is one exception: Lake Maracaibo, which opens onto the Caribbean Sea. Other lakes evaporate or their waters leak away through underground springs. Lakes fill up with water from rain, rivers, and ground water. Lakes are usually found near coasts, where the ground-water level is very high, and near mountains, where there are lots of hollows in the ground. Their waters are salty from the salt in the ground. When a lake evaporates completely, all that is left is a salt plain. The Great Salt Lake in Utah is all that remains of the old Bonneville Lake that was 10 times bigger. In tropical countries, lakes reduced to a puddle can fill up overnight when it rains, like Lake Chad in Africa for instance. Basins can form in different ways. Some are the hollows left by the disappearance of a glacier, while others form when a river in a valley is blocked by a rockfall or a man-made dam. Lakes can also be found where rainwater has accumulated in the craters of extinct volcanoes or in the gaps generated by the movement of continents. This sort of lake is very deep, like Lake Baikal in Russia, which at 4,870 feet (1,485 meters) is the deepest in the world. The Great Lakes on the border between Canada and the United States originated in one huge lake, which covered an area

The melt water from a glacier may accumulate in a large basin to form a mountain lake of cold, calm water.

of 154,440 square miles (400,000 square kilometers). The biggest lake in the world, the Caspian Sea, used to be a huge inland sea that stretched from the former Soviet Union to Central Asia.

Where can marshes be found?

Salt marshes may form near coasts and in very dry regions. Fresh water marshes are common along big rivers. Marshes may also form where fresh water feeds into the sea.

A marsh is an area of land saturated with water. They may contain shallow puddles, quicksand, and small islands. Marshes can form anywhere when rainwater or water produced by the melting of ice does not flow away and so stagnates. The water level and the size of a marsh fluctuate. Periods of droughts and flooding follow each other. Animal species that live in marshes may include birds, reptiles, and amphibians. The marshes on the banks of the River Nile are rich in game. On the banks of the Amazon you can find the largest water lilies in the world. Entangled with other plants, they form floating islands.

Why does it rain?

It rains when drops of water contained in clouds become so heavy that they fall on the Earth.

Air in the atmosphere contains water vapor. When air rises and cools, water vapor in the air condenses around very tiny particles of dust. This results in millions of droplets of water and ice crystals, which group together to form clouds. If the clouds continue to cool, more water vapor condenses and the droplets of water get bigger. When their size has increased 100 times, they become so heavy that they fall as rain. Hot air rises, cools down when it is very high in the sky, and turns to rain. This may happen very quickly. This is why summer showers are sudden and heavy but do not last long. Clouds also break as they pass over mountains because the air is forced up, cooling as it rises. The strength of the rain depends on the type of the cloud. Cumulonimbus clouds bring heavy showers, while stratus clouds bring cold and unpleasant drizzle that can last all day.

Which areas have the highest and lowest rainfall?

Kauai Island, in the Hawaiian Islands, gets the most

The Camargue in the Rhône delta in France contains vast stretches of marshland which are a paradise for migrating birds.

A rainbow is a colored arch that is sometimes visible in the sky when it is raining.

rain: 460 inches (1,168 centimeters) a year. In Arica, Chile, no rain fell for a period of 14 consecutive years.

The amount of rainfall varies depending on the location in the world. There are some places in Africa, such as Freetown, South Africa, where there is as much rain in two months in the summer as there is in one year in Europe, while in others, such as Aswan in Egypt, there has been no rain for years. The Namib Desert is the driest in the world. Rainfall depends on the latitude. At middle latitudes, the rainfall is moderate. At low latitudes (around the equator), rainfall is enormous. The presence of seas and mountains changes this pattern. It rains in the Far East, even though it is at the same latitude as the Sahara. This is the monsoon, caused by cold and wet air that comes from the Indian Ocean. The deserts in Mexico and the Southwest are created by the presence of mountain ranges that prevent western winds from bringing rain from the ocean. The Gobi Desert in central Asia exists because it is very far from any sea.

What is a rainbow?

Drops of water in the air split up the light of the Sun into the colors of the spectrum – red, orange, yellow, green, blue, indigo, and violet. These colors are displayed in the sky in the shape of an arch on the opposite side from the Sun.

Sunlight is white light, which means that it is made up of all the colors of the spectrum. The drops of water act as tiny prisms. They break up the light into colors ranging from red to violet. Very rarely, double or triple rainbows are seen at the same time. They are fainter than the main rainbow and are seen outside it with the colors inverted. This happens when the drops produce double or triple reflection. Rainbows can be used to forecast the weather. If they appear in the evening, it means that the rain is coming from the west and therefore that it is nearly over. If a rainbow appears in the morning, it means that there will soon be a shower.

How does a river form?

When it rains, water flows across the land. It cuts into the soil to form little streams, which then turn into rivers. All rivers take the water back to the sea.

Rainwater falls on the Earth. It soaks in and feeds underground springs, which then form rivers. Some of this water evaporates to form clouds, which will release the water back to the Earth again as rain, hail, or snow. The spurting of underground springs is responsible for the constant flow of rivers; surface water increases the amount of water in rivers, but is not enough to make a river on its own. Rivers alter landscapes. The larger they are, the more sediments and stones they carry and the more they wear away the ground. They dig their own bed and choose their own path. Rivers can create gentle bends, but they can also dig canyons. It is possible to tell the age of a river by looking at its profile. A young river has clear-cut shapes, whereas an older river has softer shapes.

The path of a river over thousands of years wears away the rock beneath, forming a canyon.

What is a canyon?

A canyon is a deep valley, or gorge, carved out by a river over thousands of years.

As a river flows, it wears away the river bed. If the rock of the river bed is quite soft, like sandstone or limestone, the river can cut a deep vertical channel. One of the most famous canyons in the world is the Grand Canyon in Arizona. Here the Colorado River has worn away the solid rock to make a canyon 280 miles (450 kilometers) long. In some places the Grand Canyon is more than 6,000 feet (1,800 meters) deep and 18 miles (29 kilometers) wide. As you descend the canyon, you see exposed layers of rock from different prehistoric ages, giving fascinating information about the past.

Is a glacier motionless?

A glacier is so heavy that it glides very slowly along the basin where it has taken shape. When it comes to the bottom, it melts and flows away.

A glacier is so huge that you cannot tell that it is moving. It was only in the 19th century that it became clear that glaciers do move. The speed at which they move depends on the temperature of the ice and the size of the valley (the narrower it is, the faster the glacier moves). Glaciers in the Alps move at speeds of 30 to 650 feet (10 to 200 meters) a year, whereas those in the Himalayas

reach speeds of about 5,000 feet (1,500 meters) a year. Ones in Greenland "race" at speeds of about 13,000 feet (4,000 meters) a year. A glacier carries a lot of debris, which it collects along mountains. This is deposited at the bottom of the glacier, forming embankments through which water from the melting ice flows out.

Have glaciers always existed?

There were even more glaciers, and much larger ones, during the prehistoric times called periods of glaciation, or ice ages.

Glaciation periods alternate with interglacial periods. In the past, the whole of the northern hemisphere and the tip of southern America froze over every 20,000 years. The highest mountains were then all covered with ice. It is thought that the Earth has known four glaciation periods. Climate changes that occur over the centuries affect glaciers. In the 1st century A.D. it was so mild that glaciers were unknown. It was much colder in the 14th and 15th centuries than it is today. Since 1920, the climate has warmed up and small glaciers have disappeared.

Some icebergs in the Arctic are gigantic. They can take several years to melt in waters above freezing. Some float to the equator.

What is an iceberg?

It is a huge piece of ice broken from a glacier that floats in the cold seas near the poles. The largest part of an iceberg is under the water.

A glacier forms when the temperature reaches 28.4°F (−2°C). Those in Greenland and near the North Pole are gigantic. When they reach the coast, they break up. The pieces, icebergs, pushed by the wind and the currents, drift out to sea. The smallest icebergs are the size of a tall building; the largest ones can be 2,000 times larger and weigh a million tons. Icebergs are not salty; they are made of snow that has turned into ice. Icebergs are like ice cubes in a glass of water; they melt very slowly in the polar sea. Satellites follow the movements of icebergs because they can be a hazard to ships. They normally disappear as soon as they reach waters above freezing, but they can take three years to melt.

Where can you find the thickest layer of ice?

The South Pole is covered by a layer of ice 2½ miles (4 kilometers) thick.

The Greenland ice cap is 5,000 feet (1,500 meters) thick. This is why the peaks of some of the mountains on Greenland stick up above the ice. In Antarctica all that melts is the pack ice, which is the ice that covers the sea. When the temperature drops below freezing, the sea near either pole freezes over. In the Arctic Ocean there is a ridge 3,000 feet (1,000 meters) below the surface. It divides the ocean into two basins, the Laurentian and the Angara. The Angara basin reaches a depth of 13,409 feet (4,087 meters) closest to the North Pole, when it is very deep below the ice.

How does a cave form?

Rainwater soaks deep underground. Some rocks, such as limestone, are dissolved by rainwater. Underground water slowly wears the rock away and forms caves.

Underground water contains high levels of carbon dioxide, making the water acidic and corrosive. The acidic water easily dissolves away limestone, creating little crevices that gradually get larger until they become grottoes or caves. Water continues to come into the cave through the surrounding rock, dripping from the top of the cave. This water forms part of the ground water. As it drips, it forms stalactites, which are long stems of minerals. Large stalactites take millions of years to form. Stalagmites are mineral deposits that rise upward from the ground under the drips.

Why are there

beaches?

Through its ceaseless movement, the sea wears away coastal rocks and turns them into pebbles, then into gravel, and finally into sand. Beaches are popular recreational spots – but they are not only for sunbathing. There are also many types of animals and plants that live there.

Waves are strongest on the shore. They can wear away rock and turn it into sand. The shape of the beach depends on the type of coastal rock. The harder the rock, the longer the eroding process of the sea will take. Coasts always contain several varieties of rock. The softer ones wear out first.

There may be some stronger rock left in the sea. In places, cliffs may enclose little creeks where beaches can be found. The softer rock has been turned into pebbles, which cover the beach. In turn, pebbles and sand contribute to the erosion of the coast. When a promontory has formed, waves come and lick it from both sides. It will gradually wear away and turn into a peak in the middle of the water or into an arch. Beaches move slowly to the right or to the left because the sea always comes from the side. This is why wooden or concrete breakwaters are built to preserve them.

Why are there

deserts?

In some regions, water evaporates as soon as it rains. Since there are only about 8 inches (20 centimeters) of rain a year in those places, nothing can grow. It is a desert.

As there are no plants or clouds to make any shade, the Sun dries out the ground. The lack of rain may be due to two factors. Either big mountain ranges block off wet currents of air, or the movement

These cliffs have been sculpted by waves and winds. It took millions of years before this result was reached.

of the air prevents the rain from falling. Because it is very hot during the day and very cold during the night, the rocks split. As soon as it rains, water filters through those cracks and is lost. Plants cannot take root here. And yet, some seeds may wait for years for a drop of water and sprout immediately. One-fifth of the Earth's land mass can be called a desert. Deserts are found in Africa (the Sahara), in Australia, in central Asia, and along the West Coast (Death Valley in California, and in New Mexico), and the western coast of South America.

Is it true that there used to be rivers in the Sahara?

We know that there used to be a lake. Because there was no rain to replace the water as it evaporated, the lake dried up.

Nowadays, the Sahara is an enormous salt hollow called a "chott." There was once a time when the Sahara was wet. The changes that took place are due to climatic changes that affect the whole of the Earth. These take place extremely gradually. Thus, there used to be large glaciers in the U.S., in northern and central Europe, and even in places where it no longer snows. Today, a few climatic changes are being observed. Scientists suggest that rainfall is increasing in temperate regions, and the likelihood of global warming is also being discussed.

Are there still deserts forming today?

Our thoughtless abuse of the environment is gradually creating new deserts. Trees that have been

Even in Spain, the desert is growing in size, as here in Andalusia.

uprooted can no longer retain water, and as a result the ground becomes barren.

Plants in dry regions must be preserved because once they have been uprooted it takes years for new ones to grow in their place. Plants are essential because their roots hold the soil together, and their leaves retain the moisture from the air. In Africa, where the population is rapidly increasing, animals kept for their meat and milk eat plants and destroy the soil, preventing regrowth. In wealthy countries, governments take measures to stop the growth of deserts. Unfortunately, the damage is most serious in the poorest countries. This is also where there is the least money and incentive to stop man's destruction of nature. Every year, the desert increases by 15 million acres (6 million hectares): 2 percent of Spain and 34 percent of Africa are threatened. The word "Sahel" means "edge of the desert." For several years the Sahara has been advancing a bit more each year into the Sahel and thus threatening its small pastures. Natural processes are also gradually turning some regions into deserts. Rocky landscapes will sooner or later be worn away by winds and turned into stony deserts.

Why is it so cold at night in deserts?

As there are no clouds, the Earth cannot retain the heat accumulated during the day. As soon as the Sun goes down, it gets cold.

When air rises high in the sky, it cools down, so moisture condenses out of the air and forms clouds. However, the air above hot desert regions moves downward, so the condensation process does not take place and clouds cannot form. As there are no clouds to block it, the Sun shines brightly all day. As there are no plants to absorb the heat, it beats down on the Earth. In some parts of the Sahara, for example in Libya, the temperature can reach nearly 140°F (60°C). But at night, it can drop well below freezing.

What is a desert of ice?

A desert is an area where nothing grows, not necessarily a hot place. Thus the poles are deserts of ice.

In a desert of ice, water does not evaporate as in deserts of sand or stone, but freezes instead. As a result, these icy deserts contain water, but not of a type that can sustain life. Here again, plants cannot sink their roots into the ground. The ice caps of the North Pole and the South Pole are deserts of ice.

The South Polar region is made up of land covered in ice, whereas the North Pole (above) is in the middle of an ocean of floating ice.

What is the difference between the North and the South Polar regions?

The North Pole is in the middle of the icy Arctic Ocean. The South Pole is on a continent buried under a layer of ice.

At the North Pole, in the Arctic, nothing grows because it is a floating block of ice. For a few weeks every year, on the neighboring islands, some rare hardy plants appear. The North Pole is slightly warmer than the South Pole because the sea does not cool down as quickly as the land, but the temperature can drop down to −99°F (−73°C). At the South Pole, in Antarctica, the lowest recorded temperature is −126°F (−88°C). Both poles have something in common: they are permanently frozen over.

How does a dune form?

In some regions, winds can shape dry sand into mounds or ridges called sand dunes, especially when there are no plants growing.

Dunes are usually made of sand, but can also be made of salt or gypsum crystals. They can be seen on beaches and in deserts, where they move with the wind. Dunes can also form beside rivers, made of sand blown by the wind from the river beds when they have dried out. Dunes on beaches form from the sand that has collected above the tide line. Many coastal dunes do not move because they are held back by the plants that grow in them. Their shape depends on the supporting rocks and soil, the underground water, and the effects of local plants and animals. Humans also use or change them. Dunes help filter rainwater, which is then turned into drinking water. The longest range of dunes starts at Calais, in northern France, and stretches as far as Denmark.

What gases does air consist of?

Air is mostly nitrogen (78 percent) and oxygen (21 percent). The final 1 percent is largely argon with small quantities of water vapor, carbon dioxide, and traces of other gases.

For humans, oxygen is the most important component of air. It is breathable and enables fuels to burn. Some human activities pollute the air. Factories and cars emit large quantities of carbon dioxide, sulfur, and nitrogen. Lead dust and ash produced by forest fires also have harmful effects. As these pollutants are heavy, they stay close to the ground, and in cities we constantly breathe them in. Such pollutants react with each other in strong sunlight and turn into an opaque cloud called "smog." Smog is coming under control in Los Angeles and Tokyo, but other cities such as Mexico City and Calcutta have serious problems.

Up to what altitude do we find air?

Air that is dense enough to be breathable can be found at altitudes of up to 16,500 feet (5,000 meters). In mountains, oxygen levels start to drop at around 6,600 feet (2,000 meters).

The answer depends on what is meant by air. The layer that surrounds the Earth, which is called the atmosphere, is 430 miles (700 kilometers) thick, but we can only breathe in a small part of this. The atmosphere, which is divided into four layers, protects the Earth from the harmful rays of the Sun. The troposphere starts at ground level and rises to an altitude of about 7 miles (11 kilometers), toward the ozone layer. It contains 80 percent of the atmospheric gases. Climatic changes occur within this layer. From 7 to 30 miles (11 to 50 kilometers) above the Earth lies the stratosphere. This layer only contains 19 percent of the atmospheric gases. Above the stratosphere lies the mesosphere. In this layer, the temperature can drop to −184°F (−120°C). At 50 miles (80 kilometers) above ground level the temperature increases again; this

These sand dunes are typical of those found in the Namib Desert on the Atlantic coast of Namibia.

The greenhouse effect. The Sun's rays travel through the upper atmosphere (1) and reach the ground (2), which reflects lower energy rays back to the sky (3). But this time not all of them cross the troposphere: infrared rays are sent back to the ground (4) where they warm up the lower atmosphere.

layer is called the thermosphere. This is where space shuttles are sent and is also where meteorites can be found. At 300 miles (500 kilometers) above the ground, there are no traces of gases left.

studying old limestone concretions that date to three billion years ago. These algae made it possible for the first animals to appear on dry land.

4 and 18 percent. There seems to be a hole over Antarctica. This could be a natural phenomenon partly due to the weather characteristic of the poles, but it is made worse by pollutants such as CFC gases. These release chlorine when they come into contact with ultraviolet rays. This chlorine turns ozone into oxygen. There used to be CFC gases in refrigerators, plastic foams, and aerosol cans. Since 1987, the CFC gases in these products have been replaced by other "ozone-friendly" gases.

Is it true that at one time there was no oxygen?

Three billion years ago, mammals would not have been able to breathe because there was no oxygen in the air.

The primitive atmosphere contained only water vapor, carbon dioxide, methane, and ammonia. Oxygen was produced by blue-green algae, which gave it off in gaseous form, while absorbing carbon dioxide dissolved in the sea. Scientists discovered this by

Is the ozone layer going to disappear?

It is getting thinner, and there is a hole above the South Pole. This natural phenomenon is made worse by pollution.

There is very little ozone in the air we breathe in, yet 15½ miles (25 kilometers) above the ground, levels increase by 500 times, forming the so-called ozone layer. The ozone layer protects us from the ultraviolet rays of the Sun, which can be harmful to humans. Satellite studies have shown that, since 1979, the ozone layer has been reduced by between

What is the cause of the greenhouse effect?

The layer in the atmosphere that is closest to the Earth prevents the infrared rays from escaping. These rays are sent back onto Earth and contribute to its warming up.

When the Sun's rays reach the Earth, they have a very short wavelength and easily get through the carbon dioxide and the troposphere. When the energy in these rays is absorbed by the surface of the Earth, some of it is sent back as infrared rays. These rays have a longer wavelength and cannot get through the atmosphere because carbon dioxide stops long waves. They are reflected back to the Earth and warm it up. Plants absorb carbon dioxide, while vehicle exhausts and smoke from factories produce it. In the past hundred years, mankind has been producing more and more cars and factories, but destroying more and more plants. Gradually, an excess of carbon dioxide is building up, and heat is accumulating in the atmosphere instead of following the natural cycle. In a few years, the warming up of the planet may have catastrophic effects. The sea, too, absorbs the Sun's rays, which warm it down to a depth of 30 feet (10 meters). It does not absorb all of this heat and sends some back into the atmosphere as infrared rays. In overcast conditions the atmosphere reflects all these rays to the sea.

What is atmospheric pressure?

Air is made up of molecules. It is the weight of all these molecules pressing down that accounts for atmospheric pressure.

On average, atmospheric pressure is about 1 ton per square foot (10 tons per square meter). At sea level the pressure is greater because there is a thicker layer of air above. Atmospheric pressure decreases with altitude as the air becomes less dense. It is measured in millibars using a barometer. At sea level, it is about 1,013 millibars. At an altitude of about 1,600 feet (5,000 meters), it is only 500 millibars. However, the pressure varies with the amount of sunshine that warms up the molecules in the air. Maps that show the variations in pressure can help forecast the weather.

Why do we get winds?

When masses of hot air rise, the pressure decreases. Other masses of cold air come down and increase the pressure. Winds blow because they are pushed by high pressures toward low pressures.

Zones that have the same pressure are called isobars. Where the isobars are close together, the

weather brings strong winds. When large masses of air move, they follow curved paths around the Earth. In the northern hemisphere air moves clockwise around high pressures and counterclockwise around low pressures. The opposite happens in the south.

In the summer, by the coast, the hot air over the land rises and the pressure drops. A mass of colder air comes in from the sea. This is the normal sea breeze. It will increase its speed and change its course as it comes across obstacles (such as mountains).

What is a chinook?

This is a warm, dry wind that blows down a mountainside. Chinooks blow frequently in the Rocky Mountains.

As a wind moves up the mountain, it cools and loses its water vapor. As the wind, which is now dry, comes down the other side of the mountain, it warms up again. This type of wind also blows frequently in the Alps, where it is called a *föhn*, and in North Africa and Libya, where they are known as *ghibli*.

How is the speed of the wind measured?

An anemometer is used to measure wind speed. It is a small windmill that rotates when the wind blows and produces a certain amount of electricity. An ammeter is used to measure the electric current produced.

Anemometers measure in degrees. When it shows 10°, the wind is blowing at a speed of 19 miles per hour (30 kilometers per hour). Knots (nautical miles per hour) are the units usually used to indicate wind speed. One knot is equal to 1.15 miles per hour or 1.85 kilometers per hour. On the simpler Beaufort scale (developed by seeing the effect the wind had on a ship's rigging), winds are measured on a scale from 0 to 12 (calm to hurricanes).

What does a force 10 wind mean?

A force 10 wind, or full gale, blows 90 to 101 kilometers (56 to 63 miles) per hour.

In force 10 winds, waves are 10 feet (3 meters) high. The Beaufort scale was established by sailors to measure the speed of the wind when ships had sails. It ranges from 0 (no wind and a calm sea) to 12, (hurricanes with winds blowing at speeds of more than 73 miles/118 kilometers per hour, huge waves, and visibility of almost zero). In between there are force 3 winds (light breezes and the appearance of whitecaps); force 7 (bigger, more violent waves); and force 9 (huge waves and strong gusts of wind). This scale is essential because the state of the sea depends on the current winds, the winds that have already blown, and those that are on their way. Its use can be complemented by instruments such as the anemometer.

What are trade winds?

Trade winds blow regularly on both sides of the equator. They only blow over one part of the Earth, but influence the whole world. Trade winds fill spaces left by rising hot air.

A sailing boat can sail without problems in force 6 winds. All you need is a good sailor!

Trade winds do not blow straight toward the equator, but slightly from east to west. This rotation is caused by the spinning of the Earth. Points on the equator travel faster than the rest of the Earth. Winds blowing from north and south toward the equator are not traveling as fast. Because the surface points are moving eastward faster than the air, a person on the Earth feels a wind blowing westward, against them. Hot air causes trade winds near the equator and winds from the west at middle latitudes. Hot air moves aside to a latitude of up to 30°. When it drops, some returns to the equator and some goes toward the poles. As the Earth keeps rotating, these winds are diverted, too, and seem to be coming from the west.

What is a tornado?

A tornado is a mini-hurricane that occurs on Earth.

The name used for hot air meeting cold air is a front. A tornado, or whirlwind, can form along a front and is made from a tall column of hot air. Powerful, high winds make it spin and move along. When it becomes fairly strong, the tornado descends and swallows everything in its path. Tornadoes are small –

generally a few hundred feet in diameter – whereas hurricanes can reach a diameter of 1,000 miles (1,500 kilometers). Tornadoes are capable of causing a great deal of damage – to people, cars, and even buildings. Tornadoes often occur in the Great Plains and southeastern states.

What causes thunderstorms?

During hot, humid weather, huge black vertical clouds appear in the sky. Strong drafts of air that rise and fall in the clouds charge them with electricity.

Disturbances in the layer of the atmosphere closest to the Earth, the troposphere, cause thunderstorms. When it is very hot, humid air rises quickly. Hot air meets with cold air and suddenly moves above it. At a height of several miles in the sky, the moisture in the air forms black clouds. These are called cumulonimbus clouds. They cool down quickly, warm up as they fall, and as a result rise again. This movement creates strong drafts within the cloud, which becomes charged with electricity. This results in heavy rain, lightning, and thunder.

What causes lightning?

The huge black clouds are shaken by strong drafts of air, which charge them with electricity.

Lightning is an electrical discharge. The electricity inside a cloud is generated by the friction of all its particles. The positive charges gather at the top and the negative charges at the lower part of the cloud. As the charges build up, the air itself is broken down and the charges suddenly cancel each other

Clouds charged with electricity cause an electrical discharge – lightning. The flash is electricity traveling from the Earth to the cloud as the charge is neutralized.

out. The electricity is discharged as a flash of lightning, rather like a short-circuit. Flashes of lightning can pass within or between clouds, or between clouds and the Earth. Sometimes you can see little bluish flashes at the top of steeples and pylons. This crackling electricity is called St. Elmo's fire.

All clouds are white, as you can see when you are traveling in an airplane. Some look dark because they are in the shadow of clouds above or because they are so dense that they absorb the light of the Sun.

Why does a flash of lightning appear before the thunder is heard?

Thunder is the sound made by lightning. The reason why you can see lightning before you hear it is that light travels faster than sound.

Light travels at around 190,000 miles per second (300,000 kilometers per second). Sound only travels at a speed of about 1,120 feet per second (340 meters per second) in air. If lightning occurs a few miles away, the flash will be seen immediately, but it will take a while before the thunder is heard. The difference in speed allows us to assess how far away the lightning is. The sound of thunder is the result of air being heated to high temperatures by the lightning.

The air expands at supersonic speed, producing a shock wave, which becomes a thunderclap.

What is a thunderbolt?

When an object is struck by lightning, we say it has been hit by a thunderbolt.

This occurs thousands of times each day. Lightning usually strikes trees, posts, and buildings. Yet every year people are killed by lightning. Never shelter under a tree when there is a storm: sharp and high objects attract thunderbolts. To prevent lightning from striking houses, lightning rods are used. They guide thunderbolts safely into the ground without striking anything.

What are clouds made of?

A cloud is made of droplets of water or tiny crystals of ice in suspension in cold air, far above the Earth.

The moisture in the air mostly comes from evaporation of the sea. Some moisture comes from plants, animals, and water on the land. This water vapor mixes with the air. As warm, moist air rises, it comes into contact with cold air. The water vapor condenses into droplets, or ice crystals if the temperature is very low. This condensation forms clouds. When it is hot, the air rises quickly, forming cumulus clouds, which are flat underneath and rounded on the top. Air that rises slowly forms

a layer of stratus clouds which cover the sky. These clouds usually form near the Earth, about 6,000 feet (1,800 meters) above sea level. When the clouds rise very high, their names are given the prefix cirro: cirrostratus and cirronimbus. Cirrus clouds are fine, light clouds, high up in the sky, sometimes at altitudes above 30,000 feet (10,000 meters). For clouds that are at mid-altitudes, the prefix is alto: altocumulus and altostratus. Very tall, anvil-shaped clouds are called cumulonimbus clouds. They may have a base close to the ground, while the cloud extends for another 60,000 feet (18,000 meters).

Why are snowflakes so light?

Snowflakes are lighter than rain drops because they are made of crystals and because they contain air.

Snowflakes are not as light as they look. If they were, they would not fall onto the Earth. They are made of crystals of ice that are too heavy to float. They twirl around because they are made mostly of air. If you look at one with a magnifying glass, you will see that air is trapped between the crystals. The shape of

Careless skiers who venture away from the designated ski slopes run the risk of being buried under an avalanche.

these crystals gets more complicated as it gets colder. Snow crystals have six branches with geometrical patterns. You will never find two identical snow crystals.

What causes avalanches?

Not all the snow that falls on mountains melts. Some of it accumulates on slopes. Sometimes, and without warning, this mass rolls down the mountainside.

Scientists studying the causes of avalanches have made a list of high-risk areas according to a numerical scale. The risk is low (from 1 to 4) when the snow is stable, but the risk can be increased by accident, by a skier for instance. The risk is higher (5 to 8) if the snow is not stable and

when the accumulation of snow is greater. A natural avalanche can then occur – or there could be risks of flooding and torrential rains when the snow melts.

What is the difference between a cyclone, a hurricane, and a typhoon?

They are all the same. A cyclone is called a hurricane in the United States and a typhoon in Asia.

This phenomenon only occurs in tropical regions. A depression can turn into a dangerous storm if it forms above a hot sea. When the water reaches temperatures of about 77°F (25°C), tropical storms meet in a whirlwind that gets its force from hot, humid sea winds. A hurricane is capable of crossing an ocean. On reaching the other side it turns into a spiral that may be 1,000 miles (1,500 kilometers) in diameter. Inside, winds blow at speeds of over 190 miles per hour (300 kilometers per hour). Whirlwinds carry clouds that pour out torrential rain. A hurricane is most violent toward its center. Air rises in the central column at around 100 miles (160 kilometers) per hour, then comes down in the eye of the hurricane. The core, about 20 miles (30 kilometers) in diameter, remains calm. Hurricanes can cause extensive damage and may last for up to 20 hours.

How does

fog form?

In the same way as clouds, since fog is a cloud that has formed close to the ground.

When damp air cools above the land or the sea, fog or mist forms. The water vapor in the damp air turns into tiny visible droplets as the air cools – cold air cannot hold as much water vapor as warm air. The cold foggy air is heavy and stays close to the ground.

What is black ice?

It is a layer of invisible ice that covers the ground when the temperature drops to 30°F (–1°C).

Normally, water on the surface sinks into the ground, but when it is very cold, it freezes before it can do so. Water on roads can freeze instantly and can be dangerous for motorists. It usually appears in the morning and melts during the day. However, if it is extremely cold or if there is a patch of black ice in the shade, it could remain all day.

What is the

difference between

dew and frost?

They are both formed from water vapor in the air that condenses when it is cold. The night chill leaves plants covered with dew. When it is very cold, this freezes and becomes frost.

Dew and frost do not fall from the sky, but are formed from the moisture in the air. Dew appears early in the morning or in the

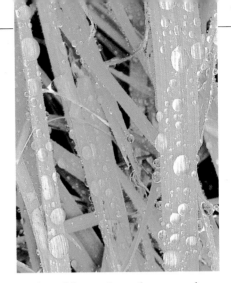

In humid weather, there can be so much dew that the grass is as wet as if it had rained.

evening in wet regions. It is always cooler during the night because the Sun is not there to warm up the air. The moisture that covers plants turns into droplets because cold air cannot contain as much humidity as hot air. Frost forms on plants when water vapor in the air turns into ice crystals when it is extremely cold. When the temperature drops very suddenly, frost forms instantly on cold surfaces such as windows and windshields.

How large can a

hailstone be?

Hailstones as big as pigeon eggs are common. However, hailstones as big as footballs and weighing 25 ounces (700 grams) have also been seen.

Violent drafts in thunderclouds send raindrops up to the top of the cloud where it is so cold that the rain freezes. The ice falls and meets rising raindrops, which may freeze on the outside. More drafts send the growing ice balls up and down until they are so heavy they fall to the ground as hail. Average-sized hailstones can destroy crops, and large ones can kill. Hail comes in different sizes: ice granules are between 1 and 4 millimeters in diameter, fine hail is made of frozen drops of water, and hailstones are usually between ¼ and 2 inches (5 and 55 millimeters) in diameter.

Why is summer hot and winter cold ?

This is because the Earth is tilted. When one hemisphere is tilted toward the Sun, it has summer; when it is tilted away, it has winter.

It takes a year for the Earth to orbit around the Sun. Its rotation follows an ellipse (oval). At each extreme of the ellipse, in June and December, the Earth is farthest away from the Sun. These are the summer and the winter solstices. The heat we get depends largely on whether the Sun's rays reach us directly or not. Because the axis of

the Earth is tilted slightly (23.5°), the northern hemisphere gets its heat more directly during the summer. In winter, the rays of the Sun are more slanted. In the southern hemisphere, the seasons are reversed. When it is summertime in the north, it is wintertime in the south, with cold, short days. There are also seasons at the poles. Here daytime lasts for six months in summer and nighttime for six months in the winter. For the same reason, in temperate regions, days are longer in summer. If the axis of the Earth was vertical, there would be 12 hours of daylight, and seasons would not change. Seasons depend on the amount of daylight.

Are the seasons the same in all the countries?

The seasons in the north and in the south are inverted. At the poles and at the equator, the climate does not change: it is always very cold and very hot.

The fact that the axis of the Earth is at an angle does not give us any particular seasons at the equator because, as it is at the center of the Earth, its orientation does not

In Nordic countries, the Sun does

change much. Near the equator, it is hot all year round. The only region where it is possible to say that the Sun is at its zenith (that is, vertically above us) is in the region between the Tropic of Cancer and the Tropic of Capricorn. This does not happen anywhere else on the Earth. At the opposite extreme, the poles experience the most marked seasons because they are situated at each end of the axis of the Earth. The poles are either always in constant daylight or constant shade, with the summer and winter lasting six months each. The closer you get to the poles, the more extreme the seasons become. Thus, in Norway,

not set at all for a few days before and after June 21.

summer nights are extremely short and in the north you can still see the Sun at midnight. Although there are no particular seasons at the equator, the climate at any place on the equator depends on other geographical and climatic factors, such as rainfall, elevation, and distance from the sea.

Where is the hottest spot in the world and where is the coldest one?

The coldest spot is in Antarctica and the hottest spot is in Africa.

The highest temperature ever recorded was 136°F (58°C) in Libya in 1922. The climate there is similar to that of a desert, where the temperature averages 91°F (33°C). The heat does vary in some deserts, though. Those close to the tropics experience a few variations during the day, and they can have very chilly nights. The lowest temperature ever recorded was −126°F (−88°C) at the South Pole. In Asia, winters can be harsh, with temperatures dropping to below 3°F (−16°C). In the north of Greenland, the temperature rises slightly above freezing for only three months in the year (June, July, and August). The rest of the time it is −4°F (−20°C). In the north of Siberia, temperatures can drop down to −58°F (−50°C) and even −94°F (−70°C). This is an arctic climate caused by the extreme latitude. The coldest inhabited countries are Canada and Siberia. Their climate is temperate but very cold: it is warm in the summer, but winters are extremely harsh. The differences in temperature are remarkable: in Siberia it can be −90°F (−68°C) in winter and more than 99°F (37°C) in the summer, which means a variation of 190°F (over 100°C). Singapore is at the opposite end with the least difference in temperature.

Where do you find microclimates?

Microclimate is the word used to describe the weather in an area of less than 1 square mile and which is different from the climate in the rest of the region.

It is wrongly believed that a microclimate is usually very sunny. A microclimate can be completely the opposite: a cold microclimate in a hot region. A small area might have a different climate from the surrounding region because of a mountain, a river, or a forest. Increase in altitude makes the temperature drop by about 18°F per mile (about 6°C per kilometer). At night in valleys it feels colder because cold air comes down from the valley sides. Airstreams are diverted by mountains, which means that the rainfall will be more on the windward side and it will be colder on the side facing the cold winds from the poles. High ridges can act as windbreaks. Quicksand can alter the climate because these areas absorb more heat by day but lose it at night. Cities are warmer and more humid than average because of the concentration of people and industries.

What is an anticyclone?

It is an area of high atmospheric pressure caused by descending air, which becomes warm and dry.

Low pressure zones are called depressions. The air is cold and low and the pressure is higher. Anticyclones and depressions are used to forecast the weather for the following day. On weather maps, all the places with the same pressure are joined by lines called isobars. Two isobars close together mean that there will be strong winds. The strongest winds rotate around the depressions, forming spirals. Anticyclones indicate that lasting good weather is expected. However, in winter they can bring frost conditions if they are situated above a continent.

How is the weather forecast?

Very sophisticated instruments are used to study the weather. Instruments used on Earth and satellites complement each other.

All over the world, there are meteorological shelters enclosing a thermometer and a hygrometer (to measure humidity). Information is collected from weather stations near coasts and at sea, boats and floating buoys transmit information to satellites. There are two sorts of satellites: some travel around our planet, 930 miles (1,500 kilometers) above our heads; others are stationary. Many nations have launched satellites into space. They are used to study clouds and help forecast cyclones, and are also sensitive to differences in temperature. They transmit information every 30 minutes. Weather balloons carry devices that send information back to Earth about conditions in the atmosphere. Meteorological stations are often situated at airports. Radar is used to study rainfall, even when the rain is far away. Different radar echoes are received, depending on the size of the raindrops. Radar is also used to study winds, temperatures, and humidity at various altitudes. This data is recorded several times a day and then is immediately sent all over the world. In all, 10,000 stations on dry land and 4,000 on boats are used to forecast the weather.

What is the difference between equatorial and tropical climates?

Heat and constant humidity are characteristic of an equatorial climate. Areas with a tropical climate have two seasons of equal length: one with heavy rainfall and one with droughts.

Parts of Africa, South America, and Indonesia have an equatorial climate. At the mouth of the Amazon, the temperature never falls below 64°F (18°C). There is up to 12 inches (30 centimeters) of rainfall during each of the four wettest months. South of the Sahara, Africa has a tropical climate. In Sierra Leone, it rains four months a year, but only two months in Dakar, followed by drought; it is always hot. Other climates include the arctic climate, freezing with temperatures as low as −58°F (−50°C); the marine temperate climate, with warm summers, cool winters, and moderate to heavy rainfall; the Mediterranean climate, with hot, dry summers and mild, rainy winters; the monsoon climate, with heavy rainfall and high temperatures; and the steppe and desert climate, where it rains very little.

According to scientific research, there were four main glaciation periods during prehistoric times. The northern hemisphere would have been covered with ice. When the ice melted, during warmer periods, large lakes, such as the big American lakes, appeared. Other climatic changes also occurred; for example, the Sahara used to contain bodies of water, but is now completely dry. Large climatic changes such as these take place over thousands of years.

What is the date of the last period of glaciation?

The last glaciation, or ice age, ended in 9500 B.C.

The orbit of the Earth around the Sun is altered by the pull of the other planets in the Solar System. The axis of the Earth oscillates in a cycle that lasts 40,000 years. Therefore, the glaciation periods may have been caused by the changes in the hours of sunshine. These changes follow a 100,000-year cycle. Every 20,000 years the Earth moves closer to the Sun. This results in warm interglacial periods like the current one. When the Sun moves away again, a glaciation period starts. During glaciation periods, which use up millions of tons of water, sea level can drop by about 300 feet (100 meters). The English Channel did not exist 9,000 years ago. North America was covered in ice down about as far as the present valleys of the Missouri and Ohio rivers.

Have there been any changes in the climates over the ages?

Periods of glaciation have alternated with warmer periods throughout the Earth's history.

The wet season starts when the monsoon blows toward the land. In Jodhpur, India, people are used to these torrential rains.

The World of Plants

How does a seed grow?

When the temperature and moisture are right, the outer covering of a seed breaks open. Then the seed germinates and starts to grow roots, a stem, and leaves.

The soft part of the seed is protected by a hard "envelope" called a tegument. Inside the seed is the embryo and stored food that will feed the embryo when it germinates. Once a seed has germinated, the young shoot produces leaves that have chlorophyll, and the young plant can then provide its own food. It is possible to germinate seeds by planting them in damp soil or by covering them with cotton that has been soaked in water. The young plants should be placed in sunlight.

What is the dormant stage of a seed?

It is a temporary halt in a seed's development. Some seeds can germinate as soon as the fruit is mature if the humidity, light, and temperature are good. Other seeds do not germinate immediately, but wait several weeks or months.

The conditions must be right for a seed to germinate. It may need lower or higher temperatures, a certain kind of light, or a relatively dry environment. Grains germinate in a fairly dry soil. Some lettuces germinate only in sunlight. Others prefer to be in the dark. Tomato seeds only grow once the acid from the fruit pulp has been washed off them. Toxic substances, which prevent growth, may disappear naturally when rain washes away the rotten part of the fruit. Germination is sometimes impossible if a seed pod is too thick to let water or oxygen through. Beans are an example of this — their teguments must be pierced. In the earth, the teguments can rot away, or else freezing and thawing can split the pods.

There is no finer example of the world of plants than the virgin forest of South America. Every day, tens of different species are discovered, and tens of different species disappear before they can be studied properly.

How do seeds get into our gardens?

They can be carried by the wind, by a river or stream, or by an animal or bird.

Only lightweight or "winged" seeds like those of the maple tree are carried by the wind. The spores of fungi, algae, and lichens are also transported this way.

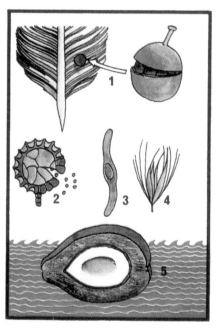

Seeds spread in different ways. (1) The husks of grass seeds can stick to a bird's feathers. (2) Light seeds can be carried by the wind for several miles. (3 and 4) These two are specially designed for being carried by the wind. (5) Coconuts, which are light and well protected, float great distances across the sea.

Heavier seeds are carried by birds who eat them or carry them in their bills with other plant material for building a nest. Some seeds have little hooks that stick to a bird's feathers. Other tough seeds are distributed by streams and rivers, and can travel for many miles. Coconuts, for example, are quite capable of floating several thousand miles in the sea without being damaged by salt. The current can, in a similar way, transport uprooted sea plants from one shore to another.

Why do plants have flowers?

A flower is the part of a flowering plant in which reproduction takes place. The flower produces a male part, pollen, and a female part, ovules.

Flowers are the sexual parts of plants. Pollen is stored in little sacks, the anthers, which are in the stamens. The pistil, the female part, contains the ovary. The stamens and pistil are protected by the corolla, made up of petals, and the calyx, which is made up of sepals. Some flowers, like the walnut tree, only have either a stamen or a pistil.

The flower is the site of pollination. The reproductive elements, the pollen, of the anthers are set free and transported to the stigma of the pistil of the same flower or another flower. The grains of pollen fertilize the flower.

The flowers of certain plants, such as grapevines, wheat, and forget-me-nots, form a group called an inflorescence. The size of flowers varies a great deal. For example, the edelweiss is a fraction of an inch in diameter while the rafflesia is 3 feet (1 meter).

Are plants always propagated by seeds?

No, a plant can grow from a cutting or a runner that may take root in the earth. A graft is a shoot put onto another plant.

With runners, roots grow from a small branch before it is separated from the parent plant. For this to happen, a low and supple stem needs to make contact with damp earth, or a piece of a stem can be surrounded by a pot of earth. In both cases, the small branch is separated from the parent plant once the roots have appeared, so it can develop into a separate plant. With cuttings, part of the stem is taken from the parent plant and planted in the earth before its roots appear. It must be hardy enough not to dry up or die. To take a graft, a bud or small branch is inserted onto another plant and the two plants grow together. The two plants must belong to the same species.

Do plants without flowers exist?

Yes, the flower is only part of a plant, which also consists of a stem, roots, and leaves. Plants without flowers are the oldest types of plant.

Algae were the first plants to appear on the Earth, followed by ferns and conifers. Flowering plants only appeared toward the end of the Mesozoic Era, about 100 million years ago. Plants without flowers reproduce in a different way. Some microscopic plants divide into two, and each half produces a plant. Other microscopic plants form buds on the mother plant and then separate once they are mature.

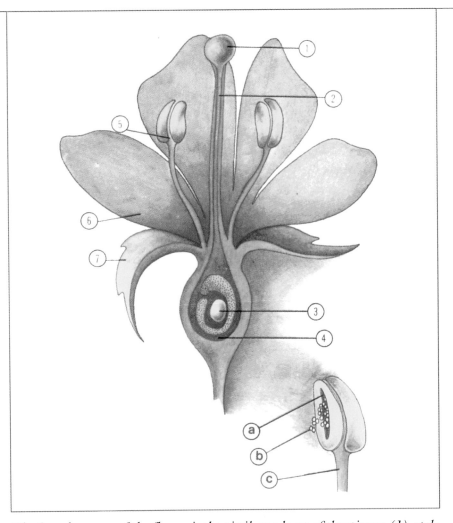

The female organ of the flower is the pistil, made up of the stigma (1), style (2), ovule (3), and ovary (4). The male organ is the stamen (5), shown in detail below: (a) the anther, (b) the pollen, (c) the filament. The whole construction is protected by petals (6), which form the corolla, and by sepals (7), which make up the calyx.

Why do ferns not have flowers?

They do not have flowers because they grow from spores. Fungi and algae are other types of organisms that grow from spores.

The spores of ferns are contained in little brown husks under the leaves. When they are mature, the husks open, and the light-weight spores are carried away by the wind. They germinate and produce a tiny green rolled-up leaf that, when it matures will produce more spores. To grow well, ferns need a damp soil, warmth, and not too much light.

What is a fruit?

When a flower has died, its center develops into a fruit. Inside the fruit are the seeds of flowering plants.

Seeds can develop into stones or pits. Examples are found in cherries, apples, lemons, and watermelons. The tomato, eggplant, olive, and green bean, which we call vegetables, are in fact fruits, because their seeds are surrounded by pulp. When mature, some fruits are fleshy, such as berries, dates, tomatoes, gooseberries, and grapes; others are dry, such as nuts, corn, and peas. Citrus fruits are a very important group. Oranges, lemons, limes, and grapefruit contain vitamin C, which is essential for humans. If we do not eat fruit, we can suffer from a lack of vitamin C. Fruits that are relatively plentiful today were rare and expensive in the 19th century.

Can fruit explode?

Once ripe, the fruit of some plants, such as broom and violet, burst and eject their seeds. Dispersed in this way, some of them will find good soil and room enough to grow.

The fruit of the horse chestnut bursts when it drops to earth, and so scatters its seeds. The hura, a great South American tropical tree, produces ripe fruits with very dry husks that explode violently when exposed to heat. The ejected fruit is so heavy it can break a window! However, the most common way for heavier seeds to be dispersed is by water, while light seeds are carried by the wind or animals.

Do bananas have seeds?

Cultivated or farmed bananas are bred to grow without seeds, so that they can be eaten as a sweet fruit. However, bananas originally did have seeds. When we cut a very ripe banana lengthwise, the black dots are where the seeds used to develop.

Bananas grown for eating only reproduce vegetatively (one part of the plant develops into a new plant) because they do not have seeds. Banana trees that are not cultivated develop a bud that flowers some months later. After flowering, the tree dies. Banana trees, with huge leaves and

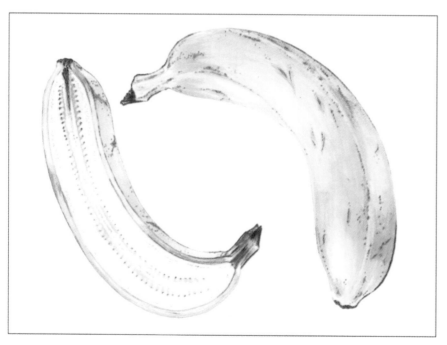

The black points in the bananas we buy are not seeds but traces of where they would have been.

clusters of fruit, originally came from tropical Asia but are now found all over the world. Their fruit have different shapes and sizes. Some types from tropical Asiatic countries produce sugarless bananas, and the pulp must be cooked for a long time before it can be eaten. These bananas contain a lot of seeds as big as pepper grains.

Are banana trees really trees?

No, despite the hardness of their central stem, which looks like a trunk, they are flowering plants. The real stem is shaped like a ball and is in the ground.

Leaves grow from the stem of the banana tree. Sheaths, shaped like crescents, fit close together and form the false trunks. The sheaths are flat and measure only a couple of inches wide and are 8–12 inches (20–30 centimeters) in diameter. The plant is strong because it has wooden fibers that play the same role as the skeleton of an animal. These numerous fibers form a vast network. The size of the plant varies between 3 and 50 feet (1 and 15 meters) in height. The banana tree produces

The flower of the banana tree grows at the end of a long vertical stem. Its weight causes the stem to bend.

its fruits in autumn and winter. They can be eaten dried, powdered, or as a puree. Its leaves are also very useful. They may be woven to make a variety of things. They are also used for thatching and umbrellas.

Where do oranges come from?

They grow on trees. Orange trees thrive in sunny countries, such as Spain, Brazil, Japan, and the southern part of the United States. As other trees do not produce fruit in winter, they are a useful source of vitamins.

Originally from China and India, the orange tree was brought to Europe by the Arabs in the 16th century. It is quite delicate and dies when temperatures drop below 30°F (−1°C). In winter in colder countries it is grown in protected orangeries. The tree is very productive; it lives for 20 to 40 years and produces 500 to 1,000 fruits, which ripen in autumn and

Grapefruits belong to the same family as oranges and lemons. Citrus fruits originally came from Southeast Asia and are rich in vitamin C.

at the start of winter. The orange tree was considered precious and was grown not just for its fruit but for its white flowers, a symbol of virginity and marriage. The skin of oranges contains an aromatic oil, and its leaves are very dark green and grow all through the year.

Why do grapefruits look like oranges?

Grapefruitlike oranges appeared a very long time ago in Polynesia and Malaysia on the same type of tree. Like lemons and mandarins, they are citrus fruits, rich in vitamin C.

Originally these fruits were acidic and bitter. It was humans who made them edible by cross-breeding. Clementines, another citrus fruit, are the result of cross-breeding between mandarins and oranges. Pink grapefruit are the result of a mutation or because grapefruit were crossed with oranges. Today, California and Israel are the main producers of grapefruit.

Is a tomato a fruit or a vegetable?

In everyday language we refer to the tomato as a juicy vegetable with a sweet or acidic taste. It is eaten raw or cooked and is used in many dishes. But in botanical terms the tomato is a fruit.

By definition, a fruit contains seeds after flowering. That is why many plants that we call vegetables are in fact fruits, for example, tomatoes, pumpkins, peppers, and beans. To the botanist, beans, peas, lentils, and garbanzo beans are all fruits. Some of these fruits come from non-fertilized flowers and do not have seeds, for example, certain types of pineapples, figs, and oranges. There are several different types of tomato. Originally from the Andes and Central America, it later became known as the golden apple or the love apple.

Did they have the same fruit and vegetables in the Middle Ages as we do today?

Apart from apples, people living in Europe during this period did not use many fruits. Vegetables were more widely available, including

carrots, cabbage, beets, leeks, onions, various salad leaves, and asparagus.

In the Middle Ages and up to about the 17th century, ordinary people in Europe ate apples and some wild fruits, such as medlars, sloes, berries, and nuts. Noblemen and wealthy people had pears, quince, nuts, and, because of the Crusades, knew about exotic fruits like dates and pistachio nuts. The introduction of orchards came as a direct result of the Crusades and the military campaigns of the Renaissance period. So peaches, plums, and apricots went to Europe. Although most of the different sorts of vegetables eaten today were already known, they were not grown very often.

Is a fir cone a

flower or a fruit?

It does not look like a flower, and it is not made of petals. It is not a flower or a fruit. However, like fruit, it produces seeds.

Tiny male cones appear on young branches in the spring. Their scales carry little sacks of pollen. On the tips of the same branches are larger cones with ovules, the female cones. When the male cones are ripe, they release clouds of pollen. The wind may carry the pollen to another tree, or it may fall on the scales of the female cones on the same tree. Once an ovule is fertilized by the pollen, the scales close and a complex system of growth begins. The seed takes three years to ripen.

What is pollen?

Pollen is the tiny male parts of a flowering plant, usually yellow but sometimes red, brown, white, or blue.

Pollen grains are made in little sacks, called anthers, in the stamens of flowers. When the flower opens, the anthers dry up, wither, and free the pollen. Some pollen may land on the female parts of the same plant, or will eventually reach another plant of the same species. The female part, the pistil, contains the stigma, style, and ovaries, which contain the ovules. A pollen grain forms a pollen tube that penetrates an ovule; fertilization takes place between the pollen and the ovule. An "egg" is made, develops into an embryo, and becomes a seed. Other parts of the ovule make

Although it is not a flower, the fir cone releases seeds when it opens and so produces the next generation of fir trees.

albumen, a special kind of tissue that feeds the embryo.

Why do flowers have a scent?

Flowers give off a perfumed smell to attract animals and insects, which when gathering nectar carry pollen grains from one plant to another.

This process means that plants are fertilized and continue to reproduce. Plants and animals need each other. Plants need to be fertilized, animals need to eat. Some plants only grow in countries where the particular animals they need live. Whereas bees and wasps are attracted to smells that we like, from plants such as the rose, acacia, or honeysuckle, other insects, such as flies, are attracted to plants with unpleasant smells, for example, the *Dracunculus*.

How does pollen reach a flower?

This is done by the action of the wind, and by insects gathering nectar. Pollen is carried from flower to flower on the same plant or to another plant. Humans may also play a part in this process.

The wind is very effective in carrying grains of pollen for great distances. But the most successful pollinators are flying insects that collect nectar. When they enter a flower, pollen sticks to their heads or backs. Later this is transferred to the pistil of another flower. When a flower is not fertilized by an insect, it may fertilize itself. The stigma bends down to the stamen. Sometimes, however, nature prevents flowers from using their own pollen on themselves; an example of this is the primrose.

Why are leaves green?

The green color is given by chlorophyll, which plays a very important role in the life of the plant. In autumn, when trees no longer make food, the chlorophyll disappears and leaves turn brown, yellow, and red.

In spring and summer, leaves use energy from light to make food that the plant needs. This is a complex process. Chlorophyll captures light and transforms it into chemical energy, which is used to

The bee gathers nectar from one plant after another and carries the pollen that allows flowers to become fertilized.

make substances needed by the plant. Only plants with chlorophyll can do this. Plants are eaten by herbivores, and herbivores are eaten by carnivores. By eating plants and animals, humans receive the energy stored away in plants.

What use are leaves?

Thanks to their chlorophyll and with the help of the Sun, leaves make food that the plant needs to grow and reproduce. This process is known as photosynthesis.

Apart from chlorophyll, two other substances take part in this process: water, which comes from the soil via the roots; and carbon dioxide, which comes from the air. With energy from the Sun, chlorophyll uses molecules of water and carbon dioxide to make the necessary sugars for the plant to live. The leaves release oxygen into the air, but they also release carbon dioxide, particularly at night. Without light, green plants cannot make food and they die. The exchange of gases in photosynthesis is the reverse of the breathing (respiration) of animals, which take in oxygen and give out carbon dioxide.

Leaves make food for the plant by photosynthesis. Here we can see the leaves of a Judas tree with their many veins.

Which tree has the biggest leaves in the world?

A native palm tree of the Mascarene Islands in the Indian Ocean, the *Raphia ruffia*, and the Amazonian bamboo share this record. Their leaves can measure up to 65 feet (20 meters) in length.

The raphia grows in Africa and equatorial South America. It has a very sturdy stem. As with many palm trees, its palms are grouped in clusters at the top of the trunk. These fibrous leaves are used for making things like bags, mats, baskets, and woven objects. There are more than 500 different sorts of bamboo in tropical regions of Asia and America, but many now grow in southern Europe. The stems are as useful as the leaves and are used to make fencing, fishing rods, furniture, and even house frames in Asia. Certain banana palms have leaves 20 feet (6 meters) long and 3 feet (1 meter) wide. But that hardly compares with the giants already mentioned!

Why do some trees lose their leaves?

If their leaves did not fall in winter, some trees would dry up and die. Their leaves

would continue to lose water, as they do in the summer, but the roots of the trees would not be able to get any new water because the earth would be frozen.

In the fall, a layer of cork grows at the base of the stalk of each leaf. This prevents water from entering the leaves, and they dry up and fall off. This growth of cork happens much later in the year under a constant light, and this is why trees that live in towns and under artificial light keep their leaves much longer. Some trees drop their leaves once a year or maybe once every two or three years. In temperate countries, leaves are shed according to the seasons. In warmer countries, the shedding of leaves is more irregular.

How does a plant feed itself?

It feeds itself in two different ways. Its roots take up water from the soil, both deep down and on the surface. Its leaves take in air.

A plant takes water from the soil and from this gets important minerals, such as nitrogen, phosphorus, sulfur, potassium, calcium, and magnesium. Iron, manganese, zinc, and copper are equally important, but are needed in smaller amounts. These substances are carried all the way up the tree to the leaves, which give off water vapor and oxygen. Leaves take in carbon dioxide from the air through a network of tiny holes. With water and carbon dioxide, plants make sugars that travel from the leaves down to the roots, and so the whole plant is fed.

Do plants breathe?

Like all living organisms, plants take in oxygen and release carbon dioxide, both day and night. But in the day, photosynthesis allows the plant to release more oxygen than carbon dioxide. That is why plants are vital for all other living organisms.

Photosynthesis is very important. Using sunlight, carbon dioxide, and water, it allows the plant to make its own sugars. When the plant needs to use its stored food, it breaks the food down and uses the energy released to make other substances. To use its food, a plant needs to respire. Respiration and photosynthesis occur at the same time when plants are in light. However, when the plant is in darkness, it can only respire. The respiration or breathing system of plants is different from that of animals. Plants breathe through their stems and leaves through many tiny holes.

In the fall, some trees lose their leaves and appear brown; only evergreens keep their leaves and therefore their color.

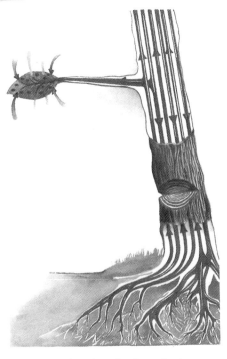

A plant's circulation is in two directions. Water and minerals are taken from the roots to the leaves (blue), while sugars made in the leaves are circulated throughout the whole plant (red).

How do plants

drink?

Fine tubes run through their stems and circulate water. Some tubes come from the roots and go up to the leaves, other tubes from the leaves circulate through the whole plant.

There are two types of tube. Large vessels take sap that contains water and minerals from the roots to the leaves. Then there are fine channels that transport sap from the leaves to the roots. This sap contains the sugar made by the leaves.

Do plants have

feelings?

Although they do not have nerves like humans, plants are sensitive to light and gas, for example, and if conditions are not right, they may die.

When there is too much carbon dioxide, plants close the holes in their leaves. When the light is too strong, the chlorophyll, which gives plants their green color, withdraws into its cells so that the plant receives less light. After a certain length of time in too much light, a plant will turn yellow. Most creepers can feel by touching things. When their tendrils or stems touch a suitable support, they curl around it and hang on. Some plants from the Mimosa family and carnivorous plants have very quick responses, but how these work is not known.

Do plants sleep?

Plants do not sleep for long stretches of time like animals, but at regular intervals throughout the day, they close up the little holes in their leaves that allow them to respire and so seem to take a rest.

This is related to the activity of a plant's cells. The division of root cells, for example, does not occur at the same rate every hour of the day. The middle of the day is a period of less activity. This time of resting probably takes place because the plant is full of food – it corresponds to the time when the plant cells are full of sugars produced by photosynthesis. Flowers also close up at night as a response to the lack of light.

How do plants live

in the mountains?

Up in the mountains, plants must be very hardy to deal with the difficult conditions. Nights are cold, but days are hot. The light is strong. The mist means the atmosphere is always damp.

Plants that grow on rocky ledges survive extremely low temperatures, often between −40°F and −76°F (−40°C and −60°C) in winter. They dry out, and the concentration of cytoplasm in the cells allows them to survive ice and freezing conditions. The most delicate parts, the buds, are surrounded by protective scales. But snowy areas can also support plants like the herbaceous willow and the crocus, which can grow through the snow. On stones and scree, plants develop a system of roots and stem that allows them to cope with sliding or moving areas of soil. They grow very quickly each time they are subjected to a landslide.

What are the most important things for a plant?

For a plant to be healthy, it needs light, water, air, a suitable temperature, and soil that contains minerals.

Light is essential. It allows the plant to make its food using the chlorophyll in the leaves and the process of photosynthesis. Sunflowers follow the position of the Sun in the sky. A plant left in darkness will die within a few days. Every plant has its own needs regarding water. Tropical plants live in an atmosphere soaked with water. Large plants are continually exposed to the Sun and bright light. Different soils have different structures. The earth of heathland is acidic and sandy. This suits broom, gorse, and fern, but other plants need earth rich in humus. Peat soils hold water very well.

Can cuttings be taken from leaves?

It is quite easy to grow roots from leaves. A cut is made in the central vein. This is put into earth, and roots grow from the point where it was cut. A new plant emerges.

The easiest plants to grow by this method are begonias. Anyone can try this. Many plants, however, cannot bud in this way.

Why do many indoor plants not grow very well?

Indoor plants often do not grow very well because it can be difficult to supply their needs, for example the right amount of light, humidity, and temperature.

Yuccas, fig trees, and cacti need strong sunshine, but flowering plants and ferns cannot live in a strong light. The plants that belong to the damp tropical forests are difficult to grow. Even if rooms are warm enough, they are very

The edelweiss, once a common mountain flower in Asia and Europe, is now quite rare.

Begonias are garden and house plants. A cutting grows very easily. One leaf in the ground, replanted or put into a vase, will soon grow into a complete plant.

barley, and bamboo have a strong, hollow stem.

Can plants become sick?

Yes, plants can be made sick by animals, larvae, adult insects, or viruses. All these organisms are capable of wounding, infecting, or damaging a plant or its seeds. Diseases may be caused by parasitic plants like mistletoe, by algae or fungi. Even the earth can harm them.

If soil is too rich or too poor in minerals, big or little spots occur on plant leaves. In some cases, part of the leaf dies. The growth of buds and small branches may be deformed. Some diseases are caused by a problem in the plant's diet. It may take in too much of one substance and then not be able to take in another more vital source of food: it may be too greedy! Some plants, such as heather and varieties of pear, do not like calcium in their diet. They need iron, and without it they turn yellow and often die. Fortunately, humans have learned how to treat most of these diseases.

unlikely to be as humid as a tropical forest. Some plants die from being given too much water, which causes their roots to rot. On the other hand, flowering plants such as begonias, hydrangeas, cyclamen, and azaleas quickly wither and die without water. Tap water is chalky and not as good as rainwater. Greenhouses and balconies, however, can create ideal conditions for plant life.

Do plants have skeletons?

Humans can walk upright because they have a skeleton of bones. Plants grow upright because little tubes force sap up the stem.

With herbaceous plants, the tubes of sap are not always strong enough to support the plant well. Certain plants have learned to deal with this. The stems of the Labiatae, for example, have a thick cross-section made up of cells filled with a substance that stiffens the stem. Thyme, rosemary, and mint grow in this way. Instead of skeletons, grains, such as corn,

Can a plant get cancer?

Cancer or a tumor in a plant can be caused by bacteria. *Agrobacterium tumefaciens* attacks 142 plants.

A pine cone soaked in an *Agrobacterium* culture can very easily produce a tumor. The *Agrobacterium* cells multiply and produce a swelling until the plant finally dies. Other tumors may appear on the plant close to the main tumor. Bacteria completely change and disturb the way cells work. The cells may even produce substances that help the bacteria.

Are there plants that can fight off disease?

Generally speaking, health problems only get as far as the surface of plants. **Insects cut them, and fungi may only attack the surface. Plants with thick skins do better than others.**

An example is the American grapevine. Its thick roots protect it against an insect that carries a disease and sucks the sap from roots. French vines, however, had thin roots that were not able to withstand the insects, so these vines caught the disease and as a result disappeared completely at the start of this century. Oak leaves can be affected by insects that lay their eggs in the leaves and cause swellings the size of a marble. The plant fights back by forming another swelling, which traps the insect's larva. To increase the resistance of plants to disease, we use hybrid cuttings. This means plants are cross-bred, using two different plants.

Mildew, caused by microscopic fungi, attacks many plants, including the leaves and fruits of vines.

Why does a tree stop growing?

It stops growing when the sap does not have enough strength to go up the trunk. The force of a redwood's sap is so strong that it can reach 300 feet (100 meters) in height. That is why these trees are such giants.

When a tree is cut, sap appears on the surface of the cut because of its pressure. It is the force of this pressure that gives adult trees their height. A vine capable of sending its sap 30 feet (10 meters) high will grow to this height, but not more. The pressure to do this comes from a group of cells in the roots. They pump the water from the soil upward through the veins of the plant. The force of the pressure varies with different plants.

What is the difference between a perennial plant and an annual plant?

Perennial plants produce flowers, then fruits, survive the winter, and flower the following year. Annual plants die after they have flowered and produced fruit. In general, annual plants are smaller.

The life cycle of an annual plant, from one seed to the next, is less than a year. In the desert, ephemeral plants have a life cycle

The Araucaria *is an ancient tree that belongs to the conifer family. It has existed for 200 million years without changing.*

of two weeks. Many annual plants germinate in spring and grow flowers. In summer, they have fruit and seeds, and after that they die. However, poppies and winter cereals germinate in autumn, flower after winter, and form fruit in the spring. Biannual plants, such as beets, carrots, and daisies, do not flower until after winter, in their second summer, and then die. Perennial plants usually flower every year. Some only flower

several years after germinating. The iris, tulip, and peony are perennials. Other plants grow throughout the year and become bushes or trees.

How do plants protect themselves?

To avoid being eaten by insects and other animals, many plants have physical defenses, such as thorns, or chemical ones such as poisons. Other plants protect themselves through the timing of when they produce fruit and flowers.

Spines, thorns, and prickles all help to protect plants from large plant-eating animals. Many plants have thick coats of wax or hair on their leaves or stems, making them difficult to eat. Citrus plants produce sticky, strong-smelling oils in their leaves and fruit that discourage insects. Other plants, such as nightshade and foxglove, contain chemicals that are unpleasant-tasting or poisonous. Certain species of plants provide a special fruit for a single type of insect. The insect in turn protects the plant from other animals.

At low tide on some beaches, you can see a variety of seaweed. Seaweed is important in the food industry.

Are algae plants?

Yes, because like other plants they have chlorophyll, which is used to make the sugars necessary for food.

Algae look different from land plants because they have a simple structure. Algae were the first plants to appear on Earth.

Can algae grow flowers?

No, algae, like fungi, grow from spores, not from seeds. The algae family is very big and reproduces in many ways.

When algae have no sexual parts, as is the case with the most primitive one-cell types, the parent cell divides into two daughter cells. When there are different sexual parts, one-celled algae divide into male and female cells. If a male and female cell meet, they can join, resulting in fertilization. With multicell algae, fertilization can take place when the movement of water causes two plants to come into contact with each other.

How do algae get their color?

Algae contain the green color of chlorophyll. They also contain other colors, such as red and brown. If there is more of one color than another, then that color is the one that is seen.

Green algae have some nondominant yellow pigment and of course chlorophyll. Certain varieties of algae, such as *Euglena,* contain chlorophyll but also have to feed on other organisms. For a long time, they were in fact classed as animals. Brown algae fall into two groups: diatoms, with decorative shapes, and Phaeophyta. Red algae are the most complex and evolved of all. Colored by phycoerythrin, they vary in color from greenish-yellow to violet.

Are there large algae?

Yes, one brown seaweed can reach 650 feet (200 meters) in length, but usually it is about 160–200 feet (50–60 meters) long. It grows 20 inches (50 centimeters) a day.

There are more than 20,000 types of algae, and they come in all sorts of different sizes. The smallest have a single cell and are only visible under a microscope. Some large algae, seaweeds, live in warm water. They use built-in floats to stay on the surface of the water, where they can photosynthesize. One seaweed contains a sticky substance that is used in ice-cream because it prevents ice crystals from forming. Seaweed is also used as a thickening and binding agent, for example in pork dishes and desserts.

What is an aquatic plant?

It is a normal plant that lives in water or beside it. Mangrove plants live in the salt waters of river estuaries, while waterlilies and reeds live in freshwater rivers and lakes.

Aquatic plants have soft flexible stems that move with the water's current. Unlike land plants, they do not have supporting tissue, and it is the water that keeps them upright. The leaves that actually float are thin and can be many different shapes. They do not have little holes for breathing. Aquatic plants often do not have any roots and absorb water and minerals through their surfaces. Sunlight is necessary for them to grow well. Some plants flower and are pollinated above the water, but most aquatic plants reproduce in a vegetative way, in other words one part of the plant grows into a new plant.

What is the biggest aquatic plant?

It is a giant waterlily known as the Queen Victoria or Victoria Regia. Its floating leaves are round in shape with a width of 3–6 feet (1–2 meters).

All waterlilies have floating leaves, but they rarely reach this size. The Victoria Regia grows in ponds and rivers of tropical America. Its leaves can breathe in oxygen, because it is not able to get enough from the marshy waters. The leaves are circular in shape and hemmed by a raised border of a few inches. A network of veins or ribs makes them rigid and takes oxygen to the underwater parts of the plant. The leaf can support the weight of a child.

What do pine needles and cactus spikes have in common?

Instead of leaves, pine trees and cacti have needles or thorns, so that they do not lose too much water when breathing. They live in dry soil. A cactus can go without water for several months in the desert.

Giant waterlilies like the Victoria amazonica *originally came from South America. They belong to the Nympheas family.*

A cactus is covered with spikes up and down the stem. Each large spike is surrounded by a little tuft of prickly hair. Within this grow the buds that give rise to stems, which grow if the main stem is cut. The big spikes are like leaves and the little tufts of gray hair like buds. Pine needles grow on short little branches supported by horizontal branches. They even grow on the trunk.

What are

succulents?

These are green plants filled with water, and it is this that makes them look thick or fat, like the cactus. A cereus cactus 50 feet (15 meters) tall can contain 650 gallons (3000 liters) of water. This is what allows succulents to survive in hot and dry places such as Africa and South America.

Their roots hold water in a fascinating way. They can be 10 or 15 times longer than the plant itself and can reach running water and water tables far away. The surface area of succulents like the ceruses and the prickly pear is small in relation to their volume, reducing water evaporation. Their leaves are thick and plump, but can be reduced to spikes, as with cacti. Sometimes a succulent plant has no leaves. These plants are covered with wax, resin, and gum, which reduce respiration. Succulents grown indoors need a mixture of airy soil, vegetable mold, coarse sand, and gravel, and need to be placed in a pot with holes in it. They should be watered from time to time, but very little in winter or they will die.

What is a

climbing plant?

It is a plant that does not have strong enough stems for it to stand up on its own. It leans on a nearby supporting surface, such as a wall, a rock, or another plant. Ivy can easily and quickly cover a whole building.

Ivy is quite happy in the shade and is useful for hiding damaged surfaces, which it clings to with its creepers. Other climbing plants, such as morning glory, grip with the stems of their leaves, while the vine has little clinging branches. Wild and domesticated clematis is found everywhere and is admired for its variety of shapes, color, and scent. The stems of some plants wind around each other for support. The hop is a climbing vine, grown for its aromatic flowers that are used to give beer its slightly bitter taste. Other climbing plants, such as honeysuckle, the robust bougainvillea, the nasturtium with its red and scarlet leaves, and several types of rose, are grown as decoration. Climbing plants can sometimes damage the surface on which they climb.

The clematis is a climbing plant with large scented flowers. It is a popular garden plant.

What plant has the longest branches?

The species of flowering plant that holds the record for the longest branches is the giant wisteria. It is found in mountainous regions of the western United States. Its stems reach 500 feet (152 meters) in length and stretches more than 550 square feet (50 square meters).

Chinese wisteria is similar in size. Its branches, which look like creepers, can reach up to 490 feet (150 meters) in length. They are covered with clusters of scented mauve flowers. The plant can weigh as much as 50 elephants.

The record for the longest tree goes to a palm that lives in hot regions, such as India and Africa. The rattan palm has creepers measuring more than 300 feet (100 meters) long and 2 inches (5 centimeters) thick. The rattan plants climb over other trees by means of hooks on their leaves. Rattan creepers are very supple and are used to make furniture and baskets.

Do prehistoric trees still exist?

Yes, the ginkgo is an example. It is a tree from China and Japan, and it was saved and looked after by Asian Buddhists. Without their care, this sacred tree, dating back to the Mesozoic Era, would certainly have disappeared. A great number of very old trees are today in danger of extinction.

There was a surprise some years ago when the Chinese *Metasequoia* was found to be flourishing in the Yunnan forests. The *Araucaria*, an exotic American tree of the conifer family with spaced-out branches, also existed in the Mesozoic Era.

Many North and South American trees are prehistoric. They had existed in Europe but disappeared in the ice ages of the Quaternary Period. In the lignite mines of the Ruhr in Germany, numerous traces of plants like *Liquidambar* and sequoias have been found. Tens of millions of years ago, they grew in that area.

For between 10,000 and 20,000 years now, human

The Ginkgo biloba, *a Chinese and Japanese tree, is a real botanical dinosaur! It dates from the Mesozoic Era. Like the* Araucaria *it has changed little.*

influence on nature has resulted in the loss of many plants. Firs, however, are being grown much more widely. They are popular because they grow easily where natural vegetation has been destroyed.

In what way is mistletoe a parasitic plant?

This little bush with small green branches wraps itself around the branches of apple trees and poplars. To feed itself, it draws on the sap of the host tree: it is a parasite.

But it only takes part of the food it needs. It does have its own chlorophyll. It is only partly a parasite because it is useful to the tree on which it lives. It seems that in winter, after the host tree has lost its leaves, the evergreen mistletoe is able to pass on some chlorophyll by a process of assimilation. But when it is too prolific, it can destroy the host tree. To destroy mistletoe it must be firmly uprooted. In Roman and Gallic times, according to the mythology of the period, mistletoe on an oak indicated the presence of a god. Mistletoe has spread into Europe, North Africa, and temperate Asia.

The bonsai is a tree originally produced by cutting branches and roots according to a Chinese method that is thousands of years old.

How are bonsais produced?

These trees are grown in little shallow pots and trimmed according to strict instructions. They only reach 16–20 inches (40–50 centimeters) in height. Originally this was a Chinese art form, but now it is more closely linked with the Japanese.

A bonsai is cut to look like an old tree. To do this, rings are placed around its branches. The flow of sap is limited and the branches are weakened by the rings. People enjoy comparing the little plant to its double growing in the wild.

The procedure described above does not work with pines. These plants have to have their branches bound with iron wire before being trimmed into the desired shape. After a few years, the shape appears. The wire lightly strangles the tree and limits the development of buds. When pine needles become too big for the size of the plant, they are cut in half or in thirds. Bonsai are very delicate and must be looked after every day.

What is the biggest tree in the world?

The record for the tallest tree is held by the perfumed eucalyptus of Australia. Some have been known to reach 500 feet (150 meters), which is half the height of the Eiffel Tower!

These trees, which grow in warm climates, are very important. Their leaves and fruit possess unique medical properties that can be used to treat breathing problems. Redwoods are also among the tallest trees and reach up to 300 feet (about 100 meters). The tallest, nicknamed the New Tree, has reached 370 feet (112 meters) in height. The diameter of the redwood is so big – up to 40 feet (12 meters) – that a road has been created through one of them in California.

In some forests in Oregon, on the west coast of the United States, there are conifers, such as *Abies*, that grow to a height of 300 feet (about 100 meters). Their diameters, however, do not really compare with those of the redwoods.

What trees have lived longest?

The redwoods may be the oldest; some are 3,000–4,000 years old. There are many of these giant conifers in California.

Redwoods are also known as sequoia; their name derives from a scholar of the Cherokee tribe, Sequoiah. To work out the true age of the tree, its heart or center must be examined, but of course some of these have disappeared. They may be dated, however, with carbon-14.

Dragon trees of the Canary Islands are several feet tall and 4,000–5,000 years old. In Africa there are ancient baobabs, not very tall, whose age is difficult to gauge because they are hollow.

The redwood is one of the oldest living trees in the world and also one of the biggest. It can reach 300 feet (100 meters) in height and about 40 feet (12 meters) in diameter.

What tree grows quickest of all?

The bamboo, a giant of a plant, that looks like a reed or sugarcane. It grows equally well in Asia and South America. Its growth rate is 14 inches (35 centimeters) a day.

In two months a bamboo plant can reach 65–70 feet (20–22 meters) in height. The swiftest-growing bamboos grow 35 inches (90 centimeters) a day. The largest of them can be 150 feet (45 meters). The bamboo is an important tree for the Japanese, who use it for a variety of purposes. The first paper was made from it. Bamboo shoots are a vegetable and are now widely

There are about 20,000 species of orchids, many of which bear beautiful flowers, such as the one shown above. Many species have become endangered in the wild due to loss of habitat, but they are widely cultivated in greenhouses, houses, and gardens. Certain wild species are protected.

available in the West. Its knotty roots, the rhizomes, are used in making knife handles, tools, and even umbrellas. Its stems are used to make furniture.

The *Albizzia falcata* can grow tens of feet in 12 months. A type of *Hespero-yucca whipplei* can grow almost 13 feet (4 meters) in 14 days – nothing compared to the bamboo!

Why are orchids so highly prized?

These plants are famous for their strange shapes and startling colors. Orchids are found throughout the world, but the biggest and most beautiful blooms grow in hot tropical rain forests.

In the past orchids have adapted to different environments: river banks, undergrowth, and forests. Gardeners grow them in greenhouses to increase the numbers of them and create new varieties. The great care taken with these plants explains their high cost, especially for hybrids. Their shapes can be quite fantastic. Their colors reveal subtle and delicate differences. They are sometimes a mixture of two or three colors.

How do orchids feed themselves?

Small orchids, which live in the wild in the ground or on the barks of trees, are extremely fragile. To survive, they need the help of a fungus.

This relationship begins very early. The hardiest small orchids are lucky enough to be infested by a fungus and are not harmed by it. This communal way of life goes on for the early stages of the plant's life or, with some species, for all its life. The orchid obtains all the food it needs from the fungus. Its stem no longer contains chlorophyll: it is said to be mycotrophic. In tropical rain forests, orchids grow on trees like many other parasitic plants. Their roots partly hang from branches. Their tendrils, made of a spongy tissue, can catch running water. They also feed from humus, mineral substances, vegetable remains, and dead leaves rotting on the host tree.

Are flowers protected by law?

Some flowers are threatened with extinction, such as the edelweiss and some varieties of wild orchid. The law protects them.

More than 20,000 flowers are currently threatened with extinction. This is because land has been cleared for cultivation, because of the use of herbicides, and because the soil and air are polluted. Several flowers are protected by nature reserves. Some poisonous plants are protected for their medicinal value, for example, the foxglove with its long hanging flowers, and the aconite, with its upper petals in the shape of a helmet.

How do we recognize a bulb plant?

When it is pulled out of the earth, the stem of a bulb plant ends in a ball covered with a sort of brown skin. This contains a flower bud and a short stem, both of which are surrounded by tightly packed leaves. It is

this ball or bulb from which the plant grows when it is put back into the earth.

The best-known plants with bulbs are the tulip, lily, gladiolus, narcissus, daffodil, and onion. Bulbs contain food supplies that allow the plant to survive the winter. In spring, they can grow again. Leaves, a stem, and a bud appear from beneath the soil. The bud enlarges and opens. When the flower is pollinated, the leaves feed the plant, which stores food in the bulb. The leaves fall, and the plant disappears above the ground but goes on living in the bulb and roots, which will produce another plant the following spring. It is much quicker to grow a plant from a bulb than from a seed. It would take three to seven years to grow a tulip from seed, for

example. The bulb may also be cut into pieces to produce new plants.

Do plants grow in the desert?

In dry places and deserts, plants have different ways of dealing with the heat. Many have long roots that drink rain as soon as it falls.

Leaves and stems are covered with a waxy watertight skin so they do not lose water. To reduce transpiration (loss of water), the leaves may shrink, curl up, or even become spikes. Succulents, such as cacti, store water, which makes them look swollen. Annual plants only germinate after it has rained. Then, as soon as they have a few leaves, they develop very quickly in two or three days. Other plants that grow in the desert are hardy perennials.

What is a stone plant?

This very small plant lives in South Africa. It can cope with very bright light. Its

An onion bulb, on the left, and a daffodil bulb on the right.
(1) Leaf.
(2) Sheath around leaves.
(3) Leaves of previous year.
(4) Scaly leaves and husks of bud of previous year.
(5) Scaly leaves rotting away.
(6) Roots.

few pale, thick leaves are covered with a sort of transparent tissue. It looks like a little stone.

The leaves of a stone plant, almost cylindrical in shape, look like a rosette. Chlorophyll is found only in the parts of the leaves that are underground. The transparent tissue, which covers the outside of the plant, acts as a filter so it only takes in a moderate amount of light. Photosynthesis occurs in the underground arrangement of chlorophyll. Bright flowers emerge from this cluster of leaves.

Lithops, or the stone plant, is a desert plant that can survive for years without a drop of water. It revives with the slightest touch of rain.

Are there many poisonous plants?

Some plants contain poison. Many fungi, such as *Amanita*, do. Buttercups and lily of the valley are also poisonous. To eat them or to suck their leaves or flowers would bring sickness or even death.

Equally toxic are meadow saffron, a plant that likes wet fields, elder, foxglove, oleander, and deadly nightshade or, to give it its Latin name, *Bella donna*. The berries of honeysuckle and ivy are also poisonous. Some deadly night-shades grow in the wild, but the plant is also grown for its medicinal properties. Deadly nightshade has black berries and can grow up to 3 feet (1 meter) in height. When used in small measures, poisonous plants may cure sickness and relieve pain. Some of their beneficial properties have been known since ancient times.

Why are foxgloves not often grown in yards?

Although it is tall and beautiful, this plant is not often grown because its leaves contain a powerful poison. Children, more vulnerable than adults, must avoid getting these flowers near their mouths.

The foxglove is deadly at a dose of half an ounce (14 grams) of dry leaves or 1½ ounces (40 grams) of fresh leaves. Anyone poisoned will have problems with digestion and vertigo and become very weak. He or she should be kept completely still until the doctor arrives. The flower is finger-shaped, and the foxglove, or *Digitalis*, takes its name from the Latin word for finger, *digitus*. In Europe, in the wild it often grows in acidic or sandy soil. It is also found in undergrowth, woods, and groves. Properties are extracted from the leaves to make medicine used to fight heart disease. It slows the heartbeat and makes it regular.

Are there other plants that can kill?

Hemlock is the most poisonous of all plants; one

fifth of an ounce (**6 grams**) of fresh leaves can kill an adult. Certain fungi, such as death cap, are equally fatal.

Hemlock poisoning acts quickly. The symptoms are varied but often include vertigo or loss of sight. It takes six hours to die, but the mind remains unharmed until the very end. Socrates was poisoned by hemlock. It is easy to confuse it with edible roots, with of course disastrous conse-quences. Today it can be seen at the side of the road. Little hemlock, which sometimes grows in gardens, may be confused with parsley.

However, hemlock does have outstanding therapeutic qualities. It is used to combat asthma, chronic bronchitis, and whooping cough. It calms spasms in the digestive system, aids neuralgia, relieves pain, and brings down swellings.

Why should some house plants be avoided?

Certain house plants are dangerous for children and animals because their leaves contain a sort of poisonous milk.

This milky fluid, called latex, is secreted by the plant's cells. A child or a pet getting a certain quantity in the blood stream would become very sick. Latex, mostly from Araceae, is generally dangerous. However, these plants are rarely fatal; because the latex irritates the skin, it is usually quickly washed off before it can cause any lasting damage. House plants should not give off toxic gases either, as these will eventually poison the atmosphere.

Is it true that opium comes from a type of poppy?

Opium comes from the great white poppy that grows to a height of 3–5 feet (1–1.5 meters). This drug, often smoked in a pipe, is extremely danger-ous. Growing and selling poppies for opium is against the law.

Foxgloves contain toxic elements, which is why these plants are rarely seen in yards. They are used in medicine for the treatment of heart disease.

The red poppy, common in fields at springtime, belongs to the poppy family. Unfortunately, modern intensive farming is causing it to disappear.

The opium is taken from the latex, which seeps out of the poppy's stem, from its leaves, and in particular from its seed case. Its medical properties are well-known. Morphine is made from poppies and is used in hospitals as a strong painkiller. Codeine, a milder painkiller, is also made from poppies. The many little black seeds in the poppy's seed case, on the other hand, produce an excellent cooking oil, as good as olive oil. The seeds are also used to decorate and give taste to cakes and bread. And of course many varieties of poppy are just grown because of their beautiful flowers. The field poppy, a small variety with wrinkled flowers, has a very full seed case.

Why did the people living in the Caribbean Islands want to kill off one of their trees?

One of the trees that grows on the Caribbean Islands has a bark that produces a poison. This poison can badly burn human skin. Because the islands are a tourist attraction, the local people wanted to get rid of the tree.

The tree is about the size of a walnut tree and comes from Central America. Its fruits, although they look like ordinary apples, are poisonous. The tree is also dangerous because of the latex that leaks out of the cracks in the bark. If a person touches the poison, they will be seriously burned and the wound takes a long time to heal.

Is it true there are meat-eating plants?

There are not many of them, and they are not very big, but meat-eating plants do exist. They eat little insects or pieces of meat. Some move to trap an insect, but others draw an insect to them by their smell.

The sundews and the butterworts are meat-eating plants found in temperate and tropical areas throughout the world. They are a few inches in diameter. The leaves are covered with hair that ends in a little drop of sweet perfume. Insects are swiftly trapped in these hairs. The butterwort's leaves are covered with sticky juices. Originally from South America, the sundew has leaves with joints that function like jaws and snap shut on an insect. Meat-eating plants that do not move are pitcher plants, shaped like a waterglass. Insects and little animals are caught and decomposed by the plant's bacteria so that the plant can obtain food from them.

What is a lichen?

Generally, it looks like a sort of fine, gray-green moss that grows on stones, tree trunks, and sand. Lichen is formed by a partnership between algae and fungi.

They live in symbiosis; each helps the other. The fungus protects the algae against dryness and, because they have chlorophyll and can make sugars, the algae supply the fungus with food. Lichen is often the first plant to grow in hostile conditions. It is found in burning deserts and on icy mountain tops. Lichen comes in different shapes and sizes, and there are three types. There is a lichen that is encrusted on stones and glass, even stained glass in a cathedral; a leafy type with hairs; and a fruity type that can make little clusters.

How does lichen reproduce?

Of the fungus-algae pairing, it is the fungus that allows the lichen to reproduce, but only when it is in the presence of the algae.

Of the two organisms that make up lichen, only the fungus has a sexually reproductive system. The algae reproduce asexually. When the fungus reproduces sexually, it releases spores into the air. If the spore lands near a suitable alga, it grows around the alga, forming a new lichen plant. The lichen can also reproduce by producing growths that break off the main lichen structure and are carried away by insects, animals, or the wind to places where they can grow. The lichen can also produce small structures made of some algae surrounded by a web of fungus. These structures are also dispersed by the wind or animals.

What is the difference between a fungus and plants?

A fungus has no chlorophyll, so it cannot photosynthesize to produce its own food.

This is why they look so soft and feeble. They do not have thick structures of cellulose, which give plants their firmness. They do not make sugars or produce starch. But they do manufacture glycogen, as human muscles and liver do. This is what gives some species their rotting smell. Like humans, they eat food from plants. They

The sundews are carnivorous, or meat-eating, plants. Their smell attracts insects, which the plant then traps and digests.

Before eating a mushroom or fungus that you have found, it should be shown to a specialist. Here are a few examples of edible mushrooms. (1) Field mushroom. (2) Truffle. (3) Cep or penny bun. (4) Caesar's mushroom. (5) Parasol mushroom. (6) Chanterelle. (7) Horn of plenty. (8) Puffball. (9) Morel.

can do this because they have enzymes that break down different substances. Some fungi feed on rotting tree trunks and other plants. Others attack living but wounded plants. Others, such as mildew and blight, live off the food other plants have made for themselves.

How do fungi reproduce?

When conditions are right, certain types of fungi can reproduce sexually. Eggs are fertilized by male and female cells fusing, and if this is successful spores are produced.

Fungi are very prolific. They send out an incredible number of spores. A puffball produces about seven million spores, a cap mushroom billions. A fungus can also produce spores by an asexual process. Some fungi, such as yeast, reproduce vegetatively by "budding." In this process, a bulge forms on the cell. A cell wall grows and separates the bud from the original cell. The bud then develops into a new cell.

Fungi can also reproduce vegetatively by producing a sort of fungoid thread, called hyphae. The hyphae form a tangled mass, which develops and forms a fruiting body. Each fruiting body has a spore case, which matures and breaks open, releasing thousands of spores. There are entire families of fungus that can only reproduce either asexually or vegetatively.

Are all mushrooms good to eat?

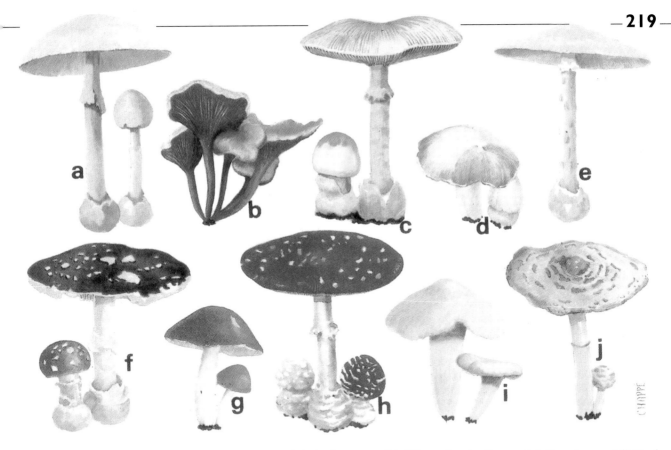

Here are some deadly or very dangerous fungi: (a) *Spring cap.* (b) Clitocybe dealbata. (c) *Death cap.* (d) *Red-staining inocybe.* (e) *Destroying angel.* (f) *Panther cap.* (g) *Cortinairus speciosissimus.* (h) *Fly agaric.* (i) Entoloma sinuatum. (j) Lepiota helveola.

No, some mushrooms like many *Amanita* are poisonous. A human can easily die from eating one. It is essential to know the difference between a good and bad mushroom.

But some animals can eat poisonous fungi with no ill effects. For example, the death cap is eaten by slugs, who have a very different nervous system than ours. Hares and rabbits also eat deadly fungi. That is why a medicine made from rabbit was for many years the only antidote to death-cap poisoning. Bright colors are not a sign that a fungus is dangerous – Caesar's mushroom is brightly colored and yet delicious to eat.

The only way of being certain about a fungus is to study the different types. If there is any doubt, a mushroom should not be eaten.

What is mold?

It is a tiny fungus that grows in damp places. You have probably seen one type of mold on an old loaf of bread. This mold looks like thousands of little green and black seeds, or like pins embedded in a pincushion. People sometimes call molds such as these pinmolds because of their appearance.

Like all fungus, mold or mildew does not make food for itself. That is why it grows on living food that it can eat. This results in a chemical reaction. Mold such as you might find on cheese gives cheese its smell. Mold also attacks any material that was once living, including wood, paper, and leather. Certain molds prevent the growth of microbes that might compete with them. They do this by releasing antibiotics. *Staphylococcus* microbes are stopped once they come into contact with the mold known as penicillin. And that is where the medicine of the same name comes from.

Where do coffee and chocolate come from?

They come from fragrant plants that grow in hot and slightly humid countries. These crops need good soil and plenty of care.

Coffee originally came from Abyssinia (now Ethiopia). Then it was grown in Arab countries and introduced to the West Indies in the 18th century, and subsequently to tropical Central and South America. Brazil has become the biggest producer of coffee in the world. Coffee beans grow on bushes that like deep rich earth. When ripe, the fruit looks like a red cherry. They are picked individually, then browned, and finally roasted, which gives the beans the unique smell we know so well.

Chocolate comes from the cocoa bean, which originally

A young girl from Madagascar grading coffee beans.

comes from South America. Cocoa beans are crushed and roasted and a paste is produced. Sugar and butter are added, and dark chocolate is the result. It was introduced to the U.S. and Europe in the 17th century, but was not used much until the beginning of the 20th century.

Does sugar come from plants?

Yes, it does. It comes in particular from sugarbeet, which is a root, and from sugarcane, a reed that grows from 10 to 20 feet (3 to 6 meters) tall. This plant was first grown in China, and is now grown in Egypt and Sicily.

For a long time sugarcane was known as "the honey of the east." Europeans were aware of it from the time of the Crusades. It was introduced to the West Indies and South America in the 15th century. When ripe, its stem is filled with a syrupy liquid. The canes are harvested, cut into pieces, crushed, and pressed. The liquid obtained is concentrated sugar crystals, reddish in color. This makes a thirst-quenching drink that is very popular in Brazil. Cuba and Brazil are the main producers of sugarcane, along with India and Mexico.

Sugarbeet, like sugarcane, needs a lot of attention and can easily become diseased. It is now grown in northern Europe and in South America and in Africa. Non-refined sugars, brown sugar, and the sugar juice from cane are often reddish-brown in color.

What is orange flower water?

It is a highly scented water taken from the flowers of the bitter orange tree or bigarade. The juice is used for cooking. In small measures, it flavors cakes and sauces that need an orange taste.

This liquid is made by distilling the leaves of bigarade. It is turned into a vapor and the condensation collected. Through this process a perfumed oil that is volatile and heavy is obtained. Oil from lemons, lavender, violets, and mint is extracted in the same way. Their uses vary. Some may be used in medicines and others simply for flavoring food. Turpentine is distilled from the resin of a certain variety of pine.

Where is tea grown?

Tea is grown particularly in slightly humid parts of the world, such as India, China, and Sri Lanka. It is also grown in Russia, Kenya, Japan, and Indonesia.

In Japan tea was drunk by nobles and Buddhist monks, who used it to stop feeling drowsy when they were at a meeting. Left to itself, a tea plant may grow up to a height of 100 feet (30 meters), which is really too high to be picked by hand. On plantations tea plants do not grow more than 3–6 feet (1–2 meters). Tea harvesting needs many skillful hands because only the young leaves are picked. The first leaf of each final bud gives the tea its taste or Pekoe quality. There are basically two sorts of tea: green tea made simply from dry leaves, and black tea, which is fermented.

What is the sap of the rubber tree used for?

Its sap is like a thick milk. By putting it through a chemical process, the sap is changed into rubber from which we make shoe soles and many other things.

This glossy tree, some 65–100 feet (20–30 meters) tall, is crowned with bright green leaves. To do well, it likes a temperature of about 75°F (about 25°C) and a very moist soil. The rubber tree grows best in the rainy season and in the undergrowth of virgin forest. When the tree is six years old, its trunk is cut at slanting angles at intervals of 4 or 6 inches (10 or 15 centimeters). The sap, or latex as it is also known, immediately starts to run and is collected in little containers. When it is smoked over green wood, the latex coagulates into thin layers. Sometimes the sap is thickened by agents other than smoke. This raw rubber is like synthetic rubber but does not have the same qualities.

What plant is the most eaten in the world?

Wheat is very widely grown, but rice is the plant most eaten in the world. Rice is the staple food of China, Japan, and India. It grows in

Tea-picking in Vietnam. Harvesting is always done by hand, and great skill is needed since only the tips of the leaves are used.

a moist soil or in paddy fields partly under water.

Originally from hot countries, this plant is now grown throughout the world. It is a nutritious food and eaten everywhere. It belongs to the cereal family and there are 20 different sorts. It remains in a seed-bed for 15 to 40 days, then when it is about 10 inches (25 centimeters) tall, it is transferred to the paddy field, which is drained when the crop is ready for picking. Several harvests a year are possible.

White rice is eaten without its husk, but brown rice still has its husk and is rich in minerals. Brown rice is better for you, particularly if it has not been sprayed with insecticides. Rice production throughout the world is more than 500 million tons a year. The principal producers are China and India.

Where is corn from originally?

It comes from Central and South America. Wild corn, or maize, was gathered and eaten by tribes living in central and southern Mexico 10,000 years ago.

Corn is something of a curiosity. Unlike other cultivated plants, its original type is not known. Its botanical history over the last several thousand years has been partly deduced. The corn cob has many seeds tightly joined together over a stem, and these are surrounded by a sheaf of leaves. This plant cannot reproduce without human help. It is in fact one of the oldest domestic plants. Flour from it is an important source of food in some regions: for example, it is used to make polenta in Italy.

Where does the potato come from?

This vegetable grows under the soil. It was originally from South America and was introduced to Europe in the 17th century.

Potatoes are swellings of stems and roots, known as tubers. They are grown vegetatively by planting tubers each year. In the ground they are vulnerable to frost and certain parasites such as mildew or blight. Although rich in water and starch, potatoes contain little protein. They are easy to grow; you can do it at home. Just put a potato in a little container filled with water, but leave part of it outside the container. It will not be long before leaves and shoots appear. Another way is to cut a potato in half, making sure each

Terraced rice fields in the Philippines. Rice is the most widely eaten food in the world.

part has an "eye" or sprout on it; later each of these pieces will turn into a plant.

Is it true that bread grows on trees?

No, breadfruit is called that because its raw fruits have the color and taste of bread. However, it is more like potato once it is cooked. Its Latin name is _Artocarpus_. In Greek _artos_ means bread and _karpos_ means fruit.

This plant, originally from the Pacific Islands, is now grown in the West Indies, India, and Malaysia. Its fruits are 4–8 inches (10–20 centimeters) in diameter and weigh 6–8 pounds (3–4 kilograms). The breadfruit tree has spade-shaped leaves and produces fruits after four years.

The jack, a fruit-bearing tree found in tropical regions, Malaysia, India, and the West Indies, is similar to the breadfruit. It is distinguished by its smaller leaves. Three varieties exist, which produce enormous fruits, sometimes weighing up to 65 pounds (30 kilograms). The seeds of these two species, about the size of chestnuts, are used for food.

Breadfruit is well named. It has a floury taste.

Is there really milk in coconuts?

Yes, but it is not like the milk from a cow or goat. It is called coconut milk, and to drink it you must break the shell.

This fruit grows on a palm that can reach 80 feet (25 meters) high and is crowned by about 15 leaves. Sometimes it is just grown for its elegant looks. There are about 3,000 types that grow in humid, coastal areas, particularly in Africa and Asia. Its fruit has many uses. Its fibrous padding can be used to make string and brushes. The shell is used to make buttons or parts for belts. The flesh inside the shell is used in cakes and candy. The dried kernel of the coconut is used to make an oil that is then used in soap products and margarine. Coconuts can float in the sea for miles before they end up on land where they can germinate.

Why do we have to peel pineapples?

Fresh pineapples are covered by a blue-green, sword-shaped skin that protects the flesh. This skin must be removed before we can eat the flesh because we cannot digest the skin and because it may contain unpleasant chemicals.

This tasty exotic fruit was discovered in 1493 in Guadeloupe and was brought to Europe at the beginning of the 18th century. A healthy plant can measure 3 feet (1 meter) in diameter and height. Its tough leaves form a crown with spikes. One type of pineapple can be grown indoors. The tuft of leaves should be cut and left to dry, then it should be planted under a bell-jar at 77°F (25°C) with lots of light. The pineapple fruit may be eaten fresh or preserved and is quite sweet. It is often used in cooking, to flavor pork or poultry for example. Its juice may be used to make wine, different sorts of alcohol, or even vinegar.

Why are some plants called aromatic?

Aromatic plants have a strong and usually pleasant smell. They include aniseed, mint, thyme, vanilla, and lavender, to name just a few. They may be used fresh or dry.

Their good properties are well known. In the kitchen, their flowers, leaves, stems, and even

Coconut palms do not just supply milk. Their fibrous bark has many industrial uses. Coconuts from Asia are not covered in hair.

Verbena is one of the many types of aromatic plants used in making herbal teas.

their roots, in particular ginger, are used as spices in many dishes. Cilantro, basil, laurel, celery, tarragon, fennel, and parsley are also aromatic plants. Aromatic plants also provide scents for perfumes and other toiletry products, and medicines.

What is a

medicinal plant?

It is a plant used in medicine. In the last century when there were no drugs, medicinal plants were very useful. There are a lot of these types of plants, for example orange, lime, blackcurrant, periwinkle, chicory, and eucalyptus.

Today some of their healing powers can be explained. Tannins from oak bark and leaves from the walnut stop wounds and burns from becoming infected. Aromatic oils from fennel and angelica have various effects. Aniseed calms the nervous system, juniper is good for arthritis and diabetes, and angelica is used to treat impotence, hypertension, and indigestion. Bitter ingredients are good for the digestive system and the appetite, for example root of gentian, *Centaurea*, marigold. The problem with using medicinal plants is how much to use: too much or too little could be dangerous. Medicines from the pharmacy, however, contain purified amounts that have been carefully measured. With a prescription they may be used safely.

Can verbena be

used to make

herbal tea?

Verbena, like many other aromatic plants, may be used to make tea. Its leaves and flowers are infused in boiling water.

When people refer to verbena, they usually mean lemon verbena,

which comes from southwestern South America. Its good qualities were noticed in the Middle Ages, when it was used for a number of illnesses, particularly those connected with the nervous system. Along with verbena, a popular herbal tea is lime-blossom, which is relaxing, and borage, which causes sweating and so helps rid the skin of impurities. Other aromatic plants used in teas include aniseed, lemon, camomile, and mint. They can be prepared in several ways: the plant may be shredded and can be made as an infusion, by boiling, or as a solution.

Can you grow mint

on a balcony?

Yes, as long as there is enough sunlight. Care must be taken to water the pot as mint needs moisture to grow. It is also possible to grow many other herbs such as parsley and cress.

Mint has been grown since ancient times and has a strong smell. Cultivated types are richer in oils than those found in the wild. It is widely used in cooking and in drinks because of its pleasant taste. Pharmacists use peppermint as

A field of lavender. Lavender is a plant with a fine fragrance, much loved in gardens.

an antiseptic and to fight bacteria. There are more than 20 species of mint found in temperate zones. Seeds can grow if they are just put into some earth or moist cotton. Sometimes they may need help and this is done by cutting the husk or tegument with a knife. The kernels of avocados, lentil seeds, beans, and even pineapple leaves can all be used to start a plant.

Does pepper

grow on trees?

Black, white, gray, and green peppers are all from climbing plants that flourish in the warm tropical climates of India, Africa, and South America. They can reach 20 feet (6 meters) in plenty of light, but usually only reach half that height on a plantation. The Chinese were the first to cultivate pepper, before the Christian era.

The common kitchen pepper has been in use throughout the world since ancient times. The Greeks, in particular, were very fond of it. It comes from the dried berries of the pepper bush. The first harvest takes place when the plant is about three years old, and it produces about 2 pounds (1 kilogram) of pepper every year for 20 years. Its stems are creepers about 30 feet (10 meters) in length, which give it support. In India, the pepper plant wraps itself around neighboring trees. The seeds of the gray pepper still have their husks, but the white pepper does not and is less strong in taste.

Why do you have

to plow a field?

The soil in a field or garden is dug over to mix air into it. This happens down to a depth of 6–20 inches (15–50 centimeters) and allows new plant shoots to break through the earth.

Plowing the soil makes it more airy and open. It also gets rid of unwanted plants on the surface. Plowing helps release important minerals, for example from manure, that are essential for new plants to grow. Water will distribute the minerals in the soil so that the young plants will have a supply of food.

Why are pesticides used?

Pesticides are used to protect vegetables and fruit from insects, microbes, and parasites. Fortunately, they are washed off before the vegetables are sold.

But they are dangerous! Pesticides can stay in the soil or on the plant. Water carries them down into the earth, which can become contaminated. Even if they are only slightly toxic, pesticides are dangerous if they last a long time. Some do not disappear and cannot be broken down, but instead remain in the water and on agricultural land. They may affect the health of animals that feed on the plants, or fish that live in contaminated water.

Is it always necessary to treat diseased plants?

Yes, but the doses used must be small. Parasites, insects, and fungi must be kept under control, but without harming the plants or the animals and humans that eat them.

Each time insecticides are used to kill insect pests, the insects become more resistant to that particular poison. This results in even stronger pesticides being used. DDT is an example of this. At first it was very successful in the battle against insects. Then something better had to be

Plowing regenerates the soil, airs it, and makes it easier for planting.

found. Next came HCH, then lindane, and both products were more poisonous than the one before, not only for insects but also other animals. Doses had been increased, but the aphids had adapted so they were immune to the insecticides. The aphids continued to attack grain crops in such numbers that some crops were completely ruined.

Why do we select certain plants?

Certain varieties of plants are chosen in preference to others so that new tastes and new colors may be created or strains developed that are less vulnerable to diseases.

Fruits are chosen according to how easy they are to pick, transport, and distribute, as well as for their taste and color. The varieties most resistant to disease are popular because they may be produced more economically. After a certain time, parasites adapt to new plants. It then becomes necessary to change plants on a regular basis to avoid an epidemic of parasites. A new variety may also be more

attractive than a traditional one. Ornamental plants are chosen for their color, shape, and how long they will last. Attention has to be paid to the type of plant, for example whether the flower is upright rather than hanging down or hidden in the foliage.

Why is fertilizer necessary?

Fertilizers, such as manure, enrich the soil so that plants can grow more quickly and are more healthy. They are used to keep production levels high for the growing population of the world.

When a plant dies naturally, it rots away and its organic parts return to the soil and enrich it. But when humans interfere, hay and straw from crops are destroyed or taken away and nothing organic returns to the soil. Fertilizer is then used to make up for this. In modern times there has been an excessive use of fertilizer, particularly fertilizers made of minerals rather than organic substances. Farmers want to see the yield of their crop increased. The soil is a complex mixture of clay, sand, and humus. Soil and humus are essential for the well-being of the plant. Traditionally this mixture was fertilized with seaweed, manure, and organic substances. Now this is considered to be too costly and time-consuming.

Covering a rice field with insecticides. This sort of spraying is a source of pollution because the wind often carries the product farther than intended.

What are the dangers of a monoculture?

Monoculture means that the same sort of plant, such as corn or potatoes, is grown in huge fields. If one microbe attacks a plant, the whole field can be lost.

Traditionally, several sorts of plants were grown together in the same area. They were weeded by hand and not treated with insecticides. When one plant variety was attacked by parasites, at least the other types remained. Another danger is that that the crops grown as a monoculture tend to be cultivated in huge stretches of land without hedges. Natural predators that feed on pests are left with nowhere to live. The pests are then free to multiply and destroy the crops. Humans have replaced the natural defenses with chemicals, which are harmful to the plants and the consumer. Without realizing it at first, by using chemicals we have caused only pest and weeds resistant to toxins to live. Finally, if the weather is more violent than usual, the harvest from a monoculture may be completely ruined.

During springtime in northern Europe, rape fields stretch as far as the eye can see. These vast tracts of cultivated ground without trees or hedges for support and protection often become eroded, and the best soil may be blown away.

What are greenhouses good for?

Plants can be grown in greenhouses whatever the season. They are sheltered under glass or plastic, so they receive natural daylight. Winter or summer, the temperature inside a greenhouse is always good.

The sunlight comes through the glass or plastic roof and heats up the greenhouse. The walls and roof keep in the heat, so that inside the greenhouse is at a higher temperature than outside. The Italians were the first to exploit this idea, when the price of glass was cheap. By the end of the 17th century, greenhouses were erected in the gardens of large houses, so that exotic fruits, such as pineapples and figs, could be grown. The upkeep of a greenhouse was no more expensive than transporting foodstuffs that rot easily. Greenhouses then became places where exotic plants were grown that could not survive in a temperate climate. And while a plant is sheltered from variations in the weather, its future is protected whatever the circumstances or conditions.

Can all plants be grown in greenhouses?

Some plants cannot be grown in greenhouses because it is too difficult to recreate the conditions they need, such as very moist soil, a constant temperature, and sunshine. They could of course be grown in a laboratory under controlled conditions.

Some plants from tropical rain forests are used to a high and constant humidity. The slightest wind or draft withers them in minutes. Mushrooms are difficult to grow under glass. A few species have been partly cultivated, but most mushrooms cannot be grown by artificial methods. Some algae or seaweed are easier to grow artificially, probably because sea conditions are not too difficult to recreate. Plants that are easy to grow in this way may well be the food plants of the future.

Where do the plants that people grow and eat today come from?

Most vegetables and fruits that people eat today did not grow in their countries in the past. The voyages of great ships in previous centuries discovered many plants.

Cabbages are European, and the bean probably is, too. Asparagus, leeks, and celery come from Mediterranean areas, and lentils, peas, and broad beans from Asia Minor. North and South America gave the rest of the world the potato, zucchini, peanut, and cassava. The Americas also provided fruit such as pineapples, papayas, avocados, and strawberries. From China came oranges, mandarins, apricots, and peaches, while cherries and plums came from the Middle East. The grape is a native of the Mediterranean.

Thanks to greenhouses, it is possible to grow many plants without fear of bad weather; so we can have flowers and fruits whatever the season.

The cereals wheat and barley are from the Middle East, oats and rye from Europe, corn from South and Central America, and rice from Asia.

Why do we prune trees?

Most trees grow very well if left alone, but for different reasons we can change their shapes by cutting their branches.

Trees are cut in gardens to make them look attractive, or so that they blend in with their surroundings, or to make the tree stronger. In the 17th century it was fashionable to prune trees to give them a very regular shape similar to the architecture of gardens and buildings. Sometimes they were shaped to look like people or animals. In fruit gardens, young trees are pruned in a very strict way. The size and shape of an adult fruit tree affects the quantity and quality of the fruit. The fruit may remain small if the tree is not sturdy enough to bear a big crop. Pruning branches can make them short and strong and well able to support a large crop. It also gets rid of any dead wood and keeps the tree healthy.

Some trees are cut to a certain shape for decorative purposes, to make a garden or park look more interesting or attractive. Pruning can also be used to strengthen trees such as fruit trees.

Why have some plants become rare?

Some types of plants disappear naturally and are replaced by other more adaptable types. Unfortunately, the truth today is that humans are responsible for the destruction of a great deal of plant life.

The use of weedkillers and pesticides has practically killed off wild poppies and bachelor's buttons that used to grow in wheat fields. Humans alone have done this. Certain mahogany trees have disappeared from Africa and South America forever. Many plants are now extremely rare. When goats were brought to the island of St. Helena, the result was the destruction of about 30 different types of plant. New types, obtained by a natural process of mutation and selection, need time to develop and reproduce. People clear forests for farms and cities, and cut down trees for fuel and to make furniture and paper. As a result, ancient conifers from tropical and temperate zones are disappearing fast, and there are not even as many California redwoods as there used to be.

Natural Wonders of the World

Where is the highest mountain in the world?

Mount Everest, in the Himalayas between Tibet and Nepal, is regarded as the world's highest mountain. In 1953 Edmund Hillary and the sherpa Tenzing Norgay became the first climbers to reach its summit, 29,029 feet (8,848 meters) above sea level.

Mount Everest was named after a British military engineer, Sir George Everest, who became surveyor-general of India. In 1987 an American expedition to K2, on the border of Pakistan and China, challenged Everest's title as the highest peak, since their satellite survey gave K2's altitude as nearly 29,200 feet (8,900 meters). Later that year the Research Council in Rome concluded that Everest was higher. In Hawaii there is a mountain taller than Everest — Mauna Kea (the white mountain). Although the part above sea level rises to a mere 13,797 feet (4,205 meters), the submerged part of Mauna Kea gives the mountain an overall height of 33,483 feet (10,205 meters).

At 29,029 feet (8,848 meters) Mount Everest (left) can only be regarded as the world's highest peak if the volcanoes of Hawaii are excluded – since the summit of Mauna Kea rises 33,481 feet (10,205 meters) from the floor of the Pacific Ocean.

Which is the highest summit in Europe?

Mont Blanc, on the border of France and Italy, is Europe's highest peak, with an altitude of 15,775 feet (4,808 meters).

Stretching from the Mediterranean to the Danube and from Nice to Vienna, the Alps describe an arc 745 miles (1,200 kilometers) long. This vast mountain range covers an area of approximately 70,000 square miles (200,000 square kilometers), divided between eight European countries — Germany, Austria, Switzerland, Liechtenstein, Slovenia, Croatia, Italy, and France. More than 100 of its peaks exceed 13,000 feet (4,000 meters) – all of which have been climbed by "alpinists," who today take ever-greater risks in tackling them. The first climber to reach the summit of Mont Blanc was the Frenchman Jean Balmat on August 8, 1786. In 1808 Marie Paradis became the first woman to set foot on the summit.

What did Moses do on Mount Sinai?

According to the Bible, Mount Sinai was where God met Moses and gave him the two tablets of stone on which were engraved the Ten Commandments.

Exodus, the second book of the Old Testament, tells how the Hebrews fled from Egypt, in search of the land "flowing with milk and honey" that God had promised to Abraham. Moses, at the head of tens of thousands of men, women, and children, led them across the Sinai Desert – a journey that took them 40 years. When they arrived at the foot of Mount Sinai, Moses climbed the mountain to meet God, who had called him to the summit. While the people of Israel waited for Moses to come down from the mountain, where he remained for 40 days and 40 nights, they were terrified by smoke and flames erupting from the top of the mountain. The commandments that God gave to Moses on Mount

Sinai formed the foundations of Jewish law, providing a succinct summary of basic morality and religious beliefs.

What is the Sugar Loaf?

The Pão de Açúcar, or Sugar Loaf, is a curiously shaped peak that rises dramatically above the city of Rio de Janeiro, in Brazil. It is one of the *morros* (isolated rocks) that stand guard over the Bay of Guanabara.

Two cable cars lead to the summit of Sugar Loaf Mountain, 1,300 feet (395 meters) above sea level. The second of these cable cars takes you to a terrace that offers a panoramic view of one of the world's most beautiful cities. In the distance is Corcovado (the hump-backed mountain), which is almost twice as high as Sugar Loaf. On top of Corcovado stands a gigantic figure of Christ, arms outstretched. Equally visible are the *favelas*, the slums packed with tin-and-plywood shacks that cling to the hillsides. Not far from Sugar Loaf Mountain is the glamorous Copacabana, Brazil's most famous beach.

Mount Pelée, on the Caribbean island of Martinique, suddenly erupted on May 8, 1902. Within minutes a cloud of burning ash fell on St. Pierre, killing nearly all its inhabitants.

How many people were killed by Mount Pelée in 1902?

On May 8, 1902, the volcano Mount Pelée exploded, killing 15,000 people in the small city of St. Pierre on Martinique – about 15 percent of the island's entire population.

There were some warnings of the impending catastrophe in the days preceding it: boiling mud, strong odors of sulfur, earth tremors, columns of black vapor issuing from the volcano, the drying up of the lake in the center of its crater. On the fatal morning, violent explosions woke the city of St. Pierre on the island of Martinique in the French West Indies. An enormous cloud of molten lava raced down the side of the volcano at more than 60 miles per hour (100 kilometers per hour), and wiped out St. Pierre within moments. Only a few escaped – among them a prisoner who was protected by the thick walls of his cell, and some sailors offshore who clung to the wreckage of their boat.

It is thought that the symmetrical columns of the Giant's Causeway, in Northern Ireland, were formed by the sudden cooling of lava after a volcanic eruption more than 50 million years ago.

Which is Africa's highest mountain?

Situated in Tanzania, not far from the border with Kenya, at 19,340 feet (5,895 meters) Mount Kilimanjaro is the highest mountain in Africa. Its name is Swahili for "the mountain that shines."

Until the mid-19th century many geographers doubted Kilimanjaro's existence, maintaining that a snowcapped summit was an impossibility so close to the equator. Five contrasting ecologies succeed each other on the slopes of the mountain: first an arid plain, then virgin forest, swampy moorland, alpine desert, and, toward the summit, arctic tundra. At the top a crater exhales heat and sulfur – for, if the semi-submerged Hawaiian volcanoes are disregarded, Kilimanjaro is the world's tallest volcano.

What is the Giant's Causeway?

On the coast of County Antrim in Northern Ireland rise prism-shaped columns of basalt. Their arrangement is so perfectly regular that this marvel of nature seems to have been created by mysterious giants.

Legend does indeed claim that a giant drove these columns into the bed of the sea in order to build a highway stretching across the water to Scotland, where similar formations are found on the island of Staffa. A more realistic hypothesis is that these astonishing rock formations were produced by the solidifying of lava after a volcanic eruption. The spectacular rows of columns stretch for 900 feet (275 meters) along the coast and 490 feet (150 meters) into the sea. The columns are about 14 to 20 inches (35 to 50 centimeters) in diameter, and most of the columns do not exceed 20 feet (6 meters) in height, although some are as much as 40 meters (12 meters) high.

Which is the largest volcano in the world?

The world's largest volcano is Mauna Kea, Hawaii. Its diameter is more than 60 miles (100 kilometers) and its overall height is 33,483 feet (10,205 meters). Lava from Mauna Kea covers an area of more than 2,300 square miles (6,000 square kilometers).

Aptly known as "the beacon of the Mediterranean," Stromboli, a famous volcano in Italy, has been active since Roman times.

Hawaii consists of some 20 volcanic islands, which owe their existence to a hot point in the Earth's mantle. Due to volcanic activity, much of the Hawaiian archipelago is covered with solidified lava and is uninhabitable. The islands' tropical climate has favored the creation of seaside resorts and the development of the city of Honolulu on Oahu.

Are there any active volcanoes in Europe?

The three most famous volcanoes in Europe are Stromboli, Vesuvius, and Etna in Italy, and they are all still active. Iceland also has a number of active volcanoes.

The highest point on the island of Sicily, Mount Etna is the largest active volcano in Europe. Its height (currently 10,960 feet/ 3,340 meters) changes after each eruption. The first recorded eruption of Etna was in about 700 B.C., and the volcano has erupted more than 250 times since then.

Vesuvius dominates the skyline of the city of Naples, which lives under constant threat of damage from an eruption. Although dormant much of the time, like Etna it can suddenly become active. The historic eruption of Vesuvius in A.D. 79 destroyed Pompeii and Herculaneum; the one in 1631 left at least 3,000 dead. Since then there have been 23 major eruptions, of which the most recent was in 1944.

Stromboli is one of seven volcanic islands (known as the Lipari Islands) off the northeastern coast of Sicily. The only one still active, it comes to life regularly, sending a flow of glowing lava and incandescent stone into the sea. When erupting, Stromboli has a magical beauty, especially when it is seen from the sea at night.

Where is Mount Fuji?

On a clear day Mount Fuji's snowcapped summit – 12,390 feet (3,776 meters) high – can be seen from Tokyo, Japan. About 55 miles (90 kilometers) to the west of the city, it is the country's highest mountain and largest volcano. Its last eruption took place in 1707.

Mount Fuji has become a symbol of natural beauty and the subject of countless paintings. The Japanese have preserved the sacred traditions associated with the mountain, and more than 50,000 pilgrims climb to its summit every year. The Japanese call the mountain Fuji-san, or Fuji-yama. The mountain's top, which is often hidden by clouds, has a crown of snow that melts in summer. Mount Fuji is not Japan's only volcano – the country, which is composed of islands, rests on an unstable portion of the Earth's crust. Some 200 volcanoes are dotted throughout the archipelago, more than 60 of them still active. Mount Fuji lies on the island of Honshu.

What is the Chaîne des Puys?

In the north of the Auvergne region of the Massif Central, in France, rises the Chaîne des Puys, a chain of 80 "young" volcanoes – about 9,000 years old – of which the best known is the Puy de Dôme, 4,807 feet (1,465 meters) high.

The volcanic formations here have varied forms, ranging from domes and pyramids to steep-sided pinnacles known as lava plugs. The Puy de Pariou is composed of two volcanoes, one inside the other; at the summit the crater forms a funnel 295 feet (90 meters) deep. Extending over 971,100 acres (393,000 hectares), the Auvergne nature reserve is a national park. South of the Chaîne des Puys, in the center of the park, are more ancient volcanoes – those of the Dore Mountains, three million years old – dominated by the Puy de Sancy, 6,188 feet (1,886 meters) high, which is the highest point in the Auvergne. Farther to the south, in the Cantal region, rises a mountain range 20 million years old. The volcanoes of the Massif are now regarded as extinct, but could become active again.

The mountains of the Chaîne des Puys in France's Massif Central include 80 volcanoes, some of which were active 9,000 years ago.

Why do some beaches have black sand?

Sand comes mainly from the erosion of rocks, which produce sediments that are variously colored. Because of its volcanic origin, the sand on beaches near volcanoes tends to be black.

Examples of black-sand beaches include the ones at the foot of Mount Soufrière on the Caribbean island of Guadeloupe, some of the beaches of Tahiti and Lanzarote, and the beaches of the island of Stromboli, near Sicily.

Other beaches have soft white sands, looking almost like flour, that are composed of the shells and skeletons of marine animals pounded to dust. Some of the most beautiful white-sand beaches are found in Polynesia, and in the Maldives in the Indian Ocean. Other beaches, like the ones along the Pacific coast of Oregon, have greenish-gray sand. In New Mexico there is a dazzling desert called White Sands. The principal component of its sand is gypsum, the mineral used for making plaster of Paris and blackboard chalk.

The Sept Îles (Seven Islands), off the coast of Brittany, France, provide a refuge for thousands of sea birds. One of the seven islands, Rouzic, is home to more than 12,000 nesting pairs.

Which are the most spectacular geysers?

The word geyser comes from Geysir (gusher), a thermal spring in Iceland that spurts water up into the air – sometimes 180 feet (55 meters) high. In volcanic regions molten lava heats the Earth's crust, causing boiling water to shoot up from underground. This occurs, for example, at Lake Bogoria in Kenya and at Geyser Flat, near Rotorua, in New Zealand. However, some of the most spectacular geysers are in Yellowstone National Park, Wyoming.

Yellowstone, the largest and oldest of the national parks in the United States, boasts 84 geysers, the most famous of which is Old Faithful. For more than 100 years it has shot water and vapor up to 100 feet (30 meters) into the air, 20 to 23 times a day. The highest geyser is Steamboat. It can project steam and water to heights of more than 300 feet (100 meters). Splashing, boiling, and whistling noises accompany these spectacular displays. Deposits left by the water from a geyser often take an attractive or unusual form.

What is special about the Sept Îles?

Situated off the north coast of France, not far from the port of Perros-Guirec in Brittany, the Sept Îles (Seven Islands) are a famous bird sanctuary. They provide a refuge for many sea birds.

The islands – Rouzic, Malban, Bono, Île aux Moines, Île-Plate, Îles des Cerfs, and Rochers des Costans – form a small archipelago where many species of sea birds (including gannets, razorbills, gulls, cormorants, petrels, kittiwakes, and oystercatchers) find refuge. There is also a small colony of seals. Rouzic is known as the Island of the Birds because it is home to more than 12,000 nesting pairs. Visitors are only allowed on the Île des Moines (Monks' Island).

A few miles from the Sept Îles, a special bird sanctuary has been established on Île Grande (Big Island). Here birds that have been damaged by oil slicks are treated.

Where can "natural amphitheaters" be seen?

One of the best natural amphitheaters is at Gavarnie in the Pyrenees mountains, in France. Created by an ancient glacier, its form evokes the ancient man-made amphitheaters.

Cliff walls more than 3,300 feet (1,000 meters) high rise from the base of the amphitheater. When the snow melts, they are veiled by waterfalls. Falling from a height of 1,385 feet (422 meters), the

Some geysers can spurt boiling water as much as 300 feet (100 meters) into the air.

Grande Cascade – the highest waterfall in Europe – vaporizes into a mist. Made fashionable in the 19th century by the Empress Eugénie (the wife of Napoleon III), the amphitheater of Gavarnie attracts numerous visitors. But Gavarnie is not the only natural amphitheater in France. Others are the Cirque de Navacelles on the Les Causses plateau, and the Fer-à-Cheval (Horseshoe) in Haute Savoie in the Alps.

Where is the largest rock in the world?

The world's largest rock is Uluru (Ayers Rock), in northern Australia, about 280 miles (450 kilometers) southwest of Alice Springs. The visible part of the rock rises to a height of 1,175 feet (358 meters) – but, like an iceberg, the part that cannot be seen is much larger, plunging 6,890 feet (2,100 meters) below the ground.

This rock – one single piece of stone – is a reddish-brown color. It is thought to be 600 million years old. Storm rains, which tumble in cascades from the rock, maintain a ring of green around it. The rock changes color in the changing light of the day, glowing spectacularly in the evening when lit by the setting sun. In Cuba another huge solitary rock, the Gran Piedra (Great Stone), has been estimated to weigh 61,355 tons.

Which continent is gradually being split in two?

A fissure 6,200 miles (10,000 kilometers) long runs across East Africa. Stretching from the Middle East to Mozambique, it is known as the Great Rift Valley. Two of the rocky plates that make up the Earth's crust are moving apart, causing some of the Earth's mantle to collapse. This threatens, eventually, to divide Africa into two.

This great fissure – visible from spacecraft 84,000 miles (135,000 kilometers) from Earth – is caused by underground forces that have torn at the Earth's crust, resulting in volcanic upheavals and lava eruptions. Some 30 active

Some 600 million years old, Uluru (Ayers Rock) in Australia's Northern Territory is the largest rock in the world.

volcanoes, together with sulfur springs that are changing lakes into swamps, indicate that this process is very much alive. Each year the two sides of the rift are pulled a few inches farther apart.

What is the San Andreas Fault?

The San Andreas Fault is a crack in the Earth's crust that runs for nearly 620 miles (1,000 kilometers), from the Gulf of California to Point Arena, north of San Francisco, before ending in
the bed of the Pacific Ocean. The "fault" results from friction between two of the plates that make up the Earth's crust – which constantly move in relation to each other.

The coast of California forms part of the Pacific plate, which is sliding in a northwesterly direction at a speed of a couple of inches per year, while the rest of the state of California is slowly sliding southeastward. Geologists believe that millions of years from now California will become an island in the Pacific. Sometimes the plates lock together – and only work free when the resulting tension produces an earthquake.

How was the Grand Canyon created?

The Grand Canyon in northern Arizona in the Southwest, extends for 270 miles (440 kilometers) along the winding Colorado River. For 65 million years the waters of the river have worn away the rock of a desert plateau, carving a huge chasm, in places 5,900 feet (1,800 meters) deep.

Created almost entirely by the action of the flowing water, the Grand Canyon is the largest gorge in the world. Differences in the resistance of the various stones to erosion have created a variety of slopes and contours, massive screes, and towering perpendicular walls. Two billion years of the Earth's history are inscribed on the canyon's multicolored stratified walls, which are like a corridor through geological time. Only the gorges of the Yangtze River, in China, rival its spectacular grandeur and beauty.

Which is the world's longest river?

The Nile flows 4,145 miles (6,670 kilometers) from its farthest source, in Burundi, Africa, to its delta in Egypt. From Lake Victoria, its largest source, the river passes through deserts and swamps, tumbles down waterfalls, and flows through a narrow fertile valley, before forming a

The Grand Canyon, carved out by the Colorado River, is the largest canyon in the world. In places it is 5,900 feet (1,800 meters) deep.

Each second more than 660,000 gallons (3,000,000 liters) of water pour over the edge of Niagara Falls.

Each second the Amazon River discharges about 4,240,000 cubic feet (120,000 cubic meters) of water into the Atlantic Ocean. The volume varies, depending on the season. When the waters are high, the rate of discharge can rise to 7,000,000 cubic feet per second (200,000 cubic meters per second).

The Amazon traces its source to the snowcapped Andes in Peru. Together with its 1,100 branches and tributaries, the river drains a basin of 2.5 million square miles (6.5 million square kilometers) — an area almost as large as the continent of Australia, or half the land surface of the United States. The Amazon carries more water than the Nile, Mississippi, and Yangtze put together. The Amazon is navigable for more than half its length, as far as the port of Iquitos in Peru. More than 1,500 species of fish have been identified in the Amazon — including flesh-eating piranhas and the world's largest freshwater fish, the pirarucu, which can be as much as 16 feet (5 meters) long and weigh 440 pounds (200 kilograms). Among the river's most dangerous predators are alligators and anacondas, snakes that sometimes reach 20 feet (6 meters) in length.

triangular delta and emptying into the Mediterranean Sea.

The ultimate source of the Nile remained a mystery until the discovery of its southernmost headstream, the Luvironza River in Burundi, in 1937. The two main "arms" of the Nile — the Blue Nile (which rises in the mountains of Ethiopia) and the White Nile (which flows from Lake Victoria) — meet at Khartoum, the capital of Sudan. The Nile is navigable in Sudan and Egypt,

except when the waters are low. Without the annual flooding of the land, the civilizations of ancient Egypt could not have survived. Almost as long as the Nile, the Amazon River flows 4,000 miles (6,450 kilometers) from its source in Peru to the Atlantic Ocean.

Which river pours the most water into the sea?

Which other long rivers are there?

The longest river system in the United States is formed by the Mississippi River and its tributary, the Missouri. Totaling more than 3,700 miles (6,000 kilometers), it is also the longest river system in the world.

Native Americans called the Mississippi "the Father of Waters." Together with its tributaries (which include the Ohio, the Arkansas, the Illinois, and the Tennessee rivers) and the canals that link them, it forms a transportation network more than 12,400 miles (20,000 kilometers) long. One tenth of the goods manufactured in the United States are transported on the Mississippi's waters. It irrigates one third of the country and ends in an enormous swampy delta, with a maze of channels that empty into the Gulf of Mexico near New Orleans. It was on the Mississippi that Mark Twain, the author of *Tom Sawyer* and *Huckleberry Finn*, learned to pilot boats.

On the other side of the world, the waters of China's longest river – the Yangtze, or Chang Jiang – flow 3,900 miles (6,300 kilometers) from the Himalaya Mountains in Tibet to the Pacific Ocean.

Are Niagara Falls the highest in the world?

Niagara Falls are not the world's highest waterfalls, although they are the most famous. The highest are the Angel Falls, in Venezuela, which are 18 times taller than Niagara.

Victoria Falls on the Zambezi River in Africa are a spectacular sight. The water falls from a height of more than 400 feet (120 meters).

Every second 660,000 gallons (3,000,000 liters) of water pour over the edge of Niagara. The falling water makes a deafening noise, which inspired the Native American name "Thundering Waters." Situated on the border between Canada and the United States, Niagara consists of two sets of falls. The Horseshoe Falls, on the Canadian side, are the most beautiful – though 10 feet (3 meters) shorter than the American Falls.

Which is the world's highest lake?

The highest navigable lake in the world is Lake Titi-caca, on the border between Bolivia and Peru. This huge landlocked lake is situated at 12,507 feet (3,812 meters) above sea level and is more than 880 feet (270 meters) deep in places. It has an area of more than 3,000 square miles (8,000 square kilometers).

Lake Titicaca was sacred to the Incas. According to Inca legend, the people of the Andes originated on one of its islands, called "the Island

Fjords – long narrow fingers of sea flanked by cliffs or mountains – are especially numerous in Norway.

from forests to fields, dunes, and large open spaces. Several great manufacturing cities have developed in this region, which is one of the most industrialized in North America. Detroit, near Lake Erie, is the capital of the automobile industry. On the shores of Lake Michigan is Chicago, the third-largest city in the United States.

of the Sun." The banks of the lake are thickly covered with reeds (*totoras*), which the Andean Indians used for centuries for making boats. In these woven reed boats they crossed the lake, fished, and traveled to the floating islands (*uros*) where some of them lived and cultivated gardens. In the Himalayas there are lakes at higher altitudes, but most of them are frozen. The highest is Panch Pokhri, 17,760 feet (5,414 meters) above sea level.

What are the names of the Great Lakes?

The Great Lakes – Superior, Michigan, Huron, Erie, and Ontario – are situated along the border between the United States and Canada. Connected to the Atlantic by the St. Lawrence Seaway, together they are the size of an inland sea.

These five freshwater lakes resulted from movements in the Earth's crust that followed the last ice age, creating a series of enormous basins. With a surface area of 31,400 square miles (81,350 square kilometers), Lake Superior is the largest lake in the western hemisphere. Its shores are partly in the United States and partly in Canada. The landscape around the lakes is varied, ranging

Which is the deepest lake?

With a maximum depth of 4,870 feet (1,485 meters), Lake Baikal in southeastern Siberia is the world's deepest lake. Bays and peninsulas are cut out of the shoreline of this lake, which has an area of 12,000 square miles (31,500 square kilometers).

An immense reservoir of fresh water, Lake Baikal freezes over late in the year – but packs of ice then persist until July. In high winds, waves can rise to a height of 16 feet (5 meters). More than 50 species of fish live in its waters – the best known being the sturgeon, from whose eggs caviar is prepared. The only freshwater seal, the Baikal seal, also inhabits the lake.

In which countries are fjords found?

Pronounced fee-ords, these fingers of sea reaching inland between cliffs or mountains are especially numerous in Norway. But fjords are also found in other parts of the world, including New Zealand. The longest fjord, which penetrates 194 miles (313 kilometers) inland, is in Greenland.

The Norwegian fjords originated in prehistoric times, when Norway was a plateau standing high above sea level. Torrents of water cut narrow gorges to the sea, which became glaciers during the Great Ice Age. Gradually the gorges became wider, forming valleys. As the climate warmed, the ice melted, giving way to the sea. The Sjorn Fjord, north of Bergen, is the largest in Norway. It reaches 124 miles (200 kilometers) inland and in places is 3 miles (5 kilometers) wide; its cliffs are up to 3,300 feet (1,000 meters) high.

Fjords are also found on the coasts of Alaska and Maine, and in British Columbia, in Canada.

What are the Everglades?

A sea of reeds, an ocean of grass, the Everglades cover part of the southern tip of Florida. The humid, subtropical climate of these marshlands favors the growth of lush vegetation, providing a habitat for a profusion of aquatic birds.

According to early maps, the region was known as the River Glades (meaning "river marshlands") or Ever Glades ("eternal marshlands"). Today it is a national park. Its 2,300 square miles (6,000 square kilometers) of grass-covered waters are dotted with small islands called hammocks, where pine, mahogany, evergreen oak, and mangrove grow. The ecosystem of the Everglades shelters more than 300 species of birds and approximately 600 species of fish. Alligators and crocodiles are also found here.

Where are the most beautiful lagoons?

The lagoons of Polynesia must be the most beautiful. They surround or are enclosed by atolls (ring-shaped coral reefs), like

Alligators, crocodiles, plants, fish, and birds all thrive in the protected habitat provided by Everglades National Park.

those of the Tuamotu archipelago, and lap the shores of mountainous islands such as Tahiti and Bora-Bora.

Situated to the northeast of the Society Islands, the dozens of atolls of the Tuamotu Islands form a perfect universe of coral, sea, and sand. The most beautiful of these is Rangiroa, which encloses an 890-square-mile (2,300-square-kilometer) lagoon. Some of the islands of Polynesia are ringed by a barrier reef – a coral reef enclosing a coastal lagoon, across which the Polynesians paddle their *pirogues*. The most beautiful of these is Bora-Bora. There are also small coral islands called *motu* with vegetation clinging to them, sometimes even a few coconut palms stirred by the breeze.

The salinity of the Dead Sea is so high that it is extraordinarily buoyant. Salt crystals continually form on its surface.

Which sea is so salty that it makes you float?

The Dead Sea is so salty that you can float in it without sinking. Its shore, lying 1,300 feet (400 meters) below sea level, is the lowest inland place on the surface of the Earth. Lying on the frontier between Israel and Jordan, this inland sea has an area of more than 390 square miles (1,000 square kilometers).

The average salinity of the Dead Sea is between 24 and 26 percent, 10 times higher than that of the oceans. The Dead Sea is the saltiest body of water on the Earth. No aquatic life exists in it, and the mountains surrounding it are almost bare of vegetation. Its salinity is so high that salt does not always remain dissolved in the water and forms crystals on the surface. Chemical plants built on the shore extract mineral salts used in the manufacture of glass and fertilizers. In 1947 the Dead Sea Scrolls – including ancient copies of some of the books of the Old Testament – were found in the caves at Qumran nearby.

Where is the deepest ocean canyon?

To the east of the Mariana Islands there is a deep, curving canyon in the floor of the Pacific Ocean, known as the Mariana Trench. The deepest part, 7 miles (11 kilometers) below the ocean's surface, is called Challenger Deep.

Discovered by a British oceanographic vessel in 1951, this great submarine canyon is 1,585 miles (2,550 kilometers) long and nearly 45 miles (70 kilometers) wide. Its deepest point, 36,000 feet (11,034 meters) below sea level, is the lowest point on the Earth's surface. Jacques Picard – who, with Donald Walsh, descended almost to the bottom of the trench in 1960 – declared that he had seen "an immense emptiness that defies understanding."

Which are the

biggest glaciers?

The world's longest glacier is the Lambert Glacier in Antarctica. Along with the adjoining Mellor and Fisher glaciers, it extends for more than 300 miles (500 kilometers).

Iceland's Vatnajökull Glacier is the largest in Europe, covering 4,600 square miles (12,000 square kilometers). Violent storms drive huge blocks of ice – detached from Greenland, less than 190 miles (300 kilometers) away – onto its coast. There are numerous large glaciers in the Himalayas. In the United States the Malaspina Glacier Complex in Alaska covers some 1,900 square miles (5,000 square kilometers). In the Alps the largest glaciers are the Aletsch Glacier in Switzerland, 15 miles (24 kilometers) long, and Mont Blanc's Mer de Glace and Glacier du Géant (which have a combined length of 9 miles/14 kilometers).

Which country

consists of

7,000 islands?

The Philippine archipelago is sometimes called "the 7,000 pearls of Asia." These islands make up a national territory of nearly 116,000 square miles (300,000 square kilometers). Added together, their coastlines are longer than those of the United States.

According to legend, the Philippines were created when two giants fought over pearls they had just harvested – with such violence that the pearls were scattered in all directions. The southernmost island is 1,900 miles (3,000 kilometers) from the northernmost island, while the easternmost island is about 1,100 miles (1,800 kilometers) from the westernmost one. Only about 100 of the islands are inhabited. The Philippines do not form the world's largest archipelago. That honor belongs to Indonesia, which consists of more than 13,000 islands. The land surface of the Indonesian archipelago amounts to almost 770,000 square miles (2,000,000 square kilometers).

What are the

Desolation Islands?

In 1772 the French explorer Yves-Joseph de Kerguélen-Trémarec discovered an

Situated in the western part of the Pacific Ocean, the Philippines consists of 7,000 islands – and so has thousands of beaches.

archipelago of "floating mountains" while exploring the southern Indian Ocean, and named them the Desolation Islands. Part of the French Antarctic territory, they are now called the Kerguelen Islands after him.

Almost uninhabited, the Kerguelen archipelago extends over 2,700 square miles (7,000 square kilometers). The largest island is dominated by a volcano. The winds are violent and the climate so cold that even in summer the temperature rarely exceeds 50°F (10°C). There are no trees or bushes, and vegetation is sparse – apart from the islands' bitter wild cabbage. Rabbits, penguins, whales, and albatrosses are the dominant forms of wildlife. Scientific research stations have been set up to study the flora and fauna, and for the observation of the weather, geomagnetism, and the aurora australis (southern lights).

Where can you go boating underground?

Deep inside the caves at Padirac, in France, there is a subterranean river that flows into the Dordogne River. Visitors embark on rafts in order to explore the wonders of the cave.

Visitors explore the caves at Padirac by boat. Some of the underground caverns in the Dordogne extend for miles.

After descending by stairs or elevator to the river, 360 feet (110 meters) below the ground, visitors walk to a jetty where their voyage begins. Boarding an unsinkable raft, they glide along the river, admiring the marvelous rock forms sculpted by the water over thousands of years. Disembarking at the Lac de la Pluie (Rain Lake), in a grotto always dripping with moisture, they discover echoing caverns adorned by splendid stalagmites and stalactites, then emerge into a cathedrallike chamber with a domed ceiling 308 feet (94 meters) high. Beneath this dome is a lake, some 92 feet (28 meters) below the river bed. Despite the number of sensational caves discovered during the past century, the *gouffre* (chasm) at Padirac – which was opened in 1898 – retains pride of place among the world's most remarkable caves.

Which is the largest desert?

The word desert evokes an arid landscape where the Sun scorches the sand and nothing grows – yet the

largest and emptiest desert on Earth is the continent of Antarctica, with an area of almost 5,400,000 square miles (14,000,000 square kilometers). The Sahara is the largest sand-and-stone desert. It has an area of more than 3,500,000 square miles (9,000,000 square kilometers).

The greatest dimensions of the Sahara are approximately 3,200 miles (5,150 kilometers) from east to west, and 1,400 miles (2,250 kilometers) from north to south. The altitude ranges from 433 feet (132 meters) below sea level in the Qattara Depression in Egypt to 11,205 feet (3,415 meters) above sea level at Mount Emi Koussi in Chad. The temperature can rise to more than 113°F (45°C) at noon and fall below freezing at night. Deserts of sand are not immobile: a high wind can transform an entire landscape. The driest desert in the world is the Atacama Desert in northern Chile, which has less than ½ inch (1.3 centimeters) of rain a year.

Deserts are usually sparsely inhabited. Penguins are just about the only permanent inhabitants of Antarctica, but nomadic peoples traverse the Sahara. Most of the population is concentrated around the oases.

Does Death Valley live up to its name?

A sun-baked wilderness of rocks and dunes, this hostile region in southeastern California was named Death Valley by pioneers who suffered from the searing heat. The temperature can rise above 132°F (56°C).

Although surrounded by mountains, Death Valley is 280 feet (85 meters) below sea level. Its landscape is varied, ranging from the vast salt flats called the Devil's Golf Course, to the Painter's Palette, where the colors of the rocks alter in the changing light. During the night and the cool early hours of the morning, coyotes and foxes are active. The roadrunner – a long-billed ground bird that catches mice and lizards – walks tirelessly along the desert roads.

What is the Kalahari Desert like?

A vast arid plain situated between the Orange and Zambezi rivers in southern Africa, the Kalahari Desert is made up of a variety of environments – swamps to brushland to enormous areas of sand. Extending for more than 190,000 square miles (500,000 square kilometers), it covers the greater part of Botswana and is the world's largest continuous expanse of sand.

Some people picture the Kalahari as a vast torrid desert covered with undulating dunes that provide refuge for herds of antelope, pursued by lions or leopards, or for tribes of people such as the Kung and San. Others see it as a

The bed of an ancient salt lake, Death Valley in southern California is one of the hottest places on Earth.

mysterious, forgotten world. It is one of the last unspoiled regions of Africa. Its inaccessibility, its expanses of red sand, and the scarcity of water have saved it from exploitation.

Are there deserts in Europe?

Once covered with endless expanses of forest, Spain is the only country in Europe with desert land-scapes. Arid conditions and soil erosion have especially affected the province of Almeria in the south of Andalusia.

The rugged landscapes of Andalusia, in southern Spain, have provided desert settings for films such as *Lawrence of Arabia*. In places the similarities with the landscapes of Arizona are so striking that "spaghetti Westerns" were filmed here. Thanks to irrigation, some desert areas have been made to bloom, and the arid land of the south has become one of the country's most productive agricultural regions. In southern Andalusia plants are often protected with plastic. These improvised greenhouses conserve water and facilitate the cultivation of tomatoes, straw-berries, and melons, enabling Spain to export fresh produce even in winter.

Located in Navajo territory, Monument Valley in Arizona has been a favorite place for filming Westerns.

Where are Westerns filmed?

Westerns are now filmed in various locations, including North Africa and southern Spain. Many of the classic Hollywood Westerns were shot in Monument Valley, the red sand-and-stone desert stretching from Arizona to Utah.

The desert landscapes, rugged mountains, and giant saguaro cactuses of Arizona have provided a setting for countless Westerns, but Monument Valley has been particularly popular. Here wind and sand have gnawed away at the soft stone for millions of years to sculpt huge towers and spires of rock that rise from the carpet of red sand. In Old Tucson, a small city of the Far West, an open-air museum serves as the setting for many modern Westerns.

Where are the tallest sand dunes?

The world's tallest sand dunes are found in the Sahara Desert. Part of the "sea of sand" at Issouane

Over 330 feet (100 meters) high, the Dune du Pilat, near Arcachon in France, is the tallest sand dune in Europe. Like all other dunes, it constantly changes shape as it is remodeled by the wind.

Seen from a distance, Meteor Crater appears merely to be a gently sloping hill – but as you climb over the brow you discover an amphitheater of gigantic proportions. Scientists have found evidence confirming that this crater was caused by the fall of a giant meteorite around 20,000 years ago. Sediment at the bottom of the crater shows that a lake formed there about 12,000 years ago. The drier climate since then resulted in the present landscape.

N'Tifernine, in Algeria, they are 3 miles (5 kilometers) long and over 1,500 feet (450 meters) high. The large groups of dunes found in the Sahara and other large deserts are referred to as sand seas.

Rising to a height of more than 300 feet (100 meters), the Dune du Pilat, near Arcachon in France, is Europe's tallest sand dune. Backed by forest, it stretches for more than 2 miles (3 kilometers) along the Atlantic coast. Like all other dunes, the Dune du Pilat constantly changes as the wind remodels the dune's shape. Long ago it was covered with forest, and we know that people lived there because archeologists have found tools and utensils dating from the Neolithic period. At the base of the dune grows a pine forest, which was planted there to help keep the sand in place. At one time the local people used to walk through the forest on stilts, so that they could keep an eye on their flocks of sheep.

Where can you see a crater like the ones on the moon?

Meteor Crater in Arizona is a giant hollow more than 3,000 feet (1,000 meters) in diameter and 700 feet (200 meters) deep – created in exactly the same way as the craters of the moon.

What is the Petrified Forest?

Around 200 million years ago, a forest flourished where Arizona's Painted Desert is today. The remains of that forest – now petrified, or turned to stone – can be seen in Petrified Forest National Park.

Scattered among the multicolored rocks that give the desert its name are the petrified trunks of giant prehistoric conifers. Crystallized logs – transformed into shimmering quartz, jasper, or agate – and fragments of petrified wood lie strewn on the ground. Among them have been found the fossilized remains of dinosaurs, which long ago lived in the forest that covered this desert landscape.

Buried in the earth, the remains of the trees gradually became permeated with minerals, which replaced the wood and preserved its form. As a result today, millions of years later, the growth rings that marked the annual development of these primeval trees can still be seen. A living record cast in stone, they show that some of the trees were as much as 230 feet (70 meters) tall.

The Parc National de la Vanoise (Vanoise National Park) was the first of the three nature reserves established to protect the animal and plant life of the French Alps.

Which was the first national park?

Yellowstone National Park, in the Rocky Mountains, in Wyoming, Idaho, and Montana was the world's first national park. Established in 1872, it covers an area of 3,469 square miles (8,984 square kilometers).

Yellowstone National Park also has the largest thermal area in the world, containing mud volcanoes, hot springs, sulfur pools, and geysers. Fauna in the park includes wapiti, bison, and over 200 species of birds. The United States has about 50 national parks and about 300 other protected areas, covering a total of 125,000 square miles (325,000 square kilometers) of land. They include the Grand Canyon National Park, the Everglades, and the Great Smoky Mountains.

Some of the most stunning national parks are found in Africa. Kenya's national parks cover an area of more than 13,000 square miles (34,000 square kilometers). The largest of these is the Tsavo National Park, which stretches from the semi-arid plains in the southeast of the country to the Chyulu Hills and foothills of Mount Kilimanjaro in the west, covering an area of 8,000 square miles (2,100 square kilometers). It contains such animals as black rhinoceros (for which the park is a refuge), buffaloes, cheetahs, elephants, zebras, leopards, lions, and hippopotamuses. Tanzania contains the Serengeti National Park, which covers an area of 5,700 square miles (15,000 square kilometers) and is famed for its animal migrations at the start of the dry season.

The French Alps are home to a number of national parks, including the Parc National de la Vanoise (Vanoise National Park), in Savoy. Some 310 miles (500 kilometers) of marked trails allow visitors to appreciate the park's characteristic flora, including splendid mountain orchids. The park is also home to chamois, ibex, marmots, and golden eagles.

Which is the largest virgin forest?

The Amazon basin is a vast forested region that extends for more than 2,300,000 square miles (6,000,000 square kilometers) over five countries of South America. It covers parts of Bolivia, Peru, Colombia, and Venezuela, and two-fifths of Brazil.

Temperatures in the Amazon basin remain stable throughout the year, ranging from 68 to 82°F (20 to 28°C). Heavy rains fall here all year round. This rain forest is in effect the world's greatest nature reserve. One tenth of the planet's bird species live in its foliage, and more than 2,500 species of fish have evolved in the Amazon river system. An area the size of Greece has been deforested within the space of 10 years. As a result, many plant and animal species are in danger of extinction, as are the human populations native to the region.

Which is the largest forest of all?

From Finland to Japan, from the Baltic to the Pacific, millions of miles of forest extend across Siberia. The taiga – the largest forest on Earth – offers a landscape in which the only variation is the density of the trees.

The taiga remains partially unexplored. Composed mainly of birch and pine, it is inhabited by moose and reindeer, bears, silver foxes, and wolves; to the east live tigers, panthers, and lynx. The vegetation here is strange. Dead tree trunks are often seen within living trees, and the forest floor is covered with a carpet of moss and lichens.

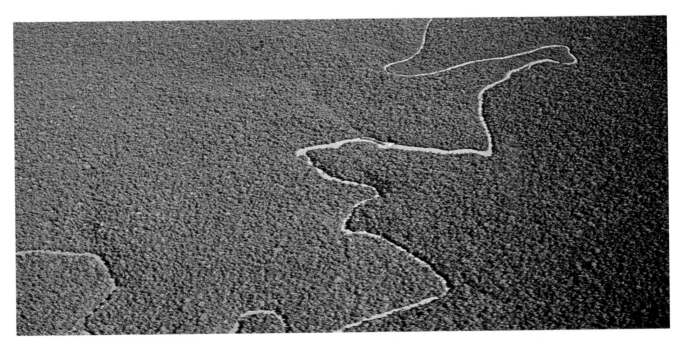

The great rain forest of the Amazon basin in South America stretches over five countries. It is the largest virgin forest in the world, but it is constantly being reduced by excessive deforestation.

Protecting Our Planet

What is ecology?

Ecology is the study of living creatures and their interaction with their environment. It is, therefore, also the science of the protection and conservation of nature.

Ecology is a very complex science that requires a thorough study of all the species in our environment, from the largest to the smallest. It is concerned with the problem of maintaining biological balances, the conservation of nature, and the protection of animal and plant life. It makes use of very sophisticated equipment, including electron microscopes, computers, satellites, and submarines.

Ecologists at work. In order to protect our environment, we need to know it better by studying it thoroughly.

What changes led to the appearance of life on Earth?

Life appeared on Earth about three and a half billion years ago, in the oceans that formed as the Earth cooled down. This primitive life used the carbon dioxide in the atmosphere and produced oxygen – the gas animals need for life.

Volcanoes on the young Earth poured out gases to form the first atmosphere, and water vapor condensed to form the first oceans. The mixture of hydrocarbons and cyanides on the planet gradually turned into increasingly complex organic molecules, and about 3½ billion years ago bacteria and blue-green algae developed. These were the first life forms. Some species of blue-green algae were able to convert water and carbon dioxide from the atmosphere into food using energy from sunlight. This process is known as photosynthesis, and it releases tiny bubbles of oxygen as a by-product. Eventually the blue-green algae created an environment rich in oxygen that supported the evolution of more complex plants and animals.

Why are some species endangered?

This is part of natural selection, whereby the

A bird eating a fish forms one of the links in the food chain.

weakest or the least well-adapted species disappear as others that are better adapted take their place. Survival involves adapting to the environment.

The evolution of a species is linked to that of its environment, and is affected by atmospheric, thermal, and geological changes. Not all species can evolve with these upheavals, and some are totally unable to adapt to new conditions of life. In the history of the Earth there have been many great changes, which is why large numbers of species have already disappeared since life first appeared on Earth. Today, species become endangered primarily as a result of the activities of human beings.

What does ecological niche mean?

An ecological niche is the place occupied by a species in its habitat, or ecosystem, including all chemical, physical, and biological components.

In order to study an ecosystem, it is necessary to observe not only the plants and animals, but also the wider environment including the soil type, water resources, and the climate. This way, we can find out how the different factors interact. It is then possible to understand how the natural environment works and thus avoid potentially harmful human interventions and predict ways in which we can maintain the natural balance.

What is a food chain?

There are creatures that eat plants, and others that feed on the plant-eaters. This dependence on other species for food is called the food chain.

This chain starts with plants, which convert the energy of the Sun into food. The plants are eaten by animals, called herbivores, and in turn these animals are eaten by carnivores. Small carnivores are often eaten by larger ones, as the food chain becomes longer. Animals that eat both plants and animals are called omnivores. There are vast numbers of organisms at the bottom of the food chain and far fewer at the top. This is part of the ecological balance.

How did life begin on the land?

Life on Earth originated in the sea. The first primitive plants developed into species capable of photosynthesis, and as more species evolved, some colonized the land.

Plant life was able to proliferate in the sea because of the huge quantities of minerals deposited in it by rivers, springs, geysers, and volcanic eruptions. The first plants with roots evolved about half a billion years ago, as they gradually adapted through successive stages from sea life to the tidal cycle, and finally to life on dry land. Plants, arthropods (arachnids and insects), and amphibians were the first species to populate dry land. Fossils of these early land species date from about 350 million years ago, in the Devonian Period. Some primitive forms of plants that still exist today appeared 300 million years ago in the Carboniferous Period, including ferns, horsetails, and mosses.

Has anyone witnessed life first coming to a new land?

In the 19th century, after a volcanic eruption on the island of Krakatoa in the Sunda Strait, a new island was born from the remains of the volcano.

Krakatoa is a volcanic island between Java and Sumatra. It suffered the second most violent volcanic eruption in the history of the world when the Krakatoa volcano erupted in 1883. Thirty years later, a new island, called Anak Krakatoa (Child of Krakatoa), was formed in the crater. This was colonized by plant species brought as seeds by the wind and by sea birds.

Anak Krakatoa, the Child of Krakatoa, appeared 30 years after the eruption of the Krakatoa volcano. It was not long before life appeared again on this virgin land: sea birds and winds carried the first seeds; growing plants attracted more birds.

Which species are the first to colonize virgin lands?

Plants are generally the first species to arrive on and colonize virgin land. The seeds of plants may be brought by the winds, seas, or animals, especially sea birds.

When animals or plants die, their remains putrefy through the action of bacteria, producing humus. This enriches the soil, providing the minerals and other organic matter necessary for the growth of plant species. A seed can germinate and grow if it has sunlight, water, and the necessary minerals and gases. Plants are always the first to grow after any natural catastrophe.

In the Antarctic, penguins are the masters. These birds live in colonies around the coast and islands of Antarctica.

What are the main animals in the polar regions?

The Arctic in the North, and the Antarctic in the South, are the polar regions of our planet. They are both so cold and barren that very few animal species are able to live there.

The Arctic is the warmer region, and it is populated by humans and several other species of mammal. Herbivores (such as reindeer, hares, and lemmings) feed on lichens and roots. The Arctic wolf, a carnivore, is the predator of reindeer. Seagulls, puffins, and terns also live in the Arctic skies. The Arctic ice field is populated by polar bears and seals. There are many fish in its waters.

Is there life in Antarctica?

Antarctica, also called the South Pole, is the coldest region on the planet. It is covered with a thick layer of ice. In area Antarctica is larger than either Europe or Australia, but humans have never colonized Antarctica. No mammals live on the land of the Antarctic.

Very few plants grow on the Antarctic mainland, of which mosses are most common. Also on the mainland are algae and lichen, a few insects, and some small animals. By contrast, the surrounding waters are teeming with wildlife. The ocean currents, rich in nutrients, support vast numbers of plankton, encouraging many species of fish, shrimps, and tiny submarine organisms to live there. Whales and seals also live in the Antarctic. These animals are perfectly adapted to the cold conditions. Several species of sea birds (penguins, albatross, terns, and petrels) also live there.

Are any of these species threatened with extinction?

Big whales are. There used to be large numbers of them, but for a long time they were hunted without any thought given to the preservation of the species.

Blue whales, humpback whales, right whales, and sperm whales have been hunted for their meat and fat, used in making many pharmaceutical and cosmetic products. Many species of whale are now on the verge of extinction. Attention has been drawn to their plight, and whaling is now regulated by very strict laws at an international level, even though they are often breached.

Whom does Antarctica belong to?

Different parts of the Antarctic have been claimed by various countries, but they have agreed by international treaty that Antarctica should be used for peaceful purposes only. These countries have also agreed to share their scientific research on Antarctica.

The Antarctic is an extremely interesting area. Several countries have set up scientific missions there to study the climate and the skies. However, because of the extremely harsh conditions, missions cannot stay for more than a few weeks or months.

Has Antarctica already been polluted?

Unfortunately, it has. The very presence of missions there has caused pollution.

When people live somewhere for any length of time, they leave their mark on the environment. Waste and debris from installations have often been left behind by Antarctic missions. Traces of lead, sulfur, and mercury that come from factories thousands of miles away have been found in the ice of the pole.

Where is the largest water reserve?

In the Antarctic, where the ice fields and icebergs make up two-thirds of all the fresh water in the world.

The large continental glaciers at the South Pole were formed when accumulated snow turned to ice. As they slowly flow toward the sea, these glaciers break up and form icebergs – mountains of

At a depth of 5,900 feet (1,800 meters) below the surface, fish, shellfish, octopuses, and worms live near the famous "black smokers" that warm up the sea.

unsalted ice. They float on the sea with only a tenth of their volume above the water, the rest lying beneath the surface. A few years ago, an American organization towed a huge iceberg to Saudi Arabia, where it was used as a freshwater reserve. However, the experiment has not been repeated.

Are the great depths of the sea inhabited?

Only in the last century was it possible to prove that there are animals living in the great depths of the sea. Some of these species have a bizarre appearance.

In the depths of the ocean there is no sunlight, and no plants can grow, but some animals have adapted to the great pressure, lack of light, the cold, still water, and scarcity of food. Most of the fish are dark in color or semi-transparent, and are blind or have enormous eyes to make the most of what light there is. Some deep-sea fish feed on the plants and animals that sink down from the sea above, while others rise to the surface at night to search for food. Some have developed huge teeth and mouths, and swallow prey as large as themselves. One such species is the viper fish, which has such long teeth that it cannot close its mouth. The most common in-habitant of the great depths is the rattail fish, or grenadier, found at depths of 10,000–13,000 feet (3,000–4,000 meters). A relative of the cod, it has the most sensitive eyes of all animals. The largest of the animals in the ocean depths is a cephalopod mollusk, the squid, which can reach 13 feet (4 meters) in length and weigh up to 350 pounds (160 kilograms).

When did people start interfering with the environment?

Humans started to modify their environment during the Neolithic Age, when people began to settle in one place, and as a result developed a new life style.

The Neolithic Age dates back to the period 5000–2500 B.C. As they settled in communities, Neolithic peoples started cutting down forests to create clearings where they built villages, kept animals, and grew crops. A social system appeared, and craftsmanship and commerce developed. Settling down in communities had revolutionary consequences not only for human life, but also for the environment, which changed dramatically as forests were cut down to become farmland and cities and roads were built.

Are forests disappearing everywhere in the world?

Although forests are being cut down in many parts of the world, in some Western countries forests are actually getting larger because of constant reforestation. In some places, forests are now even larger than they were in the Middle Ages.

A temperate forest in the fall can be a blaze of color. Unfortunately, forests throughout the world are being severely reduced.

Reforestation started at the beginning of the 20th century in Europe. In the Middle Ages, wood was the only fuel, and as a result it was used in great quantities. Consequently, forests near cities, villages, castles, and monasteries were decimated in the 16th, 17th, and 18th centuries. A great deal of wood was also required for building large ships. A different kind of danger, namely pollution, started threatening forests as the industrial age dawned. We are now aware of the risks involved in deforestation on a massive scale, and many countries are taking measures to try and prevent it.

How can you make a forest grow again?

Fallow lands quickly revert to a wild state. They soon become covered with bushes and undergrowth beneath which seeds from trees, carried by the wind or by animals, can grow undisturbed.

This is natural reforestation, which depends on the rhythm of the seasons. Artificial reforestation of sites is also practiced. Young shoots, or sometimes even young trees, are planted, which then follow their natural growth cycle. The regular alignment of trees is characteristic of reforested areas. The purpose of reforestation is usually industrial, but sometimes it is also carried out in areas that have been destroyed by fire, pollution, or massive deforestation. The Amazon rain forest, which was cut down with little thought for the future, will not grow again because the thin layer of fertile soil is eroding very quickly.

When did air pollution start?

Large-scale air pollution started in the U.S. and Europe in the 19th century, with the development of heavy industry.

Air pollution started with the Industrial Revolution, when people started turning raw materials into consumer goods on a large scale. The use of coal as fuel in the textile, engineering, and metallurgical industries began a process that worsened with the invention of the car and the use of petroleum instead of coal in industrial fields.

Air pollution is mainly caused by factories and cars. The most visible waste is not always the most dangerous: the large white plumes you can see coming out of the chimneys of factories are often nothing but steam.

Is today's landscape different from what it used to be?

Human activity has caused great changes in the landscape in many parts of the world. A large proportion of the land used to be covered with forests, but the growth in population and the development of

agriculture and industry have changed that forever.

As agriculture has developed, people cut down huge stretches of forests to grow crops and breed animals, and eventually to build cities. This has reduced the amount of the Earth's land area covered by forest from 60 percent to 25 percent. People have also made use of mountains, turning them into pastures and terrace cultivation, and have claimed land from the sea by draining certain areas. People have also created artificial lakes by building dams, and have altered the landscape by transplanting plant species from one region to another. People have drained marshes and exploited the soil and the riches under the ground (quarries and mines). All these activities through the ages have substantially altered the original landscape.

Can we stop the advance of the desert?

This would need a massive reforestation scheme. In some regions, though, the ground is already too dry and barren.

Signs of global warming can already be seen, as certain regions seem to be drying up. This is worsened by the destruction of forests, which prevents the condensation process that results in rain. Herds of animals eating vegetation contribute to the drying up of the ground, which gradually becomes unproductive. The reduction of animal herds could slow down the desertification process, but this is not really possible in regions where

A small oasis in the middle of the Algerian desert. Constant irrigation is now essential to grow crops, whereas 10,000 years ago, this spot might have been a forest.

people already suffer badly from starvation. It would require colossal investment to solve this problem.

Is it possible to grow crops in the desert?

Yes, it is possible, but it is a very expensive and time-consuming process.

Crops have been grown in Saudi Arabia and Israel (fruit trees, vegetables, cereal). Fresh water must be drawn from springs buried deep down in the ground unless desalinated sea water is used. Those barren lands must be constantly irrigated and enriched with fertilizers. All these constraints make any attempts at agriculture very expensive.

What animal species live in the desert?

The largest deserts are on the African and North and South American continents and in Australia. Various species have developed in these regions and have become adapted to the landscape and climate.

The varied wildlife in the African deserts includes insects and reptiles (lizards and snakes). Among the small mammals are rodents like the jerboa. There are also larger herbivorous mammals such as the addax, which is now an endangered species. An animal well adapted to the desert is the camel. The Mojave Desert in the Southwest shelters many species: lizards and snakes, among which are rattlesnakes; rodents (squirrels and kangaroo rats); kit foxes and coyotes, carnivores that feed on other animals and on carrion; and birds, including raptors (buzzards and hawks) and hummingbirds.

When lions are not busy hunting gazelle or zebra, they rest in the tall, dry grass of the savanna.

What is an oasis?

It is an area of land in the desert that is made fertile by the presence of water near its surface.

In the desert, an oasis is an area of life. Travelers stop there to drink and rest. Animals, too, find food and water. The vegetation in an oasis is mainly thorny undergrowth and date palms. Many oases support human settlements and farms.

Where is the savanna?

It is an extensive open tropical grassland in Africa.

This picture, taken in the humid pampas in Argentina, gives only a small indication of the vast extent of the pampas.

In the savanna, dry seasons follow rainy seasons, and the vegetation is capable of surviving both extremes. Examples include high grass, thorny acacia trees, and the famous baobabs. These also provide shelter and support for animals.

What animals live

in the savanna?

Many different species of animals live in the savanna. Most of them are herbivores.

The most impressive of all herbivores is definitely the elephant, which feeds on shoots, fruit, roots, and the bark of trees. The giraffe, with its long neck, can reach the highest branches. Other herbivores that share this large grassland include buffaloes, zebras, gazelles, hippopotamuses, and rhinoceros, which all graze on the lush grasses. They are hunted by carnivorous animals, such as lions, cheetahs, and hunting dogs. Hyenas and vultures, scavenging animals, fight for the leftovers. Savanna trees are populated by baboons, and many species of birds live here (flamingos, herons,

ibises). Migratory birds come to the savanna as a refuge during the winter.

What are

the pampas?

They are the flat, treeless plains in South America, stretching from Argentina to Uruguay. They cover about one-fifth of the land area of Argentina.

Low rainfall and a large number of herbivorous animals make it difficult for any type of vegetation to develop in this vast, flat, treeless plain. Hot summers follow mild winters. The pampas can be split into two different zones: the dry pampas in the west, where the soil is sandy and there are only a few thorny trees; and the humid pampas in the east, where there is more rainfall and the soil is rich and fertile. The vegetation in the pampas is similar to that of the Asian steppes and the prairies of the western U.S. Fields of wheat, corn, and alfalfa cover much of the fertile eastern pampas.

What types of animal species live in the pampas?

Many herbivores and a few predatory carnivores live in the pampas, together with the great herds of cattle.

The predatory animals are the puma, which is quite rare now, and the maned wolf, which is omnivorous as it will eat fruit if it can find no animal prey. The largest animal in this region is the pampas deer, another species that is rapidly disappearing. The rhea, a flightless bird similar to the ostrich, is well known for its quick turn of speed. Other pampas animals include the armadillo, which has peglike rootless teeth and a covering of strong armor plates over most of its body, and the viscacha, a rodent similar to the chinchilla, which lives in burrows.

Is it possible to reclaim land from the sea?

This can be done by building dikes around land submerged by the sea, and then draining it.

In Holland, people have reclaimed large areas of land from the sea through an extensive program of dike building. These areas of land, called polders, have been enclosed by dikes and drained through a process of pumping and draining of the waters. Polders are very fertile lands situated below sea level, and are used for growing crops and keeping animals such as cattle and sheep. In Hong Kong, skyscrapers have been erected on drained land.

Hong Kong is constantly growing; new skyscrapers rise up on land reclaimed from the sea.

Have people also changed the shape of mountains?

In some places people have deforested mountains in order to increase the amount of land suitable for cultivation, resulting in a

modification of the land-scape.

The roots of trees can prevent the erosion of the ground by the rain because they hold back the earth. Once mountains have been deforested, it is necessary to build terraces in order to grow crops. When there are no trees, the erosion of the ground and the movement of fertile ground down into the valleys is prevented by small walls of stones. Some changes to the mountains have caused avalanches and landslides.

A view from the air of the famous Trans-Amazonian Highway, which splits the Amazonian forest into two.

How is the land used after forests have been destroyed?

Forests are destroyed for a variety of purposes: cutting down of trees for fuel or for raw materials, making way for mining of minerals or ores, or simply to increase the area of land that can be cultivated. Forests can be destroyed by fires or pollution.

In some regions, people burn down forests in order to reclaim the land for agriculture. Forest fires result in a very fertile compost through the mixture of earth, ash, and plant debris. Sometimes, forests that have accidentally burned down are replanted.

Why is the destruction of forests dangerous?

The massive destruction of forests results in an ecological imbalance, which causes flooding, landslides, and desertification.

In forests, the ground is covered with vegetation of different sorts: trees with their long roots, smaller plants, mosses, fungi, and dead leaves. The plant roots soak up the rainwater. Once trees and plants have disappeared, the ground can no longer retain water, and when there is heavy rainfall, torrents of mud and landslides can threaten neighboring villages and crops. The landscape then becomes barren; this is the beginning of the desertification process.

How have farmers produced more food?

The increasing world population has meant that farmers have had to provide more food. The area of cultivable land has been expanded, increasing crop yields and developing new species.

People have considerably enlarged cultivable areas by clearing large spaces and have increased crop yields by using fertilizers. Scientists have also selected the strongest

Paper mills are major sources of coastal and river pollution. Here you can see the consequences of waste outflow from a paper mill in France.

because they are used in such large quantities that they cannot be eliminated from the soil. They soak into the ground and mix with the water below the water table. Sometimes they are carried by rainwater into rivers and cause pollution there. Natural fertilizers (manure, guano, and compost), and the nitrogen added to the soil by leguminous plants such as beans, do not damage the environment.

What causes the pollution of drinkable water?

Chemical fertilizers, pesticides in agriculture, and the pouring out of sewage from cities into rivers are the main causes of freshwater pollution.

Fertilizers and pesticides that have not been broken down end up in rivers and underground springs, which are the main sources of fresh water. Some local authorities do not process their sewage or the chemical waste from factories that is poured directly into our rivers. These are the most serious causes of fresh-water pollution.

and most productive plants and have found ways of improving their yield.

Why are fertilizers good and bad at the same time?

Chemical fertilizers are usually used in agriculture on a large scale. They increase productivity in the short term, but in the long term they can poison the soil.

Fertilizers increase the fertility of the soil by acting as complements to the nutrients needed by plants to grow. Most chemical fertilizers (nitrates and phosphates), at the same time as providing necessary nutrients, become dangerous

Why have insecticides been found in the bodies of polar animals?

This is a consequence of the food chain. Algae absorb toxic waste discharged into the sea. The algae are eaten by fish, which then carry the insecticide in their bodies. At the end of the food chain, these fish are eaten by polar animals.

Algae contaminated by toxic products discharged into the sea are eaten by small fishes and shellfish, which in turn are eaten by larger fishes. Some of these fishes migrate to the polar seas where they are eaten by animals from the ice field, which in turn become contaminated.

What is sea pollution?

All the factors that contribute to the degradation of the sea cause

The Shetland Islands, off the coast of Scotland, were devastated by an oil slick caused by the wreck of the Braer oil tanker in 1992.

pollution: the dumping of sewage and chemical effluent, the over-use of fertilizers, and unchecked land development.

Sea pollution is caused by the dumping of industrial and urban waste as well as by the use of fertilizers. Harmful microorganisms and toxic chemicals contaminate the sea water and damage sea plants and animals. Pollution is also caused by oil tankers that clean their tanks in the sea; by the exploitation of oil fields; and by accidents that cause the spillage of oil or dangerous chemicals at sea. Overdevelopment of coasts (tourist resorts, marinas, and artificial beaches) has led to the extinction of much of the coastal flora and fauna. Tourists leaving trash also cause pollution.

What is the most polluted sea?

The North Sea, because it receives the largest quantities of toxic waste from neighboring countries.

Belgium, France, Germany, Britain, and Holland all discharge waste and sewage water into the North Sea. In addition, two large rivers that run through highly industrialized regions of Germany and France, the Rhine and the Elbe, discharge several thousand tons of toxic metal into it every year (lead, copper, and mercury). The North Sea used to be a rich fishing ground, but today its fauna and flora populations are severely depleted. Neighboring states, however, keep a close eye on it and do their best to improve the situation. In eastern European countries, the Baltic and Caspian seas are very badly polluted and neglected (atomic piles from Soviet submarines lie at the bottom). The Black Sea, too, is polluted and is a threat to the nearby Mediterranean.

What is an

oil slick?

It is the layer of oil covering the surface of the sea after a spillage of oil.

Oil slicks happen when an oil tanker sinks at sea or near a coast, or when oil wells under the sea erupt. Some oil slicks are caused deliberately when oil tankers are cleansed of gases and residue left in their tanks by pouring them out into the sea. The famous oil slicks (the *Torrey Canyon, Amoco Cadiz,* and *Braer*) killed thousands of sea animals (fish, birds, penguins) and destroyed the sea and coastal flora. Specialists have noticed that the sea tends to quickly "digest" these catastrophes. Obviously the dead fauna does not come back to life, but the flora reappears over a period of several months to 10 years. Two years after the Gulf War, the Red Sea, which had been

covered with a layer of oil, had already lost all traces of it. Although these catastrophes were not as damaging as we might have feared, we must not be fooled into thinking that the sea can be used as a dump for toxic products.

What is the

water cycle?

Water is a compound found in three different states: liquid, gas, and solid (ice). Water evaporates from the sea and falls as rain, hail, or snow, then evaporates once again in an endless cycle.

Rainwater comes from droplets that gather into clouds. When it falls, it soaks into the ground. Some sinks deep to replenish the reserves of ground water, and some emerges again in springs, lakes, or rivers. In cold regions and at high altitudes, water solidifies and forms snow and ice. Great rivers of ice, called glaciers, gradually flow toward the sea. As they melt, they release large quantities of fresh water. The action of the Sun and the wind on lakes, rivers, and oceans causes water to evaporate, forming new clouds. The water cycle starts again.

What are

nonrenewable

resources?

These are raw materials and fuels that formed underground during the different stages of the geological evolution of the Earth. It took millions of years for these materials to form. Once they have run out, these resources cannot be replaced.

Metals, minerals, oil, and coal are nonrenewable resources that people extract from the ground and use in industry, construction, and everyday life. Growing demand has led to an increasing consumption of raw materials, with the result that many deposits are running out. Ways to reduce demand are now being sought, as are alternatives, in terms of renewable sources of energy such as the Sun and the wind, and recovering raw materials from recycled waste.

Can oil run out?

Yes, it can, because together with coal, natural gas, and

Transportation of radioactive products is carried out under high security. Here, barrels of radioactive materials, reprocessed in a plant in the Hague, are being loaded on the tanker Akatsukimaru on the way to Japan.

uranium, it is one of the sources of energy in greatest demand. It took millions of years to form, but with increasing demand, deposits will begin to run out.

Oil is a mineral of organic origin. It is composed of hydrocarbons made from plankton and algae that were changed over millions of years by the action of bacteria and heat while buried under the sea. Oil is used for making gasoline and different kinds of fuel, as well as chemicals and plastics. Oil is found in many places, from the Middle East to the Arctic, and oil companies continue to search for new sources. However, exploitation of oil reserves in harsh environments will require more expensive and more sophisticated techniques.

How can the use of oil pollute the atmosphere?

The atmosphere is polluted by gaseous and solid substances that are released into the air. Crude oil is used to make gasoline, combustible gases, and other oils, and contributes this way to air pollution.

Pollution by hydrocarbons is mostly due to oil derivatives. This includes the burning of gases in factories and emissions from cars and trucks. Oil refineries, where certain substances and residues are removed from crude oil, also produce pollution. One of the waste products, carbon dioxide, contributes to the greenhouse effect and thus to global warming.

What are the most dangerous polluting agents?

The most dangerous pollutants are the chemical wastes produced by factories and power stations, and exhaust fumes from the burning of gasoline.

Chemical plants release highly polluting gases derived from toxic acids. These contribute to the greenhouse effect, causing a thermal imbalance that is likely to result in serious climatic change. By releasing toxic gases such as sulfur, lead, and nitrogen dioxides, both factories and power stations are responsible for the acid rain that has destroyed large areas of forest in northern Europe and Canada. The release of mercury into the

water supply is also a serious problem. Transmitted to people by the fish they eat, mercury causes diseases such as cancers and congenital malformations. Pollution in cities is mostly due to the burning of hydrocarbons; this is responsible for respiratory disorders, which are becoming increasingly common and more serious.

What is acid rain?

It is an acidic rainfall, thought to be caused by the release into the atmosphere of fumes from the

In Quebec, Canada, a special rain-collecting device has been set up to analyze the acidity of rain contaminated with acids released into the atmosphere by industry.

burning of fossil fuels. Acid rain is linked with damage to trees and buildings and the killing of wildlife.

Fumes released by burning fossil fuels contain toxic gases. When they come into contact with water vapor, they turn into droplets of acidic water that damage plants. Acid rain is associated with industrialized countries. In North America and Europe, it has resulted in damage to hundreds of acres of forests, since it not only burns adult trees but also young trees and shoots.

What has been the most serious ecological disaster?

At a time when desertification is a serious threat that must somehow be stopped, the Aral Sea, on the boundary between Uzbekistan and Kazakhstan, has lost over half its volume of water. This is because two rivers that used to flow into it have been diverted for irrigation.

The Amu Daria and Syr Daria rivers, which used to flow into the

Aral Sea, were diverted in the 1960s to irrigate land designated for the cultivation of cotton. Since then, the level of the sea has dropped by 45 feet (14 meters), and vast areas of what once was the sea today look like a desert. Moreover, because fresh water no longer flows into it, the water has become saltier. As a result, many species of fish have disappeared, and fish breeding in general has stopped.

Do nuclear plants cause pollution?

They are potentially dangerous because they process radioactive materials. However, they do not pollute the atmosphere since they do not release any toxic gases.

The building, surveillance, and maintenance of nuclear plants are regulated by a set of very rigid regulations that must be enforced at all times, both inside and in the neighborhood of the plants. Strict management of the storage, transportation, and of course manipulation of these substances is required. The smoke rising from nuclear power plants does not contain any radioactive or toxic substances; it is just water vapor produced by the cooling of the reactors.

What happened at Chernobyl?

It was human negligence that caused the explosion and blaze at the Russian nuclear plant in Chernobyl. This disaster resulted in the radioactive pollution of several European countries.

In Chernobyl, in 1986, the biggest nuclear disaster ever to happen, was caused by a combination of building defects, lack of maintenance, and negligence on the part of technicians. A huge cloud of radioactive particles traveled toward northeastern Europe. Where these particles landed, they contaminated the plants and animals that came into contact with them. Many trees had to be cut down, and fruit and vegetables had to be thrown away in order to protect people from contamination. In Scandinavian countries entire herds of deer had to be destroyed.

What happens to radioactive waste?

Most radioactive waste and residue cannot be reprocessed or recycled. It has to be stored in airtight, nondegradable containers and buried deep in the ground.

This is the Russian nuclear plant in Chernobyl, which caused the worst radioactive pollution ever seen when it partially exploded in 1989. The after-effects of the explosion are still being felt today.

It takes hundreds or thousands of years for radioactive materials to become harmless. Nothing can speed up or change this process. Because of this, nuclear waste must be placed in secure, airtight containers. These containers are then stored carefully, sometimes buried in clay or salt mines.

How do animal species become extinct?

Some animal species become extinct because they are hunted by people until they are completely exterminated. Others may become extinct because they are unable to adapt quickly enough to a naturally changing environment.

People are – directly or indirectly – responsible for the extinction of about 5,000 species every year. Uncontrolled hunting and fishing without any regard for reproduction cycles and preservation of species, together with deforestation and the increasing use of land for agriculture and habitation, have greatly reduced the quantity and variety of plants available for herbivorous animals in the natural

The lynx, which used to be common in Europe, has now been completely exterminated in the wild. Attempts at reintroducing it have failed: people continue to hunt them.

environment. Reduction in numbers of these animals leads to a reduction in the numbers of carnivorous animals that feed on them.

Which animals are most at risk?

The animals most at risk are probably the large African mammals. The elephant, hunted for its ivory tusks used for jewelry and various objects, and the white rhinoceros, sought for its horn, could easily disappear in the early

A species threatened with extinction: the aye-aye in Madagascar will soon be unable to find the plants it feeds on.

21st century if poaching does not stop.

The gorillas in the Zairian mountains are hunted for their flesh and fur, and they are also dispatched to zoos and laboratories all over the world. In the Seychelle Islands the crocodile has completely disappeared; it was systematically hunted both for its skin and to free the land from its presence in the 17th and 18th centuries.

What is a predator?

A predator is an animal that hunts, kills, and eats another one (the prey). Some only hunt one single species.

A predator can be harmful to the species that it kills, but it also contributes to keeping a natural biological balance by regulating the animal population. The main predators, such as the wolf, the lynx, the bear, and birds of prey, have been hunted by people for a long time because they killed sheep, goats, and cows. People who live from hunting, fishing, and gathering fruit are also predators.

What is the aim of nature reserves?

Parks and nature reserves first appeared in the U.S. and in Europe in the 19th century. There are now 1,500 of them in the world. They are areas inside which the natural resources, wildlife, and plants specific to a particular region are protected.

With the growth of cities and towns, it has become necessary to protect regions where both animal species and landscape might have been threatened. Nature reserves usually have very tight security, and hunting, fishing, and fruit gathering are forbidden. People from cities go there for hikes and also to explore the sites. Scientists such as geologists, botanists, and ornithologists visit them to study nature. Human intervention is only allowed in nature parks and reserves if it is justified in terms of protection or maintenance (cutting wood, making paths, caring for wildlife and plants).

Is it possible to import species from other countries?

Animal and plant species have been imported by some countries for commercial purposes. Their

introduction is not always successful and can upset a region's ecological balance.

New species can be introduced, but some species of plants and animals imported by people have later escaped into the wild. Parasites, unnoticed in boxes that came from the U.S. after World War II, spread a disease that decimated plane trees in the south of France. The coypu and the muskrat, imported into Europe from the U.S. in the 19th century for their fur, overran the rivers, causing damage to river banks. It is extremely important to make sure that the real needs and the natural environment have been carefully studied before importing species. Nevertheless, introducing new plants has proved very successful with chestnuts, tomatoes, mimosa, and corn.

Cheetahs are predators that do not have a favorite prey. They hunt gnus as well as gazelles.

The first horses were taken to America in the 16th century, after the arrival of the Spanish. They were carried in ships. Some escaped into the wild and formed herds. Some Native American tribes tamed them and began to use them for riding.

in Mauritius. It was hunted for its flesh with such ferocity that there is not a single bird left today. The large penguins in the North Atlantic disappeared in the 19th century. They were hunted for their flesh, which sailors used as bait.

A type of zebra known as the quagga was also hunted to extinction in the 19th century. The quagga, which had a brown body with black and white stripes on its head and neck, was hunted for its meat and skin. A sea mammal known as Stellar's sea cow, a relation of the manatee, was discovered in the Bering Sea in 1741. Killed by sailors for food, they were extinct by 1768.

Have Native Americans always had horses?

The first Native Americans, who walked to that continent across the Bering Strait, had never seen a horse until the start of Spanish colonization.

Has hunting led to the disappearance of any animals?

Some animals have managed to survive in spite of being hunted. Other species have not been as lucky. A famous example is the dodo, a bird that used to live

Which animals benefit from human activities?

Some animals, even though they have not been domesticated, live in the vicinity of humans and feed on what food they can find.

These animals are mostly birds. Pigeons, sparrows, and swallows have adapted remarkably well to life in our cities and rely almost entirely on garbage discarded by people for their food. This is also the case for sea birds, such as seagulls, which live in ports, or those birds that follow trawlers and feed on the remains of fish thrown away by sailors. Rats and mice, in sewers and in cellars, also make the most of the human habitat.

When did rabbits first appear in Australia?

They were imported by English breeders in the 19th century. This triggered off major ecological changes.

Ever since rabbits appeared in Australia, kangaroos have had a hard time finding enough food to survive.

Rabbits managed to escape from captivity and quickly proliferated. They dug underground tunnels and ate plants that were already quite scarce because of drought. The erosion of the ground caused much harm to kangaroos, which are herbivorous mammals. In an attempt to control the proliferation of rabbits, the Australians imported foxes, not knowing that they were putting the smallest species of kangaroos at risk. Some of these have now completely disappeared. The proliferation of rabbits was finally stopped when they were infected with a disease known as myxomatosis. Con- taminated rabbits were accidentally taken to Europe, transmitting the disease to wild rabbits there and nearly causing their extinction.

Is it possible to save an endangered species?

This can be done by passing laws that will either make hunting illegal or at least reduce it. It is also essential to help the species develop safely in protected areas.

Many wild species are protected by an international agreement known as CITES (Convention on International Trade in Endangered Species), signed in 1975. This agreement tries to control trade in wildlife and certain wildlife products. For example, it bans the trade of furs of certain endangered animals, such as tigers and leopards, and the import or export of ivory obtained from the tusks of elephants or rhinoceros horns. Other treaties attempt to protect the habitat in which endangered species live. One of the first of such agreements was the Ramasar Convention, established in 1971 to protect wetlands. Various organizations publish lists of endangered species of animals and plants in an attempt to bring them to the notice of conservationists, politicians, and the general public. Large sea mammals, such as whales, dolphins, and manatees, are protected by international fishing laws. Unfortunately, some people choose to break these laws, and many species are still under threat. The best way of preventing the extinction of a species is by classifying it and introducing it into a nature reserve to allow it to reproduce in safety. A growing number of species of plants and animals are extinct in the wild and live only in captivity in botanical gardens, zoos, and animal research centers. Some of these animals and plants are bred in captivity in the hope of returning them to the wild.

Sea birds, such as gulls, were quick to realize that garbage dumps make excellent restaurants.

What type of trees grow in forests in temperate regions?

There are two main types of forests in temperate regions: forests of broad-leaved trees where the climate is mild and wet; and forests of mixed trees (both broad-leaved trees and conifers) in colder regions. Broad-leaved trees are deciduous (they lose their leaves in winter), whereas conifers are evergreen (they keep their leaves all year round).

The oak and the beech are the largest trees growing in forests. The oak is a hardy tree with lobed leaves and produces acorns. The beech has a straight trunk and white wood; it produces beech nuts, which contain an edible oil. The ash is a tall tree with a grayish-green bark; its wood is white and hard. The birch has white, peeling bark with black spots. All these trees are very common in forests of broad-leaved trees. Under-growth, ferns, and mosses also grow in forests. The conifers in mixed forests are usually pine trees, firs, cedars (very tall with

The taiga is a type of forest that stretches from Canada to Siberia. Above, the border of the Canadian taiga is covered with snow for much of the winter.

spreading branches, and scented resin and wood), and spruce, which is similar in appearance to the fir.

What is a mangrove?

It is a type of plant growth that appears on the swampy coasts of tropical countries.

By sending down aerial roots from their branches, the vegetation in mangroves rapidly forms close-growing mangrove thickets. The vegetation is perfectly adapted to saltwater swamps. Mangroves are rich breeding grounds for animal life: huge insects (mosquitoes, tropical wasps, spiders, ants, butterflies), fish, shellfish, and leeches. There are also reptiles, crocodiles, monkeys, bats, and tropical birds. There are mangroves on islands in Indonesia, in South America and Central America, and in Florida. Unhealthy conditions make mangroves inhospitable, wild areas totally unfit for human habitation.

What is the difference between the steppe and the taiga?

The steppe is the vegetation found in Eurasian semibarren areas, mostly composed of grassy plants and bushes. Taiga refers to the forests of conifers in northern Canada and in Eurasia.

Both words come from the Russian. The steppe is an extensive plain that stretches from Mongolia to the Black Sea. It is covered with a thick layer of grass burnt by the sun in the summer and lashed by freezing winds in winter. It is an inhospitable area to which few animals have become adapted. The species that do live there are rodents, roe deer, and red deer, Saiga antelopes, wild cats, wolves, and a species of crane that nests in the tall grass. The taiga is a much richer area. In spite of a much colder but also more temperate climate, a mixed forest of coniferous (pine, fir, and spruce) and deciduous (birch and larch) trees grow there. Many species live here, of which the largest is the elk, a member of the deer family with a dark coat and flat antlers. Its worst enemy is the wolverine, or carcajou, a carnivore similar in appearance to the bear.

What are typical

Australian animals?

Australia, the largest island in the world, belongs to the continent of Oceania. It straddles two oceans, the Indian Ocean to the west and the Pacific Ocean to the east. Because it is so big, **the climate in Australia is tropical in the north and temperate in the south. This explains the diversity of its fauna and flora.**

The kangaroo is a marsupial with large, powerful hind legs used for leaping, and a long thick tail. During reproduction periods, newly born offspring are suckled

A kangaroo with a young in its pouch. The kangaroo, which is Australia's mascot, does not live anywhere else in the world.

in the mother's pouch. The dingo is a wild dog that is possibly related to the domestic dog. Just like the kangaroo, which it hunts, it can live in barren regions. The temperate regions are home to the koala, a marsupial that feeds on eucalyptus leaves, and the platypus. About 700 bird species live in Australia. These include the lyrebird, multi-colored parakeets, and the kookaburra, whose cries sound like human laughter.

Why are all sorts of strange animals found on islands?

These creatures are likely to have descended from the very first species that populated the Earth. Physically isolated, they have been protected from predators of all kinds that might otherwise have exterminated them. Moreover, because their natural habitat has not changed, they have not had to alter in order to survive.

Species that have developed in isolation include various types of lemur (primitive primates) found on Madagascar in the Indian Ocean and the largest lizard in the world, the Komodo dragon, about 10 feet (3 meters) long, which lives

The Komodo dragon is the largest lizard in the world. It is a member of the family Varanidae and breeds only on Komodo Island and some of the neighboring Lesser Sunda Islands of Indonesia.

Coral reefs at low tide in Queensland, Australia.

on Komodo Island and a few neighboring Indonesian islands. On the Galápagos Islands, on the equator, unique marine iguanas 3 to 6 feet (1–2 meters) long and huge tortoises can be found, slight differences existing between species on different islands.

Where are there coral reefs?

Coral forms in warm seas. It is made of tiny animals that congregate and form reefs or atolls, ring-shaped islands around lagoons.

Corals grow in clear water, fairly near the surface to take advantage of the daylight essential to their growth. Coral reefs can be found in temperate seas, such as the Mediterranean, off Corsica and north of Africa. However, they are found mostly in warm, shallow, tropical seas. The most impressive coral reefs are found in the Caribbean (West Indies); in the Pacific Ocean (Polynesia, Africa); and in the Indian Ocean (Australia, the Philippines). The largest coral reef in the world is the Great Barrier Reef of Australia, which is about 1,200 miles (2,000 kilometers) long. A large coral barrier also stretches

across the sea near Venezuela, in the Atlantic Ocean.

Why are corals endangered?

Coral reefs shelter a very diverse flora and fauna. Many fishes come for food and shelter. However, they are put at risk by fishermen and divers.

Tourism and the jewelry trade are a serious threat to corals. Pollution also threatens the life of coral reefs and their inhabitants.

Great Events in World History

Why were the first tools made of stone?

The first people were capable of making tools, but only from materials that were at hand. Stones existed everywhere, so it was simply a matter of gathering them. Tools have been found that are as much as 500,000 years old.

Before learning how to make tools, humans used stones in their rough state. Then some humans began to look for stones suitable for specific uses and to break and reshape them. Later they refined the making of tools, using flint, which can easily be cut into all sorts of shapes. Our ancestors shaped flints with small rocks, and before long learned to fashion flint knives and arrowheads.

Why was the discovery of fire so important?

The discovery of fire was one of the most important developments in the history of humanity. People could now live with the benefits of heat and light. Fire also protected them, keeping wild animals at a distance.

No one can say when or how our ancestors discovered fire, but we know that the first hearths appeared in Europe between 450,000 and 380,000 years ago. This was a major discovery. People were no longer condemned to darkness at night, but could gather around the fire with their families and clans. When they realized that it was possible to carry fire with them, using torches, our ancestors were able to venture deeper into caves in search of more sheltered places to live. People had less to fear from animals, because fire kept wild beasts at a distance. They no longer had to eat their food raw, but began to cook. In addition, fire made it possible to smoke meat in order to preserve it.

When Columbus set foot on Watling Island (now San Salvador Island) in the Bahamas, he could not have known it was an event that would change the world.

Agriculture began to be developed during the Neolithic period. Like the discovery of fire, this was a development that dramatically changed the life of mankind.

Around 4500 B.C. farmers discovered abundant minerals in Iran and in southern Spain. It was during this period that bronze (an alloy of copper and tin) was first made. Bronze Age farmers dug copper out of rocks with wooden picks and stone hammers. Using their knowledge of fire, they heated the mineral to its melting point (around 1,980°F/1,080°C) and added an appropriate proportion of tin (and, later on, other metals) to the copper. The mixture was poured into molds to make a variety of objects.

How did humans discover the importance of metals?

Around 4500 B.C. our ancestors discovered how to extract copper from rocks by the process of smelting. They quickly realized that they could also work other metals that become malleable when heated.

The discovery of metalworking was in fact the last of a long series of steps beginning with the mastery of fire. It was only in the Neolithic period (New Stone Age), once our ancestors had learned to mine flint, that they became capable of extracting and making use of other minerals.

Who were the first people to make alloys?

The first known blacksmiths were the Hittites, who lived in Anatolia in central Turkey. They discovered how to make alloys around 3000 B.C.

For metalworking to exist on any scale, metals must be abundant.

When did farming begin?

Agriculture began in the Neolithic period (New Stone Age), when people started to settle and establish villages, undoubtedly encouraged by the onset of a milder climate. Around 6000 B.C. people began to cultivate grain, such as wheat, and to domesticate and raise animals.

The first farmers appeared in the Middle East, in the region known as the Fertile Crescent. Gradually nomadic populations that were too concentrated in certain areas sought new lands and settled on them. To grow crops and raise animals meant remaining in one place, which in turn gave rise to the need for more permanent forms of shelter – and so the first simple houses were built.

Who were the first merchants?

Written records tell us that in Mesopotamia there were important commercial exchanges between fairly distant cities. As roads and canals did not exist, long-distance trade remained an activity of the government, and only some of the population were involved.

The Sumerian king Gudea imported precious materials to build his temple, such as cedar wood from Syria and gold from the Indus Valley. Only kings could afford such luxuries. Cities did, however, exchange basic merchandise.

What was the first great battle?

The first great battle we know of took place in Sumer around 2500 B.C., between the cities of Uma and Lagash.

Questions of territorial limits have always posed problems. In addition, the riches of one city could provoke the envy of another and create the risk of invasion. Uma and Lagash had disputed a frontier for many years. In the end, Eannatum, the king of Lagash, crushed his rival. Proud of this exploit, he had an account of his victory engraved on a stele (column), which is one of the first written records.

Who were the first great navigators?

The Phoenicians were both enterprising merchants and remarkable sailors. They traded throughout the Mediterranean from the 12th century B.C. until the 1st century B.C.

The name Phoenician (meaning reddish brown) came from the color of their skin and the famous purple dye they used for coloring fabrics. Their main ports were Byblos, Tyre, and Sidon, along the coast of modern Lebanon and Syria. The Phoenicians knew how to carve ivory and used sand to make beautiful glass. Their ships carried all sorts of merchandise – Spanish metals, Greek vases, and Egyptian linen.

The Phoenicians were renowned as traders throughout the Mediterranean, from as early as the 12th century B.C. up to the 1st century B.C.

What kind of government did Sumer have?

The Sumerian civilization, which flourished in Mesopotamia during the 3rd millennium B.C., revolved around two authorities: the religious authority, whose center of power was based in a superb tiered temple (the *ziggurat*), and a warrior king who inhabited an equally splendid palace.

Although agriculture and animal husbandry played important roles, Sumer was above all an urban civilization, with a military monarchy. It originated in the 4th millennium B.C. as a loose association of about a dozen independent city-states, consisting of fortified cities surrounded by villages. Because of the frequent wars between the cities and the threat of "barbarian" invasions, the king of each city-state maintained a standing army reinforced when necessary by a peasant militia. Archeological remains reveal that the Sumerian army was composed of chariots supported by light infantry, plus heavy infantry who advanced in tight formation.

Almost all the early civilizations went through a period where animal (and even human) sacrifice was common. In this scene, dating from the 3rd millennium B.C., a ram is being sacrificed by Sumerian priests.

When did the Semites arrive in Sumer?

The country was colonized three times. Around 4500 B.C. peasants developed a rural civilization. Soon afterward the Semites (another people of the Middle East, from the Syrian Desert) arrived. The Sumerians (a non-Semitic people) arrived last, between 3500 and 3000 B.C.

Around 3000 B.C. Mesopotamia, the area between the Tigris and Euphrates rivers (now part of Iraq), was divided into two regions: Akkad to the north, Sumer in the south. The fusion of these peoples brought about the flowering of the Sumerian civilization. The Semites blended with the existing population. Thanks to the survival of clay tablets inscribed with cuneiform writing, we know a great deal about life in Sumer.

Why did the Minoan civilization vanish?

The island of Crete had a brilliant and refined civilization, of which numerous remains can still be seen. It was destroyed by a violent volcanic eruption.

Archeologists divide Cretan civilization into three periods: the prehistoric period, or ancient Minoan (2600–2100 B.C.), middle Minoan (2100–1600 B.C.), and late Minoan (1600–1400 B.C.). In 1400 B.C. the Santorin volcano wrecked the island of Crete and put a sudden end to its splendid civilization. Crete was subsequently settled by Greek colonists. Enough remains from the Minoan civilization have survived to make it possible to reconstruct the life of its people.

When was the first Egyptian kingdom founded?

The first kingdom is said to have been founded by the legendary Pharaoh Menes around 3000 B.C.

The history of Egypt spans five millennia, beginning in the Copper Age when tribes settled on the banks of the Nile. At the end of the prehistoric period, around the time when hieroglyphic writing developed, two states disputed power in the Nile Valley. In the kingdom of Lower Egypt (the area around the Nile delta), the inhabitants worshipped the god and goddess Osiris and Isis and their son Horus, whereas the kingdom of Upper Egypt in the south favored the cult of Seth, the god of evil. Pharaoh Menes is said to have united the two kingdoms around 3000 B.C., thus founding the first of the 31 dynasties of pharaohs that ruled ancient Egypt. He is said to have adopted the *pschent*, the red-and-white headdress worn by the pharaohs, to symbolize the union of the two crowns.

What did Akhenaton's reforms consist of?

Pharaoh Amenhotep IV (1372–1354 B.C.) established a new religion in Egypt with a single deity, the Sun god Aton. After doing so, he took the name Akhenaton ("he who pleases Aton").

At this time, life at the Egyptian court was luxurious and the arts flourished. The previous kings, his father Amenhotep III and grandfather Tuthmosis IV, had succeeded in keeping the Egyptian kingdom intact despite wars and conspiracies. Akhenaton did not

The burial of a pharaoh was accompanied by complex ceremonies. The sarcophagus was placed in the middle of the pharaoh's most precious possessions.

The mastery of metallurgy was to have a profound impact on human history. Ancient Egyptian blacksmiths were renowned for their skills.

future city of Alexandria. When Alexander died, in 323 B.C., one of his generals became ruler of Egypt under the name of Ptolemy I and founded a long dynasty. The era of the pharaohs was over: Egypt was Greek for three centuries, before falling under the rule of Rome. Nevertheless, the Egyptian Empire had deeply influenced Crete and, later, the Greeks.

feel drawn to a religion that worshipped many gods. So, with his wife, Queen Nefertiti, he established a cult devoted solely to Aton – one that required neither priests nor images. In so doing, he earned the enmity of the priests of Amun, the great god of the Egyptian capital, Thebes. Akhenaton therefore moved the capital from Thebes to Armana. His reforms did not survive him. The priests of Amun made Akhenaton's successor change his name from Tutankhaton to Tutankhamun.

What put an end to Egyptian splendor?

Around 1050 B.C. Egypt entered into a period of decadence, marked by conflicts and wars, that was to last for more than seven centuries, up to 332 B.C.

Royal power weakened, and the governors of the *nomes* (administrative districts) became more and more independent. In addition, the priests of Amun became more powerful than ever. From the 21st to the 30th dynasty, invasions and civil wars followed one after another. The south struggled with the north in an unending war, and the Assyrians invaded Egypt three times. In 332 B.C. Alexander the Great was greeted as a liberator. Throwing his white cape to the ground, he indicated the site of the

What ended the kingdom of Israel?

Israel and Jerusalem were invaded time after time. Finally, the Romans reduced Jerusalem to ruins and dispersed the population, many of whom became slaves.

The first king of Israel was Saul. He was followed by David (1010–970 B.C.), who was succeeded by his son Solomon (970–933 B.C.). After Solomon's death, the kingdom was divided into two – the northern kingdom (Israel) and the southern one (Judah). But the kingdoms were doomed. In 722 B.C. Israel was invaded by the Assyrians, who deported 28,000 of the inhabitants. Judah survived until 597 B.C. when Nebuchadnezzar, king of Babylon, reduced it to submission. Ten years later he destroyed Jerusalem and took most of the population into captivity in Babylonia. In 539 B.C. the Persian king Cyrus the Great captured Babylon and allowed the Jews to return from exile. After a succession of rulers, including the Egyptians and the Seleucids (from Syria), in 63 B.C. the Roman general Pompey captured Jerusalem and created the Roman province of Judaea. In 66 A.D. the inhabitants rose against the Romans, who in 70 A.D. razed Jerusalem to the ground. The fall of the fortress of Masada marked the end of the rebellion: the 953 Jewish patriots defending it committed suicide rather than surrender.

The Bible relates that when Moses led the Jewish people to the promised land, the Red Sea divided to let them pass. As yet no one has come up with a scientific explanation for such an event.

What was the

Diaspora?

If vast numbers of people leave their own country and end up scattered throughout the world, that is known as a *diaspora* (Greek for scattering or dispersal).

After the future emperor Titus crushed the Jewish rebellion against the Romans in 70 A.D., thousands of Jews were carried off into slavery all over the world. Today the name "the Diaspora" also means all the Jewish communities of the world outside Israel.

What were the

Persian Wars?

These conflicts between the Greeks and the Persian Empire lasted from 499 to 479 B.C. They began when Athens decided to help the Greek cities of Asia Minor throw off Persian rule.

At first Darius, king of the Persians, was victorious and savagely crushed the city of Miletus, on the coast of Asia Minor, in 494 B.C. He then attacked Athens. However, although their army was smaller, the Athenians won a remarkable victory at Marathon, in 490 B.C., suffering few casualties while the Persians lost over 6,000 soldiers.

To avenge this defeat, Darius's son Xerxes launched the Second Persian War and invaded Greece. The Greeks failed to stop the Persians at Thermopylae, and Athens was captured and burned. However, thanks to the ingenious strategy of the Athenian leader, Themistocles, the Persian fleet was defeated at Salamis in 480 B.C. Next year, at Mycale, the Greeks inflicted a final defeat on the Persian fleet.

Which was the first

great naval battle?

One of the first great naval battles of which we have details was the Greek victory over the Persian

fleet off the island of Salamis in September of 480 B.C.

The opening phase of the Second Persian War had gone badly for the Greeks. The bodyguard of the Spartan king, Leonidas, just 300 strong, managed to hold the mountain pass of Thermopylae for three days so the main Greek force could retreat. But this did not stop the Persians from marching to Athens and burning the Acropolis. It was at this point that the Greeks, led by Themistocles, won their victory at Salamis, destroying 200 enemy ships. The Persian king, Xerxes, withdrew, leaving behind an army that was defeated a year later at Plataea. The courage of the Greeks at Salamis was celebrated in *The Persians*, a tragedy by the dramatist Aeschylus staged in Athens in 472 B.C.

Why were Sparta and Athens rivals?

During the Persian Wars, the two cities were united by a common enemy, but later Sparta was reluctant to accept Athenian power. Moreover, the two cities were governed differently. Sparta had a military regime, while the Athens government was much more liberal.

As early as the 7th century B.C. Athens was a flourishing commercial center. Its port, Piraeus, received merchandise from all over the Mediterranean. Athens was also a political power. Democracy had developed – partly thanks to the city's increasingly rich and powerful commercial class, which pressed for greater civil rights. The harsh laws of Draco (625 B.C.) reformed the system of justice; those of Solon (594 B.C.) granted power to an assembly of free men. The Assembly gave each male citizen the chance to voice his opinions, though women and slaves had no role in public life. Athens – especially during the 5th century, when it became a center for philosophers, artists, poets, and dramatists – remains the source of many of our ideas about democracy and the classical culture.

Sparta was ruled by an aristocracy directly descended from Dorian invaders. Since the 9th century B.C. it had been organized as a military oligarchy (a state governed by a small group of people). The Spartans were obsessed with military virtues. Women were not thought important, and female infants were often left to die. Spartan children received a narrow education that emphasized one sole value: service to their country. At the age of seven, boys were sent to barracks to begin their military training. At 20 they were enrolled in the army, where they were expected to serve until the age of 60.

In the 5th century B.C. the Peloponnesian War (431–404 B.C.) broke out between Sparta and

Leonidas, king of Sparta, died fighting, with 300 of his soldiers, at the Battle of Thermopylae in 480 B.C.

Athens. The Spartans emerged victorious, but after a brief period of power they were defeated by the Theban general Epaminondas, at the Battle of Leuctra, in 371 B.C. The expansion of Macedon, under Philip II and Alexander the Great, ended Sparta's influence. They were absorbed into the Roman Empire in 146 B.C., and the city was later destroyed by the Visigoths in the 4th century A.D.

Who unified Greece?

Philip II, king of Macedon and father of Alexander the Great, succeeded in extending his power over the whole of Greece by exercising political skills as well as military means.

A small kingdom at the northern end of the Greek peninsula, Macedon had been crushed by the power of Sparta, Athens, and Thebes. When Philip gained the throne, at the age of 23, he was faced with huge problems. A fearless soldier, he succeeded in molding the Macedonian army into a force totally devoted to its leader. But he was also a skilled politician who knew how to negotiate. In 356 B.C. Philip annexed the

The Etruscans preceded the Romans in Italy. They have left us many remarkable works of art, such as this jewelry box in bronze.

gold and silver mines of Mount Pangaeus in Thrace. Later he manipulated discord among the Greeks in order to impose his own authority. By doing so, he established a durable peace in Greece. An admirer of Greek culture, he invited numerous Greek artists and scholars to his court, including Aristotle, who served as tutor to his son, Alexander. In 336 B.C. Philip was planning a war against the Persians (long-time enemies of the Greeks) when he was assassinated, the victim of a conspiracy organized by his wife. He was succeeded by Alexander, aged 20, who was already well prepared in the arts of government and war.

What did the Etruscans pass on to the Romans?

The Etruscans preceded the Romans in Italy, settling there around the 8th century B.C. Their influence was felt in religion, architecture, and politics.

The Romans preserved Etruscan culture in a variety of ways. For example, the purple toga worn by Roman emperors and the toga worn by Roman officials were of Etruscan origin. The Etruscan art of divination was practiced by the Romans. Following established principles, specialized priests studied the entrails of sacrificed animals and the flight of birds to predict the future. The Roman atrium – the interior courtyard around which the rooms of a house were grouped – was also Etruscan in origin, as were the arch, the dome, and vaulted ceilings. The Etruscans had a highly developed civilization. Artefacts – frescoes, sculptures, statuettes, jewelry, mirrors, and many other objects – have survived to testify to the richness of their artistic tradition. But no one has yet been able to decipher their writing.

Why did the Romans destroy Carthage?

In the 3rd century B.C. two great powers, Rome and Carthage, vied for control of the Mediterranean. In 218 B.C. Hannibal's Carthaginian army invaded Italy. The Romans resolved to repel the invasion and to destroy Carthage itself.

Hannibal crossed the Pyrenees and the Alps with his soldiers riding on elephants. Rome feared his arrival, but Hannibal was not equipped to besiege Rome. The war dragged on, and in the south of Italy, the Carthaginian army gradually weakened. In 210 B.C. a young Roman general, Publius Cornelius Scipio, was given the task of driving the Carthaginians from Spain. Scipio captured Carthago Nova (now Cartagena), a fortified city. He then defeated Hannibal's brother, Hasdrubal, at Baetula in 209 B.C. Thus Spain fell under Roman rule. Scipio realized the only way to entice Hannibal from Italy was to attack his home city, and declared "Carthage must be destroyed." His army of 30,000 men crossed into Africa and went

The Gauls were deeply religious. One of their most important rituals was the gathering of mistletoe by the druids.

from victory to victory. In 203 B.C. 60,000 Carthaginians died when his army set fire to two camps. Alarmed by Scipio's success, the Carthaginians recalled Hannibal. In 202 B.C. he was defeated at Zama, surrounded by Roman troops. Scipio imposed harsh terms on Carthage. The city was made to give up its overseas possessions and was forbidden to take any military action without authorization from Rome. It was also forced to pay indemnities, in silver, and surrender its elephants and galleys. Scipio returned in triumph to Rome.

Where did the Gauls come from?

The Gauls were Celts, a people who probably originated in southwestern Germany. They settled mainly in the northeast of the area that is now France, the rest of which was already inhabited by the Basques, the Iberians, and the Ligurians.

From the Bronze Age, the Gauls migrated gradually, in successive waves, at first filtering into an area then arriving in greater numbers. Around 250 B.C. the Belgae, the last of the Celtic tribes to emigrate, settled in the Rhône Valley and Languedoc. By the late 3rd century B.C. the area later known as France was inhabited by Celts and populations with which they had merged.

What was life like in Gaul?

When the Romans colonized **Gaul** (today's **France**), the Gauls were not a barbaric people but a well-organized society.

Although the tribe was the basic element of political life among the Gauls, the family was of great importance. The authority of the father was paramount – but women also played important roles and were considered equal to men. The Gauls were a religious people who believed in the immortality of the soul. The druids (their priests) taught that death did not exist and life on earth was a passage to eternity. The Gauls developed agriculture and various farming implements. The Celts also developed industries such as metalwork, glassmaking, and the manufacture of clothing. Not much is known about their language as their literary tradition was oral. Their art is characterized by a taste for geometric forms.

Why was the leader of the Gauls defeated?

In 52 B.C. Julius Caesar, believing Gaul to be tranquil, left for Italy. The Gauls, led by Vercingetorix, took advantage of the Roman departure to mount a revolt. Forced back on the town of Alesia, Vercingetorix was caught in a siege, from which he could not escape because the Romans had built a double wall, 9 miles (15 kilometers) long.

For six years, between 58 and 52 B.C., Julius Caesar marched across Gaul. But reacting against harsh Roman rule, the Gauls rebelled under Vercingetorix. The capture of Avaricum (Bourges) forced the leader of the Gauls to fall back to the Auvergne. Despite a victory at Gergovia, he became trapped in the town of Alesia, surrounded by Roman troops. He is said to have taken his best weapons and thrown them at Caesar's feet. His surrender marked the end of the Gauls' bid to regain their independence, and a Gallo-Roman civilization was born that lasted for 300 years.

What were the "Germanic invasions"?

Attracted by the riches of Roman Empire, from time to time "barbarian" peoples invaded Italy and Gaul.

Defeated at Alesia, Vercingetorix threw down his weapons at Julius Caesar's feet in surrender. He was taken to Rome, where he died in prison.

Rome was a magnet to tribes from central and eastern Europe: the Saxons, the Franks, the Vandals, and the Burgundians from the Upper Danube. During the reign of Marcus Aurelius (A.D. 121–80) the Roman Empire was threatened by pressures from these German peoples. Later, in the middle of the 4th century, the Huns (a nomadic people from Central Asia) thundered westward. The Goths, who had converted to Christianity, comprised the Ostrogoths, who struck out toward the plains of Hungary, and the Visigoths, who ended their exploits in Aquitaine, France. Alaric, leader of the Visigoths, hesitated before attacking Rome (which he did in A.D. 410), having no wish to see "a city that had ruled a great part of the world for 1,000 years sacked by an army of foreigners."

The Franks, who occupied the northeast of the land that later became France, were excellent warriors.

After Saint Peter's crucifixion, in A.D. 64, his successors stayed in Rome – except between 1309 and 1376, when there were rival popes in Rome and Avignon. The authority of the pope came to be disputed by the eastern Orthodox Church. In the 11th century the patriarch of Constantinople – regarded by Rome as an archbishop – presented himself as the pope's rival, leading to a division between the eastern and western churches.

Why is Rome the seat of the pope?

Jesus entrusted Saint Peter to establish the Christian Church, and he is regarded as the first pope or head of the Church. To spread the teachings of Christ, Saint Peter traveled to many parts of the Roman Empire and settled in Rome.

Why did the Western Roman Empire collapse?

The Roman Empire grew so large that it was difficult to control. In addition, Roman life had become increasingly soft, which made the empire easy prey.

In the west, the frontiers seemed to burst open everywhere. The empire might have been able to withstand isolated attacks, but it was overwhelmed by the many barbarian invasions. In A.D. 410 the Visigoths pillaged Rome. Then in 476, Odoacer, chief of a Germanic tribe (the Heruli), seized control of the city. Numerous other tribal leaders carved out kingdoms from the remains of the empire. The Vandals settled in North Africa, the Visigoths in Spain, the Franks in Belgium and northern Gaul, the Burgundians in the valleys of the Saône and Rhône, the Lombardians around the River Po, and the Angles and Saxons in Britain.

How did the heritage of antiquity survive?

After the invasions that caused the collapse of the Roman Empire, the Christian Church played an important part in preserving the cultural heritage of the classical world.

By destroying the idols of the Romans' gods and the cult of the emperor, the Church contributed to the decline of the empire. But it also Christianized the barbarians and passed on to them much of the Roman culture. The tribes that invaded western Europe did not impose their cultures on the region: the barbarian kings issued their edicts in Latin and kept the existing administrative institutions.

What was the Eastern Roman Empire?

In A.D. 330 the Emperor Constantine established his new capital, Constantinople, on the western shore of the strait of Bosphorus. The "new Rome" was built on the site of Byzantium, itself an ancient city in Turkey. This was the start of the Eastern Roman Empire, which was to survive for a thousand years after the fall of the western empire.

For more than 11 centuries Constantinople was the beacon of the Eastern Roman Empire, until 1453, when it was captured by the Turks. Although the Eastern Empire experienced confused and difficult periods, several emperors achieved prosperity and glory. Of these perhaps the greatest was Justinian I, who ruled from A.D. 527 to 565. During his reign, Constantinople dominated the Mediterranean and prospered. From the 9th to the 11th century a series of emperors restored the city to the glory it had known under Justinian. During this time, the golden age of the Eastern Empire, the capital had over a million inhabitants.

Who were the Franks?

The Franks, like the Celts before the Roman conquest, were a rough-mannered people who lived in tribes.

Good fighters, their weapons were short-handled axes and heavy iron javelins. Brought within the Roman Empire as a bulwark against invasions from the east, the Franks did not halt these invasions and themselves settled in Gaul.

How was France founded?

Clovis, a young Frankish chief with a taste for power

In A.D. 496 Clovis, the king of the Franks who united France, became Christian. He was baptized by Remigius, bishop of Reims, on Christmas Day.

and **pageantry, began the unification that produced the kingdom of France.**

When Clovis became king of the Salian Franks (now Belgium), in A.D. 481, at the age of 15, Gaul was divided into four principalities: the kingdom of the Visigoths in the southwest (now the Provence region of France); the kingdom of the Burgundians in the east; the domain of Syagrius (the last Roman ruler in Gaul) at the center; and the domain of the Franks in the northeast. Clovis resolved to unite all the Franks living in Gaul. In 486 he defeated Syagrius at Soissons, then in 507 curbed the power of the Visigoths, killing their leader, Alaric II, at the Battle of Vouillé.

Clovis gained control of most of France and made Paris his capital.

When did the great period of Arab expansion begin?

The Islamic religion – founded by Muhammad, who proclaimed the existence of a single God, named Allah – was to cement Arab unity. After the prophet's death in A.D. 632, Islam became an irresistible conquering force.

Within 10 years of Muhammad's death, the Arabs had conquered a great part of the Middle East, including Syria, Mesopotamia, and Egypt. They then swept across Persia. In 642 the Umayyad dynasty established itself at Baghdad, which became the capital of the Muslim empire. The invaders appeared to be invincible and made themselves masters of the Mediterranean basin. They did not succeed, however, in conquering Constantinople. The Arabs then targeted North Africa and in 670 founded the holy city of Kairouan, in Tunisia. Finally, they crossed the Strait of Gibraltar into Spain in Europe.

Who halted the Arab invasion of Europe?

In A.D. 711 the Arabs sacked the Iberian peninsula and Visigoth rule crumbled. The invaders (Moors or Saracens) continued north until Charles Martel stopped them at Poitiers, France, in 732.

The Arab invasion of Europe was halted by the Frankish leader Charles Martel at the Battle of Poitiers in A.D. 732.

After conquering Spain, the Moors marched into southwestern France, where they spread

The Vikings (or Norsemen) sailed from Scandinavia in the long ships. They established colonies in Normandy and in parts of the British Isles.

destruction. Narbonne was taken, Toulouse besieged, and Nîmes and Carcassonne pillaged. The Moors took the Rhône valley in central France without resistance. The Franks then regrouped their forces under Charles Martel (grandfather of Charlemagne) and Eudes, Prince of Aquitaine, crushing the Arab army in seven days. The Moors withdrew to Spain, establishing the emirate of Córdoba, which for 200 years would rival the power of the caliphate of Baghdad. Charles Martel's victory prevented the Arabs from continuing north and also signaled the growing power of the Frankish people.

What ended the

Byzantine Empire?

After outliving the Western Empire by a thousand years, the Eastern Roman, or Byzantine, Empire disappeared, wrecked by the Crusaders and threatened by the Serbs and by the Turks, who captured the capital in 1453.

After its inauguration in A.D. 330 by Emperor Constantine, Constantinople was to alternate between periods of glory and confusion. From the 9th to the 11th century the Byzantium Empire flourished. The Crusades worsened relations between western Europe and the Byzantine Empire. The Fourth Crusade became an exercise in conquest and pillage. On April 12, 1204, Constantinople was attacked. When Palaeologus retook his capital in 1261, the empire

was weakened and only survived for two more centuries. Despite the resistance of Constantine XI, on May 29, 1453, Constantinople was seized by the Ottoman Turks under Mehmet the Conqueror, who renamed it Istanbul. The sacking of the city continued for three days, and thousands of inhabitants were taken into slavery. It became the capital of the Ottoman Empire.

Who were the

Vikings?

The Vikings (or Norsemen) originated in Scandinavia. They plowed the oceans for more than 400 years, from the 8th to the 11th century A.D.

Audacious sailors, the Vikings sailed on drakkars (warships) about 65 feet (20 meters) in length. These "long ships" were highly decorated, often with figures representing terrifying beasts mounted on the prow. Warriors, navigators, and traders, the Vikings sailed from Russia to the Atlantic. Under Eric the Red they discovered Greenland, where they established a colony whose population swelled to 10,000 by the end of the 12th century.

Why did Normandy get its name from the Norsemen?

The Norwegians, Danes, and Swedes were adventurous traders as well as intrepid sailors. They touched the coasts of many parts of western Europe and visited its ports and trading cities. They traded furs, amber, and reindeer horn for silks, glassware, and weapons. The Vikings seized Nantes in 843 and spread into the center of France.

Louis the Pious, king of France, tried to hold off the Norsemen but could not stop the invaders. Paris was pillaged several times between A.D. 845 and 887. Germany, England, and Italy all suffered the ravages of the Vikings. Around the year 900 the appearance of a Danish fleet forced the king of France, Charles the Simple, to negotiate with the Norse leader Rollo. The region of France known since that time as Normandy was given to Rollo in exchange for recognizing Charles as his feudal overlord.

A Viking tribe from Sweden called the Varangians settled in Russia. One of their leaders, Rurik, was elected king of the Slavs in A.D. 861.

Who were the Magyars?

In the mid-9th century A.D. Asiatic horsemen appeared by the Black Sea, just as the Huns had done 500 years before. They were the Magyars, the founders of the kingdom of Hungary.

These nomads, having crossed much of central Europe, settled in the region of Hungary now known as the Great Plain, through which flow the Danube and Tisza rivers. They settled there, under a chief named Arpad, in A.D. 896. But the Magyars were used to adventure and for more than 50 years launched raids on parts of Europe. Italy and Germany suffered greatly from their attacks. In 955 the

Hungarians attacked in strength. A chronicler relates: "They were so numerous that they seemed invincible, save if the Earth were to swallow them up or the sky collapse over their heads." Nevertheless, the German king Otto I inflicted a decisive defeat on the invaders at the Battle of Lechfeld. The Hungarians withdrew to the Great Plain, and their raids ceased. In A.D. 1000 Stephen I became the first king of Hungary.

How did Otto I become Holy Roman Emperor?

Henry the Fowler, Duke of Saxony and from A.D. 919 king of Germany, wanted

to revive the tradition of a powerful Holy Roman Empire once promoted by Emperor Charlemagne. But Henry died in 936, just as he was about to claim the crown. Twenty-six years later his son, Otto I, received the imperial crown, which had not been worn since 924.

Supported by the Church, the dukes of Saxony had achieved preeminence among the peoples who constituted the kingdom of Germany. Otto proved to be a powerful protector of Christianity, safeguarding the autonomy of Rome and the papal states. In return, in February 962 he received the imperial crown from the hands of Pope John XII in Rome and was hailed as Emperor and Augustus, as Constantine and Charlemagne had been.

Who was the first czar of Russia?

Russia emerged as a recognizable state at the end of the 9th century A.D., but the czars did not appear until seven centuries later.

Between the 9th and the 16th century Russia underwent many difficult periods. Its first leaders, Oleg and Igor, rose to power in Kiev. Igor's son Sviatoslav (who reigned from 962 to 972) became the founder of the first Russian state, which adopted Christianity, under Vladimir, around 988. In the 12th century Mongol invasions spread terror throughout Russia. Kiev was completely destroyed in 1240, and Moscow was burned to the ground. The Mongols dominated the principalities of Russia and forced the Russians to pay them tributes. The last of the Mongol invaders, Tamerlane, king of Samarkand, sacked Moscow in 1382. In 1547, at the age of 17, Ivan IV adopted the title Czar of the Russias. His cruelty earned him the name Ivan the Terrible. He massacred more than 1,000 of the Russian nobles, the Boyars, to force the rest into submission. In 1552 Ivan retook Kazan from the Tartars, and in 1556 annexed Astrakhan. Although driven back from the Baltic Sea by the Swedes, he extended his empire east beyond the Ural Mountains by annexing Siberia in 1581.

What was meant by chivalry?

Knights were warriors who fought in groups for a

Knights were the great heroes of the Middle Ages. They had to vow that they would follow the teachings of the Church and defend the weak.

common cause. Chivalry – the code of conduct and principles of knighthood – played a major role from the 9th to the 15th century.

Knights belonged to the nobility. From a very early age the future knight was initiated in the arts of war. He accompanied his father on the hunt and participated in tournaments. After completing his education, the apprentice-knight received his helmet and armor. A knight had to pledge himself to honor the teachings of the Church and to defend the poor and the weak. He became a knight in a ceremony called "dubbing" in which the knight received his chivalric name and was given his sword.

Why were castles built?

Castles were erected for defensive purposes. Most of them were built on elevated ground – which hampered attack and made it difficult for would-be assailants to approach unobserved.

In northern Europe in the Middle Ages, vassals had to obey their lord, and in return he had to protect them. So, although the lords built these strongholds for their own protection, in times of unrest the peasants and serfs who were their subjects could seek refuge within the castle walls. The first stone castles appeared in the 11th century, with massive ramparts and high battlements from which defenders could rain down arrows and boiling oil on attackers below. Just as the castle seemed to be being perfected as a means of defense, more and more powerful methods of attack were developed – such as artillery. Consequently, during the Renaissance many castles were transformed into palaces or stately homes.

Why did Christians join the Crusades?

At the time of the Crusades (which lasted for almost two centuries), Jerusalem was held by the Turks. In order to liberate the "city of Christ," volunteers set out in great numbers. It was believed that all who died during a Crusade would go straight to heaven.

However, there were other, less holy, motives, such as a thirst for

The Fourth Crusade set out for Jerusalem, but ended up pillaging Constantinople (above) in 1204.

The proclaimed goal of the Crusades was to liberate the tomb of Christ in Jerusalem from the Muslims. The Crusaders entered the Holy City in 1099.

conquest. The rich principalities of northern Italy, such as Genoa and Venice, wanted the Mediterranean swept clean of Muslim fleets. The papacy wanted to recover formerly Christian lands. In addition, the Crusades provided a means of redirecting the energies of rebellious barons. There were five main Crusades between 1096 and 1272, plus several lesser ones. Many Crusaders did not survive these expeditions. The Turks, disease, heat, and hardship decimated them. Ahead of the main First Crusade a mass of people, the "People's Crusade," set out without proper equipment or provisions, and were almost completely wiped out. Some of the Crusaders returned with new literary and artistic ideas, thanks to their contact with Arab civilization.

What did Magna Carta achieve?

Magna Carta (the Great Charter) was a document designed to limit the power of the English crown. Written in Latin and consisting of 62 articles, it was imposed on King John by aggrieved barons, with the backing of the Church.

Signed by the king at Runnymede, near Windsor, on June 15, 1215, the charter was designed to protect the interests of the nobility, the clergy, and the middle classes, but it did nothing for the serfs, who formed the majority of the population. However, it did specify that no freeman should be arrested without reason or imprisoned without trial. The Magna Carta eventually came to be regarded as a symbol of individual freedom and even as a forerunner of the Declaration of the Rights of Man issued by the French Assembly in 1789 at the outset of the French Revolution.

Why were the Jews persecuted in the Middle Ages?

Although Christianity had evolved from Judaism, in medieval times many Christians believed that the death of Christ had been sought by the Jewish people as a whole – rather than a small faction closely associated with the Roman government of Judaea.

In the Middle Ages there was a good deal of hostility toward the Jews. Gradually they were barred from public offices and excluded from agriculture and industry. In order to make a living, many Jews became pawnbrokers or bankers, though usury (charging interest on loans) was regarded as a sin by Christian and Muslim religions. The

Jews were also criticized for keeping to themselves – despite the fact that they were often forced to live in ghettos. The treatment of the Jewish population eventually improved in western Europe, but pogroms – bouts of vicious persecution – persisted in eastern Europe (in Poland and Russia, for example) until the early 20th century. In the 1930s, anti-Semitism was to manifest itself in a particularly horrific form with the rise of Hitler, the German dictator, culminating in the death of more than six million Jews in Nazi concentration camps during World War II.

How large was the Mongol Empire?

When Genghis Khan died, in 1277, the Mongol Empire stretched from the north of China to the Caucasus Mountains in Georgia. The Mongols ruled for three centuries over an empire where peace was enforced by means of intimidation.

In medieval times Mongolia was populated by nomads, led by chiefs called khans. These nomads believed that their mission was to dominate and pacify all the peoples of the world. In 1206 one chief, Temujin, assumed the title of Genghis Khan ("universal ruler") and set about conquering his neighbors. The Chin Empire in northern China crumbled in 1215, when he captured Beijing. He then proceeded to destroy Bukhara and Samarkand, while another of his armies reached Kiev.

The power of the Mongols stemmed above all from their military organization and discipline. Their first written code of law, the Yassak, was published in 1219. It outlawed murder, looting, and other kinds of violence, as well as adultery and drunkenness.

After Genghis Khan's death his sons continued his policy of conquest. Western Europe was threatened by Batu, one of his grandsons, who turned back from the gates of Vienna when he heard that his father had died.

Did the Hundred Years' War really last 100 years?

This war in fact lasted more than 100 years. It began in 1337, when Edward III of England refused to pay homage to the king of France, and ended in 1453.

The cause of the war dated from 1328 when Charles IV, king of France, died leaving two daughters. Under French law, only male heirs could inherit the throne. When Charles' cousin Philippe de Valois was chosen as successor – instead of Edward III, king of England, Charles' nephew – the English were furious, and in 1340 Edward claimed the French crown. Edward won a series of victories – Sluys (1340), Crécy (1346), Calais (1347), and Poitiers (1356) – and under the Treaty of Brétigny (1360) was given half of France. Between 1360 and 1380 the French conducted a war of attrition and recovered some territories. A truce followed, but the conflict flared up again when Henry V invaded France and won the battle of Agincourt in 1415. For the next 15 years, with France virtually in a state of civil war, the English seemed to have the upper hand. But in 1429 Joan of Arc turned the tide of the war against the English .

What happened at the Battle of Crécy?

The English victory at Crécy in 1346 came as a

shock to the French. Their knights were slaughtered; killed by the first cannon to appear on a battlefield, by archers, and by infantry.

At the start of the Hundred Years' War, with a population four times greater than that of England, France appeared to be the stronger of the combatants. Yet during the first 20 years of the war, France consistently experienced defeat. At the Battle of Crécy the French knights were helpless under the arrows that poured down on them from the English archers. Their frightened horses threw them to the ground – where, unable to get up, the knights lay trapped in their armor at the mercy of the English.

Joan of Arc played a major role in driving the English from France. She is shown here on the ramparts of Orléans, which she recaptured from the English.

How was

Switzerland

founded?

In 1291 three Swiss regions, known as *cantons*, signed the Perpetual Covenant, declaring their freedom and promising to help each other against any foreign ruler. Together, they won their independence from the Habsburgs, who ruled Germany and Austria. This formed the backdrop to the legend of William Tell, which symbolized the Swiss longing for independence.

According to the legend, William Tell refused to obey a proclamation issued by Gessler, the tyrannical Austrian ruler of Switzerland. Gessler compelled Tell, a famous bowman, to shoot an arrow through an apple balanced on the head of Tell's young son. Tell did so, and then shot Gessler dead.

In 1648 the Treaty of Westphalia confirmed the end of the Habsburgs' domination of Switzerland. Just over 150 years later, in 1803, Napoleon declared the 22 cantons of Switzerland a "democratic federation." In 1815, at the end of the Napoleonic Wars, the Congress of Vienna guaranteed the independence and "perpetual neutrality" of the new nation.

Which city most influenced the Renaissance?

During the 14th and 15th centuries, under the patronage of the Medici family, the arts flourished in Florence, Italy. Florentine architecture, painting, and sculpture was to influence the whole of the western world.

In 1267, when it became an independent republic, Florence was already one of the most prosperous cities in the Italian province of Tuscany. A merchant city organized into guilds, it made no distinction between artists and craftsmen. For each, it was necessary to undergo an apprenticeship lasting 13 years. The leaders of Florence fostered the growth of arts that became described as the Renaissance. Cosimo de' Medici (1389–1464), for example, commissioned the construction of various monuments, including the Convent of San Marco. The city's cathedral, churches, palaces, and squares all bear witness to the artistic life of the city in the 14th and 15th centuries.

When was Venice's golden age?

From the 13th to the 16th century, Venice was a great maritime and trading power and one of the richest cities in Italy.

The Crusades helped Venice develop an empire. The Crusaders asked Venice to supply them with ships, and in exchange captured the fortress of Zara, on the east coast of the Adriatic. In 1204 the Franks and the Venetians divided the Byzantine Empire between them. Venice's golden age was the 15th century, when its empire included Crete, Cyprus, part of Croatia, and part of northeastern Italy. But the wealth and power of Venice aroused the jealousy and fear of its neighbors, who allied against the city in 1508. In response, Venice entered into a series of unstable alliances that contributed to its decline.

Who backed Christopher Columbus?

The great navigator who discovered the New World was Italian, the son of a Genoese weaver, but it was the Spanish monarchy who financed his explorations.

The court of the powerful Medici family in Florence, Italy, was among the most brilliant in 15th-century Europe.

In his first voyage to the Americas, Columbus set sail with three ships – the *Pinta*, *Niña*, and *Santa María* – all crewed with Spanish sailors and financed by the Spanish government. In October 1492, after 50 days at sea, Columbus sighted land – and thought he had reached India, which is why the islands of the Caribbean became known as the West Indies. In later expeditions Columbus reached the coasts of Central and South America. But it was another Italian with Spanish connections, Amerigo Vespucci, who gave his name to the lands that Columbus discovered. Columbus died in Spain in 1506 and was buried in Seville.

The proclaimed goal of the conquistadors was to spread Christianity among the Indians of Central and South America. In fact, they cheated, raped, murdered, and enslaved them.

Who were the conquistadors?

The conquistadors ("conquerors") were Spanish and Portuguese soldiers sent to seize lands in Central and South America to find new sources of wealth.

In the 16th century the treasuries of Spain and Portugal were empty due to the cost of wars and luxurious royal courts. It was imperative to find some new means of obtaining gold. This was the main motive for the voyages of explorers such as Columbus and for sending conquistadors to distant lands. Hernán Cortés (1485–1547) invaded the Aztec Empire, in Mexico, and within two years totally destroyed their civilization. Hernando de Soto (1500–42) played a major role in the exploration of Central America and helped Francisco Pizarro (1478–1541) to subjugate Peru. Pizarro soon realized how to exploit the weaknesses of the Inca. In 1533 he penetrated into the heart of the Inca Empire and reached the capital, Cuzco. A few years later he was assassinated, but by then Peru was in Spanish hands. The conquistadors cruelly suppressed the native populations of Latin America. They set out with the intention of spreading Christianity, but in reality were unscrupulous and greedy men.

Did Cortés kill Montezuma?

It is not known exactly how the Aztec emperor Montezuma died – but, despite the brutality of the conquistadors, Cortés appears not to have been directly responsible for his death.

In Aztec mythology a plumed-serpent god Quetzalcóatl once ruled on earth in human form – then vanished, promising that he would return bringing glory and

Despite the difficulties of their location, the Inca developed a great civilization and a far-reaching empire. They had a complex political system, in which power was shared between the central authority of the emperor and local rulers. The Inca were skillful builders and goldsmiths, and evolved a sophisticated system of agriculture and irrigation. They built a network of roads that linked distant parts of the empire. The Inca spoke Quechua and worshipped the Sun. The death of Emperor Atahualpa at the hands of Spanish conquistador Francisco Pizarro marked the end of the Inca Empire.

Montezuma, the Aztec emperor, greeted the conquistador Hernán Cortés as a god. It is not known exactly how Montezuma died.

peace. The Aztecs thought Cortés might be the god, so they welcomed him and showered him with gifts. Some historians believe that, when Cortés was absent from Mexico, Montezuma's people rebelled and the emperor was mortally wounded, either by a rock or by a blow from a sword. Alternatively, he may have been killed while attacking Cortés's troops.

Who were the Inca?

In the late 13th century the Inca settled in the region of Cuzco in the heart of the Andes Mountains in what is now Peru, at an altitude of 11,000 feet (3,400 meters).

Did the Inca and Maya know each other?

The Maya lived in Central America, in what is now Guatemala, Mexico, and Belize, and the Inca lived in South America, in what is now Peru. They seem to have lived isolated lives, unaware of each other.

Several civilizations that developed in pre-Columbian Central America were decimated by the Spanish conquest. These Central Americans (Meso-Americans), such as the Olmecs, Maya, Toltecs, and Aztecs, are thought to have been related, as there are similarities in their artistic skills, architecture, and religious practices. The Maya, for instance, were influenced by the Olmecs, who settled along the coast of the Gulf of Mexico. The peoples of Central America had contact with each other, but were isolated from the rest of the world. The Maya and Aztecs had no knowledge of the Inca.

Why didn't the

Inca and Maya

use the wheel?

The Indians of Central and South America had developed artistically refined civilizations. It is surprising that neither the Inca, the Aztecs, nor the Maya discovered the wheel.

When we study the cities of the Inca, such as Machu Picchu, or the pyramids of the Maya, it is astonishing that such structures were built without such basic aids as the wheelbarrow – these peoples had no knowledge of the wheel.

What happened

to France's North

American colonies?

France was the first country to establish colonies in North America, but gradually lost them.

In 1608 Samuel de Champlain founded Quebec. Previously, on July 24, 1534, Jacques Cartier had claimed the east coast of Canada in the name of the French king, François I. This was the beginning of what came to be known as New France. Like Columbus and Magellan, Cartier hoped to find a route to China via the American continent. Between 1534 and 1541 Cartier made several voyages to Canada. In the course of the 18th century, after a series of wars and treaties, France progressively lost its hold on the vast territory of New France.

Who was Suleiman

the Magnificent?

He was sultan of the Ottoman empire and ruled from 1520 to 1566. The court of Suleiman the

Magnificent was renowned for its luxury and splendor. Moreover, Suleiman was a great ruler who administered his empire with authority and justice.

At the height of its power, during the 16th and 17th centuries, the Ottoman Empire was the most powerful empire in the world. It was an Islamic empire, controlling Asia Minor (now Turkey), the Balkans, parts of northern Africa and present-day Iran, Saudi Arabia, and Syria. The empire started in Turkey about 1300. The first Ottomans were nomadic Turkish tribes, led by Osman, the founder and first sultan (ruler) of the empire. The Ottomans gradually conquered the Byzantine Empire during the 14th and 15th centuries, finally capturing Constantinople (now Istanbul) in 1453. The empire continued to expand, reaching its peak of power and wealth under Sultan Suleiman I.

The Incas developed an ingenious system for sending messages, using knotted strings.

Why did the "Sun never set" on the empire of Charles V?

Prince of the Low Countries and king of Spain and Sicily, Charles V became Holy Roman Emperor in 1519, aged 19. It was said that "the Sun never set" over his empire, because its territories were so huge.

Charles was already a great monarch when the possibility arose of succeeding his grandfather, Maximilian Habsburg, as Holy Roman Emperor. The crown was elective and there was a rival candidate: François I, the young king of France. However, Charles had the advantage of being of a line of German and Spanish rulers, and was also very rich. This won him election. He was crowned twice: first at Aachen, in Germany, in 1520 and then by the pope himself. Charles traveled constantly, between Spain, Germany, and Italy, and even to North Africa. After ruling for more than 35 years, he abdicated in October 1555 and retired to a monastery, where he died two years later.

Suleiman the Magnificent and François I were both enemies of Charles V (above) and formed an alliance against him.

Why did Henry VIII quarrel with the pope?

King Henry VIII of England broke with Rome when the pope refused to annul his marriage to his first wife, Catherine of Aragon.

Henry's first wife, Catherine of Aragon, whom he married in 1509, gave him no male heir. Having fallen in love with Anne Boleyn, a maid of honor to the queen, he demanded that Pope Clement VII annul his first marriage. When he was refused,

Henry repudiated the authority of the pope and in 1534 declared himself head of a new, independent church, the Church of England.

Before his quarrel with the pope, Henry had been a staunch Catholic and had even been given the title "Defender of the Faith" by Pope Leo X after rebutting the ideas of Martin Luther.

What happened to the Spanish Armada?

The "invincible" Armada was the great war fleet of Philip II, king of Spain. Composed of 130 vessels, it lost its reputation for invincibility when it attacked the English fleet in July 1588.

Philip II had two main reasons for attacking England. First, Queen Elizabeth I had beheaded Mary Queen of Scots, whom Philip had dreamed of putting in Elizabeth's place. In addition, in knighting the privateer Francis Drake, Elizabeth had expressed official approval for the plunder of Spanish shipping.

England at this time was on the verge of economic collapse, whereas Spain had never been more powerful. However, the

Armada made several errors, including hesitation and poor strategy, which worked to the advantage of the English. The Spanish fleet was damaged in a battle in the English Channel, losing 63 ships, while the English lost none. Badly battered by storms, only half of the Armada managed to return to Spain.

Who were the

Moguls?

The Moguls, who ruled India for over 300 years, came from Turkestan. Famous Mogul emperors included Babur, Akbar, Jahangir, Shah Jahan, and Aurangzeb.

Babur (the Lion), the first Mogul emperor, was descended from two conquerors, Tamerlane and Genghis Khan. After conquering Afghanistan, he advanced into India and entered Delhi in triumph in April 1526. Akbar (Babur's grandson) became known as "the Great Mogul," because of his conquests and enlightened rule. The Moguls were Muslim, but they ruled a mostly Hindu nation. Eventually, the empire declined due to internal rivalries and external pressures. The last Mogul emperor was deposed in 1857.

Although reputed to be invincible, the Spanish Armada was badly defeated in a great battle in the English Channel in July 1588.

Why were the

Europeans ordered

to leave Japan?

The rulers of Japan feared that the Christian mission-aries and European traders might bring armies with them to conquer Japan. They also thought that to keep order in Japan, they should isolate themselves. In the 1600's, all Europeans were forced to leave Japan, and the country cut itself off from the rest of the world.

European traders and Christian missionaries began arriving in Japan in the late 1500's. However, the shogunate, the rulers of Japan, soon saw the threat of invasion by the West. In the 1630's, Japan cut all ties with all other nations, apart from the Dutch, and Japan became isolated. The Japanese were not allowed to leave the country, and those who lived abroad were forbidden to return. Trade relations with the West were not renewed until the mid-1850's.

How did pirates differ from privateers?

Pirates illegally scoured the seas in search of vessels to plunder, whereas in the 16th and 17th centuries governments at war with Spain licensed privateers to raid Spanish treasure ships. Francis Drake, for one, was given a privateer's license by Queen Elizabeth I.

There were also semiofficial freebooters and buccaneers such as Henry Morgan – who later became lieutenant-governor of Jamaica. Captain Kidd, on the other hand, was sent in 1695 to hunt down pirates in the Indian Ocean, but turned to piracy himself. There were also Dutch and French pirates and privateers.

How did the United States come into being?

With the Declaration of Independence of July 1776, the colonists began their rebellion against the British monarchy. The 13 British colonies in America fought for seven years (1775–83) to win independence from Britain. This was recognized by the Treaty of Paris in September 1783.

The American colonists were few, but they knew the land and had support from France. The new nation came into being in 1788. In April 1789 George Washington, commander-in-chief of the American armies during the fight for independence, became the country's first president.

What did the French Revolution achieve?

By overthrowing an oppressive monarchy, and declaring that all people are equal (liberty, equality, fraternity was the call), the French Revolution brought hope to all.

The French Revolution (1789–1799) was not without drama or horror. During the Reign of Terror (September 1793 to July 1794), some 40,000 people died. But spurred by America, the Revolution's idea of equality and freedom for all made an impact worldwide.

Pirates scoured the seas and ransomed ships for their own profit – while privateers did the same on behalf of governments and kings.

Which were the French general Napoleon's most

notable victories

and defeats?

Napoleon Bonaparte was crowned emperor of France on December 2, 1804 – and from then until 1809 he advanced from political to military success. At the battle of Waterloo, he suffered his final and humiliating defeat.

On December 2, 1805, at Austerlitz (Battle of the Three Emperors), Napoleon triumphed over Austria and Russia. During the next four years he extended France's power across much of Europe. In March 1814, when the powers allied against him reached Paris, Napoleon admitted defeat and was forced into exile on the island of Elba, off the coast of Italy. He escaped and on March 1, 1815, landed in the south of France, raised an army, and marched on Paris. The four great powers of the period (Austria, Prussia, Britain, and Russia) renewed their alliance against him. A battle finally took place at Waterloo, near Brussels, on June 18, 1815. Despite the courage displayed by the French, especially by Napoleon's Imperial Guard, his army was defeated. He was exiled to Saint Helena, an

At Austerlitz in 1805, Napoleon won one of his greatest victories, defeating the combined might of Austria and Russia.

island in the South Atlantic, where he died.

When was slavery

abolished?

Slavery was abolished in the British Empire in 1833; by the Emancipation Proclamation in the United States in 1863; in Saudi Arabia in 1963; and in Mauritania in 1980. But it still exists in parts of Africa, Asia, and South America.

The Portuguese were the first to capture Africans for sale as slaves, in the 15th century. Other traders soon followed suit. In the 17th and 18th centuries, ships left Europe filled with merchandise destined for Africa, where their cargo was exchanged for black slaves. Among those who campaigned for the abolition of slavery were William

When the Germans besieged Paris in September 1870, Léon Gambetta, the French minister of war, made headline news by escaping from the city by balloon.

Lloyd Garrison and Frederick Douglass in the United States and William Wilberforce in Britain.

What was the Industrial Revolution?

The advance of technology in the late 1700s permitted the development of new industries in Europe and the United States.

In Europe, Britain was at the forefront of the Industrial Revolution. Iron and textile industries were among the first to benefit from new technology. The invention of railroads added to industrial growth. In the 19th century, the development of electrical and chemical industries revolutionized manufacturing and laid the foundations of modern technology. These innovations also brought suffering – many workers (including small children) led miserable lives.

How was Germany unified?

The German empire was created as a result of the Franco-Prussian War.

The Franco-Prussian War (1870–1) began as a dispute between France and Prussia, a German state. All the other German states joined in, and it became a war between France and Germany. The result was a disaster for the French, who were defeated at Sedan in March 1871. Germany forced France to give up Alsace and Lorraine. The four German states became a united German nation under Prussian leadership, and Wilhelm I was crowned the first *kaiser* (emperor) of the new German empire.

What event started World War I?

The assassination of Archduke Franz Ferdinand – heir to the throne of Austria – and his wife, Sophie, in Sarajevo, 1914, triggered World War I. But tension had long existed between France and Germany.

Nationalist movements had created an explosive situation in central Europe. The conflicts revolved around Serbia, a new state, formed in 1878. Two alliances had formed. On one side, France, Britain, and Russia; and on the other, Austria-Hungary, Germany, and Italy. Many crises had preceded the war, including colonial disputes in the Balkans. In addition, France had a dispute with Germany, having been forced to hand over Alsace and Lorraine in 1870. The war was expected to be short – but the carnage continued for four years, leaving ten million dead.

What was the October Revolution?

During 1917 a series of revolutions took place in

Russia. In the last of these – the October Revolution – the Bolsheviks, headed by Lenin, seized power.

Czar Nicholas II hoped World War I would strengthen the monarchy, but in February 1917 he was deposed and Alexander Kerensky took power. However, the soviets (the elected revolutionary councils) opposed Kerensky and demanded an end to the war. From April, the soviets pressed for a revolution. This erupted in November (October by the old Russian calendar) when the Bolsheviks stormed the Winter Palace in St. Petersburg. The government was deposed and replaced by the Soviet of People's Commissars, headed by Lenin.

The assassination of the Austrian Archduke and his wife in Sarajevo, in June 1914, was the pretext for the outbreak of World War I.

What was the

League of Nations?

The League of Nations was established in 1919 by the Treaty of Versailles, which was drawn up by the victorious countries at the Paris Peace Conference at the end of World War I. It sought to guarantee peace and international security by preventing war.

Woodrow Wilson, the president of the United States, and the other founders of the League of Nations sought greater openness among states and more cooperation among nations. In 1933 Germany left the league in order to rearm; six years later World War II broke out. In practice, the League of Nations lacked the means to be effective.

How did Hitler

seize power?

In 1933 Adolf Hitler, the leader of the National Socialist Party (Nazi Party), seized power. He accused Communists of setting fire to the Reichstag (parliament

building) and arrested them and became sole master of Germany.

The Weimar Republic (1919–33) had been born out of Germany's defeat. Then, in the 1920s Germany suffered a grave economic crisis. The country was ripe for a takeover by extremists. Hitler, leader of the Nazi Party since 1921, became Chancellor in January 1933. Using the burning of the Reichstag as a pretext, he had his opponents arrested and closed down opposition newspapers. German aggression under Hitler caused World War II. Hitler remained dictator of Germany until 1945 when, faced with defeat, he committed suicide.

Hitler seized power in Germany in 1933. Above, Hitler in company with Marshall Keitel and General Jold.

Who were Germany's main allies during World War II?

Italy (under Mussolini) and Japan were Germany's principal allies.

On the other side were the forces of "the free world": Britain and the countries of the British Commonwealth, France, the Scandinavian and Benelux countries, the Soviet Union (after Germany invaded Russia in 1941), and the United States (which entered the war in December 1941).

How did Japan enter World War II?

On December 7, 1941, a Japanese aircraft bombed Pearl Harbor, an American naval base in Hawaii. The next day the United States declared war on Japan, an ally of Germany.

Germany wanted to dominate Europe; Japan wished to control Southeast Asia. Within months of attacking Pearl Harbor, Japan had occupied Burma, Malaya, Singapore, and the Philippines.

When were nuclear weapons first used?

On August 6, 1945, the United States dropped the first atom bomb, on Hiroshima in Japan, killing 80,000 people. Three days later, another bomb was dropped on Nagasaki, killing a further 75,000 people.

Many who escaped immediate death died later of radiation. President Truman had hesitated to unleash such terrible weapons, but reasoned that they would end the war and so save American lives.

What is the role of the United Nations (UN)?

The UN's main role is to preserve peace and international security. It also has agencies, such as UNICEF (United Nations International Children's Emergency Fund) and the World Trade Organization.

The United Nations was established in 1945 to replace the League of Nations. Its headquarters is in New York.

On December 7, 1941, Japan launched a surprise attack on Pearl Harbor in Hawaii, gravely damaging the American fleet. Next day, the United States declared war on Japan.

The UN Building in New York was constructed in 1957 to house the United Nations. It is 505 feet (154 meters) tall.

What was the Cold War?

It is the name given to the intense power struggle that developed after World War II between groups of Communist and non-Communist nations. It is called the Cold War because it did not actually lead to fighting.

On one side was the U.S.S.R. and its Communist allies, and on the other were the U.S. and its democratic allies. There was a mutual distrust and hostility between the two sides. Each group saw the other as a threat to its security and way of life. The tension eased during the late 1980's when the U.S.S.R. began to reduce its military presence in Eastern Europe. The Cold War ended with the collapse of Communism in Eastern Europe in 1989, the reunification of East and West Germany in 1991, and the breakup of the Soviet Union in 1991.

Who presided over the end of Communism in Russia?

In March 1985, when Mikhail Gorbachev became general secretary of the Communist Party, the Soviet Union was in a grave economic crisis, which led to the collapse of the Communist system.

Gorbachev began a restructuring (*perestroika*) of Soviet institutions, along with "openness" (*glasnost*) in everyday life and international relations. But the Communist system could not survive, and in December 1991 the Soviet Union was dissolved. Boris Yeltsin then came to power.

Why has peace in the Middle East proved so elusive?

After the Jews were banished, Palestine was inhabited by Arabs for nearly 2,000 years. Following the creation of the State of Israel in 1948, many Palestinian Arabs were forced into exile.

Wars between Israel and her neighbors (such as the Six-Day War in 1967 and the Yom Kippur War in 1973) caused great bitterness, as have acts of violence by extremists on both sides. Attempts at reconciliation — such as the 1978 Camp David Agreements and the 1993 peace accords between Israel and the Palestine Liberation Organization — have

From 1964 to 1973, during the longest war ever fought by American troops, the United States poured men and armaments into Vietnam to stop the Communist North from annexing the South.

alternated with bitter attacks that have obstructed peace.

How long did the Vietnam War last?

Direct American involvement in Vietnam lasted from 1964 until 1973, when the U.S. withdrew its troops.

During the Indochina War (1946–54), France fought to keep control over the last of its colonies in Southeast Asia. Under the 1954 Geneva Agreements, which ended that war, Vietnam was split into two states. North Vietnam was ruled by a Communist regime and South Vietnam by a dictatorial regime backed by the United States. Fearing that Communism would spread throughout

Southeast Asia, the United States sent military advisors to help South Vietnam ward off invasion from the North. News of attacks on American warships in the Gulf of Tonkin in 1964 led the United States to send the first combat troops. American troops were withdrawn in 1973. In 1976 the reunited country became the Socialist Republic of Vietnam.

Daily Life in the Ancient World

Where did Australopithecus live?

Scholars regard Australopithecus as our earliest ancestor. This species lived in East Africa, in what is now Ethiopia, Kenya, Tanzania, and the east part of South Africa.

Before Australopithecus, man's ancestor was barely distinguishable from apes. Australopithecus was the first species to have truly adopted an upright posture. This allowed the brain to develop and freed the hands for work and self-

defense. The climate was hot and humid, and the vegetation was like that of a savanna – vast prairies with tall grass, dotted with trees and marshes. The oldest and most complete skeleton of Australopithecus was found in Ethiopia in 1974. It was named Lucy after the popular Beatles' song "Lucy in the Sky with Diamonds."

Who made the first tools?

Two or three million years ago, man began to make tools – at first crudely shaped small stones, then flint tools cut on both sides (bifacial tools).

The name *Homo habilis* (Latin for "skillful man") has been given to these early toolmakers. Their tools were very basic and imprecise in form. Gradually, tools became more specialized, with a variety of sizes and shapes suited to different uses. Around 500,000 years ago, man learned how to use fire, a discovery of great importance. Fire provided heat for warmth and for cooking food. Tools and weapons fashioned from wood could be hardened in its flames, which also kept wild animals at bay.

How were stone tools made?

The stones used as tools by prehistoric humans were usually shaped by striking stone with stone. The Stone

Hunting was a vital activity in prehistoric times. For a long time our ancestors lived in natural caves in the sides of rocky cliffs.

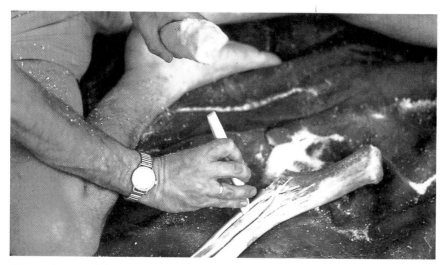

To understand how our ancestors made tools, archeologists have tried to make them the same way. Here a tip is being made for an assegai (throwing spear). Using a flint chisel (above), a piece of bone is cut from a deer's antler. After being soaked and softened in water, the piece of bone then has to be straightened (below), using another tool (made from a cow's rib).

tasks, and more efficient for shaping even more precise tools, or weapons such as arrowheads. Stone Age people also learned to rework the edges of tools to restore their sharpness when they began to grow dull. Much later (around 15,000 years ago) they began to polish the stones after cutting and shaping them, which meant they could make even finer and more precise tools.

What did our ancestors eat?

Prehistoric paintings and engravings that have survived on the walls of caves reveal the principal activities of their creators: hunting, animal husbandry, and food gathering. Meat and fish were the basis of their diet, together with what they could gather growing wild in the fields and forests around them.

Age takes its name from this technique.

The toolmakers held the future tool tightly between their feet or braced it between other stones. To shape the tool, they struck at it either with another stone, which they used as a hammer, or with a strong bone suited to the work. Stones such as flint or obsidian (a dark, glassy volcanic rock) were preferred; once they had been shaped, they made hard and durable tools that could cut effectively. Flint tools evolved over time, gradually being made sharper, better adapted to specific

In the early 20th century, many nomadic tribes still lived this way. Everything that could be found in forests and clearings — wild berries, mushrooms, fruits, nuts, and various plants — was either consumed fresh or dried to be eaten during the cold season. Salt occurs in a natural state in some regions and has been used since early times to preserve meat and fish. Sugar, on the other hand, was found in nature only in the form of honey (cane sugar only appeared in European food after the discovery of the New World).

How did the first men make fire?

It was during the period of *Homo erectus* (who was a descendant of *Homo habilis*) that our ancestors discovered fire. The oldest hearths that have been found are those in the cave at Escale at the mouth of the River Rhône in France, and at the 360,000-year-old site in the Chou-k'ou-tien cave in China.

Before this time our ancestors may have made use of fire caused by natural phenomena such as lightning and may even have tried to preserve it, but there is no evidence to confirm this. To light fires man probably used a technique that certain African tribes practiced at the beginning of the 20th century and some Polynesian tribes still practice today. A piece of green wood was held tightly between the feet. A small hole was cut into the wood, into which was pushed a stick of hard wood. Turning the stick very quickly between the hands, the green wood was heated until it began to smoke and burn. The small flames were then fed with dry leaves and straw to build up the fire. Striking two stones of flint together, producing sparks to light straw and tinder, is another technique.

Who was Neanderthal man?

Around 100,000 B.C., a type of human appeared on Earth who resembled modern humans, though their skull was flat and their eyebrow ridges and jaw were far heavier than ours.

Neanderthal man used language, had a relatively well-developed social life, lived in huts, and buried his dead. The earliest known graves belong to the Neanderthal period. But suddenly around 35,000 B.C. all trace of Neanderthal man disappeared from Europe and Central Asia (the limit of his range) – and scientists now believe that the true ancestor of modern man was not Neanderthal man, but Cro-Magnon man, who superseded them.

Reconstruction of a typical scene from daily life in the time of Neanderthal man.

How old is modern man?

Modern man is directly descended from _Homo sapiens_, who appeared in Africa 100,000 years ago.

Homo sapiens evolved from this time, developing language and making increasingly sophisticated tools. _Homo sapiens_ developed art and created social and religious rituals. Settling in stable communities, they developed agriculture around 10,000 B.C. From then on, humans were no longer totally dependent on the hunt and what was in season. They could store food, make bread, and raise settlements, which grew into villages. Eventually this led to commercial exchanges, especially of materials such as metals, between communities.

How did the Native Americans arrive in America?

Native Americans do not constitute a separate race, but are descended from the Mongol populations of Central Asia. About 40,000 years ago they emigrated from Siberia to Alaska, possibly on foot during the last ice age and perhaps also in kayaks similar to those still used by the Inuit (Eskimos) in the early 20th century.

This migration may have been a search for new hunting and fishing grounds. Having arrived in their new continent, the Native Americans spread along the mountain ranges in the west of North and South America, finally reaching Patagonia around 6000 B.C. Their migration from the Arctic to the edge of the Antarctic was thus completed. In the richer lands of South America, the Native Americans formed diverse and rich societies, such as those of the Aztecs and Incas. The discovery of South America by Spanish conquistadors ended this adventure, with the destruction of the main civilizations.

How long has Australia been inhabited?

About 53,000 years ago, due to a fall in sea level, two reefs (Sunda and Sahul) emerged between Australia and the continent of Asia. This meant peoples from Southeast Asia could reach the shores of Australia, making the crossing in light craft, around 40,000 B.C.

The volcanic activity of the region then produced further upheavals, and the peoples of Australia found themselves scattered over several islands, including Tasmania and Melville Island. One Australian tribe has a legend, which may have been handed down for thousands of years, relating how a serpent rainbow cut their island off from the continent and how the island was then populated with marsupial lions and other giant marsupials, the ancestors of the kangaroo. In prehistoric times the Australian Aborigines lived by hunting and foraging, and succeeded in adapting to daunting climate changes. When Europeans arrived in Australia about 200 years ago, the Aboriginal lifestyle had hardly evolved beyond the Stone Age.

What does Paleolithic mean?

The Old Stone Age – known as the Paleolithic period

(from the Greek words for "old" and "stone") – lasted for more than two million years. It was during this period that people began to use and make stone tools.

The Old Stone Age is divided into several periods (Perigordian, Solutrean, Magdalenian, etc.), named after places where Paleolithic sites have been found in Europe. Using carbon dating, archeologists can now establish the dates of these sites fairly precisely. The climate varied throughout this period, being sometimes temperate and sometimes cold. Evidence shows that Paleolithic people traveled great distances, over a long period of time, and populated most regions of the world. Hunters and fishers, they followed herds or migrated in search of new hunting grounds. During this period art and social life also evolved.

Fat-burning lamp from the Stone Age, discovered in the Caves of Lascaux.

When did prehistoric people learn to draw?

We do not know when people first began to draw. Designs traced in snow or sand disappear within days, and paintings or drawings on animal skins last only a few years. The only evidence we have of prehistoric art is found on the walls of caves, of which the earliest are 30,000 years old.

The best-known caves in the Western world are in France, Spain, and the Sahara Desert. The Caves of Lascaux, near Montignac in the Dordogne region of France, are among the best finds to date. Here there are representations of animals that were hunted by prehistoric man: mammoths, bison, aurochs (European wild oxen, now extinct), deer, and other mammals. Some paintings are magnificent, often using the contours of the cave walls to emphasize the form or movement of the animals. Sometimes we find representations of people – such as the painting of a man kneeling before a bison at Lascaux. Many believe that the representations of animals sought in the hunt may have had magical significance.

What did cave dwellers do for light?

Most of the time prehistoric people remained at the entrance of caves, where they lit large fires at night to provide light and heat. To paint or engrave images on the cave walls, they penetrated into the interior of the caves, through dark, narrow passages, so they needed to carry the light with them.

At first they used juniper torches, which they could carry into the caves to avoid getting lost in the dark. Such torches gave off a bright light, but lasted only a brief time. They also invented a fat-burning lamp, consisting of a wick of soaked hair in a bone bowl filled with animal fat. This primitive lamp also burned quickly, but it provided better light than a candle and it was easy to carry a reserve of fat in a leather pouch to refuel it.

How old are the paintings at Lascaux?

Discovered in 1940, the paintings in the Caves of Lascaux (in the Dordogne region of France) had survived without deterioration, and unseen by man, for 17,000 years.

The discoverers of the caves found these examples of prehistoric art perfectly preserved, their original colors still vibrant. It is thought that this "cathedral of prehistory," as it has been called, was a sanctuary decorated by a hunting people and that the paintings had a magical and spiritual meaning for them. The elegance and force of the animals represented (bulls, deer, great cats, horses, bison) have inspired admiration for more than half a century.

What weapons did prehistoric humans use?

In the Neolithic period they had well-formed weapons that assured successful hunting. Traps (pits covered with branches, for instance) were used to capture large animals such as mammoths, but strong weapons were needed to kill them once they were captured.

Arrows, sometimes poisoned, were the weapons most often used. This can be seen in a painting in the Caves of Lascaux: a bison pierced by an arrow has turned on the hunter, who is shown crouching in front of the animal. The arrows used by prehistoric hunters were either hardened in the fire or had a flint tip, which was sometimes finely worked. Stone Age hunters also used harpoons made from bone or from a deer's antler, axes, and throwing and thrusting spears. At the beginning of the Bronze Age, superior weapons appeared, including swords and daggers, as well as more effective spears, axes, and harpoons.

Animals are often represented in cave paintings like the ones at Lascaux, but we do not actually know why Paleolithic man decorated caves. Could they have been sanctuaries dedicated to the gods of the hunt?

There are still people who live in lake dwellings – such as in these houses in the village of Ganvie, in the Republic of Benin.

Several burial grounds from the Upper Paleolithic period have been discovered. The body was placed at the bottom of a hole, on its back, or sometimes in a folded position. In some cases it was buried in its best garments. Skeletons have been discovered wearing strands of pearls or surrounded by objects that must have belonged to the deceased.

Where did people live in the Paleolithic period?

Homo habilis has left no trace of his dwellings, and elaborate shelters would not have been necessary given the warm climate in which he lived. The series of cold periods that occurred 100,000 years ago forced man to seek shelter in caves and beneath overhanging cliffs. In addition, stretched skins were used to provide shelter from wind and rain.

When the weather turned warm, the herds of mammoths and reindeer migrated toward northern Europe – where caves and cliff shelters were harder to find. Here humans began to construct solid huts; structures of beams covered with skins anchored to mammoth tusks. These huts could be taken down relatively quickly, permitting families of hunters to follow the herds of game.

What are the oldest burial sites?

The main evidence of prehistoric religious rites is the existence of numerous burial grounds. The oldest discovered to date are Neanderthal tombs 40,000 years old.

What did Paleolithic people wear?

For a long time our ancestors were content simply to throw animal skins over their shoulders. The invention of the awl made it possible to punch holes in the edges of a skin through which thongs could be threaded.

Initially such fastenings consisted of leather cords, thongs, or tendons from a bison or reindeer. Later the invention of the needle made it possible to sew skins together. The animal skins brought back by the hunters were stretched and then scraped with flint. Thus cured and softened, they were dried in the shade, then cut into clothes. The craft of weaving developed much later. A piece of cloth discovered in Europe has been dated to around 5000 B.C. – but the weave of the fabric is so fine and regular that we can assume it was made using a technique developed long before that date.

What does

Neolithic mean?

The New Stone Age – known as the Neolithic period (from the Greek for "new" and "stone") – began around 8000 B.C. It is sometimes referred to as the Age of Polished Stone.

In the Neolithic period, people began to polish stones to make tools, whereas previously they had chipped or cut them. It was also during this period that man began to practice agriculture and animal husbandry. The climate had warmed, and the great herds of reindeer and mammoths had disappeared. The domestication of animals was a revolutionary development, assuring human communities reserves of food throughout the year. Cooking also developed during this period, which is notable for its baked-clay pottery. In the New Stone Age

human activity became more varied. Impressive monuments were constructed: menhirs (great stones standing alone or in lines) and dolmens (tables of stone), like those found at Carnac in France; tumuli (burial mounds); and temples such as Stonehenge in the south of England.

What is a tumulus?

A tumulus is a huge man-made mound of stones and earth. As time goes by it becomes covered by grass. Since the Neolithic period, humans have constructed these enormous mounds of stone to protect the remains of their leaders.

Tumuli have long remained a mystery. Why were such gigantic structures created? Numerous civilizations throughout the world, from the Stone Age period to the Bronze Age, built tumuli. They exist in places as far apart as the Americas, France, Germany, the British Isles, and the plains of Siberia. In South America strange mounds of earth have been found that were probably the work of pre-Columbian tribes. Construction of tumuli usually followed a similar pattern. The site at Gavrinis, on the Gulf of Morbihan in France, is typical. A tunnel leads from an entrance set in the side of the mound to a chamber at the center surrounded by large stones. Stones and earth were then laid on top of this structure over a

Numerous remains of the Neolithic era are found in Ireland – such as the entrance of the stone tunnel of the burial mound at Tara, shown here.

period of time, perhaps lasting many years. Later, nature covered the tumulus with grass and it blended into the landscape.

When did people begin to domesticate nature?

When wild game became scarce, our ancestors began to try to tame and breed some of the animals they had hunted. Later, when villages became more or less permanent, man began to cultivate the soil.

From the 11th millennium B.C. the inhabitants of Mesopotamia (in what is now Iraq) and Palestine (now Israel) harvested cereals. Sickles, stone mortars, and pestles indicate that grain was gathered and ground into flour, even if they do not prove that agriculture was practiced systematically this early. Frescoes at Tassili in the Sahara provide evidence of the astonishing changes that took place in that part of Africa. They show herdsmen of the 10th or 11th millennium B.C. watering cattle and leading them to pasture. The

The Sahara was not always a desert, as is clear from the frescoes at Tassili in Algeria depicting agricultural life in prehistoric times.

Neolithic period was a time of great land clearing. People used axes to cut down trees, flint scythes and sickles for harvesting, and millstones and grinding mills for making flour. The breeding of pigs for food also began during this period. Ceramics and pottery appeared in the 6th millennium B.C., making it possible to transport and store water and to cook food other than over an open fire.

Where were the first villages?

Throughout the Paleolithic period, humans were content with the caves or overhanging rocks and in primitive tents of animal skin. At the start of the Neolithic period they began building villages, and remains of human settlements dating from this time have been found throughout Europe. As protection from attackers, inaccessible sites were preferred, such as isolated hilltop crags. They also built villages on stilts in the middle of lakes.

Lake villages were made up of rectangular houses built on tree trunks driven deep into mud. On top of these supports, platforms were constructed from tree limbs and stout branches. The walls of the houses were either made of thick sticks or daubed with a mixture of clay and straw that dried to a hard surface (a technique still used by builders less than a century ago). Finally the roof beams were covered with reeds. A jetty linked the houses to the shore. These houses were built in great numbers in Switzerland, France, Italy, Germany, and Britain.

When were the first villages built?

The earliest remains of villagelike settlements were discovered at Jericho, in Israel, dating from 7000 B.C.

Layers of human settlements built over thousands of years eventually formed hills, which archeologists call tells. The excavation of the tell at Jericho – which is 70 feet (21 meters) high – has revealed that the site was occupied from the end of the Mesolithic period (Middle Stone Age) until the end of the Bronze Age (around 1000 B.C.). During this span of time the inhabitants of the village practiced agriculture and raised goats. The earlier houses at Jericho were round or oval and the later ones rectangular.

What are the oldest monuments?

Contrary to popular belief, the first standing-stone monuments were built not by the Celts, but around 4000 B.C. at the end of the Neolithic period.

In the Gulf of Morbihan region in France are found extraordinary standing-stone monuments called megaliths (Greek for "large stones"). These include menhirs (stones standing alone or in groups), dolmens (stone "tables"), cromlechs (circles of stone pillars), and tumuli (burial mounds).

Why were these structures, made of huge stones sometimes transported hundreds of miles, erected? The dolmens may have been funeral monuments; single menhirs perhaps celebrated an event, such as a victory. Some have been Christianized. The alignment of menhirs may have been important in the observation of stars and eclipses. This may be the purpose of Stonehenge, in England, where each stone in the giant double circle weighs more than 50 tons. These stones were transported from two quarries – one about 12 miles (20 kilometers) from the site, the other at a distance of 120 miles (200 kilometers) – and some may have come from Ireland. Tumuli served as funeral monuments and sometimes held more than one funeral chamber. The tumulus at Gavrinis in France has an entrance passage of square-cut stone covered with engravings. Although these monuments were not built by the Celts, they played a major role in Celtic ceremonies.

Stonehenge, on Salisbury Plain in southern England, is one of the most ancient standing-stone monuments. We know nothing of the people who built it, but they must have possessed sophisticated technology, given the complexity of this structure.

When did the Bronze Age begin?

It was between 2500 and 2000 B.C. that our ancestors discovered how to make bronze, which is an alloy of copper and tin.

Bronze was developed in Mesopotamia (the region between the Tigris and Euphrates rivers, in what is now Iraq), the center of bronze work in the 3rd millennium B.C. Bronze was good for tools, weapons, or jewelry. It could be formed into any shape, and the objects used for barter. The two main fabrication methods were pouring melted bronze either into an open mold or into two symmetrical molds. A third, the lost wax method, was more complex.

Where did the Iron Age originate?

The Iron Age began about 1200 B.C. among the Hittites, who developed blacksmithing and exploited iron-ore deposits in the Caucasus region and Anatolia (modern Turkey), part of the Hittite empire.

Bronze helmet dating from the 5th century B.C., found near Tène in Switzerland.

Iron objects dating from the 4th millennium B.C. have been found in Iraq and in Egypt, but these were made from meteorite ores rather than from iron excavated from the earth. Use of iron spread through the Mediterranean world and Egypt. A text dating from 900 B.C. reveals that iron then had a value eight times greater than that of gold. One reason that iron became valuable was the increasing scarcity of tin (necessary for the manufacture of bronze). Iron made possible the manufacture of the various tools that the agricultural society of the time needed, such as scythes, axes, tongs, saws, and nails, as well as items for military use.

Who were the first miners?

There is evidence of enterprising industrial activity dating back to the Neolithic period.

Neolithic people began to dig into the earth in search of flint, salt, clay, and various stones. Their digging tools were very basic – made from bone, animal horn, or stone – and the mine shafts they excavated were no more than 24 to 30 inches (60 to 80 centimeters) in diameter, barely wide enough to permit the passage of an adult person. Nevertheless, they dug to depths of 40 feet (12 meters) and sometimes extended the mines with horizontal galleries. Flint mines dating from the 5th millennium B.C. have been found in Portugal, Sicily, Belgium, and virtually all of northern Europe. Mining for metals began later – in the 3rd millennium B.C., as exposed sources of metal were exhausted.

When was

pottery invented?

As early as the Upper Paleolithic period (the later part of the Old Stone Age), people were making objects from clay. Shards of vessels and statuettes have been found at several sites dating from about 11,000 B.C.

These early remains are isolated and rare. Initially pottery making was not practiced continuously – probably because, for nomadic peoples, ceramic vessels were less convenient for transporting water than water skins made of leather. Around the 7th millennium B.C. people began to settle, build villages, and develop a more elaborate domestic life. Pottery became common throughout the eastern Mediterranean (in Turkey, Syria, and Greece) and the Near East. The first pots bear no resemblance to the ceramics of the classical Greeks – but they did make possible the development of cooking, especially soups and stews. The earliest potter's wheel was discovered at Ur in Mesopotamia and dates from around 3500 B.C. One early pottery technique was to hollow out a ball of clay; another was to coil rolls of clay in spirals, then smooth them into the desired shape. The technique of turning pots on a wheel was developed later.

When was

weaving invented?

The earliest woven fabrics, found in Egypt, date from around 5000 B.C. The quality of the weaving indicates that by then our ancestors had long known how to weave natural fibers.

Bone needles dating from the Paleolithic period have been found that are too fine to have been used for sewing leather thongs. Natural fibers do not survive long, and we can only imagine what the first fabrics were like, but they must have included fishing lines, fibers such as flax in Europe and cotton in India and Peru, and

A baked-clay vessel from the Neolithic period, discovered in a cave in France.

roughly twisted woolen yarn. There is no direct evidence of the existence of looms before 4400 B.C., but one is depicted on Egyptian pottery from that time. The most primitive type of loom consisted of two wooden sticks set into the ground connected by a horizontal bar placed across their tops, from which hung rows of thread weighted with small balls of baked clay to keep them vertical. The weaver would pass the weft through the suspended threads.

What were fibulas and torques?

Fibulas and torques were objects of personal adornment first made in the Bronze Age. A fibula is a pin or buckle that was used for fastening a large cape. A torque is a rigid necklace.

Originally the fibula was a thick pin with a flat head that was sometimes decorated. Later, especially among the Celts, it evolved into a richly decorated brooch. The Celts, who were fond of jewelry, have left many fibulas. The torque was a round collar of gold, silver, or bronze. Both torques and fibulas have been found in Celtic tombs.

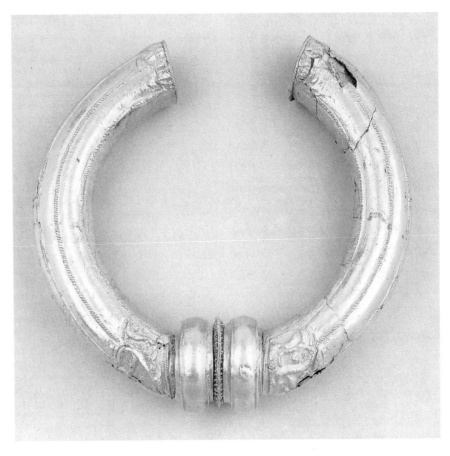

Gold torques, like the one above, were among the most common items of Celtic jewelry in Neolithic times. They were probably worn by men.

Who invented writing?

Western religious tradition places the location of the Garden of Eden and the Tree of Knowledge in Mesopotamia, now part of Iraq, between the rivers Tigris and Euphrates (the name Mesopotamia is Greek for "between two rivers"). So it is not surprising that it was people from Mesopotamia – the Sumerians – who invented writing, around 3500 B.C.

Soon afterward, perhaps inspired by the Sumerian example, writing appeared in various regions of the world: in Egypt, in China, and then in India (around 2500 B.C.). The writing of the Sumerians is described as cuneiform (Latin for wedgelike) due to the wedge-shaped signs that the scribes engraved on tablets with reed sticks. The signs resembled things they stood for. It was gradually realized that representing the sound of words, instead of the shape of objects, gave more scope. This crucial change did not occur for another 2,000 years. Writing was used to make inventories of possessions and armaments, and to record laws and edicts. From an early date it was also used as a means of diplomatic communication. Writing remained a secret code among those who held power.

How was the earliest writing deciphered?

The most ancient Mesopotamian cuneiform writing was deciphered by Henry Rawlinson, a British soldier, scholar, and diplomat.

Perched on a ladder, at a height of 330 feet (100 meters) above ground level, he copied a huge cuneiform inscription in three languages that covered a rock face at Behistun in Iran. He was then able to decipher first the ancient Persian text, then the second script used (Elamite), and finally the third (Babylonian). Later

excavations at the end of the 19th century made it possible to decipher Sumerian script with the help of Babylonian/Sumerian dictionaries compiled in antiquity.

Where does papyrus come from?

The papyrus is an aquatic plant that grows in abundance along the banks of the Nile river. From the 3rd millennium B.C., the Egyptians used its leaves as a writing surface. The leaves had to be beaten and dried in the Sun before use.

Before the invention of papyrus, people used wooden tablets and

Engraved on this stone is the deed of sale of a house and field – sold 4,500 years ago.

the bark of trees as writing surfaces. The Latin word *liber* first meant bark and then book; "library" comes from this word. The Chinese wrote on bone, tortoiseshell, and ivory. In the 2nd century B.C. the Greeks started using parchment (dried sheepskin), which later played an important role in the making of books from the 4th century A.D. Fabrics and copper, gold, and silver plates were used as writing surfaces in Southeast Asia; fabrics were also used in Egypt and the Islamic countries and by the Romans. Paper was first used in China, but not until the 1st century A.D. The most ancient text on paper that has survived dates from around A.D. 105–110.

When were the

first musical

instruments made?

Musical instruments such as whistles made from reindeer's hoofs and flutes made from birds' wing bones have been found dating from the later part of the Paleolithic period.

Song and dance probably began much earlier. The Egyptians have left us paintings and engravings depicting musicians playing wind and string instruments. Primitive wood and reed clarinets, flutes, and trumpets were played to entertain kings and enliven work in the fields. We know that by 2500 B.C. the Greeks had devised numerous instruments, among them the lyre, the harp, the cithara, flutes, pan pipes, and cymbals. Almost nothing remains of ancient Egyptian music, but the Greeks left a rich musical heritage and even developed a theory of music that provided the basis of modern musical scales.

When were the

first cities built?

The most ancient cities appear to have been the ones established in Mesopotamia during the 4th millennium B.C. Remains of ancient cities built with kiln-baked bricks have also been found in the Indus Valley.

One reason why so few vestiges of the ancient cities of Mesopotamia have survived is the materials with which they were built. Most structures were made of compacted earth or mixtures of clay and straw that do not endure. Kiln-baked bricks were used, but were reserved for royal buildings and

This painting on the walls of a tomb in Thebes in Egypt, dating from the 15th century B.C., shows a young woman playing a harp.

temples. Between 3000 and 2500 B.C. asphalt was discovered in Mesopotamia, allowing the construction of efficient water and sewer systems. People in the Indus Valley also developed such systems for their cities. Few vestiges of their civilization remain.

How did people

travel in

Mesopotamia

and ancient Egypt?

Mesopotamian traders, adventurers, and soldiers traveled mainly on foot, but

also rode on horseback, and used river barges and horse-drawn chariots.

By the 4th millennium B.C., a great deal of traveling was going on between the Mediterranean and the banks of the Indus River. The Greek historian Herodotus described river navigation in the region: "The boats of the Babylonians go down the river right to Babylon. They are a round shape and are made entirely of leather." Boats of this kind are still used in the marshlands of the Euphrates delta. The Egyptians began to build sailing craft in the 3rd millennium B.C. Egypt's location between the Mediterranean and the Red Sea made it a maritime nation. The ships' sails were made of woven flax or papyrus. A team of rowers went into action when the winds were not favorable.

With whom did the Mesopotamians trade?

Early Mesopotamian kings sought to demonstrate their wealth and power by importing valuable objects and precious stones and materials from distant lands.

No effort or expense was spared in adorning their temples and palaces. Rare stones were used for their steles (monumental columns) and in statues and statuettes representing gods and kings. These precious materials – gold, copper, carnelian, lapis lazuli, silver, alabaster – were brought from Iran, Afghanistan, India, and Siberia. Inscriptions, engraved on stone and clay tablets, tell us about their commercial exchanges: of cedar wood and stone brought from Syria; diorite (a dark volcanic stone) and wood from Arabia; and copper and gold from the Indus Valley.

Who invented the alphabet?

An alphabet consisting of simplified cuneiform symbols, dating from 1350 B.C., has been discovered in Syria. We also know that the Phoenicians used an alphabet of 22 characters from around 1100 B.C.

The alphabet was not a sudden invention. Initially, the earliest form of writing, Sumerian, was pictographic: made up of small

Bas-relief from the palace of Sargon II at Khorsabad, in Iraq, showing Assyrian ships transporting lumber for building purposes.

drawings representing objects and more abstract concepts. It then progressively became more alphabetic, with signs representing sounds instead of objects. Alphabetic writing made possible much more precise expression of thought, and is also easier to learn than pictographic writing because fewer symbols are needed. Alphabetic cuneiform script was used by several peoples who spoke different languages. The development of writing in Egypt is very interesting. By the 4th millennium B.C. the Egyptians had developed an alphabetic system of writing, yet still continued to use difficult pictographic script. The Greek alphabet, derived from that of the Phoenicians, was the first to represent vowels.

How was glass discovered?

It was the discovery of enamel, or rather the glazes used by enamelists, that led to the invention of glass in Mesopotamia and Egypt.

The glass manufactured in those distant times bore little resemblance to the glass we know today – possessing neither the fineness nor the transparency, since the process of fusion was not yet fully understood. In the 14th century B.C., during the reign of Tutankhamun, the Egyptians finally succeeded in making transparent glass. Phoenician merchants soon began to trade in glass throughout the Mediterranean – which is why the Romans thought they had invented it. Once the technique of glassblowing was discovered, flasks, glasses, and all sorts of containers could be made.

Which were the first gods?

From the earliest times our ancestors worshipped the forces of nature: water, fire, wind, rain, and the Sun. All that they desired or feared was governed by gods, whom they worshipped.

Anu (god of the sky) and his sons, Enlil (god of the wind), Nanna-Sin (the Moon), and Uta-Shamash (the Sun), ruled the sky and were the most powerful of the Mesopotamian divinities. Next in importance were the terrestrial gods of plants and water, upon whose goodwill man was directly dependent. The Mesopotamian gods are represented on cylindrical royal seals that can be "read"

Gods have always inspired fear and respect, as can be seen from this statuette of a Mesopotamian man kneeling in devout worship more than 4,000 years ago.

when rolled on plaster to obtain a print. Their attributes included the horned tiara (the more important the god, the more tiers of horns), the rays of the Sun god, the sheaf of wheat carried by Nisaba (goddess of grain), and the waves around Enli (god of water).

Who were the first doctors?

Originally medicine was an activity of magic and sorcery rather than a scientific method of treatment.

However, from a very early time healing ointments were prepared from plants, soils, and animal organs.

Human bones from the Paleolithic period reveal that a primitive surgery was also practiced. In 1948 in the ruins of Nippur, in Iraq, writing tablets were discovered inscribed with a list of Sumerian pharmaceutical products. We have learned from Mesopotamian texts that two kinds of medicine were practiced in that civilization: a practical medicine where the patient was examined and medicines prescribed, and a religious medicine where a priest or sorcerer examined the entrails of sacrificial animals and invoked the gods to expel the demons responsible for the sickness.

What were early calendars based on?

The first calendars were based on the movements of the stars and planets. Even early societies used a calendar, as they needed to set times for festivals and to establish dates for the collection of taxes.

The Mesopotamians developed a calendar based on the movements of the Moon. The months varied between 29 and 30 days, making a year of 354 days. Because the solar year is 365 days long, several days had to be added at the end of each calendar year. Other countries adopted different types of calendar, some of them based not on the movements of the stars but on the seasons and crop cycles. Our

Hippocrates was born on the Greek island of Kos in the 5th century B.C. He wrote the first "scientific" treatise on medicine.

current calendar, called the Gregorian calendar, was introduced by Pope Gregory XII on October 15, 1582. An error in the preceding calendar had caused a difference of 11 days, and the pope decided that Thursday, October 4, 1582, would be followed by Friday, October 15, 1582 – eliminating 11 days. Britain only adopted the new calendar in 1752, Russia in 1917, and Thailand in 1940.

Who were the first astronomers?

The scribes and astronomers of Mesopotamia, who invented the calendar, studied the stars and planets. But if the great megalithic monuments of the Stone Age were in fact observatories, then astronomy must have developed at a much earlier date.

It is believed that the megaliths of Stonehenge and other prehistoric sites were used to observe celestial phenomena, especially eclipses, but the lack of written evidence makes it impossible to know. The astronomy of the Babylonians is widely confirmed, and representations of the Sun and stars have been found on Babylonian pottery

In one of the earliest images of war that have survived (dating from around 2200 B.C.), Naramsin, king of Babylon, is shown trampling on his enemies. His horned helmet is a sign of divinity.

Who started the first war?

War surely goes back to the earliest days of humanity. The first wars of which we have historical knowledge were the ones between the Sumerians and the Semitic peoples of Mesopotamia around 2500–2300 B.C.

The victories of Sargon I, king of Akkad, created a Semitic empire extending from Lebanon to the Persian Gulf. After his death, a succession of other leaders seized power in the region. The most famous of these was Hammurabi, king of Babylon, who made himself ruler of all Mesopotamia. Victory steles (commemorative columns) engraved with images of armies on the march show the Sumerians with chariots and infantry, armed with spears and shields, and iron helmets.

What kind of money was used in ancient times?

According to ancient Greek historians, the Lydians were

6,000 years old. The Egyptians developed the science of the stars from an early date, too. The tomb of Ramses II was built in the 12th century B.C. as an astronomical observatory. In 130 B.C. Hipparchus, a Greek astronomer, listed 800 stars. Building on this, the Egyptian scholar Ptolemy, who lived in Alexandria, compiled a list of 1022 stars in the 2nd century A.D. His theories about the nature of the universe remained unchallenged until the 16th century.

the first people to use money – that is, to use metal worked into a specific form as a means of exchange for commercial transactions.

Before money came into circulation, our ancestors used a barter system – a field of barley could be exchanged for animals or for gold or silver or clothing. A similar system was practiced in prehistoric times, with captured animals, tanned hides, or tools serving as currency. Pearls were later used as a means of exchange, as were shells, sacks of gold powder, and precious metals. The oldest coins that have been found date from the 6th century B.C. These bear the image of a lion, the emblem of Sardis, the capital of Lydia, in Asia Minor and were issued by Croesus, the last Lydian king. The use of coins spread throughout the Mediterranean basin. Once the Greeks began to mint coins, the practice spread rapidly to the East.

Did anyone shave in the ancient world?

The razor is not a recent invention. Razors 2,500 years old have been found in Denmark, not far from a peat bog from which carefully shaven human bodies were exhumed. The body of a 4,000-year-old man found, perfectly preserved, in an Austrian glacier in 1991 was shaven. Egyptian frescoes also show men who were clean-shaven or who had neatly trimmed beards.

Shaving was a privileged activity. Only the very wealthy could afford the services of a barber, and razors were far from being as easy to use as the ones available nowadays. It required great skill to cut a beard with sharpened flint, as in prehistoric times, or with a piece of glass or honed bronze. It was only in medieval times that the cutthroat razor made its appearance; and not until the 20th century that the safety razor, changeable blades, and throwaway and electric razors became available.

How did people keep clean in ancient times?

The desire to bathe and wash one's clothing seems

The Romans frequently visited public thermal baths. Shown here is one of the rooms in the baths at Pompeii.

to date far back in time. Before the discovery of soap, our ancestors used natural cleansing materials – including plants, clay, ashes, and animal urine.

Plants such as soapwort and quillai (soapbark) are used in some modern shampoos; and clay is used by Arabs for washing the body and hair, which it leaves perfectly clean. Soap itself was an invention of the Gauls that the Romans were quick to adopt. However, they used it solely for personal hygiene. Wool was cleaned with animal urine; and clothing was either boiled or scrubbed with blocks of clay and rinsed in a river or stream.

Washing with soap is not the only way to cleanse the body. The Romans preferred thermal baths, where they perspired abundantly in a hot, humid atmosphere and then rubbed themselves down thoroughly. This method is still used in many parts of the world.

This terracotta sculpture from Boeotia (in Greece), dating from the end of the 6th century B.C., shows bakers kneading dough, with a flute player setting the rhythm for their work.

What tools did

the Gauls use?

The Gauls, inhabitants of early France of the 2nd century B.C., possessed highly developed tools, and employed sophisticated woodwork and metalworking techniques that hardly changed over the next three centuries.

The Gauls mastered many techniques: casting, founding, and assembling metals, tin-plating (the process of coating a surface with a smooth layer of tin), and enameling. Superb metallurgists, they worked all kinds of metals – bronze, iron, copper, silver. The Gauls' plows, wagons, and chariots were better designed than those made anywhere in the Mediterranean world and inspired the admiration of the Romans. The construction of casks was a familiar art to them, although it is a highly sophisticated technique that requires the ability to fit wood together precisely and a deep understanding of the reactions of wood and heated metal.

When did bread

first appear?

It is known that the ancient Egyptians had ovens and baked leavened bread, but it is quite possible that bread-making goes back to much earlier times.

Millstones and flat plates for grinding grain into flour have been found at many prehistoric sites. But it is not certain that our ancestors used the flour to bake bread. Breadmaking has long been a family affair, and in many countries of the world it remains an essentially feminine activity. In the Louvre Museum, in Paris, France, is a terracotta sculpture showing a row of ancient Greek women kneading dough to the rhythm of a flute. The dough was usually prepared at home and left to rise. Afterward, if the family did not have a bread oven, the loaves or cakes would be taken to the village oven – in the Middle Ages, these were known as "common ovens" – where they were baked in huge collective batches. To recognize their bread when it came out of the oven, each family marked it with a distinctive sign, such as crosses or parallel lines.

Taxation existed even in ancient times. These Assyrian peasants are shown taking part of their harvest to the tax collector (figure on the left).

Who made the first wine?

Historians think wine was first made in the Caucasus around 6,000 years ago.

Assyrian bas-reliefs from the 1st millennium B.C. suggest a complete mastery of the process of wine making. Egyptian pictures depict people harvesting and crushing grapes and storing wine in vessels. The Bible tells of winemaking in Palestine. But it was the Greeks and Romans that were dedicated to wine producing. Both civilizations extended vine growing throughout the Mediterranean basin and into Gaul (now France). The Romans developed the cultivation of vines and winemaking, seeking to maintain or improve the quality of their wine. Christianization in its turn promoted the spread of wine growing throughout Europe. Wine, identified with the blood of Christ, was used in the sacrament of Communion, so churches had to be assured of a supply. The Church increased the planting of vines, because it was more reliable to have wine available locally.

Since when have people paid taxes?

Taxes have existed since ancient times. A sovereign provided protection for his subjects. In exchange, his subjects were called on to enrich his estate and to

meet the cost of the troops who assured the defense of their village, region, or kingdom.

Taxes were originally paid in kind – a proportion of the harvest, a certain number of cattle, and so forth. Later they were paid in money. One of the oldest taxes was the tithe – a tenth of one's produce or revenue. In Biblical times tithes were paid to support the Hebrew priesthood. In the Middle Ages the tithe system was adopted by the Church to support the clergy. This religious tax has survived in a voluntary form known as tithing. One unpopular kind of tax was conceived in Europe in the Middle Ages: a period of obligatory service to the local feudal lord for the upkeep of his estates and to provide him with servants.

Did slavery exist in ancient times?

We do not know how far back slavery goes, but it can be assumed that with the first wars prisoners were taken and forced to do the most unpleasant work. Also at an early time, people undoubtedly exchanged slaves for goods, workers being viewed as a form of wealth.

Although the ancient Greeks invented democracy, they were also great employers of slaves. Many hands were essential to the accomplishment of many tasks, ranging from building temples to agricultural work, serving in the mansions of the rich, and rowing galleys. In ancient Rome slaves who had rendered valued service to their masters were sometimes freed or "manumitted." One can imagine the exhilaration felt by these *libertini* (freedmen) – who nevertheless often remained attached to the household of their former master, although with enhanced social status. A number of violent slave revolts occurred in

In Rome, a master frees one of his slaves – while an envious comrade grimly labors on.

Roman times, the most famous being the rebellion led by the gladiator Spartacus in 73 B.C.

When were the first sewers built?

Rome was the first city to build a proper underground sewerage system. The oldest and largest Roman sewer, the Cloaca Maxima, was built around 600 B.C. to drain the area around the Forum.

Nowadays, no one dreams of throwing their waste water out of the window, as was commonly done in medieval times. In towns, used water was then drained away, more or less effectively, by an open drain running along the middle of the street (the surrounding paving stones sloped toward it). Walking down these muddy streets was no doubt a delicate operation.

When was running water introduced?

Because water is essential for survival, people have always tended to settle near lakes and rivers. In other

locations, our ancestors dug wells or built cisterns (tanks for collecting rainwater).

The cistern was the method most widely adopted in antiquity. In addition to private cisterns, cities in Palestine, Egypt, and Asia Minor had huge public cisterns from which water could be drawn for the irrigation of crops. Running water represented an enormous improvement in living standards. In Egypt, Mesopotamia, China, and the Indus Valley traces have been found of the water-channeling from distant sources as early as the 4th millennium B.C. Water was transported through pipes and by canals and aqueducts (in Mesopotamia ceramic water pipes have been found dating from the 3rd millennium B.C.). Roman aqueducts were often superb works of architecture. One of the most famous is the Pont du Gard, which supplied water to the town of Nîmes, in southern France.

When were

forks invented?

Table forks were in use in Constantinople in the 10th century A.D., and first appeared in Europe in the 11th century.

Even today many peoples of the world do not use forks – the Chinese, for example, eat with chopsticks, and the Arabs prefer to eat with their fingers. Forks were known in antiquity, but were mostly used for cooking. In Europe the use of the fork for eating is said to have been introduced to the Venetians during the 11th century by a Byzantine princess – who astonished them by using a fork to bring food to her mouth. The same astonishment struck the French court when forks were imported by King Henry III in the 16th century. In England, in 1669 foreign visitors complained about the lack of forks.

Why were knives

so important?

The first flint tools made by Stone Age people were probably an early form of knife, used for cutting items such as meat, wood, and leather.

The first knives would have been no more than oval lumps of flint that happened to have a cutting edge all around. But knives have continued to evolve ever since, growing progressively longer and more refined. The knife has always been the companion of humans. All sorts of materials – including bone, bronze, iron, steel, gold, and silver – have been shaped in its manufacture with a view to making it sharper or more refined.

The Pont du Gard in France is a great example of Roman building techniques and architecture. It channeled water from the neighboring hills.

How long ago were spoons introduced?

Teaspoons, tablespoons, soup spoons, ladles... How did we ever manage without spoons?

The basic form of the spoon is not new: the ancient Egyptians, Greeks, and Romans all used spoons, but only for cooking or preparing medicines and cosmetics. European nobility began using spoons for eating in the Middle Ages – beautiful spoons in gold, silver, or crystal, their handles decorated with gems. At that time, spoon handles had an inconvenient cylindrical shape. The flattened handle did not evolve until around the 17th century.

What did the first nails look like?

The use of nails goes back to the Bronze Age. As soon as people had mastered the basic skills of metalworking, they began to make nails to fasten wood.

The oldest form of writing is known as cuneiform because of its

The first spoons were not used for eating. This small Egyptian spoon decorated with a young girl standing on a boat is in fact a cosmetic spoon.

wedge-shaped signs. However, the characters used in cuneiform script (which look rather like modern carpet tacks) also bear a resemblance to the heads of the nails forged in antiquity and the

Middle Ages. In antiquity iron, copper or silver nails were sometimes used as decorative items. Nail-studded trunks were very much in fashion and are still prized in India and other countries. For fastening wood, mortise-and-tenon joints secured with dowels (wooden pegs) give much more durable results than nails, because all the components are wood and therefore expand and contract at the same rate.

Were scissors known in antiquity?

Ancient scissors consisted of a single piece of metal that operated like a pair of tongs. The blades cut as they overlapped.

Scissors of this type have been found dating from around 1000 B.C. Even today, when shearing sheep, shepherds in many parts of the world use shears that are exactly like the scissors used in the ancient world. Scissors with two separate, pivoting blades have only been made since the 14th century. Since then, as with knives, various designs have been developed for specific tasks – such as sewing, trimming nails and hair, and cutting paper or cloth.

Men and Women Who Made History

Who is the first person whose name we know?

Probably Enmerkar, king of Mesopotamia, who wanted to secure the submission of a rival king.

Enmerkar sent a messenger to the ruler of the city of Aratta. The two kings could not agree, and the messenger had to go back and forth between them. The messenger had difficulty in remembering the long messages, so Enmerkar inscribed what he wanted to say on clay tablets. It may be that this is how written records began.

What is Hammurabi known for?

Hammurabi – founder of the first Babylonian Empire, which ruled Mesopotamia – compiled one of the earliest (possibly the first) written codes of law.

Mesopotamia (the region between the Tigris and Euphrates rivers, in what is now Iraq) was the cradle of the civilizations of Sumer, Akkad, Babylonia, and Assyria. When Hammurabi assumed the throne of Babylonia in 1792 B.C., the kingdom was growing more

and more powerful. Nevertheless, the task that faced him was not easy. He was confronted by numerous small neighboring kingdoms, all wanting to dominate Babylonia; and in a series of battles he defeated the kingdoms of Larsa, Mari, and Assyria. Hammurabi was an Amorite (the previous kings had been Sumerians) and it was in Akkadian, the new language of the country, that he drafted his code of laws in which crimes were accorded specific penalties. The limits of the law were thus established. The code was engraved on a stele (column) of basalt (a hard, black stone), which has been discovered at Suse in the southwest of Iran. Hammurabi, who referred to himself as "he who established justice on earth," is represented at the top of the stele before Shamash, the god of justice. He is also known for the

Attila, king of the Huns, was known as the Scourge of God. With his army of horsemen, he attacked the Romans and then the Gauls – but, due to the bravery of Saint Geneviève, he did not succeed in taking Lutetia (Paris).

correspondence he conducted with his neighbors — before proceeding to dominate them.

Why did Pharaoh Cheops build a pyramid?

The Egyptians believed that life after death was only possible if the body and the soul remained united. They therefore mummified their dead and protected the mummies – which is why the pharaohs of the Old Kingdom constructed the colossal tombs that are the pyramids. The most famous of these is the Great Pyramid of Cheops.

Regarded by the ancients as one of the seven wonders of the world, the Great Pyramid is 453 feet (138 meters) tall and occupies a site of around 10 acres (4 hectares). On the plateau of Giza, near Cairo in Egypt, there are three large pyramids (those of Cheops, Khephren, and Mykerinus) and three smaller ones of their queens. A corridor leads to an antechamber that opens onto the funeral vault containing the sarcophagus of the deceased pharaoh.

The Great Pyramid of Cheops is the most famous of the three large pyramids situated on the plateau of Giza, near Cairo.

The pyramids of Egypt are among the most visited sites in the world, yet they still retain their mystery. The techniques employed by the ancient Egyptian builders are only partly understood, and we do not know how they hoisted the blocks of stone into position.

When did Nebuchadnezzar live?

There were two kings of this name, but Nebuchadnezzar II (605–562 B.C.) is the one remembered in history. Like Hammurabi, one thousand years before him, he was a powerful king of Babylonia.

Mesopotamia (the region between the Tigris and Euphrates rivers) is, with Egypt, the site of the first recorded civilizations. People there created complex agricultural irrigation schemes and founded cities. Around the end of the 4th millennium B.C., they invented a system of writing. From the time of the kings of Sumer in the 3rd millennium B.C. until the time of Nebuchadnezzar, the king was both a warrior and the administrator who ran the country. Nebuchadnezzar made Babylon the greatest city of the ancient world. With its hanging gardens and its grandiose royal buildings, it was the political capital and the religious center of the country. Although pillaged and destroyed by (among others) the Hittites and the Elamites, the city was always reborn. The administrative structures perfected by Nebuchadnezzar are known thanks to the extensive records that survive on clay tablets written by scribes.

Who was Assurbanipal?

The last great king of Assyria, Assurbanipal (669–627 B.C.) regarded himself as the uncontested master of the world.

Assurnazirpal II and his sons Salmanazar III, Sargon II, and Assurbanipal extended the Assyrian Empire right across the Middle East. Under Assurbanipal, Assyria experienced its most brilliant period – and it was he who established Nineveh, on the banks of the Tigris, as his capital. To make sure their history would be remembered, the kings of Assyria inscribed the major events of their reigns on clay tablets. The walls of Assurbanipal's palace at Nineveh are decorated with huge bas-reliefs recording the king's achievements. The architecture of Nineveh was of colossal proportions. Like all Mesopotamian cities, it was surrounded by ramparts protecting a citadel. Inside the citadel were built a ziggurat (tiered temple) and other temples, and Assurbanipal's palace.

Why is Tutankhamun famous?

Dead at the age of 18 after ruling for just nine years, this Egyptian pharaoh would not be known today if his rich tomb had not been discovered in the Valley of the Kings in 1922.

On November 5, 1922, the British archeologist Howard Carter discovered the tomb of Tutankhamun, the last-but-one pharaoh of the 18th dynasty, who reigned over Egypt around the middle of the 14th century B.C. It was a priceless treasure that Carter and his sponsor, Lord Carnarvan, unearthed. The young monarch's funeral mask, in gold embossed with precious stones, is the most famous and most brilliant of the treasures displayed in the National Museum in Cairo. Tutankhamun was originally called Tutankhaton, but the priests made him take the name of the god Amun. The previous pharaoh, Akhenaton (1372–1354 B.C.), had opposed the cult of Amun and favored that of a Sun god, Aton, which did not require priests. After Akhenaton's death, the priests reasserted the cult of Amun. For 3,000 years, Egypt had been ruled by a king (the pharaoh) regarded both as a

The treasure discovered in Tutankhamun's tomb brought the young pharaoh lasting fame.

descendant of the great Sun god Ra and as a god himself. Revered and worshipped, the pharaoh was master of all – people, animals, and things. When he died, he became a divinity of the Kingdom of Shadows. Given the power and attributes of these kings who ruled absolutely, their tombs were understandably lavish.

Who was Nefertiti?

Nefertiti was the favorite wife of Akhenaton, the pharaoh who sought to establish the cult of the god Aton. Queen Nefertiti was a great beauty, as can be seen from the famous bust of her displayed in the Egyptian Museum in Berlin.

This queen, whose image can also be seen at the National Museum in Cairo, exerted a strong influence on her husband, Akhenaton. They lived in the 14th century B.C. and attempted to suppress the cult of Amun in favor of Aton.

Until the end of the 18th century, the history of ancient Egypt was restricted to a list of kings, classed in 31 dynasties, because no one had been able to decipher the writing of a civilization that lasted 5,000 years. This writing, in the form of hiero-

Moses was saved from the waters of the Nile by the pharaoh's daughter. Later he became the leader of the Israelites and led them to the Holy Land.

glyphics, kept its secrets until 1799, when an expedition sent to Egypt by Napoleon discovered the Rosetta Stone, which was inscribed in Greek as well as hieroglyphics and the more easily decipherable demotic Egyptian script. A French scholar, Jean-François Champollion, used the Rosetta Stone to decipher hieroglyphics.

What did

Moses do?

Born in Egypt of Jewish parents, Moses ("saved from the waters") narrowly escaped being killed – the fate that the pharaoh of the day had ordered for all Jewish male infants. Hidden in a cradle, Moses was found among the bulrushes at the edge of the Nile and raised by the pharaoh's daughter. As an adult, he organized the exodus (departure) of the Israelites from Egypt.

According to the Old Testament, while minding sheep in the desert Moses saw a bush that was on fire but remained unburned. He heard the voice of God say to him: "I have seen the misery of my people living in Egypt. Go, I send you before the pharaoh to demand that my people, the children of Israel, leave Egypt." As a result, Moses led the Israelites from Egypt around

1250 B.C., in search of their "promised land." The waters of the Red Sea are said to have parted to let them pass. Moses was then summoned to Mount Sinai by God and given two tablets of stone bearing the Ten Commandments.

Who was Abraham?

When Abraham (or Abram) reached the age of 99, God announced to him that he would be the father of a multitude of peoples. He is seen as the ancestor of both the Arabs and the Jews.

According to the Old Testament, Abraham left his home in Ur (now Iraq) to found a state whose people believed in one God. With his entire tribe, he finally reached the land of Canaan (now Israel). His grandson, Jacob (or Israel), is regarded as the ancestor of the Jews; a son, Ishmael, is seen as the ancestor of the Arabs.

What was the

Judgment of

Solomon?

Solomon, who ruled Israel from around 970 to 931 B.C.

and built the first temple in Jerusalem, was reputed to have been a just and wise king. As evidence of his wisdom, the Old Testament relates the following story.

Two women claimed the same child. Solomon decreed that the infant should be cut in half and divided between them. One of the women agreed, but the other abandoned her claim in order to save the child. Solomon concluded

According to the Bible, Abraham was ready to sacrifice his son on the orders of God. At the last moment God stopped Abraham from killing Isaac.

that the true mother was the one who would not allow the child to be killed.

Who was the greatest king of Persia?

Darius I, "Darius the Great King, King of Kings," dominated an empire made up of 23 nations. He ruled Persia (Iran) from 521 to 486 B.C.

The Persian Empire was founded by Cyrus the Great (Cyrus II), who lived from around 556 to 530 B.C. It covered a vast territory, including the Middle East and part of Greece. With the conquests of Darius it reached northwestern India. This huge empire, composed of peoples of different races, languages, and religions, remained peaceful for over two centuries. This unity was due to the administrative brilliance of its kings. Their strength was based on an efficient and highly mobile army. The royal guard was composed of archers and pikemen, who appear in the friezes of Darius's palace. The soldiers of the royal guard were called "the Immortals," because as soon as one soldier fell, another took his place. Darius continued the work of his predecessors, both as a military commander and as an administrator. The empire was divided into provinces, or satrapies, that acted as administrative areas. From the offices of the royal palace, orders and decisions were dispatched throughout the empire to each satrapy, each of which was ruled by a satrap (governor) appointed by the king. The organization of the empire was very precise, and at its summit sat the all-powerful sovereign. Darius had a magnificent palace constructed at Persepolis.

As king of Israel, Solomon is said to have gained a reputation for the wisdom of his judgments.

Did King Minos really exist?

This legendary king of Crete, famed for his wise judgments, was the son of Zeus, the god of gods in Greek mythology. Because of his wisdom, after his death Minos became a judge in Hades (the Underworld). His legend is closely intertwined with the origins of Cretan civilization. It is

not known whether a king called Minos existed outside legend.

What is known is that Minos gave his name to the Minoan civilization in Crete. His name is also linked to the legend of the Minotaur. Minos imprisoned the Minotaur (half-human, half-bull) below his palace in Knossos, in a labyrinth built by the craftsman Daedalus. Every seven years, the monster – the son of Pasiphae (Minos's wife) and a sacred bull – demanded the sacrifice of seven young boys and seven young girls. When Theseus (the future king of Athens) ventured into the labyrinth, Minos's daughter Ariadne, who was in love with Theseus, gave him a thread that allowed him to retrace his steps after killing the Minotaur. He and Ariadne then fled from Crete.

A great hero of the Trojan War, Ulysses survived dangerous adventures before returning to his island of Ithaca and his wife Penelope.

Who were the first Greek kings?

Between 1400 and 1200 B.C., powerful kingdoms grew up in Greece, dominated by the Achaeans, whose major cities were Mycenae and Argos. Agamemnon is the most famous of these early, legendary kings.

It was Agamemnon who ordered the famous war against Troy described by Homer in the *Iliad*. According to legend, the reason for this military expedition was the abduction of Helen by Paris, the son of the then king of Troy, Priam. Helen was the wife of Agamemnon's brother Menelaus, who was king of Sparta. Furious, Menelaus demanded that the kings of the other Greek cities help him recover his wife. The kings and princes of Greece – Agamemnon, Menelaus, Ulysses (king of Ithaca), Nestor (king of Pylos), and many others – set sail with their armies and for ten years laid siege to the city of Troy, the remains of which still exist in Turkey on the shores of the Aegean Sea.

What were the wanderings of Ulysses?

One of the mythical heroes of the Trojan War, Ulysses underwent amazing adventures returning from Troy. These inspired Homer's epic poem the *Odyssey*.

Known for his cunning, Ulysses (the Latin version of the Greek name Odysseus) was the king of two small islands in the Ionian Sea, Ithaca and Dulichium. It took him 20 years to travel home from Troy. First, storms and contrary winds drove him to the coast of Africa,

Homer, the most famous of the ancient-Greek poets, recites his poems to an attentive audience.

where his crew abandoned him. From Africa he made his way to Sicily, the land of the Cyclopses – the one-eyed giants. Next as a result of visiting Aeolus, god of the winds, Ulysses lost 11 ships. The enchantress Circe then kept him spellbound for a year. Then, avoiding the twin dangers (rocks and whirlpools) of Scylla and Charybdis, he arrived at the island of the sea nymph Calypso, who detained him for seven years. Setting off on a raft, Ulysses escaped drowning but managed to reach the island of the Phaeacians where he was greeted by Nausicaa, daughter of Alcinous, the island's king. With Alcinous's help he was at last able to return to Ithaca. There he was reunited with his wife, Penelope.

What was the sword of Damocles?

The sword figures in a story about Damocles, a courtier of Dionysius, tyrant of Syracuse, who lived at the start of the 4th century B.C.

Envious of the splendor in which Dionysius lived, Damocles kept on telling him that kings were the happiest men on earth. Tired of Damocles' envy, the king offered to exchange places with him for a day. Delighted, Damocles accepted and presided over a royal feast. Suddenly, to his horror, he saw a sword suspended over his head by

a single hair that might snap at any moment. The courtier instantly realized that Dionysius lived in perpetual fear of assassination or losing his throne. To say that you have a sword of Damocles hanging over your head means you feel threatened by imminent danger.

Who was Homer?

The greatest poet of ancient Greece was probably born in Asia Minor, not far from Troy – the city (now in Turkey) whose siege provides the central story of the *Iliad*. Seven cities claim to be his birthplace.

Was Homer blind, as legend relates? Did he actually write all 27,800 verses of the *Iliad* and the *Odyssey*? Or did several poets compose these epics? The work of Homer was the culmination of a long oral tradition. From the 10th century B.C., bards traveled to courts to sing the exploits of legendary heroes. In the *Iliad* much of the action centers around the wrath of the Greek hero Achilles who, during the siege of Troy, withdrew to his tent and refused to fight. Achilles' anger is due to the Greek commander, Agamemnon, having abducted Briseis, a prisoner of war captured by the Greeks, with whom Achilles is in love. Unlike the *Iliad*, the *Odyssey* is the story of only one man, Ulysses, whose weaknesses are matched by his resourcefulness. However, in the end his escape from the dangers he encounters is due to intervention by the gods on his behalf. The *Odyssey* is in effect an adventure story told in verse. Whether there was a poet named Homer we shall never know, but these two poems represented an important advance in Western culture and were among the first great stories about gods and men.

Who was

Hippocrates?

The most famous doctor in antiquity, Hippocrates was said to be descended from Aesculapius, the god of medicine. He is regarded as a forerunner of modern medicine.

Hippocrates was born on the Greek island of Kos (in the Aegean) in 460 B.C. and died around 377 B.C. His observations on the treatment of fractures and dislocated joints are still valid today. He also noticed that men burdened with heavy responsibilities suffered heart ailments

more than others. Today doctors still take the "Hippocratic oath," a pledge that they will observe a rigorous code of conduct. In accordance with his code, Hippocrates treated the poor without charge and was scrupulously honest. The Persian king Artaxerxes II offered Hippocrates the post of doctor to his armies, but he refused to serve a country that was at war with his own.

What was the

Age of Pericles?

Pericles was an outstanding military leader and one of the greatest statesmen of ancient Greece. He was born around 495 B.C. and died, in Athens, in 429 B.C.

At the end of the Persian Wars (499–479 B.C.), the Persian army had been driven from Greece, but Athens lay in ruins. Pericles, who was from a distinguished family, undertook to restore the city to its former grandeur. Repeatedly re-elected *strategos* (leader of the army) over a period of 30 years, Pericles governed with wisdom. Realizing that the city's future rested on its maritime strength, he built a powerful navy and a large commercial fleet. In 445 B.C. he negotiated a 30-year peace with

Under Pericles the arts, architecture, and wealth of ancient Athens prospered to such an extent that the city's golden age is known as the Age of Pericles.

Sparta – but in 431 B.C. the treaty was broken. Two years later, he died of plague while Athens was under siege. His reign is seen as the golden age of Athens (Pericles' contemporaries called him "the Olympian"). During the 5th century B.C., the Athenians attained their highest achievements in drama, sculpture, ceramics, and painting. Under Pericles the best architects of ancient Greece rebuilt the Acropolis and its temples in magnificent style.

Plato, philosopher and disciple of Socrates, left an important body of written work. Here he is shown debating philosophical ideas with another great Greek philosopher, Aristotle (on the right).

Who were

Socrates and Plato?

Two of the greatest philosophers of ancient Greece, they both lived and taught in Athens. Socrates was born around 470 B.C. and died in 399 B.C. Plato, who was one of Socrates' disciples, was born around 428 B.C. and died around 348 B.C.

Socrates did not leave any written work, but his ideas are still well known today. The master taught his disciples to know themselves and to enrich their spirit through reflection. However, his unflinching honesty and habit of asking probing, ironic questions earned him the enmity of the Athenian authorities. He was condemned to death for "impiety" and "corrupting the youth." His death was both dramatic and heroic: he serenely drank the cup of hemlock poison that was handed to him and died in conversation with his students.

Plato belonged to a noble family and was well educated. After studying the teachings of other philosophers, he met Socrates in 408 B.C., became his disciple and recorded his master's thoughts in his "dialogues." Due to illness, he was not present at Socrates' death. After traveling extensively, he founded the Academy, a teaching institute that he directed for 20 years. Plato left an important body of work, and his theories – known as Platonism – have provided the foundations of most modern philosophical thought.

What countries

did Alexander the

Great conquer?

In just 10 years, with an army that rarely exceeded 400,000 men, Alexander the Great conquered the Persian Empire and led an expedition that reached India.

Although he only lived to 33, Alexander astonished the world with his conquests. After being educated by the Greek philosopher Aristotle, he became king of Macedon (at the northern end of the Greek peninsula) in 336 B.C., aged 20, when his father, Philip II, was murdered. He completed the conquest of Greece begun by his father. He then disembarked in Asia Minor near the ancient city of Troy. Marching 12,000 miles (20,000 kilometers), he conquered the entire Persian Empire. Egypt welcomed him, and Mesopotamia offered no resistance. He afterward reached the Punjab in India, where his army, tired of harsh winters, forced him to turn back. Babylon became the capital of the new empire, and Alexander died there, probably of malarial fever, in 323 B.C. The legendary image remains of Alexander on his horse Bucephalus, an animal which he succeeded in training when he was only 12. Alexander's vast empire did not survive him. Upon his death it was divided up among six of his generals, known as the Diadochi. Today many cities (such as Alexandria in Egypt) still bear his name.

Are Romulus and Remus fact or fiction?

Romulus and Remus were part of the legendary story of the founding of Rome. If the two brothers did exist, they would have lived in the 8th century B.C.

According to legend, Amulius, the youngest son of King Procas of Alba Longa, a city in ancient Latium, killed his brother, Numitor, and seized the throne. Amulius also killed Numitor's son and forced Rhea, Numitor's daughter, to become a vestal virgin. These priestesses were forbidden to have children, but Mars (the god of war) made Rhea the mother of twins, Romulus and Remus. Amulius threw Rhea into prison and cast the twins adrift in a cradle on the River Tiber. They were found by a she-wolf who, having lost her own young, fed the infants her milk. Romulus and Remus fought over the right to found Rome, and Remus was killed. According to the legend, Rome was founded on the Palilia (the festival of Pales, goddess of sheepfolds and pastures), on April 21, 753 B.C.

Who were the real founders of Rome?

The Etruscans are thought to have founded Rome.

The Etruscans settled in Italy at the end of the 8th century B.C., to exploit the copper and silver mines of the region as well as the iron mines of the island of Elba. Skilled seamen and metalworkers, they traded ores and metal objects. They prospered and their cities flourished. Arezzo and Volterra are Etruscan cities, as are Pisa, Fiesole, and Bologna. Toward the end of the 7th century, the Etruscans seized a scattering of

Conqueror of the Persian Empire, Alexander the Great flew from conquest to conquest. He became king of Macedon at the age of 20 and died in 323 B.C. at the age of 33.

hilltop villages overlooking the River Tiber. They established a new city (the future Rome) and surrounded it with ramparts. They continued to develop the city under three kings (Tarquinius Priscus, Servius Tullius, and Tarquinius Superbus), and built a forum (public meeting place) and elegant stone houses. Then in 509 B.C. the inhabitants of the city rebelled – and the Etruscans, who were not great warriors, found themselves dominated by the Romans.

The vanquished Etruscans nevertheless greatly influenced their conquerors. The Romans retained the organization of the Etruscan army. Deeply religious, the Etruscans practiced the art of divination – to know the future and the will of the gods, specialized priests called haruspices observed the flight of birds and interpreted the meaning of their positions, numbers, and speed. The Etruscans believed in life after death, so they laid out tombs with care. The excavation of tombs, at Tarquinia and Cerveteri, in Italy, has given us information on the lives of the founders of Rome. Great architects, the Etruscans bequeathed to the Romans the architectural techniques of the arch and the ribbed vault. They were also accomplished hydraulic and sanitary engineers.

What is a Pyrrhic victory?

Pyrrhus, king of Epirus in northwestern Greece, was born around 318 B.C. His victories against the Romans were more a cause for grief than rejoicing, because they cost so many lives.

Pyrrhus "the Eagle" dreamed of conquering an empire. The Greek cities of Italy, threatened with Roman conquest, appealed to the king of Epirus for support. Pyrrhus marched on Rome and won, at a cost of heavy casualties. A second battle took place, which the king of Epirus won narrowly – again with terrible casualties. The king declared "One more victory like this and we are lost." A Pyrrhic victory has therefore come to mean a victory that is so costly that it is of questionable value.

Who defeated Hannibal?

One of the greatest generals of ancient times, the Carthaginian leader Hannibal found his match in the Roman general Scipio Africanus. Their two cities, Carthage in North Africa (it is now in Tunisia), and Rome in Italy, were in a fight to the death.

Hannibal went from North Africa to Spain and, using elephants, crossed the Alps into Italy and

After defeating the Romans, Hannibal was himself defeated in 202 B.C. by the Roman military leader Scipio Africanus. Later, in 146 B.C., another Scipio burned Hannibal's native city, Carthage, to the ground.

The great scientist Archimedes was known for his discoveries in the physical sciences. He was killed by a Roman soldier at the end of the siege of Syracuse.

Why did Archimedes cry "Eureka!"?

The Greek scientist exclaimed "Eureka!" ("I've found it!") when he stepped into a bath – because he had realized that it was possible to determine the volume of a body by measuring the displacement of water. His discovery is known as "Archimedes' principle."

marched south to Rome. But Scipio succeeded in halting the Carthaginian advance. At 17 Scipio had proved his courage by saving the life of his father. Now, aged 24, he was given a command in Spain and succeeded in taking the city of Carthago Nova (now Cartagena), which Hannibal had fortified. Scipio attacked the city in broad daylight, at the moment when his foes expected it least, and took it at the first assault. Hannibal himself was still in Italy, however. To make the Carthaginians recall Hannibal from Italy, Scipio decided to invade Africa, with 30,000 men, choosing as his target the city of Carthage itself. The two armies met at Zama,

about 300 miles (480 kilometers) from Carthage, in 202 B.C. Hannibal was defeated, despite careful preparation for the battle. The Carthaginians were forced back to Carthage, 35 years after setting out from the city. Scipio did not demand Hannibal's surrender, but imposed a harsh treaty on Carthaginians. The defeated city was forced to abandon all claims to possessions outside Africa and to pay heavy indemnities; Scipio also demanded that Carthage surrender its galleys and elephants. Returning to Rome, Scipio was greeted with unprecedented adulation. With the defeat of Hannibal, Roman power was unchecked.

Born in Syracuse, in Sicily, in 287 B.C., Archimedes made numerous discoveries in mathematics and the physical sciences. He also devised systems of cogs and pulleys to reduce physical labor, and had the idea of using mirrors across great distances to burn enemy ships. Archimedes was killed by a soldier when, after a three-year siege, the Romans took Syracuse in 212 B.C. He didn't hear the soldier's approach.

What did Euclid invent?

A brilliant mathematician, Euclid established the basic

principles of geometry that are still taught today.

The famous Greek mathematician lived in the 3rd century B.C. and founded a school at Alexandria, in Egypt. His *Elements of Geometry* consist of 13 books. He also wrote works on music, optics, and astronomy that have been lost.

Why do we say "as rich as Croesus"?

Croesus was king of Lydia, in Asia Minor, around 560 B.C. A country with numerous gold mines, Lydia was the first Mediterranean state to mint gold coins.

During Croesus' reign, Lydia rose to the peak of its powers and wealth through gold mining and extensive trade. Croesus also conquered some Greek cities and extended his empire. He admired Greek art and culture and gave generously to Greek temples. He formed an alliance with Babylonia, Egypt, and Sparta. However, his allies did not help him when he attacked Persia, and the Persian king Cyrus responded by seizing Sardis, the capital of Lydia. Legend tells us that Cyrus spared Croesus, preferring to make him his advisor.

Why did Julius Caesar and Pompey become enemies?

Together Julius Caesar and Pompey became the two most powerful men in Rome. But once they had gained power, their friendship turned to rivalry.

An outstanding general, Pompey re-established order in Spain, rid the Mediterranean of pirates, and conquered Syria and Palestine, where he took Jerusalem in 63 B.C. Returning to Rome, he formed a triumvirate (three-man government) with Crassus and Caesar, but the death of Crassus left Pompey and Caesar competing for power.

When Caesar left for Gaul with his legions, Pompey assumed power. Caesar hesitated to return to Rome, because to do so without the authority of the Senate meant that he would be declared the enemy of the Republic. In the end, Caesar marched on Rome and defeated Pompey – who sought refuge in Egypt, where he was killed.

Which was Virgil's most important work?

Virgil was the finest Latin poet. Born near Mantua in 70 B.C., he died in 19 B.C. His longest poem, the *Aeneid*, ranks in importance with Homer's *Iliad* and *Odyssey*.

A popular Roman general and statesman, after his brilliant victories in the Mediterranean Pompey became the enemy and rival of Caesar. In the end he fled to Egypt, where he was assassinated.

It was the need to escape Herod's planned "Massacre of the Innocents" that prompted Mary and Joseph's flight into Egypt (above) with the infant Jesus.

Virgil wrote the *Aeneid* after Emperor Augustus suggested that he should write an epic poem in his honor. It tells how Aeneas, a Trojan prince, came to Italy after the fall of Troy and celebrates the founding of Rome. The *Aeneid* is divided into 12 "books." Virgil traveled to Greece in search of inspiration and worked on the poem for 10 years. Aware that he was dying and had not had time to polish it, he wanted the manuscript to be burned — fortunately, his friends ignored his wishes.

How did

Cleopatra die?

Cleopatra committed suicide by allowing herself to be bitten by an asp. Cleopatra was Egypt's seventh queen of that name.

The young queen of Egypt had just been driven from her throne when Julius Caesar arrived in Alexandria. Cleopatra wanted to meet him and to make him an ally.

Fearing assassination, Cleopatra is said to have had the idea of sending Caesar gifts, including rugs – in one of which she hid herself. After Caesar's murder, Cleopatra married his associate, Mark Antony. Following their defeat at the Battle of Actium, both Antony and Cleopatra committed suicide.

Why did Herod

want to kill the

infant Jesus?

Herod I, king of the Roman province of Judaea, was born in 73 B.C. and died in A.D. 4. According to the Bible's New Testament, hearing that the Wise Men were looking for the newborn "king of the Jews," he decided to kill the infant to ensure the continued reign of his heirs.

The New Testament tells how Herod told the Wise Men that he needed to know the child's whereabouts, so that he could bow down before him. The Wise Men found Jesus in a manger in Bethlehem. When the Wise Men did not return, Herod ordered his soldiers to kill every child in Bethlehem less than two years old.

Warned by an angel of Herod's intentions, Mary and Joseph fled to Egypt – which is how Jesus escaped what came to be called the "Massacre of the Innocents."

Who assassinated Julius Caesar?

On March 15, 44 B.C., Julius Caesar was stabbed to death in the Roman Senate by a group of aristocrats who felt he had become too powerful. Seeing his friend Brutus among the conspirators, the emperor is said to have cried, "Et tu, Brute?" ("Brutus, you too?").

A brilliant general and politician, Caesar was also an historian and autobiographer. He accomplished the conquest of Gaul (modern France) and returned to Rome with his army to eliminate his rival Pompey. Caesar won victory after victory, put Cleopatra on the throne of Egypt, and just before the conspiracy that killed him, was made dictator for life.

Why were Roman emperors called Augustus?

"Augustus," a Latin word meaning "inspiring respect and admiration," became part of the title of every emperor of Rome.

The first Roman emperor was Julius Caesar's great-nephew, Octavian. Julius Caesar adopted Octavian as his son and made him his heir. Octavian revenged the death of his great-uncle and made himself master of Rome and its provinces. On becoming emperor, he took the title of Augustus and ruled over one of the most brilliant periods of Roman history, which became known as the Augustan Age.

Who was Spartacus?

A Greek slave who had become a gladiator, Spartacus led the largest slave revolt in Rome's history.

Protected by only a shield and helmet, in the arena Spartacus had proved to be a match for better-armed gladiators. In 73 B.C. he escaped and led the most successful slave rebellion in ancient times. For two years he held off troops sent against him, but was defeated and killed by Crassus, a wealthy politician who had allied with Pompey and Caesar to share power.

The adopted son of Julius Caesar, Augustus brought peace and prosperity to Rome. Future emperors all took the same title.

Was the Emperor Nero as bad as history claims?

Nero deserved his evil reputation. Born in A.D. 37, he died in A.D. 68 after a murderous career.

It was only because his mother, Agrippina, poisoned the Emperor Claudius, who had adopted him, that Nero gained the throne. He then poisoned his half-brother Britannicus, who seemed a threat, and killed his mother. In A.D. 64, a fire broke out in Rome. Nero played the lyre while he watched the capital burn. The first persecutions of the Christians began under Nero, who accused them of having started the fire. His regime of terror eventually provoked resistance. In the end, proclaimed an enemy of the Republic by the Senate, he committed suicide.

When did the Roman Empire end?

The western part of the Roman Empire finally succumbed to the pressure of barbarian invasions around

A great philosopher and teacher, Prince Gautama Siddhartha, who became known as the Buddha, was born in Nepal around 560 B.C. His teachings, which form the basis of Buddhism, spread through India, China, and Japan. This huge reclining statue of the Buddha is in Sri Lanka.

A.D. 476. Odoacer, chief of the Heruli (a Germanic tribe) and commander of the imperial guard, deposed the last Roman emperor, Romulus Augustulus.

In the 1st century B.C. some Germanic tribes began to migrate south from northern Europe. During the next 500 years, they hurled themselves at the Roman Empire. In the 3rd century A.D. the Franks and the Alemanni penetrated into Gaul. During the 4th and 5th centuries, other Germanic peoples, also under pressure from the Huns, filtered into the Roman Empire. The Visigoths ravaged Italy, seizing Rome in

A.D. 410. The Angles and the Saxons seized Britain. The Vandals devastated Gaul and Spain. The Ostrogoths poured into Italy. In 476 the western part of the empire finally collapsed.

When did the Buddha live?

The Buddha ("the enlightened one") is the name given to Prince Gautama Siddhartha, the founder of Buddhism, who was born in Nepal around 560 B.C. He died in India around 478 B.C.

The son of a king of the Sakya clan, Gautama became a monk at the age of 30. The Buddha stressed the importance of meditation and self-discipline, and taught that one could reach *nirvana* (enlightenment) by purifying one's thoughts and actions. His teachings spread through India, China, and Japan, to form the basis of Buddhism.

Who was Confucius?

Confucianism is seen as a system of moral and philosophical teachings, rather than a religion. Its founder, K'ung Fu-tzu, or Confucius, lived at approximately the same time as the Buddha.

Confucius taught that people should conduct their lives along "a course of moderation." An idealist, he believed that it was possible for anyone to be good, loyal, and generous. His disciples looked upon him as a saint, and temples were erected in his honor.

Why was Attila known as "the scourge of God"?

The Chinese philosopher Confucius believed that any person could become good, loyal, and generous.

Attila, king of the Huns, was born near the River Danube in A.D. 395 and died in 453. Feared by all, he was called "the Scourge of God."

The Huns lived on the banks of the River Danube, in what is now Hungary. Attila had completed his education at the court of the Emperor Honorius in Rome, where he developed a hatred of the Romans. He later attacked them in the East, in Gaul (now France), and in Italy, terrorizing the population. According to legend, wherever Attila passed with his hordes of horsemen, the grass never again grew. He was eventually defeated by the Visigoths in France in 451.

Which city was founded by the Emperor Constantine?

Constantine the Great, the first Roman emperor to become a Christian, built a new capital at Byzantium, situated on the Bosphorus, where Europe and Asia meet. In A.D. 330 Byzantium became Constantinople. In 1453 it became Istanbul.

It was Constantine who ended the persecution of the Christians. Constantinople rivaled Rome and was richly endowed with beautiful architecture. Later, on the death of the Emperor Theodosius, in A.D. 395, the Roman Empire was divided into the Western Empire (with Rome as the capital) and the Eastern Empire. The Western Empire collapsed in the 5th century under barbarian invasion – but the Eastern Empire survived until 1453, when Constantinople was captured by the Ottoman Turks.

What made Harun al-Raschid famous?

Harun al-Raschid is the man who inspired the *Arabian Nights*. He also developed Baghdad (now the capital of Iraq) into a magnificent city. He was born in A.D. 766 and died in Persia in 809.

In four years 100,000 workers, directed by great Arab architects, built a beautiful city on the banks of the River Tigris, though little of it now remains. In the *Arabian Nights* (also known as *The Thousand and One Nights*), Scheherazade relates the life of the Caliph of Baghdad, weaving into this account the legends and tales that her master loved, such as the stories of Aladdin and the Magic Lamp and Ali Baba and the Forty Thieves.

Was Saint Peter the first pope?

Simon of Galilee, called Peter, was the leader of the Twelve Apostles. Born in Judaea, he died in Rome in A.D. 64. He is regarded as the first Bishop of Rome – and so, in effect, the first pope.

After the death of Christ, Peter traveled throughout the Roman world to spread Christianity. Jesus had given him the name of Kephas,

"rock," to signify that he would be the rock upon which the Christian Church would be founded. After the fire of Rome in A.D. 64, he was arrested and condemned to death by crucifixion.

Which saint survived being thrown to the lions?

To try to halt the spread of the Christian religion, the Romans resorted to persecutions. The young Saint Blandine was among the first to be condemned.

Many of the early Christians died horribly. They were crucified, burned alive, pierced with arrows, devoured by wild beasts, or flayed. Huge crowds of spectators went to watch Christians thrown to the

The leader of the Twelve Apostles, Saint Peter is regarded as the founder of the Christian Church. He died in Rome, crucified upside down.

lions in the arenas. At Lyons, in France, in A.D. 177 some 48 Christians were martyred this way. Among them was a young girl named Blandine. When she was thrown to the lions, they ignored her. She was stretched on the rack, then thrown to an angry bull.

When was

Muhammad born?

The founder of the Islamic religion, Muhammad was born in Mecca (now in Saudi Arabia) around A.D. 570. He died in Medina (also in Saudi Arabia) in 632.

Orphaned young, Muhammad traveled with the caravans of Arabia. He often heard Jews and Christians speaking of their faith and of a single God. Around A.D. 610 he received the revelation that there was but one God, named Allah. Muhammad meditated in a cave on Mount Hira and prayed to Allah to reveal himself to the Arabs, as he had to the Jews and Christians. The angel Gabriel appeared to Muhammad and asked him to go out and convert the world. He then began to preach faith in the one true God, and renunciation of a selfish life. The Koran, the holy book of Islam,

After much fighting, in 1099 Godfrey de Bouillon, leader of the First Crusade, liberated Jerusalem from Turkish control.

contains all Muhammad's revelations. His teachings provoked the anger of the authorities in Mecca, and in 622 he was forced to flee to Medina. This flight (the Hegira) is seen as the start of the Muslim era and of the "holy war" or struggle to defend and spread the faith.

Who headed the

First Crusade?

Godfrey de Bouillon was a French nobleman who, with his brothers, headed the First Crusade. The Crusade was launched to liberate the tomb of Christ in Jerusalem from Muslim control.

Godfrey, the eldest son of the Count of Boulogne, visited Jerusalem with a group of pilgrims. He could not afford the admission price to the Holy Sepulcher, and on asking the guard if he could enter for free, he received a thrashing. He could not forget his humiliation, and in 1096 he returned to Jerusalem at the head of the First Crusade. In 1099 Godfrey captured Jerusalem from the Turks and was elected ruler of Jerusalem, with the title of "Defender of the Holy Sepulcher." He died a year later.

Where was Genghis

Khan's empire?

Genghis Khan began to lay the foundations of the Mongol Empire in 1206, when he organized the Mongols into

a federation. By the time of his death, in 1227, his empire stretched from the Yellow Sea of China to the Black Sea of Russia.

Genghis Khan began by establishing kingdoms in China and Manchuria (today the largest province of northeastern China). In 1206 he adopted the title of Genghis Khan ("universal ruler"). His hordes, fearsome horsemen from Mongolia, conquered northern China, Afghanistan, and western Iran. Notorious for killing, looting, and burning, they spread terror in their path. Genghis Khan's sons expanded the empire further – conquering southern China, Iran, Iraq, and Syria – so that it reached the frontiers of Arabia and eastern Europe. The Mongols were, however, great conquerors but poor administrators. At the end of the 13th century, the empire broke up into smaller parts, and the rulers became absorbed into the culture and civilizations of their subjects.

Where is the story of William the Conqueror told?

The story of William the Conqueror's invasion of England is told in the Bayeux Tapestry, in Normandy. This embroidery on cloth, about 230 feet (70 meters) long, records the various episodes of the conquest in 58 scenes.

Descended from the Vikings, William was born in France in 1028 and became Duke of Normandy in 1035. In September 1066, claiming that his cousin, King Edward the Confessor, had promised that he would succeed to the English crown, William embarked with his troops near Dieppe, France, and crossed the Channel to England in a flotilla of boats. After defeating the English at the Battle of Hastings, during which their king, Harold II, was killed, William was crowned king of England in Westminster Abbey on Christmas day, 1066. As Duke of Normandy he owed fealty (obedience) to the king of France, but as king of England he was his equal. William died in Rouen, France, in 1087, after a reign lasting 20 years.

Who was the last Aztec emperor?

The last Aztec sovereign was Cuauhtemoc. Born between 1495 and 1502, he was hanged in 1525 on the orders of Spanish conquistador Hernán Cortés.

The Aztecs were an ancient people of Mexico. In 1325 they founded their capital, Tenochtitlán – near today's Mexico City –

The 58 scenes of the Bayeux Tapestry provide a vivid pictorial record of the invasion and conquest of England by William the Conqueror and the Normans in 1066.

and dominated the country until the arrival of the Spanish, led by Cortés, in 1519. In 1520 Cuauhtemoc, then high priest, succeeded his uncle Cuitlahuac as ruler of the Aztec Empire. But his resistance to the Spanish troops could not prevent the empire's destruction in 1521. Cortés became governor general of New Spain. Cuauhtemoc refused to submit to his rule and was hanged in 1525.

Who opened up the trade route to India?

Henry the Navigator (1394–1460), the son of King John I of Portugal, encouraged navigators to discover a trade route to India by sailing south on the Atlantic Ocean to the Cape of Good Hope and around the continent of Africa.

He wished to avoid having to make extortionate payments to the Turkish merchants who controlled the Mediterranean trade routes, and he also wanted to spread Christianity to the peoples of Africa. Eleven years after Henry's death, the Portuguese became the first Europeans to cross the equator (in 1471). In 1487 Bartholomeu Dias rounded the Cape of Good Hope, but failed to reach India. In 1497 Vasco da Gama reached India via the Cape of Good Hope. In 1500 another Portuguese navigator, Pedro Cabral, was carried by the current to Brazil (which he claimed for Portugal) and then landed in Mozambique, in eastern Africa, before sailing on to Calicut (Calcutta), where he negotiated the first trade agreement between India and Portugal.

Who reached North America before Christopher Columbus?

Eric the Red, the Norwegian explorer born at Jaeren in Norway around A.D. 940, discovered Greenland around 985, and Canada around 1000.

Wanted for murder, Eric fled Norway with his father and took refuge in Iceland, where they learned of islands still further to the west. Setting out to explore these lands, Eric reached the southern tip of an icebound land, which he named Greenland to attract settlers there. From there the sailor-settlers found their way to the American continent, landing around A.D. 1000 on the coast of Labrador (between the Atlantic Ocean, Hudson Bay, and the Saint Lawrence River). Eric died in Greenland around 1010.

Vasco da Gama embarks from Lisbon in 1497, bound for India.

Why wasn't America named after Columbus?

America was named after Amerigo Vespucci, an Italian explorer, by a German mapmaker. Vespucci did visit the West Indies, Venezuela, and Brazil, but not until 1499.

Maps published in 1507 labeled the New World "America Terra." This was because of an account of Vespucci's voyages describing how he discovered the New World. It was actually Christopher Columbus who was the first to reach the New World, on October 12, 1492, after a direct crossing of the Atlantic sponsored by the sovereigns of Spain. The Spanish gave his name to Colombia, the state that they founded in South America in 1510.

Who was the first to circumnavigate the globe?

The Portuguese navigator Ferdinand Magellan (1480–

Columbus discovered the New World on October 12, 1492. On his return, he made a gift of the new lands to the king and queen of Spain.

1521) generally gets the credit, though perhaps it should go to his Spanish captain, Juan Sebastian del Cano, who completed the voyage after Magellan died.

In 1519 Charles V, king of Spain, supplied Magellan with ships so he could seek a new trade route, via Cape Horn, the tip of South America, for importing spices from India. After passing through the strait that now bears his name, Magellan sailed into the Pacific Ocean (which he named), but was killed in the Philippines. Only one of his ships, captained by del Cano, got back to Spain safely, in 1522.

What did Gutenberg invent?

Johannes Gensfleisch Gutenberg (1400–68) did not invent the printing press – but between 1430 and 1440, in Strasbourg, he perfected a method of printing with movable metal type.

In partnership with Johannes Fust, in Mainze, Germany, around 1450, Gutenberg printed a Bible running to 1,282 pages. Although this represented a landmark in printing, only ten copies of Gutenberg's Bible have survived.

What happened to Henry VIII's wives?

Henry VIII married six wives in succession and had two of them beheaded. Born in 1491, he became king of England in 1509 and Ireland in 1541.

Henry's marriages to his first and fourth wives, Catherine of Aragon (mother of Queen Mary I) and Anne of Cleves, were annulled. The two wives whom he had beheaded were his second wife, Anne Boleyn (the mother of Elizabeth I), and his fifth wife, Catherine Howard. His third wife, Jane Seymour, died 12 days after giving birth to a son (Edward VI). Henry's last wife, Catherine Parr, survived him.

Who was Ivan the Terrible?

The son of Ivan III, "Sovereign of All Russia," Czar Ivan IV – known as Ivan the Terrible – was only three years old when his father died. He assumed power in 1547, at the age of 17.

Ivan's first wife, Anastasia, exercised a calming influence on him. But after her death in 1560 he became suspicious of everyone and began a reign of terror that lasted until his death in 1584. On Ivan's orders, his guards massacred more than 1,000 of the Boyars, the powerful Russian nobles whom he suspected of plotting against him. As he aged, his mental state grew worse, and in the course of a dispute he killed his eldest son.

Who founded Protestantism?

The Reformation, the great religious movement that took place in Europe in the 16th century, gave rise to the Protestant churches. Its founder was the German preacher Martin Luther.

The son of a miner, Luther studied to be a lawyer; but one day, walking through the countryside, he was caught in a violent storm and vowed to become a monk if he survived. He entered an Augustine monastery at Erfurt in 1505 and went to Rome in 1511. The luxury of the papal court shocked the young monk, who sought a simpler faith. In October 1517 the people of Wittenberg, in Germany, found

Henry VIII was a colorful English monarch. He is seen here greeting François I of France when they met, with much pageantry, in June 1520.

95 theses (arguments) compiled by Luther nailed to the church door. In them the basis of Protestantism was set out. These reforms spread throughout Germany, then Europe. Another Protestant leader was the French theologian John Calvin, who founded a strict religious community in Geneva. Expelled from the city for his extreme ideas, he was invited back there in 1541.

Why was Simon Bolívar known as El Libertador?

Simon Bolívar was hailed as "El Libertador" (the liberator) because he helped several South American countries achieve independence from Spain. Born in Caracas, Venezuela, in 1783, he died in Colombia in 1830.

After studying in Madrid, Bolívar returned to Venezuela and led an uprising to drive out the Spanish. He was then elected president of the new republic. He crossed the mountains into Colombia and drove out the Spanish from there, too. He was not the only one to be helping countries to independence. José de San Martin brought

Sitting Bull (Tatanka Iyotake) was a courageous opponent of the settlers who came to the West.

liberty to Chile and Peru, while Bolívar's lieutenant Antonio José de Sucre liberated Ecuador.

Who was Sitting Bull?

Sitting Bull (Tatanka Iyotake) was a great chief of the Dakota Sioux. In 1836 he and Crazy Horse (Ta-Sunko-Witko) led the Sioux at the Battle of the Little Bighorn.

Sitting Bull (1834–90) opposed the settlers who came to the

West. The Native Americans of the plains of North America led a nomadic existence, which was threatened by the settlers. Many of the Native American tribes were destroyed.

Who united Italy?

The great champion of a united Italy was a patriotic soldier, Giuseppe Garibaldi. He helped expel the Austrians from northern Italy, and twice tried to free Rome from papal rule.

In 1860, at the head of 1,000 "redshirts," Garibaldi liberated Sicily and Naples. In 1862, Victor Emmanuel II, king of Sardinia, became the first king of a unified Italy.

What is Abraham Lincoln remembered for?

Lincoln is remembered for issuing the Emancipation Proclamation that ended slavery in the United States. His election as president in 1860 precipitated the Civil War (1861–65) between the northern states (the Union)

The American Civil War (1861–1865) tore the United States apart. General Grant led the armies of the North, while General Lee commanded those of the South.

Czar Nicholas II had abdicated in March 1917. The government was placed in the hands of "soviets" (revolutionary councils), and Russia (the Union of Soviet Socialist Republics, or U.S.S.R.) entered a period of over 70 years of Communist rule. Lenin masterminded the transition and served as head of the first Soviet government.

and the southern states (the Confederacy).

The cultivation of cotton in the South had brought in its wake the development of slavery. Plantation owners needed cheap labor and imported slaves from Africa. The northern states, opposed to slavery, eventually won the bitter Civil War. Lincoln was assassinated just as the war was ending.

Who were the two leading generals in the Civil War?

At the end of the Civil War General Ulysses S. Grant commanded the forces of the northern states, and

General Robert E. Lee commanded those of the South.

After defeating Lee, Grant accepted his surrender on April 9, 1865. Lee's plantation in Arlington, Virginia, is now the US National Cemetery. Grant was twice elected president of the United States (in 1868 and 1872).

Who led the Bolsheviks?

The Bolsheviks were the revolutionaries who seized power in Russia in the "October Revolution" of 1917. Their leader was Vladimir Ilyich Ulyanov, known as Lenin.

Who were the Free French?

The Free French were the forces who continued the war against Germany after France fell in 1940. Their leader was General Charles de Gaulle (1898–1970).

In May 1940 German forces occupied France. Refusing to accept the armistice with Hitler, de Gaulle took refuge in England. On June 18, 1940, he broadcast a call to the French people to resist. He organized French soldiers outside France into the Free French forces, who, with the "Underground" in France, continued the war against Germany. In August 1944, de Gaulle marched into Paris with his troops as Allied forces ended German occupation.

Who was Gandhi?

Mohandas Gandhi (1869–1948) helped free India from British rule and is regarded by Indians as father of their nation.

Indian people call Gandhi "Mahatma," which means "great soul." Gandhi taught that people should not accept injustice, or resort to violence, but should oppose it nonviolently and with courage. He spoke out against the injustice of British rule and encouraged his followers to break the law deliberately, but without violence. His special method of nonviolent resistance inspired the Indians to seek independence. The United Kingdom granted India its freedom in 1947. Gandhi was assassinated in 1948 by an Indian who resented Gandhi's teachings of tolerance for all races and religions.

Who was the greatest scientist of the 20th century?

Albert Einstein (1879–1955) is perhaps the greatest scientist of recent times. A German physicist who be-came an American citizen, his theory of relativity had a profound impact on modern science.

Although the atomic bomb was made possible by Einstein's discoveries, after World War II Einstein campaigned for nuclear weapons to be banned.

What was President Kennedy's greatest challenge?

When Kennedy announced in 1962 that the United States intended to land a man on the Moon by 1970, the technology to achieve such a goal did not exist – yet the goal was achieved.

In politics John F. Kennedy also took on some daunting challenges. In foreign affairs he dealt firmly and calmly with the Soviet Union during the height of the Cold War. He took a firm line, especially in the crisis of 1962 when he forced the Russians to withdraw nuclear missiles from Cuba. In the domestic field, Kennedy was a dynamic leader and promoted the civil rights of black Americans. He was assassinated in Dallas in 1963.

Who was the first man to walk on the Moon?

On July 21, 1969, American astronaut Neil Armstrong became the first man to set foot on the Moon.

The Apollo space program was an extraordinary technological feat and also a great human achievement since Armstrong and his fellow astronauts needed to be superbly trained and perfectly fit to carry out all the operations involved. Since then many space missions have been launched, both manned and unmanned, some to distant planets.

Einstein during his conception of the theory of relativity (left), and at the time of his campaign against nuclear weapons (right).

Historic Monuments of the World

Which is the most important megalithic monument?

Stonehenge, the circle of megaliths (huge stones) on Salisbury Plain in southern England, is one of the most mysterious remnants of prehistoric Europe.

This gigantic stone structure was erected about 5,000 years ago, toward the end of the Stone Age, but was modified several times in the 1,500 years that followed. The outer circle, more than 100 feet (30 meters) in diameter, is composed of enormous single stones (monoliths), topped by linking stone slabs. The inner circle consists of smaller stones. At the center are five pairs of vertical stones, each supporting a horizontal block. Just outside the circle stands the Heel Stone, which aligns with the point on the horizon where the sun rises on Midsummer Day. We do not know exactly what the function of Stonehenge was. It may have been used for Sun worship, or for astronomical observation.

What were the stones at Carnac?

Erected during the 3rd millennium B.C., the alignments of menhirs (standing stones) at Carnac, in France, extend over 2½ miles (4 kilometers). The site contains more than 5,000 monuments. Some of these megaliths (huge stones) are arranged in parallel rows leading to a cromlech (semicircle).

The height of the menhirs at Carnac varies from 18 inches (45 centimeters) to nearly 40 feet (12 meters). Some of the upright stones weigh as much as 100 tons. Even if some of these stones were erected close to where they originated, the act of raising them must have involved a great effort. The exact purpose of the alignments of the megalithic monuments at Carnac remains a mystery. Suggestions include that

The mosque at Córdoba, constructed between the 8th and the 10th century, was once one of the greatest mosques in the world. In 1234 it was transformed into a Catholic cathedral and renamed Our Lady of the Assumption.

they were an army of petrified soldiers, sacrificial altars, religious monuments consecrated to the worship of the Sun or the Moon, or instruments of astronomical measurement.

Who discovered the Caves of Lascaux?

In 1940 at Lascaux, in France, five boys discovered the entrance of a cave and decided to explore it.

The boys found themselves in a large grotto with a high roof resembling the hull of a ship. There they discovered the extraordinary frescoes of charging bulls and other animals that decorate the walls of the cave. The paintings were dated to the Magdalenian period (about 17,000 years ago). The caves soon attracted crowds of visitors. However exposure to acidic gases and humidity caused the paintings to deteriorate, so in 1963 the caves were closed. A concrete shell reproducing the exact shape of the grotto was constructed and facsimiles of the paintings were made, employing the techniques used at the time of their

The Dolmen of Crucuno, at Carnac. Dolmens are tablelike megalithic monuments composed of one or more slabs of stone resting on vertical blocks.

creation. Consequently people are again able to admire the astonishing images created by our ancestors, and the original paintings have been preserved. Only scientists now have access to them – but as rarely as possible because they remain extremely vulnerable.

Are there other prehistoric caverns?

There are numerous prehistoric caves scattered throughout the world. Paintings dating to the Stone Age can be found on the walls of caves as far apart as Lascaux in France, Altamira in Spain, Toquepala in Peru, and Tassili in the Sahara.

In 1985, a diver on the southern coast of France discovered the entrance of a tunnel, at a depth of 118 feet (36 meters), leading to a grotto that had no water in it. Six years later, the same diver, while exploring the cave system further, discovered engraved on the walls sketches of horses trotting beside ibex, herds of bison, stags and other deer, chamois, and even a seal. Specialists in prehistoric archeology confirmed that these paintings date from the late Stone Age.

Have any lake villages survived?

The first lake villages appeared around 3000 B.C., located mainly in the Alps and the Jura Mountains, on

or beside lakes and marshes. Numerous remains of such settlements have been found underwater – in Lake Zurich, for example, and Lake Paladru in France.

Well-preserved objects and tools have been found at these sites, enabling archeologists to reconstruct daily life there. The discoveries made at Lake Paladru indicate that the dwellings were built on stilts driven into the ground. The stilts supported a construction of wooden beams fastened with rope and covered with reeds. These dwellings were built around 2700 B.C. At the open-air museum in Unteruhldingen, on the shore of Lake Constance in Switzerland, there is a reconstruction of a Bronze Age lake settlement. Lake villages built on piles still exist in Africa, Asia, and South America.

Which is the largest dolmen in Brittany?

Dolmen means "stone table." The Merchants' Table near Carnac is the most famous of the dolmens in Brittany, a region in northwestern France. It is believed to have been a funeral chamber that was covered by a burial mound.

The Merchants' Table is composed of three large horizontal slabs of stone supported by 17 stone pillars. One of the supports is decorated with engravings of ears of wheat, and beneath the table one can just make out the shape of a cart and two feet of an animal. The engravings are thought to date from between 2500 and 1500 B.C. Dolmens also occur in the Massif Central of France and in Ireland. An astonishing "portal dolmen" can be seen at the Burren in County Clare.

Which is the most ancient pyramid?

Around 2680 B.C. an architect named Imhotep built a stepped pyramid at Saqqara in Egypt. It is 200 feet (62 meters) high and, with the surrounding temple complex, covers an area of 37 acres (15 hectares).

Imhotep lived during the reign of Pharaoh Djoser, who died around 2680 B.C. In addition to being an architect, he was a doctor, high priest, and royal advisor, and may have been the first to create a

The stepped Pyramid of Djoser at Saqqara was built almost 5,000 years ago. It is thought to be the most ancient pyramid in Egypt.

monumental building in stone. The inspiration for it came from tombs covered by a mound of sand, but Imhotep had the idea of building a pyramid in the shape of gigantic stone steps so the pharaoh's soul could ascend to the heavens. The architect also reproduced elements from nature in stone, including columns in the form of bundles of reeds and decorated with engravings of lotus flowers.

Which pyramid

is the largest?

The largest pyramid was probably the one at Cholula in Mexico. Dedicated to the plumed-serpent god Quetzalcóatl, it was built some time between the 2nd and 6th centuries A.D.

In terms of volume, it was twice as large as the Pyramid of Cheops in Egypt. Its base occupied about 45 acres (18 hectares), and its sides were approximately 1,000 feet (300 meters) long. Composed of seven superimposed pyramids, it rose to a height of 180 feet (54 meters). A sumptuous temple at the summit enclosed a gigantic statue. It was built with huge bricks of sun-baked clay that probably came from the other side of the volcano Popocatepetl.

It is thought that each brick was passed from hand to hand along a "human chain" consisting of at least 20,000 men. Sadly, all that remains today is an enormous mound with a church at its summit. However, there are other pyramids in Mexico – such as the Mayan one at Uxmal – that have been better preserved.

What is the Valley

of the Kings?

The Valley of the Kings shelters the tombs of the pharaohs of Upper Egypt. It lies to the west of the Nile, near the site of the ancient Egyptian city of Thebes.

Carved into the side of a mountain, whose summit is shaped like a pyramid, these tombs consisted of long, gently sloping galleries divided into compartments and ending in one or more chambers. The stone sarcophagus enclosing the mummy of the king was placed in the last chamber and surrounded with furniture, arms, and jewelry. The pillars and passages of the tomb were decorated with frescoes representing the voyage to the afterlife. Sadly, over the centuries the tombs of the Valley

The Mayan pyramid at Uxmal, on the Yucatán peninsula in Mexico, is about 1,000 years old. It has been beautifully preserved.

The walls of the tombs in the Valley of the Kings were decorated with frescoes.

of the Kings were plundered. The only tomb discovered intact has been that of Tutankhamun, dating from the 18th Egyptian dynasty (1350 B.C.).

Did the Tower
of Babel exist?

Many archeologists and historians believe it may have been the great ziggurat (tiered temple) at Babylon, completed in the reign of Nebuchadnezzar in the 6th century B.C.

The Bible relates that the descendants of Noah started to build a tower that would reach to the heavens. But this angered God and He punished the builders, making each of them speak a different language. This story in part coincides with what is known about Babylonian ziggurats. Moreover, Babel is the Hebrew for Babylon. Built in honor of the god Marduk, the ziggurat in Babylon would have had seven tiers leading up to a small temple, which was the god's wedding chamber and the point where the earth and heavens joined in union.

Was the city of
Troy just a legend?

Troy was a real city in Asia Minor. The discovery of its remains in Turkey in the

1870s gave a historical foundation to the story of the Trojan War related in Homer's poem the *Iliad*. The first traces of the city date from 3000 B.C.

The *Iliad* tells of the siege of Troy, following the abduction of Helen, a beautiful Greek princess, by Paris, son of the king of Troy. For 10 years the Greeks tried without success to get into the city. In the end, the Greeks, led by Ulysses, pretended to withdraw, leaving behind a huge wooden horse. Deceived, the Trojans dragged the horse into the city, thinking it was an offering to their gods. That night, soldiers hidden inside the horse emerged and opened the gates of Troy to the Greek army, who captured the city. Excavations indicate that Troy was sacked twice, around 1210 B.C. and 1100 B.C.

The building of the Parthenon was supervised by the sculptor Phidias. With its Doric columns, it is a perfect example of classical Greek architecture.

What were the Seven Wonders of the World?

The seven wonders of the ancient world include the pyramids at Giza in Egypt, the temple of Artemis at Ephesus in Turkey, the tomb of Mausolus at Halicarnassus (now Bodrum, in Turkey), the hanging gardens of Babylon, the statue of Zeus at Olympus in Greece, the Colossus (giant statue) of the Sun god Helios in Rhodes, and the lighthouse at Alexandria in Egypt.

Of these famous monuments, only the pyramids at Giza, some remains of the temple of Artemis (which was destroyed in A.D. 262), and some fragments of sculpture from the tomb of King Mausolus remain. Although they evoke an image of terraced splendor, we know little about the hanging gardens of Queen Semiramis (600 B.C.). We do know that the statue of Zeus — in gold, marble, and ivory — was 40 feet (12 meters) high and was destroyed in a fire. The Colossus of Rhodes tumbled to ruins during an earthquake in 224 B.C. — as did the great lighthouse at Alexandria, built to a height of 400 feet (122 meters) on the island of Pharos.

When was the Parthenon built?

The most famous temple of the Acropolis, the religious center of ancient Athens, the Parthenon was rebuilt after being destroyed during the Persian Wars in the 5th century B.C. Dedicated

to the goddess Athena, the "new" Parthenon took nine years to build, starting in 447 B.C.

This elegant Doric temple, in gleaming marble, looks out over the capital of Greece. It was originally decorated in bright colors. Inside, in the sanctuary, stood a statue of Athena in gold and ivory. The beautifully sculpted friezes that decorated the temple are now divided between the Acropolis Museum, the British Museum in London, and the Louvre in Paris. In the 6th century the Parthenon was transformed into a church, and in the 17th century it became a mosque. Today it is one of the world's most visited monuments.

Who performed in the theater of Epidaurus?

Built around 300 B.C., the theater at Epidaurus in the Peloponnese could seat 12,000 people, who came to see plays such as the tragedies of Aeschylus, Euripides, and Sophocles, and the comedies of Aristophanes.

The plays performed at Epidaurus were written in verse and were either about current events or inspired by traditional legends or mythology. The action was usually commented upon by the leader of the chorus, which sang, danced, and spoke directly to the audience. The masks worn by the actors indicated to the audience whether their roles were tragic or comic. Both male and female roles were performed by men. The theater at Epidaurus is the best-preserved ancient Greek theater. Its acoustics are so good that the slightest whisper is audible in the back row. Each summer, performances are given there.

When was the Great Wall of China erected?

The Great Wall of China is often spoken of as the eighth wonder of the world. Started in the 4th century B.C., it was built mainly in the 3rd century B.C. and was extensively restored in the 14th century A.D. It is said to be visible from the Moon.

In 221 B.C., after completing his conquest of China, Emperor Shih

Epidaurus has one of the best-preserved theaters of the classical world. It could seat 12,000 people, who flocked there to see tragedies and comedies by the great dramatists of ancient Greece.

Huang-Ti decided to strengthen the ramparts built in northern China as protection against barbarians. To do so, he joined sections of wall together to make a continuous 1,850-mile (3,000-kilometer) barrier. Many of the 300,000 men assigned to the task died while working on it. The resulting wall, between 20 and 60 feet (6 and 18 meters) in height, snaked through the hills, and for many centuries defined the northern border of China. A road on top of the wall facilitated the movement of horsemen and chariots between small forts erected at regular intervals along it. Abandoned for several hundred years, the wall was restored by the Ming rulers of the 14th century.

Who built the Pont du Gard?

The Pont du Gard, in France, is one of the most elegant examples of Roman architecture. It was built in 20 B.C. by Marcus Vipsanius Agrippa, the son-in-law of the Emperor Augustus.

Its three levels of superimposed arches rise to a total height of 160 feet (49 meters). The Pont du Gard was built to supply water to

The Via Ostiensis connected Rome with its port at Ostia. Like the Via Appia, it is one of the most ancient Roman roads still existing today.

the Roman city of Nemausus (Nîmes). Agrippa was Augustus's closest friend and advisor. As well as contributing to many military successes, he was entrusted with many important public-works projects, such as the construction of roads and aqueducts.

Which is the oldest road?

The Via Appia, or Appian Way, in Italy, is the most ancient road that still exists. Begun by Appius Claudius in 312 B.C., it was known as

the *regina viarium*, the "queen of roads."

The Appian Way began in the heart of Rome and initially reached as far as Capua. It was later extended to what are now Taranto and Brindisi. The road led to Greece and the markets of the East. It helped consolidate Rome's territory and aided the movement of troops. Today, bordered by tombs and luxurious private villas, the road still runs through beautiful countryside dotted with cypresses and pines. Some of the original basalt paving stones can still be seen. Many of the major highways of Europe follow the path of ancient Roman roads.

What was the Colosseum?

An oval amphitheater that could seat 50,000 people, the Colosseum was primarily used for combats between gladiators or between people and wild beasts. But it was also used for athletic games and even for naval battles (for which the center of the arena would be flooded). It was built, by some 20,000 slaves, in A.D. 80.

The spectators were seated according to social rank, arranged in sections to the left and right of the imperial box. In the event of rain, a velarium (awning) was stretched over the arena. The men and animals fated to participate in the spectacles were kept in cells beneath the arena and were hoisted into the arena by an elevator worked by weights and pulleys. In A.D. 249, to celebrate the thousandth anniversary of the city's founding, the most incredible – and bloodthirsty – spectacle took place in the arena. Some 2,000 gladiators took part, and during the combats 32 elephants, 10 giraffes, 60 lions, and 10 tigers were killed.

Which Roman amphitheaters are the best preserved?

The amphitheaters at Arles and Nîmes, both in France, are the best preserved of all the Roman arenas.

The amphitheater in Nîmes was built in the time of the Emperor Augustus. Some 24,000 spectators could be accommodated in its four tiers of seats. During the Middle Ages the building was transformed into a fortress that could house more than 2,000 people. Every year, during the Festival of Nîmes, bullfights bring the arena back to life. Arles has an oval amphitheater dating from 46 B.C. Like the one at Nîmes, it was transformed into a fortress in the Middle Ages; subsequently it was converted into a citadel enclosing more than 200 houses. Three tall towers remain from the days when the amphitheater served as a fortress. In other respects, it has been fully restored.

Have the holy places changed since the time of Christ?

Visitors to modern Jerusalem may find it difficult to picture the city where Christ lived 2,000 years ago. Many of the holy places are thronged with tourists.

A busy marketplace has to be crossed in order to reach the Church of the Holy Sepulcher, believed to stand on the hill of Golgotha where Jesus was crucified and buried. Passing through a narrow door into a sanctuary shared by Catholics, Orthodox Christians, Armenians, and Copts, the visitor is struck by the conflicting styles belonging to the different churches. Is that really where the cross was set up, that hole behind an altar laden with heavy candelabra? Can the tomb of Christ have resembled that marble slab? And when the visitor climbs the modern street that leads to Golgotha, it is difficult to visualize the steep, dusty path that Christ had to climb, struggling with his heavy cross.

The Roman arena at Arles, in France, is perfectly preserved and still in use – as a venue for bullfights and festivals.

Does Solomon's temple still exist?

Nothing now remains of the temple built by King Solomon in Jerusalem. The Western Wall or Wailing Wall, which is a place of Jewish pilgrimage, is in fact the remains of the foundations of the temple built by King Herod I on the site of Solomon's temple.

According to the Bible, Solomon's temple stood on the spot where Abraham prepared to sacrifice Isaac. Erected between 966 and 959 B.C., it housed the Ark of the Covenant, the chest containing the stone tablets engraved with the Ten Commandments, given by God to Moses. When the Babylonians destroyed the first temple, in 587 B.C., the Ark of the Covenant was lost. Herod built a new temple on the same site – but it was in turn destroyed, in A.D. 70, by the future Roman emperor Titus.

The royal city of Angkor, in Cambodia, contained the palace and temples of the Khmer kings.

What happened to the great library at Alexandria?

The library at Alexandria was established around 240 B.C., in the time of Ptolemy I. After being burned by Julius Caesar's soldiers in 48 B.C., it was rebuilt, only to be again destroyed in A.D. 391.

The ancient library at Alexandria is said to have contained a collection of 700,000 works in the form of papyrus scrolls. The library enriched its collection by acquiring or copying texts brought to Alexandria from abroad. It also produced works of scholarship, among them an annotated edition of the works of Homer and commentaries on the classics of Greek literature. The destruction of the library's collection meant the loss of a vast body of knowledge that had been gathered over centuries.

Which are the oldest churches?

Santa Maria Maggiore and Santa Sabina, both in Rome, were founded during the first half of the 5th century. Among the oldest churches still standing, both preserve features typical of 5th-century architecture.

The first Christian places of worship were sanctuaries rather than churches, but by the 4th century churches were being founded. These early churches were generally large rectangular halls bordered with columns taken from pagan temples. At the end of the nave, an apse contained a sanctuary regarded as the throne of Christ. Pagan temples were often transformed into churches. The Pantheon in Rome, for example, a temple dedicated to all the Roman gods, was converted into a church consecrated to the Virgin Mary and the Christian martyrs.

Where is the temple of Angkor Wat?

The ruins of the royal city of Angkor and its magnificent temple lie stranded in the middle of a forest in Cambodia, in Southeast Asia.

The royal city of Angkor, which extended over an area of 740 acres (300 hectares), was founded by Yasovarman I (A.D. 889–900) on the site of a pre-existing city. The Khmer kings of ancient Cambodia built their palaces and temples here over a period of more than five centuries. Among the many buildings (now ruins) that lie scattered in the forest, the temple of Angkor Wat is the masterpiece. Built in 1122, it was decorated with many bas-reliefs and statues. Five towers crown the structure, one of which contains a royal tomb. The city of Angkor was abandoned in the 15th century. Its buildings were left to fall into ruin, until 1992 when UNESCO placed the city on its list of protected world-heritage sites.

What is the Kaaba?

The Kaaba ("the cube") is a square shrine located in the Great Mosque in Mecca, Saudi Arabia. The holiest shrine of Islam, it is the destination of the *hajj*, the pilgrimage that all Muslims must undertake at least once.

According to tradition, the Kaaba dates from the time of Abraham. Set in one of its walls is a sacred stone that was given to Abraham by the Archangel Gabriel; originally white, it was turned black by the sins of humanity. After expelling the pagans who gathered in Mecca to worship the stone, the prophet Muhammad proclaimed the absolute dominion of Allah. Today the Kaaba is veiled in thick black drapes. The Muslim pilgrims who come to touch the stone must carry out a strict ritual. Dressed in unsewn white cloth, the pilgrims circle the Kaaba seven times, then climb to the summit of

The ruins of Pompeii hint at the beauty and prosperity of the city before it was buried by the eruption of Mount Vesuvius in A.D. 79.

the mountain where Muhammad received the revelation of the Koran.

How were Herculaneum and Pompeii destroyed?

Pompeii was once a rich port and pleasure resort, and Herculaneum a bustling smaller city. Both were situated at the foot of Vesuvius, the volcano near Naples, which erupted on August 24, A.D. 79. Within 48 hours the two cities were buried under lava and volcanic ash.

This terrible disaster was vividly described by the Roman writer Pliny the Younger: "A horrifying red cloud, torn by ragged flashes of light and glowing with the breath of fire, opened to reveal towering flames, like flashes of lightning but much larger..." Within hours the volcano had wiped out all life. Buried under a layer of ash up to 23 feet (7 meters) thick, Pompeii was not discovered until 1748, while the town of Herculaneum was found earlier, in 1709. Archeologists are still excavating the two cities.

Where did the Battle of Alesia take place?

Alise-Sainte-Reine – a small town in Burgundy, France – takes its name from Alesia, the fortress where Julius Caesar trapped Vercingetorix, the leader of the Gauls, in 52 B.C.

The location of Alesia has long been debated. In the early 19th century an archeological investigation of the site revealed vestiges of military works around Alise-Sainte-Reine, as well as remains of weapons and bones of men and horses. Aerial photographs, revealing the outlines of ancient Roman trenches, have reinforced this hypothesis that this is the site of Vercingetorix's last battle. Nevertheless, the debate about the location of Alesia continues.

Did the Maya imitate the pyramids in Egypt?

Mexico and Egypt are too far apart for the Maya to

Nobody knows why the Incas built the

have known about the civilization of the pharaohs. The only link between the two civilizations is the fact that they both built pyramids – the architectural form most easily built.

The monuments of the Maya and those of ancient Egypt are not contemporaries. Not only were the building materials completely different, the periods of construction did not coincide. The Egyptians' civilization reached its

city of Machu Picchu high up in the mountains, or why they abandoned it.

peak around 3000 B.C., whereas Mayan civilization only began to flower in the 1st century A.D. Moreover, most of the pyramids in Mexico were built to serve as pedestals for temples, whereas those in Egypt were tombs. In the Mayan city of Palenque, however, a funeral chamber has been found inside a pyramid – in some ways reminiscent of the tombs in the Egyptian Valley of the Kings. As in the tombs of the pharaohs, the stone sarcophagus of the Mayan high priest discovered at Palenque contained jewelry and ornaments, and was surrounded by offerings. These similarities, however, are probably coincidental.

Which was the biggest pre-Columbian city?

The largest pre-Columbian city was Teotihuacán – the "city of the gods" – about 25 miles (40 kilometers) northeast of today's Mexico City. A great religious center, thought to have been built by the Oltecs around 300 B.C., it occupied more than 8 square miles (20 square kilometers).

Teotihuacán's golden age lasted from the 4th to the 7th century A.D. Inhabited for 1,000 years, it was sacked by the Toltecs around A.D. 750. The remains of Teotihuacán are spectacular. A flight of 222 steps leads to the top of the gigantic Pyramid of the Sun, some 196 feet (60 meters) high, which was crowned by a colossal statue of the Sun god. From the Pyramid of the Sun, the Street of the Dead leads past the smaller Pyramid of the Moon to the temple of Quetzalcóatl. This processional way is lined with temples and tombs, in which masks and knives have been found – confirming the suspicion that the Oltecs' religion involved human sacrifice.

Where is Machu Picchu?

Dramatically perched on the side of the Urubamba Gorge, in Peru, at an

altitude of 8,000 feet (2,500 meters), this Inca ghost town is about 60 miles (100 kilometers) from the city of Cuzco.

One of the world's most puzzling archeological sites, Machu Picchu was discovered in 1911 and named after the mountain upon which it stands. No one knows who built its houses, palaces, and temples (all made of stone blocks, without mortar), or who lived there, or why the city was abandoned. Most of the ruins seem to date to the 15th century, but opinions vary as to why the city was built high up in the mountains, on the side of a gorge. Was it a holy city? Or the last refuge of the Incas, fleeing from the conquistadors? The city remains an enigma.

What happened to the medieval port of Aigues-Mortes?

In 1241 the French king Louis IX created a port at Aigues-Mortes, in the south of France, with the intention of rivaling Marseilles, which was at that time still under Roman rule. Before long, the port began to silt up.

It was from Aigues-Mortes that Louis IX set out on his Crusades in 1248 and 1270, but the port was only briefly prosperous. Its access to the sea was progressively blocked by silt and sand. As a result, the town became more and more cut off from the coast. Surrounded by splendid ramparts, today Aigues-Mortes is isolated in a strange landscape of lagoons and is only joined to the sea by a canal.

Does Charlemagne's palace still exist?

Charlemagne's vast palace in Aachen, in Germany, was said by his contemporaries to have been intended to rival the architectural splendor of ancient Rome. The chapel of the palace, which was built between A.D. 796 and 805, is now part of the city's cathedral.

Copied from the magnificent Basilica of San Vitale in Ravenna, in Italy, the palace chapel was of an impressive scale for its time and is the most important structure from the time of Charlemagne's rule. Charlemagne was the first Holy Roman Emperor. His empire extended from the North Sea to Italy and from the Atlantic to the Carpathian Mountains. He established his capital at Aachen in 794 and died there in 814.

The fortified city of Aigues-Mortes, in the south of France, is a splendid example of medieval military architecture. It was intended to be a great port, but was eventually cut off from the sea by deposits of silt and sand.

How old is Hagia Sophia in Istanbul?

The Hagia Sophia was built in the 6th century by the Emperor Justinian, whose ambition was to create the most beautiful edifice in the world. For its inauguration he organized a magnificent celebration that lasted several days. Viewing the finished building, the emperor is said to have declared, "Solomon, I have done better than you!"

Church or mosque? The Hagia Sophia in Istanbul was built as a church and became a mosque after the fall of Constantinople in 1453.

Constantinople (now Istanbul) was then the capital of the Eastern Roman Empire. The Hagia Sophia, sometimes called Santa Sophia, was built as a Christian cathedral on the site of an earlier church, dating from the time of the Emperor Constantine, which had been destroyed by fire during the civil war in 532. The great brick cupola, 184 feet (56 meters) high and 108 feet (33 meters) in diameter, collapsed several years after being erected but was immediately rebuilt. After the fall of Constantinople in 1453, the building was converted into a mosque. It now serves as a museum. The building has evolved over the years, including the addition of four minarets.

How long did it take to build Notre Dame?

The construction of the great cathedral of Notre Dame, in Paris, France, lasted almost 200 years, from 1163 until 1325. Badly damaged during the French Revolution, the cathedral was restored in the 19th century.

Building began in 1163, and by 1250 the nave and choir were complete. But subsequently it was decided to extend the nave, and work on the side chapels continued until 1325. The cathedral's west façade is particularly remarkable, with its triple portal, and the gigantic rose window, which is among the most beautiful examples of European Gothic art.

Which are the most impressive medieval castles?

Hradcany Castle in Prague and the fortress at Ghent in Belgium are among the oldest in Europe. Both were founded in the 9th century A.D.

In England, Heldingham, Dover, and Rochester castles and the Tower of London, founded by

William the Conqueror, all have splendid Norman keeps. In Wales, Edward I built powerful fortresses such as Harlech, Conwy, and Caernarfon (one of the best-preserved). Scotland is especially rich in castles, ranging from solitary towers to elegant residences graced with dozens of turrets.

Which is the largest cathedral ever built?

The Cathedral of Saint John the Divine in New York (begun in 1892) covers an area of 120,900 square feet (11,240 square meters). Its nave, 600 feet (183 meters) in length and nearly 125 feet (38 meters) high, is the longest in the world.

Only slightly smaller is Seville Cathedral, in Spain, which has an area of 112,185 square feet (10,422 square meters). At the start of the 15th century, when the religious authorities in Seville decided to tear down the great mosque and replace it with a cathedral, they declared: "Let us build a church so large that those who see it will think we are insane." The result was an awe-inspiring building. The nave is 413 feet (126 meters) long and 272 feet (83 meters) wide, with a vaulted ceiling 98 feet (30 meters) high. The largest basilica is St. Peter's in Rome, which covers 250,000 square feet (23,000 square meters). It has an overall length of about 700 feet (215 meters), and a nave over 590 feet (180 meters) long. The cross on top of the dome is more than 440 feet (135 meters) from the ground.

Which are the oldest churches built of wood?

By the 14th century there were numerous *stavkirke* (wooden churches) in Norway. The pyramid-shaped roofs crowning these intriguing structures were covered with wooden tiles, resembling a fish's scales, and adorned with dragons like the ones that graced the prows of Viking long ships. The oldest of these churches is in Borgund. It was built around 1150.

The origins of the *stavkirke* still puzzle experts. Were they pagan temples, or were they simply the first churches built after the

Carcassonne, in southwestern France, is a splendid example of the walled cities of the Middle Ages. After being allowed to decay, in the 19th century its fortifications were restored to their former glory.

Louis XIV, the "Sun King," transformed the hunting lodge at Versailles into a sumptuous palace. It took 36,000 workers 50 years to complete the project.

conversion of the Vikings to Christianity in the 13th century? They are found on the southern coast of Norway and in the valleys extending inland. Some fine examples have been moved from their original sites and re-erected in the open-air folk museums in Oslo and Lillehammer.

What was a

fortified city like?

The European fortified cities of the Middle Ages were completely enclosed by thick walls or ramparts. The walls defined the boundaries of the city and protected against invaders.

An example of a fortified city can be seen at Carcassonne, near Toulouse in southwestern France. This city was fortified between the 11th and 13th centuries. Two miles (3 kilometers) of castellated walls encircle the city, with more than 50 towers keeping watch over the surrounding countryside. Except for the souvenir sellers, the city within the walls seems still to live much as it did in the Middle Ages.

Why did Louis XIV

build a palace at

Versailles?

As a young man Louis XIV loved to stay at the hunting lodge built by his father, Louis XIII, 13 miles (21 kilometers) from Paris. In 1661 he decided to transform this modest hunting lodge into a sumptuous palace. Work on the palace continued for the rest of his reign.

In August 1661 the king visited Vaux-le-Vicomte, the magnificent château that had just been built for his finance minister, Nicolas Fouchet. Envious and impressed, Louis commissioned the men who had created Vaux-le-Vicomte to convert Versailles into the most beautiful palace in the world. Initially, a central block was built with a vast terrace on one side and a marble courtyard on the other. Later, two large wings were added, as were additional upper stories. The terrace was enclosed to create the famous Hall of Mirrors. Outside, forests were transplanted into the surrounding park. In 1682 Versailles became, in effect, the seat of government, housing around 1,000 courtiers and 4,000 servants.

During the Renaissance, the kings of France built magnificent palaces, or châteaux, in the Loire Valley, in central France. Many of them, such as the Château de Chenonceau (above), were influenced by Italian architecture.

French influence was not confined to palace architecture. The Austrian court also adopted French manners and etiquette. In the 19th century Ludwig II of Bavaria (1845–86) had a hall of mirrors and a bedroom similar to those of Louis XIV installed at his palace in Linderhof.

the Loire Valley became the architectural playground of the royalty and nobles of France. The area's châteaux reflect the interplay between the heritage of medieval France and the creative innovations of the Italian Renaissance.

Which palace was modeled on Versailles?

The architectural style known as French classicism was created by Louis Le Vau, the architect of Versailles, and was imitated throughout the world. One building modeled on Versailles was the Palace of Schoenbrunn, Vienna, completed in 1750.

Why does the Loire Valley have so many châteaux?

Spectacular castles – such as Chambord, Chenonceau, Blois, and Amboise – testify to the rich history of the Loire Valley.

Known as the garden of France because of its great natural beauty, from the 15th to the 17th century

Is Venice actually built on water?

Venice is built on 118 small islands separated by 117 canals, straddled by 400 bridges. The city is surrounded by a lagoon, cut off by sandbanks from the Adriatic Sea. Nearly all its sumptuous palaces have water lapping at their foundations, and most of the buildings are constructed on stilts.

Water taxis, water buses (*vaporetti*), and graceful gondolas provide transportation for Venice's residents and visitors. The Grand Canal is the city's principal artery. More than 200 palaces line its banks. Even festivals such as the *Sensa* – the marriage of Venice and the sea – are held on water. During the *Regata Storica,* gaily decorated boats and gondolas participate in races, and for the *Redentore* a bridge of boats is strung across the Giudecca Canal. Today the canals that made Venice famous threaten its continued existence. Rising waters are attacking the foundations of the buildings, and the whole city is gradually sinking into the Venetian Lagoon. Dams are being built to hold back the water and protect Venice from flooding, and the Italian government and international organizations are working to preserve the city's buildings.

Are there any other cities like Venice?

A number of other cities are built on water. In Amsterdam, as in Venice, water predominates. Bruges, in Belgium, is called the Venice of the North. Bangkok, the capital of Thailand, is known as the Venice of Asia.

The Dutch city of Amsterdam is built on 90 small islands (28 fewer than Venice). The canals are laid out like a spider's web, composed of concentric and parallel canals. Along their banks are houses built by wealthy merchants. In Bruges the canals reflect the pale-red brick of the stately houses that line their banks. In Bangkok many of the klongs (canals) have been blocked off or filled in to make way for streets and avenues, but there still remain a number of polluted klongs. In California there is a city entirely built on canals. Its name is Venice.

Which abbey took over an island?

Off the coast of the bay where the French regions of Normandy and Brittany meet rises Mont-Saint-Michel – a desolate rock on which a fortified abbey was built in the Middle Ages.

Until the 8th century the only building on the rock was a hermitage – then Aubert, bishop of nearby Avranches, had the idea of erecting an abbey dedicated to Saint Michael. Its construction was extremely difficult, and it took a great deal of ingenuity to crowd the monastic buildings onto the

Known as the Venice of the North, the Flemish city of Bruges built its prosperity upon its canals – which, in their own way, are no less charming than those of Venice.

narrow platforms and ledges of the rock. Over the centuries the abbey was modified several times (every surface that could be built on was used to enlarge it). During the Hundred Years' War, strong walls were added to protect it from attack. Pilgrims flocked to Mont-Saint-Michel, and during the 15th and 16th centuries a village sprang up, clinging to the steep slopes leading to the abbey church.

Who built the Taj Mahal?

Standing on the banks of the River Jumna, near Agra in India, the Taj Mahal has long been regarded as the world's most beautiful funeral monument. It was built by the Mogul emperor Shah Jahan in memory of his favorite wife.

When Shah Jahan's third wife, Mumtaz Mahal, died giving birth to their ninth child, the inconsolable emperor decided to build a mausoleum of such perfect beauty that it would immortalize his love for her. Some 20,000 masons and artists worked on it for 16 years, from 1632 to 1648, under the direction of several architects. The monument is magnificent, the white marble giving it a magical lightness and purity. Surrounded by formal gardens, it rises at the end of a long pool in which its image is reflected.

Where can one see the most beautiful mosque?

With its forest of 850 columns in marble, granite, and jasper, the Great Mosque at Córdoba, in

Built by the Mogul emperor Shah Jahan in memory of his favorite wife, the Taj Mahal is one of the world's most beautiful buildings.

Spain, is one of the world's most beautiful religious buildings. It was built between the 8th and 10th centuries.

This mosque was one of the great monuments of the Islamic world until 1238, when it was transformed into a Christian cathedral. For three centuries Córdoba had been the largest and most important city of Europe. It was also a great center of learning, with numerous universities and libraries, and a place where Muslims, Jews, and Christians lived in harmony. Tragically, however, after the capture of the city by Ferdinand III of Castile in 1236, Córdoba began to decline.

Many other beautiful mosques are to be found throughout the world – such as the dazzling white-marble and red-sandstone mosque in Delhi, the Great Mosque in Isfahan with its turquoise-tiled dome, or the famous Blue Mosque built by Sultan Ahmet in Istanbul.

Who decorated the Sistine Chapel?

In 1508 Pope Julius II decided to have the Sistine Chapel (the private chapel

of the popes, in the Vatican) redecorated. **Some of the greatest Italian artists, such as Botticelli, Pinturicchio, Perugino, and Ghirlandaio, contributed to the redecoration – but the daunting task of painting frescoes for the high vaulted ceiling and for the wall behind the altar was entrusted to Michelangelo. The frescoes relate the story of man as told in the Bible.**

Michelangelo Buonarroti (better known simply as Michelangelo) lived from 1475 to 1564. A brilliant painter, sculptor, and architect, he also wrote poetry and produced marvelous drawings. He spent much of his life in Florence – where he worked for the Medici family – and in Rome, working for Pope Julius II. Besides the ceiling of the Sistine Chapel, masterpieces by him include sculptures such as the *Pietà* in St. Peter's Basilica and *Moses* in San Pietro in Vincoli (both in Rome), and *David* in Florence. The huge dome of St. Peter's was mainly his work. Michelangelo labored at the ceiling of the Sistine Chapel for four years (from 1508 to 1512), often standing on tiptoe or lying on his back. Despite such difficulties, the enormous frescoes radiate amazing power and vitality.

Who lived in the monasteries at Meteora?

In the Middle Ages the pinnacles of rock that rise out of the plains of Thessaly, in Greece, attracted monks in quest of solitude. At Meteora they built a group of monasteries on top of these almost inaccessible peaks.

The isolation of the hermitages symbolized the monks' decision to withdraw from the world. They vowed never to descend from their refuge and to spend their lives in meditation and prayer. Women were forbidden access to the monasteries, and food was hoisted up to them by a system of weights and pulleys. Between the 12th and 14th centuries, 24 monasteries were built at Meteora. Of these, several have been transformed into museums; only five are still inhabited by monks.

From what period does Windsor Castle date?

For more than nine centuries Windsor Castle was the principal residence

At Meteora, in Thessaly, Greek Orthodox monks lived in monasteries, like the one above, built on solitary pinnacles of rock.

of the kings and queens of England. Modified or extended by nearly all of them, it is the largest inhabited castle in the world.

Windsor Castle dates back to William the Conqueror, who built a wooden fortress beside the River Thames. Henry II rebuilt it in stone, adding sturdy ramparts and part of the enormous Round Tower. Edward III enlarged the royal apartments, and also founded the Order of the Garter. The stalls and banners of the knights can be seen in the castle's glorious St. George's Chapel, begun by Edward IV and completed by Henry VIII. Charles II transformed Windsor into a more comfortable residence. Finally, George IV and Queen Victoria allowed the architect Sir Jeffry Wyatville to make further changes, giving the castle the form it has today.

What is special about the Great Clock in Rouen?

A curious Renaissance arch, adjoining a 14th-century belfry, spans one of the liveliest streets in Rouen, France. Each side of the arch is adorned by a clock face made of intricately worked gilded lead. This clock, which has presided over the history of the capital of the region of Normandy since the 16th century, is the city's most popular sight.

Originally the Great Clock was installed within the belfry, but the citizens of Rouen found it so beautiful that in 1527 they built an arch to display it to better advantage. The time is told by a single hand, which indicates the hours, while a calendar displays the days of the week. The cobbled street that passes under the Great Clock has been a busy shopping street since the Middle Ages. Now a pedestrian precinct, it connects the old market place – where Joan of Arc was burned at the stake on May 30, 1431 – with Rouen Cathedral.

The works of the great Spanish painters and sculptors are superbly displayed at the Prado, in Madrid.

What can you see at the Prado?

With more than 3,000 paintings – mostly collected by the kings and queens of Spain – the Prado, in Madrid, is one of the world's most famous art galleries.

It contains the largest collection of paintings by the Spanish painters Goya and Velázquez, and numerous works by the great Dutch and Flemish masters.

The great painters of France (Poussin, Claude Lorraine, Watteau) and Italy (Fra Angelico, Botticelli, Titian, Raphael) are also well represented. Some of the world's best-known paintings hang in the Prado, among them *The Maids of Honor* by Velázquez, *The Third of May 1808: The Execution of the Defenders of Madrid* by Goya, *The Garden of Earthly Delights* by Hieronymous Bosch, and *The Triumph of Death* by Pieter Breugel the Elder. Specially displayed in an annex is another famous painting – *Guernica* by Pablo Picasso.

Why did the Easter Islanders disappear?

Isolated in the middle of the Pacific Ocean, Easter Island has intrigued anthropologists ever since its discovery on Easter Sunday in 1772. A now-vanished civilization lived for 1,200 years on this small island in the middle of nowhere. Who were they, and why did they sculpt those gigantic stone heads with huge staring eyes?

The stone figures were carved out of solid rock from the slopes of a volcano. The question remains as to how these enormous monoliths, each weighing several dozen tons, could have been transported and erected. Too numerous and too similar to have represented gods, they are more likely to have been figures of heroes or venerated ancestors.

Scientists surmise that the Easter Islanders arrived from islands farther west in the Pacific, or perhaps even from as far away as China. Their civilization appears to have been totally self-sufficient, and they developed a form of script that is still undeciphered. But suddenly, and for no apparent reason, in the 17th century they disappeared. Was it a plague, or did they kill each other off? Today the mystery of their origin and disappearance remains as puzzling as ever.

Who gave obelisks to Britain, France, and the U.S.A.?

Beside the River Thames in London, England, stands a pink-granite obelisk, more than 65 feet (20 meters) high; its twin stands in Central Park in New York.

Gigantic heads carved from volcanic stone are strewn across Easter Island, in the Pacific. Why they were erected remains unknown.

Both were gifts from Mehmet Ali, pasha (governor) of Egypt. In the Place de la Concorde, in Paris, France, is a similar obelisk that he gave to France.

The obelisk in London was given to Britain in 1819 – but only traveled to London in 1878, in a specially made iron pontoon towed by a steamer. Its name, Cleopatra's Needle, is misleading. It and its twin came from Heliopolis, in Egypt, but were erected by Pharaoh Tuthmosis III around 1500 B.C. The 220-ton obelisk in Paris (also pink granite) came from the temple of Ramses II in the ancient Egyptian city of Thebes, where it was erected around 1300 B.C. A crowd of 200,000 people watched it being raised into position in the center of Paris in 1836.

Who built the Arc de Triomphe?

In 1806 Napoleon commissioned a number of monuments to glorify his Grande Armée. The most famous of these is the Arc de Triomphe, which stands in the middle of the Place de l'Étoile in Paris, France.

Construction of the monument began in August 1806, but due to financial problems it was not completed until 1836. The sculptures on the façades – which were created by some 20 sculptors – were installed in 1844. Modeled on the triumphal arches of ancient Rome, the harmonious proportions of the Arc de Triomphe (which is 160 feet/48 meters high and 150 feet/45 meters wide) give it a massive yet elegant appearance. Napoleon did not live to see the completion of the arch, but the cortège bearing his ashes passed under it when they were brought to France from St. Helena in 1840.

The Leaning Tower of Pisa is slowly toppling over, despite attempts to save it. It started to lean even before it was completed.

Is the Leaning Tower of Pisa about to fall down?

Originally intended as the belfry of the cathedral of Pisa in Italy, the eight-story tower had already begun to lean before the fourth story was completed. Its extraordinary tilt (now about 16 feet/5 meters from perpendicular) is still increasing by approximately 1 millimeter per year. Despite efforts to support it, the tower is gradually toppling over.

The tower rises from the Piazza del Duomo, which includes the cathedral, baptistery, and Campo Santo (an enclosed graveyard). Begun in 1174, its construction was not completed until 1350. When the original architects became aware that the tower was leaning, they tried to provide a contrary tilt, but could not correct the problem. Despite numerous earthquakes the tower remains standing – which some regard as a triumph on the part of the architects. The reason for the tower's tilt is believed to be its weak foundations in waterlogged soil.

The foundations of Philip Augustus's fortress, dating from the 1190s, were excavated during restoration work at the Louvre in 1984–5.

How old is

the Louvre?

The Louvre goes back to the 1190s, when the French king Philip Augustus built a fortress to guard Paris from attack across the River Seine. The Great Tower was completed in 1202.

The Louvre has been endlessly modified and extended since medieval time. After demolishing the original keep, François I began to transform the Louvre into a luxurious palace, a process only completed under Louis XIV. Turned into a museum during the French Revolution, it was enlarged and embellished under Napoleon.

Modifications made between 1981 and 1993 included adding a spectacular new entrance in the form of a huge glass pyramid.

When was the

Suez Canal opened?

A canal linking the Mediterranean with the Red Sea was dreamed of – and attempted – by Pharaoh Necho (610–595 B.C.). It became a reality in 1869.

Extending for 120 miles (195 kilometers), from Port Said on the Mediterranean to Suez on the Red Sea, the canal was originally 560 feet (170 meters) wide and 65 feet (20 meters) deep. Its

opening in 1869 – for which Verdi composed the opera *Aida* – brought prosperity to the Suez Canal Company, which had been licensed to operate the canal for 99 years. In 1956 the canal was nationalized by President Nasser of Egypt. Blocked during the Six-Day War between Egypt and Israel, it remained closed from 1967 until 1974. It has since been enlarged to accommodate supertankers.

Who built the

Panama Canal?

Work on the canal – which had been conceived of more than four centuries earlier by the first Spanish explorers – was begun by Ferdinand de Lesseps in 1880. American engineers completed it in 1914.

The first teams began work in daunting conditions. Numerous landslides, a harsh climate, and frequent outbreaks of malaria and yellow fever hampered progress. Then in 1889 political scandals, centered around the French Panama Canal Company, brought construction to a halt. The United States obtained administration of the Canal Zone in 1903 and completed the work. The canal is an amazing feat of engineering. Some 50 miles (80 kilometers) long, it is 40 feet (12 meters) deep, which permits the passage of large tankers. By connecting the Atlantic and Pacific oceans, it meant ships could avoid the long passage around South America and the dangers of circumnavigating Cape Horn.

Where can you see a French château in Canada?

Dominating the skyline of the city of Quebec is an enormous hotel built in the style of the great French châteaux. During World War II, it was the venue of two important meetings between Winston Churchill and President Roosevelt.

The Château Frontenac was erected in 1893 by the Canadian Pacific railroad company on the site of the Château Saint-Louis, which had been the residence of the governors of New France. The château is named for Louis de Frontenac, governor of New France (as Canada was then called) from 1672.

What is unusual about the Ponte Vecchio?

The oldest bridge in Florence, Italy, the Ponte Vecchio has spanned the River Arno for more than 650 years. Built in 1345 after an earlier bridge was swept away by floods, it has always been lined with shops.

Originally the shops on the bridge were mainly occupied by butchers, tanners, and fishsellers. But the smell was so appalling that in 1593 the ruler of Florence decreed that they were to be rented to jewelers and goldsmiths – who are still there today. Above the shops there is a gallery that links the Pitti Palace with the Palazzo Vecchio in the main square of Florence. Dating from 1565, the gallery also served as one of the earliest art galleries. In August 1944 the bridge had a narrow escape. As the Allies advanced on Florence, the Germans planned to blow up all the bridges over the Arno – but the explosives placed under the Ponte Vecchio were never detonated.

Why is Sainte-Chapelle in Paris almost invisible?

Sainte-Chapelle was built between 1241 and 1248 by Louis IX to house holy relics, among them Christ's crown of thorns. It is enclosed within the walls of the Palace of Justice – only the roof and steeple are visible from outside.

The chapel originally stood isolated in the middle of a courtyard, with a gallery connecting its upper story to the apartments of the king. But during the 18th century, when one of the buildings that make up the Palace of Justice was erected, it was joined to the chapel. The chapel has two sanctuaries, one above the other. The upper sanctuary contains the oldest stained-glass windows in Paris, depicting 1,124 scenes from the Bible.

Who lives in the White House?

The president of the United States lives and works in the White House,

in Washington, D.C. This elegant mansion is visited by more than 1½ million people each year, making it one of the most popular tourist attractions in the United States.

The 132-room mansion, built of white limestone, stands in a 17-acre (7-hectare) landscaped park. The original building was built in 1792. It was burned by British troops in 1814 and rebuilt in 1817. During the 1820's, a wide, curved portico (porch) with columns two stories high was added to the mansion's south side, and a square portico to the north side. Further rebuilding was carried out and extensions added by successive presidents.

When was the Eiffel Tower built?

France's most famous landmark resulted from the architectural competition organized to select a spectacular centerpiece for the 1889 Universal Exhibition, held in Paris to celebrate the centenary of the French Revolution. The winning project was the huge iron tower proposed by Gustave Eiffel, an engineer known for building metal bridges and viaducts.

It took Eiffel only 27 months to erect the 980-foot (300-meter) high tower, made entirely of metal. Greeted with a mixture of wonder and derision as it rose above the city's skyline, the tower eventually came to be regarded as the symbol of Paris. Since the day of its inauguration, the tower has grown 68 feet (21 meters), thanks to the television aerial that now crowns it.

Who sculpted the presidents' heads on Mount Rushmore?

In 1920 an American historian looked at various projects that might attract tourists to South Dakota – and selected a proposal to sculpt portraits of celebrated figures from American history on the face of Mount Rushmore. The figures chosen were the four most famous presidents of the United States to date – George Washington, Thomas Jefferson, Abraham Lincoln, and Theodore Roosevelt.

The sculptor, Gutzon Borglum, a former student of Rodin,

Built in the 13th century, Sainte-Chapelle is one of the marvels of Paris. The intense blue of its stained-glass windows has never been reproduced.

carved the giant heads with the aid of dynamite and pneumatic drills. The original idea was to depict the presidents from the waist up, but in the end only their faces were sculpted on the mountain. Sixty years old when he embarked on the project, Borglum devoted the rest of his life to it and died leaving the work unfinished. Mount Rushmore National Memorial soon became one of the most popular tourist attractions in the United States. Only Cary Grant and Eva Marie Saint have ever been authorized to climb among the gigantic noses – in order to film the cliff-hanging closing scene of Alfred Hitchcock's *North by Northwest.*

Where was the first skyscraper built?

A spirit of audacity characterized the rebuilding of Chicago after the fire that devastated the city in 1871. Modern steel alloys made taller and stronger buildings feasible, and by then elevators had come into use. The first skyscraper – the ten-story Home Insurance Building, in Chicago – was completed in 1885.

Between the two world wars, a streamlined, functional style of architecture became popular, encouraging the development of new construction techniques. In 1921 Ludwig Mies Van der Rohe proposed the first steel-and-glass skyscraper; and in 1932 New York's famous Empire State Building was completed, its 102 stories rising to a height of 1,090 feet (332 meters). This remained the world's tallest building until the completion of the World Trade Center, with twin towers 110 stories tall, soaring to a height of 1,375 feet (419 meters). The design of these structures has a stark simplicity that seems to raise them effortlessly into the sky. These towers have been surpassed by the Sears Tower (1,450 feet/443 meters high) in Chicago and the twin Petronas Towers (over 1,475 feet/450 meters) in Kuala Lumpur, the capital of Malaysia. Even taller towers are planned elsewhere in the Far East.

Skyscrapers create the drama of New York's skyline. Rockefeller Center, in the foreground, rises to a mere 886 feet (270 meters). In the background are the twin towers of the World Trade Center, 1,375 feet (419 meters) high.

Who built the

Statue of Liberty?

The Statue of Liberty, which stands at the entrance of New York harbor, was given to the United States by the people of France. It was created by the French sculptor Auguste Bartoldi, who called upon Gustave Eiffel to design the metal skeleton that gives the structure its strength.

The statue took ten years to make. It was assembled in Paris in 1884 and then dismantled and shipped to the United States in 214 containers. The reassembled statue symbolizing the "liberty which illumines the world" was unveiled by President Cleveland on October 28, 1886. A flight of 167 steps and an elevator lead to the pedestal; 12 flights of steps then lead to the platform at the top of the statue, which is visited by several million people each year.

Holding its torch aloft at the entrance of New York harbor, the Statue of Liberty was a gift from the people of France to the United States.

How deep down

is the Channel

Tunnel?

Begun in 1986, the Channel Tunnel has been in use since 1994. It was bored through the bed of the English Channel at a depth varying between 80 and 150 feet (25 and 45 meters).

The Channel Tunnel is in fact not one but three tunnels. Two of these contain rail tracks for the trains that carry passengers, vehicles, and goods between England and France. The third acts as a maintenance and service tunnel. Specially designed trains take 35 minutes to travel the 30 miles (50 kilometers) separating Folkestone and Calais. Some people maintain that since the opening of the tunnel, Britain is no longer an island.

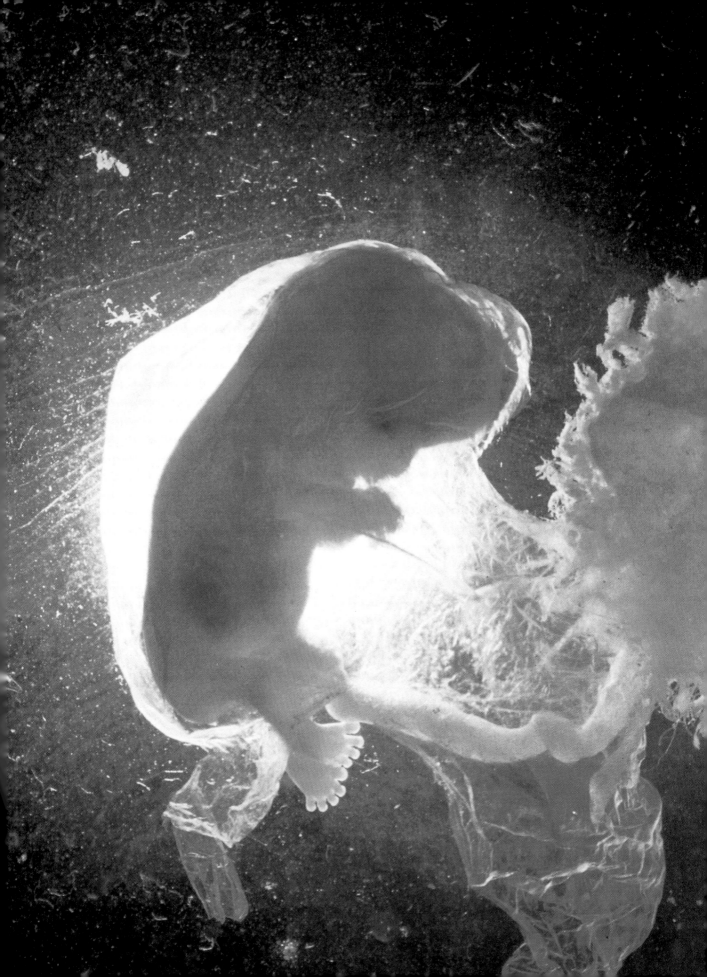

The Human Machine

What is a cell?

A cell is the basic unit of living matter. Each part of the human body contains many different types of cells, each of which has a specific role.

Whatever its shape, a cell contains a nucleus surrounded by a jellylike material called the cytoplasm. The whole cell is contained within a membrane called the plasmalemma. New cells are produced by a process of cell division called mitosis. Cells of the same kind are bound together in what is known as a tissue, and tissues are bound together to make up organs. Different kinds of cells work in different ways: cells in muscles can change their shape to allow movements to happen; those in blood are able to fight germs; those in the brain are able to receive and send all sorts of messages to various parts of the body.

How does human life begin?

It begins when an egg cell (from a woman) meets with a sperm cell (from a man). Once the egg has been fertilized, it develops for nine months in the uterus of the mother before the baby is born.

In the beginning the egg is no bigger than a pin head, but it quickly develops by a process of cell division, first into two cells, then into four, and so on. On the eighth day after fertilization, there are already 100 cells and the embryo is implanted onto the wall of the uterus. Part of the embryo develops into the placenta, which feeds the baby and provides it with oxygen. About a week after fertilization, the different parts of the body start to form. Two months later, the baby measures an inch (3 centimeters) in length. Its limbs are very tiny, but it already has eyes, a nose, a mouth, and a heart that is beating. As early as six or seven months after fertilization, the baby is capable of surviving if for some reason its mother cannot keep it inside her. The baby will be placed in an incubator, which mimics the conditions in the womb.

Life starts in the mother's womb. In this extraordinary picture, you can see a very tiny fetus only a few weeks old: it already has hands, feet, ears, and eyes.

Why are some babies born as twins?

Identical twins are formed when a fertilized egg splits into two cells. Non-identical, or fraternal, twins are formed when two eggs are fertilized at the same time by two different sperm cells.

Identical twins look the same as they have the same genetic data. They have inherited the same chromosomes from their parents. This means they have the same genes and the same hereditary features. Fraternal twins are no more likely to look the same than any brother or sister. Triplets (three babies) and quadruplets (four babies) are rare.

What happens during childbirth?

When the fetus emerges from the mother's womb, its lungs fill with air for the first time and it starts to cry. This cry means that from now on the baby is an independent individual.

Identical twins have the same genetic make-up. They look the same and behave in a similar way. When they are dressed alike, it can be difficult to tell them apart.

The childbirth process starts with a "signal" sent to the mother by the contractions of the uterus, which tell her that the baby is ready to come out. The membrane that contains the liquid in which the baby is floating breaks. The contractions, which get stronger and closer to each other, open the neck of the uterus and push the baby out. The walls of the vagina stretch to allow the baby to come through. When the baby has been born, it cries for the first time. It is now an independent individual who will breathe and eat independently from its mother. As soon as the baby is born, the midwife cuts the umbilical cord that brought it food and oxygen while it was still in the womb.

Why do babies seem to need so much sleep?

Sleep is absolutely essential for a baby's development. The time that a baby stays awake increases as it grows. A newborn baby needs a great deal of sleep.

Just like adults, babies sleep to get their strength back. While it sleeps, a baby uses very little energy, which allows it to use most of the energy it gets from food for growth. On average, newborn babies weigh 7 pounds (3.2 kilograms) and two-year-olds about 22 pounds (10 kilograms). The rapid cell multiplication needs an enormous amount of energy, and babies use a lot when they are awake.

Why do we give milk to babies?

The young of all mammals are fed with milk produced from their mothers' bodies. Humans are mammals, and our babies also need milk. Breast milk contains elements essential for the baby's growth during the first months of life: water, fat, proteins, minerals, and salts.

Mothers are usually advised to breastfeed their babies. Breastfed babies are usually healthier and are less likely to get overweight than bottle-fed babies. In the past mothers who could not breastfeed their babies themselves for health reasons, or because of their lifestyle, used to employ a "wet nurse" to feed the baby. Nowadays, powdered milk formulas for babies are very similar to mothers' milk. When babies are a few months old, they are introduced to other foods such as baby rice, vegetables, and blended meat.

During the early months babies need about 20 hours' sleep per day.

What makes us grow?

We grow as the cells in our body divide to make more cells in a process called cell division.

Growing is fundamental to life. An inadequate diet or poor conditions of life can slow it down, but cannot stop it completely. Children who suffer from severe malnourishment will not grow as much as those who are well fed. By the time a baby grows to be an adult, its size has increased by over 3 feet (1 meter). A person's adult height is roughly twice the height they were at the age of two years. The body's growth is regulated by the endocrine gland, which secretes hormones into the bloodstream.

Breast milk is the best food for young babies. Mothers are encouraged to breastfeed their babies.

What is the skeleton?

The skeleton is the frame of the human body. It supports the body and protects the most fragile parts of our organism, such as the brain, heart, and lungs.

The main parts of the skeleton are the skull, which protects the head, the shoulder blades, the rib cage (12 pairs of ribs), the pelvic girdle, the long bones in the arms and legs, and all the bones in the hands and feet. The spine is the axis of the body. It has 33 vertebrae joined in a flexible chain, and it contains the spinal cord, which is the continuation of the brain.

How many bones are there in the human body?

Our body has over 200 bones and many joints, which enable us to move.

The bones of the skeleton meet at joints, most of which allow movement. These joints can sometimes become dislocated. This is painful but can easily be remedied. Bones can also break. Fractures sometimes require an operation so the surgeon can put the two broken pieces together before putting the arm or leg into a plaster cast. The skeleton has three different types of bones: long bones, flat bones, and short bones. The long bones (such as the humerus bone and the shin bone), together with muscles

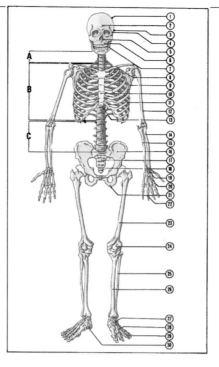

A: cervical vertebrae. B: thoracic vertebrae. C: lumbar vertebrae. (1) parietal bone. (2) frontal bone. (3) occipital bone. (4) temporal bone. (5) nasal bone. (6) maxilla. (7) mandible. (8) collar bone (clavicle). (9) shoulder blade (scapula). (10) breastbone (sternum). (11) ribs. (12) humerus. (13) end of the sternum. (14) radius. (15) ulna. (16) ilium. (17) sacrum. (18) coccyx. (19) wrist bones (carpals). (20) hand bones (metacarpals). (21) ischium. (22) fingers (phalanges). (23) thigh bone (femur). (24) kneecap (patella). (25) fibula. (26) shin bone (tibia). (27) tarsals. (28) foot bones (metatarsals). (29) toe bones (phalanges). (30) calcaneus.

attached to them, help us move and carry things. Red blood cells form in the marrow contained in these bones. The flat bones, such as the shoulder blades, have a

protective role. The short bones are important to the joints. The hand alone has 20 bones that allow it to move in different ways, making it a sophisticated tool. Bones are joined together by ligaments. Where the ends of the bones meet, they are smooth and glide over each other. The smallest bones are inside the ears; the largest is the thigh bone (femur).

Why do we have blood?

We need blood to carry food, oxygen, and other necessary materials to the various parts of the body.

Blood is made of a yellowish liquid called plasma in which red and white blood cells and platelets are suspended. Oxygen is carried to the body in the red blood cells, and waste carbon dioxide is collected by the blood from the tissues. The white blood cells help fight infection. These cells are also found in the clear liquid that appears on the surface of the skin following a scratch. Platelets cause the blood to clot when tissue has been damaged (the dark scab that forms on an injury is clotted blood). Blood also carries food, enzymes, antibodies, waste products, and heat. Blood reserves build up fairly quickly, but a severe loss of blood may result in a feeling of weakness. This is why blood transfusions are carried out on patients who have lost blood following an accident or operation.

How does blood circulate?

It circulates in the arteries, veins, and capillaries. The heart is the motor, or pump, that ensures the circulation of blood through the whole body in less than a minute.

The heart.

(1) aorta

(2) superior vena cava

(3) pulmonary artery

(4) pulmonary vein

(5) auricles

(6) ventricles

(7) inferior vena cava

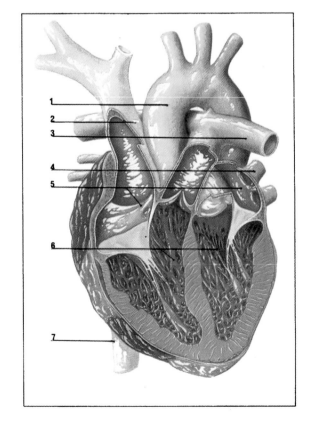

The heart has four chambers: two auricles and two ventricles. Blood enters into the right auricle, and is pumped into the right ventricle, and then out to the lungs via the pulmonary artery. In the lungs waste carbon dioxide is given off and oxygen is absorbed. Oxygenated blood comes back to the heart from the lungs via the pulmonary vein, and enters the left auricle. It then is pumped into the left ventricle, and is pumped from there to the body through the aorta. The arteries carry blood from the heart to the organs, and veins carry it from the organs and various tissues back to the heart. Capillaries are tiny

vessels that enable nutrients and gases to be exchanged with the tissues. In total, there are 93,000 miles (150,000 kilometers) of blood vessels in the human body. The usual heart rate is about 70 to 80 beats per minute (about 100,000 per day). The heart beats faster when the body needs more energy and more oxygen. The heartbeat is slower during sleep.

Why is there red blood and dark blood?

Red blood cells contain hemoglobin, which gives them a dark red color. This changes to bright red when it is combined with oxygen. Bright red blood contains oxygen, and dark blood does not.

Red blood flows in the pulmonary vein from the lungs to the heart and is pumped out to the body through the aorta. It flows through progressively smaller arteries and into the capillaries. Dark blood circulates in a similarly complex network of veins toward the heart and then in pulmonary arteries to the lungs.

Red blood cells carry oxygen throughout the whole body. In this photograph, the red blood cells here have been colored red to make the picture clearer.

What is the difference between red cells and white cells?

Red blood cells contain hemoglobin, which give the blood its color and carry oxygen. White blood cells have a protective role and help our body fight against germs.

In one cubic millimeter of blood there are about five million red blood cells and only 7,000 white blood cells (leukocytes). Red blood cells take oxygen from places where there is a high concentration of oxygen (the lungs) and release it where the concentration is lower (the tissues). The number of white cells increases when the body is fighting against an infection. When you hurt yourself, the affected area becomes red because the blood comes in larger quantities to fight off the invasion of germs. Pus is a thick yellowish liquid that appears on a wound before it heals. It is a residue that contains old white cells and germs destroyed by them.

What is a blood group?

Blood is classified into four main groups. Some of these groups are not compatible with others. When someone is given a blood transfusion, care is taken to match the blood group.

The blood group depends on whether A antigens or B antigens are present in the red blood cells. Group A blood has A antigens, and group B blood has B antigens. Blood that has both A and B antigens is called AB blood, while blood that has neither is called O blood. People with group O blood are universal donors; their blood is compatible with the other three blood groups and can be used in transfusions for all groups. Blood groups are inherited.

How does the brain work?

The brain is the most efficient of all personal computers. It controls most of the body's activities through a network of millions of nerve cells.

The brain is safely housed inside the skull and is protected by a double membrane (the meninges). The largest part of the brain, the cerebrum, consists of two hemispheres. These are divided into several areas, each with their own function. Some areas, called sensory areas, receive messages, while the motor areas send out signals from the brain to specific muscles. Other areas, called association areas, interpret impulses and make decisions. Strangely, the left hemisphere of our brain governs the right side of our body, and vice versa. The outer layer of the cerebrum, the cerebral cortex or gray matter, contains 15 billion nerve cells. Other parts of the brain include the cerebellum, which governs muscular coordination and balance; the hypothalamus, which regulates sleep; and the brain stem, which contains the nerve centers that control breathing and blood circulation. The human brain enables us to use our imagination, to think, and to remember. It also governs our voluntary movements and reactions to what we perceive.

How does the brain send messages to the body?

Messages are carried to and from the brain and spinal cord by nerve cells. There are millions of nerve cells in the body, forming a complex information network.

The central nervous system receives information and sends messages through the nerves. (1) Cerebrum. (2) Cerebellum. (3) Spinal cord. (4) Spinal nerves running in pairs from each vertebra.

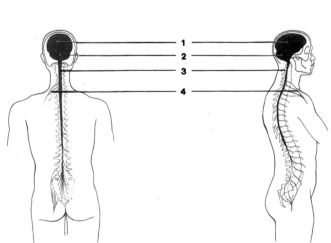

There are 12 pairs of cranial nerves that run from the underside of the brain to various organs and parts of the body such as the head, heart, lungs, and stomach. Another 31 pairs of spinal nerves run from the spinal cord to the skin and muscles. They mean that all the parts of the body are connected to each other and to the control center. The physical perception in a given place (hot, cold, rough, soft, etc.) is sent to the brain, which records and interprets the message and sends an appropriate message back (for example, telling you the bath water is hot enough). The nerve impulse, which is a sort of electrical current, travels at speeds of about 80 to 410 feet (25 to 125 meters) per second. The sensory nerves (for example, olfactory, auditory, and optic) tell the brain what is happening, and the brain tells the motor nerves (and consequently the muscles) what to do.

Why do we sleep?

Sleep seems to be a natural reaction to tiredness, particularly physical tiredness. Yet, certain animals sleep very little. The giraffe, for instance, only sleeps three minutes every 24 hours!

Living close to an airport can be a great cause of stress. Noise pollution can be so distressing that some people have to move from their home.

No one can really explain why we sleep. However, experience shows that sleep is essential for a healthy nervous system. When we are asleep, the brain receives very little information from outside and only the subconscious keeps on giving it tasks. During sleep, recent events, problems, and personal difficulties may appear in dreams. Everyone dreams, even if they do not remember doing so. Dreams are essential for a healthy balance in humans. Psychoanalysis gives a high priority to dreams and their meaning because they can express our hidden wishes and frustrations.

Why is the nervous system vulnerable to attack?

The nervous system is designed to receive information and act upon it. Sometimes it can become overloaded or messages can be confused. Attacks that result in "stress" may come from the external environment, such as noise, or from toxic substances we inflict upon ourselves, such as tobacco or alcohol.

The nervous system is a sort of mediator that acts between the outside world and our brain. It enables us to see, hear, and feel. At times there may be an excess of information, such as a very loud noise or a very bright light, which the nervous system cannot deal with. The sufferer may then experience an unpleasant sensation, anything from slight discomfort to real pain. These kinds of unpleasant

feelings act to encourage us to look for a less hostile and less stressful environment. The human nervous system can also be threatened by toxic substances such as those found in alcohol, tobacco, and drugs. They attack the nerve cells directly, generally without our even knowing it. People who smoke and drink often do so to calm themselves down; what really happens is that these toxic substances damage the nervous system, which then has to put up with even greater stress. The nervous system suffers most when the stress is permanent. It is also attacked by sorrow; the death of a close relative, for instance, can cause great nervous stress.

Why are some people left-handed?

Some people have greater and finer control over their left hand than their right, and so use their left hand to write, play tennis, or sew, for example. In these people the right-hand side of their brain is dominant.

The left hemisphere of the human brain governs the right side of the body, and vice versa. In most people, the left side of the brain is dominant. As a result, these people feel more comfortable using their right limbs, and they prefer using their right hand. It has also been noticed that both the right hand and foot in right-handed people are more developed than their left hand and foot. In left-handed people, it is the opposite. People who can use either hand are termed ambidextrous. Both sides of their brain are equally developed.

The muscles help the body to move, pulling on the different bones to create movement.

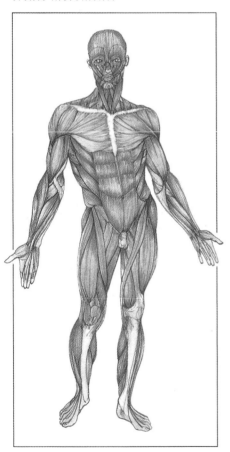

How do we move?

Our joints, muscles, and brain work together in order to allow us to move. All movements of the body result from the contraction of muscles.

There are about 500 muscles in our body that can make it move. When we contract our muscles, they become hard. The stronger you are, the larger your muscles. Our bones are connected by ligaments at movable joints. Muscles are joined to the bones by tendons, and when the muscles contract, they move the bones.

Can muscles move without our wanting it?

Some muscles can move without our wanting it or even thinking about it. For example our heart constantly beats and we never stop breathing.

There are many involuntary movements in our body. Our eyes blink and our digestive system settles down to work without conscious effort. When it is cold, some very tiny muscles start working without our even being aware of it: we shiver or we get goosebumps. Sometimes when we are tired because of a great effort, or because we have not moved for a long time, a muscle becomes hard and stops moving. This is a painful cramp.

What is skin for?

Our body is entirely covered by a soft and sensitive cover that has a protective role and allows exchanges with the environment: our skin.

The thickness of skin varies from 1 to 4 millimeters depending on its location and its role. It is quite thick under the foot and quite thin on the face. It can stretch enough to follow all the movements of the body, and it can absorb shocks. It is a barrier against humidity, cold, heat, and germs, and it can also retain water in our tissues. Its pores make it relatively permeable. One of its roles is the exchange of heat. The skin sweats to cool the body when its temperature gets too high (because of external heat, physical effort, or raised temperature). Waste materials are also excreted in sweat.

Why do we have hairs?

The bodies of our ancestors were completely covered with hairs. This hair had a protective role that has mostly disappeared today.

The hair that grows on the head is usually very long and fine – quite different from the hair on the rest of the human body. It grows by almost an inch a month. It grows faster in the summer than in winter, and faster during the day than at night. There are up to 50 hairs in each square inch. Our hair, eyebrows, and our eyelashes protect us from the cold, dust, and foreign bodies. The hairs on our head and on our body, as well as our fingernails, lack nerves and are therefore insensitive to cold and pain. This is just as well, or else we would not be able to cut them so easily!

Why is our skin so sensitive?

The lower layer of the skin, the dermis, contains a large number of nerves. These send tactile information

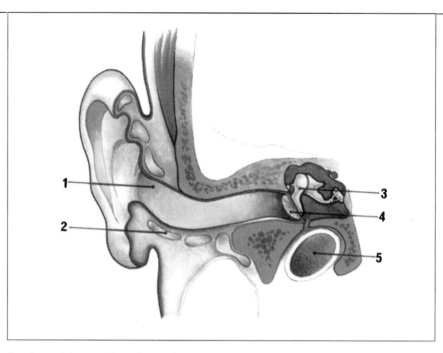

Section of the ear that shows the structure of the outer, inner, and middle ear. (1) Ear canal. (2) Cartilage. (3) Ossicles (hammer, anvil, and stirrup). (4) Eardrum or tympanic membrane. (5) Jugular vein.

about the environment surrounding our bodies to the spinal cord and then to the brain.

Our skin has two layers: an outer layer called the epidermis and a lower layer called the dermis. The cells in the epidermis are constantly being rubbed away and replaced from below. The dermis contains nerves that allow us to feel things. Millions of specialized receivers send information to our brain about temperature and the general conditions that surround our body. Thus, our skin plays an essential role in warning us about surrounding dangers. Very often the message does not even have to reach the brain. As soon as it has reached the spinal cord, nerves

that travel from it send a message that results in a reflex reaction: without even thinking about it, we remove our hand from the burning iron, we drop the very hot dish, or we start rubbing the area of our body where we feel pain.

Does skin change color?

Skin can get darker in the sun (because of ultraviolet rays), or redden because of an emotion (blood flows in), but it cannot change color because the color of skin depends on the pigments it contains.

Some skins have more brown pigments, some have more yellow pigments. An albino is a person whose skin does not contain any pigments at all. Because skin color is hereditary, nothing can be done to change it. Children from a mixed-race couple could inherit one of their parents' color or a mixture of both. Clusters of brown pigments, or melanin, result in freckles. Pigments also trigger the tanning process. Ultraviolet rays from the sun activate the release of melanin and give the skin a darker color. In an embarrassing situation, some people might blush. Blood flows into the face, which turns red.

Why can we smell things?

In prehistoric times, humans used their sense of smell to warn them about danger, or to find food. Today our noses warn us of gas leaks and fire, and we enjoy the smells of perfume and cooking.

The organ of smell is in the higher part of the nose, an area covered with olfactory cells. The olfactory nerve transmits smells to the brain. You only realize how important smell is when you lose that sense, for example, when you have a cold. You can smell something when you inhale air through the nose. Molecules of gas from an object can then reach the olfactory cells. When we eat and drink, most of our enjoyment comes from smell. Wine tasters use their noses as much as their mouths. As for specialists in perfumeries, they are able to recognize hundreds of different perfumes. Some animals, carnivorous mammals, for instance, have a much more developed sense of smell. Thus, a dog can follow the tracks of another animal over quite a long distance.

How does our tongue recognize different tastes?

Our tongue is covered with taste buds. The taste buds contain tiny receptors that are able to recognize different tastes.

There are different taste buds in different areas of the tongue: the sides are sensitive to sour tastes, the tip of the tongue is sensitive to sweet and salty foods, while the very back of the tongue is sensitive to bitter tastes. You can taste food through the combination of these different areas, but this is further enhanced by smell, which plays an equally important role in the pleasure or lack of pleasure we get from food. It is easy to tell a food that we do not like by its smell. Our sense of smell can tell us immediately whether we are going to enjoy what is cooking or not.

How do we perceive sound?

We hear sounds through our ears. Sounds run along a three-stage mazelike route in our ear, at the end of which it will reach the brain.

The ear is an extremely complex organ made up of three different parts. The outer ear transmits sounds to the eardrum, a membrane that vibrates like a drum and which is the first part of the middle ear. The vibrations of the drum are amplified and sent toward the liquid in the inner ear. The variations in pressure are felt by nerves in the inner ear. These then send a nervous impulse toward the brain, which interprets the sound it receives.

How do we see?

Our eyes enable us to see the world around us. But sight, just like the other senses, is only possible because our brain is able to interpret the messages sent to it by the eyes.

The eye can be compared to a camera. The diaphragm that opens and closes depending on the amount of light is the iris. The hole in the diaphragm, the pupil in the center of the eye, is larger when the light is dim. The eye contains a lens that enables us to see a clear picture. The sensitive film on which images are imprinted upside down, just as in a camera, is our retina. The human visual field covers 180°. It is narrower than in some animals and much broader than in others. Human eyesight is satisfactory for us, yet it is very much weaker than the eagle's. We are able to see colors, which is not the case for many species.

Why do we have two eyes?

Our eyes work together to enable us to receive a single image of the slightly different pictures received by each eye. This gives us the ability to judge the distances between objects.

The perception of depth is linked to the difference between the pictures perceived by each eye. If you hold your hand about 8 inches (20 centimeters) away from one eye and then look through a tube with your other eye, you will get the impression that there is a hole in your hand, through which you can see what happens behind the tube. Generally speaking, there is a fusion between what both eyes can see. Our binocular vision gives us an accurate three-dimensional view that allows us to judge the position and speed of objects in front of us.

What is an optical illusion?

A picture we think we can see very clearly when in fact we are mistaken. The brain interprets the image received by our eyes, and sometimes we see what we expect to see rather than what is really there.

Some optical illusions can be explained by the fact that the retina "remembers" certain elements of one image as we look at the next. If we look hard at one picture and then at another, the first is superimposed on the second. Other famous optical illusions include two lines that are really the same length placed at right angles, so they appear

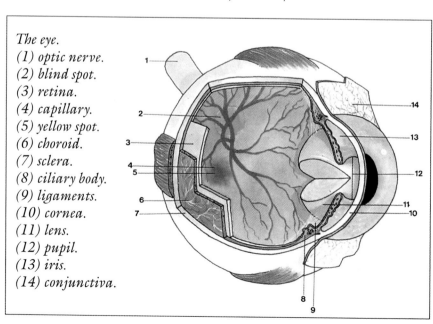

The eye.
(1) optic nerve.
(2) blind spot.
(3) retina.
(4) capillary.
(5) yellow spot.
(6) choroid.
(7) sclera.
(8) ciliary body.
(9) ligaments.
(10) cornea.
(11) lens.
(12) pupil.
(13) iris.
(14) conjunctiva.

different lengths, and images that can be interpreted in different ways (such as the vase/faces illusion). Our eyesight weakens with age, becoming less reliable.

Why do some people not see as well as others?

Some people cannot see very well at long distances because they are near-sighted. Others cannot see things that are close because they are farsighted. As people get older, the lens in the eye becomes less elastic, and they are unable to focus on nearby objects.

The main eye disorders affect either what we see at long distances (hypermetropia or far sight) or what we see at short distances (myopia or near sight), or even how we see colors (color blindness). These disorders can be due to a malformation of the lens: focused images form in front of the retina (myopia) or behind the retina (hypermetropia). Astigmatism is a disorder caused by an uneven curving of the cornea that distorts objects depending on the

angle from which they are viewed. The most common disorder is presbyopia, a condition first noticed in people in their mid-40s. It is caused by a deterioration of the lens that becomes increasingly pronounced. Nearby objects become blurred. Your optician can prescribe glasses or contact lenses that reinforce the power of the natural lenses of your eyes.

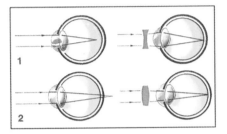

(1) Myopia. The light rays are focused short of the retina, producing a blurred image. A concave (inwardly curved) lens held in front of the eye corrects this error. (2) Hypermetropia. The image received is beyond the retina. A convex (outwardly curved) lens held in front of the eye reinforces the eye's own convex lens.

Why do we eat?

The food we eat and the air we breathe are essential for our survival. Our body needs both to develop during childhood, and to give us energy and replace old cells throughout our life.

Life relies on a process of absorption and then burning of energy. We burn calories when we make any physical effort. To do this we need two sorts of fuel: food and oxygen. Food provides us with energy for moving, thinking, keeping our body warm, and staying healthy. The internal combustion never stops, and we need to eat as regularly as possible. A newborn baby grows so fast that it needs at least seven meals a day. An adult, in order to stay healthy, must still have three meals a day. The longest gap between meals is between the evening meal and breakfast the next day. This is why breakfast is the most important meal of the day.

What happens to the food we eat?

The food we swallow is digested in the digestive tract. It is broken down into tiny particles that pass through the wall of the intestine to be transported by the bloodstream to the hungry cells.

First, food is chopped by the teeth and then moistened with saliva. It then passes down to the stomach, where it is mixed with acids and enzymes that break it down further into juices. It then goes into the small intestine. It passes through the wall of the intestine into the bloodstream, which carries it to the remotest parts of the body. Anything left over goes into the large intestine and is evacuated.

Why do we salivate?

When you are very hungry, the sight of food can make your mouth water. A dog does not hold its saliva, and you can see saliva dripping from its mouth while its owner is preparing its food.

Saliva is an important substance in the digestion of food, and the first one in the digestion process. When we see food or smell it cooking, this triggers the production of saliva in the mouth, and the mouth waters. This is called a reflex.

Can we eat anything?

Some animals only eat plants and others only eat meat. Humans are omnivorous. This means we eat both sorts of food.

Our basic food requirements are classified under four main groups: proteins, found in meat, fish, eggs, and dairy products; carbohydrates, found in bread, rice, pasta, potatoes, sugar, and chocolate; lipids or fats, found in butter, cream, and oil; and vitamins, found in differing quantities in most foods, especially in fruit and vegetables. Energy contained in food is measured in calories. Working adults need about 2,500 calories per day in order to replace their energy. They also need about 4 pints (about 2 liters) of water: this can be drunk as a liquid or taken as food.

It is often said that the modern diet is not very healthy: we eat too much meat, too much sugar, and too much fat. Yet dieticians know more and more about food, and they give us more and more advice on how to eat healthily. The real problem in today's world is malnutrition in developing countries. There people suffer from dietary deficiencies (this means that they do not have enough food or that their food intake lacks certain nutrients).

Why do we have teeth?

Teeth are needed to bite and grind our food. Mixed with saliva and ground by the teeth, food is sent to the stomach for the next stage in the digestive process.

In some animals all teeth are the same. Humans have four different types: eight sharp incisors for biting; four sharp and strong canines for tearing; and eight premolars, and 12 molars whose job it is to chew food. Bits of food caught between the teeth may ferment and cause decay. Because our teeth are so valuable and because they cannot be replaced, it is essential to take good care of them. They should be cleaned several times a day, preferably after meals and before going to bed.

Why do we sometimes get toothache?

Most of the time toothache is caused by dental decay, or caries. To start with, dental decay is a superficial infection that gradually spreads inside the tooth, forming a hole called a cavity. If it is not treated in

Another wobbly tooth! It will soon fall out, to be replaced by another one, with much stronger roots.

its early stages, the cavity can get larger and larger until it reaches the nerve. It can then become very painful.

You can help prevent decay by cleaning your teeth regularly and by cutting down on the amount of sugary foods you eat, especially cookies, candy, and sodas. Also, everyone should see a dentist at least twice a year, to check your teeth and gums and look for any decay. If there are any cavities, the dentist will drill away the damaged part of the tooth and fill the holes with silvery dental amalgam or modern fillings that contain porcelain and are nearly invisible. If the decay is extensive, it will be necessary give you a local anesthetic and numb the nerve. Visiting the dentist is not a painful process, so there is no need to worry about going for your regular check-ups.

Why do our teeth fall out?

Milk teeth have an important role. They fall out because they are only needed temporarily.

Milk teeth seem quite useless to children. What is the point in having teeth that grow, fall out, and then grow again? In fact they are very necessary. Small children can use them to chew while their jaw is still not fully grown. Milk or baby teeth prepare the way for the bigger teeth that will come later. As the jawbone grows, permanent teeth form and develop beneath the baby teeth. They then start to push the baby teeth out. In any case, the jawbone has by now become too large for them.

Why do we get ill?

The human body is a complicated machine, but it is so well organized that under ideal conditions nothing should go wrong, except for normal wear

and tear. Unfortunately, the stresses and strains of the outside world are such that the machine sometimes does break down. It suffers from sickness.

Many serious diseases (such as plague, cholera, smallpox, tuberculosis, diphtheria) have been almost eradicated from developed countries as a result of immunization programs, better hygiene, and an awareness of which animals may carry certain diseases. Children in developed countries can be immunized against most childhood diseases, including mumps, whooping cough, measles, and German measles (rubella). Once the body has suffered a particular disease, or has been immunized against one, it reacts by producing antibodies, which will immunize it for life; this means that the body will not catch the same disease again.

One of the most common symptoms of any disease is a raised temperature. When this happens, it is important to go to your doctor, as you never know what the cause of the disease might be. In some cases action must be taken very quickly. Some diseases cannot be cured, for example certain cancers, AIDS, and some mental illnesses.

What is the difference between a virus and a bacteria?

There are very large numbers of tiny beings that live in our body. They are called germs. Some can be seen through a microscope; these are bacteria, protozoa, and fungi. Others are so small they can only be seen with a much more powerful instrument, the electron microscope; these are viruses.

There are various types of medicine that can be prescribed to a patient when their body cannot fight alone against harmful bacteria and fungi. It is more difficult to fight a virus. The best way to protect the body is through immunization: this is done in the first months of a child's life by injecting the child with a small dose of dead or modified virus. The body produces antibodies against that virus, so if it should come in contact with a live virus, the body will quickly recognize and fight against it before it can multiply and cause illness.

How does our body fight germs?

Our body can fight germs in a number of different ways. Our skin and mucous membranes act as a barrier against the attack. The white cells and antibodies within the body rush to crush the enemy.

Bacteria and viruses multiply and spread very quickly inside our body, through a process of cell division. They behave as parasites and start producing waste called toxins, which cause the body's temperature to rise. If there is a wound, white cells will rush to the spot to try and swallow the germs. Our bodies also produce antibodies that recognize particular viruses and bacteria, and so participate in the fight to keep healthy.

Fortunately, not all germs are dangerous. There are billions of germs all around us (there are hundreds of millions germs on a seemingly harmless facecloth). Some bacteria might even be useful, and play a crucial role, for instance, in the digestion process.

What is medicine?

Medicine helps us fight against pain and diseases. The first drugs were all plant-based. Plants are still widely used by the pharmaceutical industry, especially in homeopathy.

Plants are now processed in laboratories, where the active ingredients they contain are extracted and then used to cure us. The difference between the primitive witch doctor and the modern chemist lies mainly in a better knowledge of the active ingredients of plants and how to extract them. Animal substances are also widely used, as well as synthetic products. These have the same benefits as natural products, but cost less to produce and are more easily controlled. Vaccines, serums, and antibiotics are a different sort of medicine, derived from living organisms such as fungi or bacteria. They are used against infectious diseases caused by harmful bacteria and viruses. Drugs are prescribed by doctors. It is strongly advised not to use self-medication as doses must be very accurate (they depend on the age and weight of the patient). Also, doctors are trained to know the exact effects of drugs on the body.

Immunization campaigns have saved millions of human lives. They have resulted in the eradication, for example, of smallpox. Injections are usually quite painless.

What are vaccines?

The principle of vaccination was invented 200 years ago by an Englishman called Edward Jenner. He noticed that young dairy maids who had suffered a disease known as cowpox (vaccinia) did not then catch another fatal disease, smallpox. He deduced that their bodies must have been immunized against it by the cowpox. By deliberately injecting vaccinia into a healthy body, it was possible to prevent smallpox.

Several different methods can be used to produce a vaccine: bacillus may be heated until it becomes harmless, or dead bacillus which causes a very mild form of the disease may be used. After the vaccine has been injected into you, your body is encouraged to start producing antibodies that will later prevent an invasion of the live virus, should you come into contact with it. Some vaccines are still necessary: those against tuberculosis, diphtheria, tetanus, and poliomyelitis. Children can also be immunized against diseases such as mumps, measles, whooping cough, and German measles (rubella).

Thanks to medicine, the average life expectancy of people in developed countries has increased.

What is today's most serious disease?

After World War II, when it became possible to eradicate tuberculosis with vaccines and antibiotics, the most feared disease was cancer. With the advance of science, it is now possible to cure a large number of cancers. A new disease that appeared in the 1980s has caused widespread anxiety because we have not yet discovered a cure for it: this disease is AIDS (acquired immune deficiency syndrome).

The AIDS virus is transmitted through blood exchange and sexual intercourse. A person who has become infected first becomes HIV positive. This means that they carry the virus, but it is not yet active. For months or even years there are no symptoms. Yet the virus is there, attacking the body's immune system. When the immune system has been weakened, diseases appear that a healthy body should normally be able to fight. It is not the AIDS virus itself that attacks the body, but rather diseases known as opportunistic diseases. Each one of these can be cured, but because there are so many, the body becomes weaker and weaker. This is why AIDS is fatal. Some drugs, the most common one being AZT, slow down the multiplication of the virus. However, these drugs have side effects and can further weaken the patient.

Why do we die?

Humans are living creatures, and by definition life has an end. Plants and animals are born, they live and get old and must all die. Whether death is accidental or natural, none of us can escape it.

As time passes, our body wears out: new cells do not replace old ones as quickly, our muscles lose their flexibility, our joints stiffen, and our bones become more fragile. Even our skeleton shrinks. As you get older, you cannot hear as well, you cannot see as well, and even food seems to be less tasty. Medical research is aimed at extending the use of these faculties and generally improving the quality of life for elderly people.

How long can people live today?

Life expectancy for humans keeps increasing. According to some scientists, we should theoretically be able to live up to the age of 150. Sickness, poor hygiene, and an unbalanced diet might be the reasons why we do not live so long.

In some places on the planet, people live longer than average, such as in Abkhazia in the country of Georgia, and Vilcabamba in

Ecuador. It is impossible to say whether this is hereditary, or whether it has something to do with the climate or with food. However, one reason for apparent long life may simply be the lack of birth registration, so it is possible that some people's ages may have been miscalculated. Scientists who study the longevity of humans are called gerontologists. Advances in the medical and surgical fields as well as a drop in childhood mortality have already lengthened human life. Within the last century, life expectancy in developed countries increased from 43 to 72 years for men and from 45 to 80 for women.

What is the difference between an hereditary disease and a congenital disorder?

Hereditary diseases are transmitted by the parents' genes. Congenital disorders appear in the fetus while it is still in the womb.

Research into genetic disorders is partly financed by charity.

The most common congenital disorders are malformations such as a harelip, a clubfoot, or something less obvious such as a crooked little finger or webbed toes. Some congenital defects are much more serious, such as the absence of a brain, which means that the newborn baby will die at birth. There are three different causes of congenital disorders: the mother may have caught a disease during pregnancy, the embryo might have been damaged by X-rays or drugs taken by the mother, or there may be some chromosome abnormalities in the fertilized egg. Some well-known diseases are to be feared because of the consequences they could have for the fetus, such as German measles (rubella). This is why young women are advised to be immunized against this disease before they get pregnant, if they have not had it before.

What is a genetic disorder?

Genetic disorders are caused by abnormalities of the chromosomes which are transmitted to children by their parents.

Both the sperm cell and the egg cell carry chromosomes, which contain information about the parents' characteristics. These chromosomes are made up of a chain of genes (DNA), each gene more or less responsible for one characteristic. Accidents may happen over the whole chain or they may be related to only one gene. These accidents are called mutations and can be responsible for the diseases transmitted by parents to their children. Hemophilia (a person's blood does not coagulate and therefore there is a permanent risk of hemorrhage), color blindness (the person cannot distinguish all colors), and Duchenne muscular dystrophy are all genetic, or hereditary, diseases.

The Peoples of the World

Where do the Inuit live?

The Inuit, also known as Eskimos, live in the Arctic, one of the world's coldest regions. The Arctic extends all around the North Pole and covers parts of Canada, Alaska, Greenland, and the north of Siberia.

Around 50,000 Inuit live in the Arctic zones of North America and Greenland, in temperatures that fall as low as −60°F (−51°C). Another 2,000 Inuit live in Siberia, the Russian part of the Arctic. In the Arctic, the year is divided into six months of daylight and six months of darkness. In summer the average temperature barely exceeds 50°F (10°C) and often falls below freezing. Although snow melts relatively often in the southern regions of the Arctic, the earth remains permanently frozen. Despite this, around 100 vigorous species of plants do grow during the short Arctic summer.

What is the climate of the Antarctic like?

The Antarctic, one of the polar regions, extends around the South Pole. It is much colder there than in the Arctic. Special thermometers must be used to measure the temperature, which can fall to −130°F (−90°C).

The Antarctic is covered with a deep layer of snow, called pack ice, where no humans or land mammals live. Scientists from all over the world participate in expeditions here, devoted to study and research of the Antarctic and its wildlife. These expeditions are conducted in harsh conditions and last no longer than a few months. The only mammals in this inhospitable region are the marine mammals: whales, seals, sea lions. Penguins, fish, and several varieties of birds such as the albatross are also found here.

An Inuit woman in Alaska. The Inuit are the last Asian immigrants to have made a land crossing of the Bering Strait, 10,000 years ago. The more southerly natives of North America crossed this strait 30,000 years before them.

What work do the Inuit do?

The Inuit, or Eskimos, are a hunting and fishing people. However, because of their contact with Western civilization, they have increasingly abandoned their traditional way of life.

Until recently, hunting and fishing was the subsistence way of life of the Inuit. However, these activities are now principally practiced by those who supply local stores. These activities provide not only meat and fish for food, but also skins used for making clothes and small boats. Today, in adapting to the contemporary world, the Inuit have become merchants, doctors, bank employees, pilots, etc. Some have become guides for the tourists who visit their regions. Children attend school, but they must often leave their families during the school year to do so, returning home only for holidays.

What do the Inuit do in their leisure time?

Fishing remains a traditional activity among the Inuit.

Many outdoor sports are popular among the Inuit, including ice hockey and sled racing, for example. But those who live in houses also love to remain warm inside, reading, playing cards, and watching television.

The Inuit still fish, and hunt seal and caribou in their leisure time. They also enjoy dog sled races and the more modern sport of snowmobiling. They play hockey with sticks and pucks fashioned from the horn and bone of moose. But the Inuit today spend most of their free time at home, where they play games, both traditional and modern. One such game entails throwing darts through holes made in caribou horns, which they hang from the ceilings of their home.

Do the Inuit still travel in kayaks?

The kayak is a small boat made of seal skins stretched over a framework – most often made of wood but sometimes of whalebone – which is propelled through the water by means of a paddle. It is still in use today, but the Inuit also now use motorboats.

Although the Inuit have kept their traditional craft such as the kayak and the umiak, they also use motorboats for longer journeys or for transporting heavy loads. Tracked vehicles or snowmobiles are often used to haul long sleds overland, replacing dogs. Long-distance travel is now by small airplanes that make regular scheduled flights throughout the Arctic region. This has lessened the isolation of many small villages. These planes are often fitted with skis in place of wheels, allowing them to land on snow and ice.

Do igloos still exist?

The igloo is a traditional dwelling that is especially used during hunts across the ice pack. It is a round shelter constructed out of blocks of ice. It has become quite rare today.

The igloo is now hardly ever found among the Inuit who inhabit the north of Canada. The ice of the igloo does not melt because, even inside the igloo, the temperature always remains below freezing. Animal fat is burned in a lamp that produces just enough heat to cook food and warm up the atmosphere a little. Today, most Inuit live in modern housing, equipped with electricity and heating. The houses are made mostly of stone, which is abundant in the Arctic.

How do the Inuit clothe themselves?

Very warmly! When it is especially cold, the Inuit sometimes wear several layers of fur garments made from the skins of seal and caribou.

The living conditions in an isolated Inuit village are harsh and more traditional. For hunting and fishing,

In Greenland an Inuit prepares to depart on an expedition with his dog team and sled.

in order to protect themselves from exposure to the extreme cold, the Inuit wear two layers of fur garments: the fur faces inward in the inner layer and outward in the exterior layer. The Inuit who live and work in urban areas tend to dress in contemporary Western clothing, but furs remain indispensable.

What do the Inuit eat?

The Inuit have always depended for food on the natural resources around them – fish, and the meat of bear, seal, and caribou. Today, modern transportation makes it possible for them to import other foods.

The bounty of fishing and hunting still constitutes a major part of Inuit nutrition. Fish and meat are eaten fresh, or preserved by the processes of salting and drying. This food is rich in the proteins and fats necessary to withstand the rigors of the Arctic climate. Modern life has made it possible for the Inuit to vary their traditional diet, notably by making available fruits and vegetables that were unknown to them until recently.

How do the Inuit receive medical care?

Formerly the Inuit cared for themselves by means of traditional remedies prepared from plants. Many young Inuit now study medicine at universities in Canada, the United States, and Russia, returning to practice in their own communities.

Although methods of treatment have improved considerably, the Inuit have unfortunately become vulnerable to new infections through contact with visitors to the Arctic region, and new diseases have arisen from changes in nutrition and modes of living. Many villages are too small and isolated to have their own medical staff. Doctors and dentists therefore travel by airplane from village to village, offering their services in regular clinics.

Who are the Lapps?

We have only a limited knowledge of the origins of the Lapps, or Laplanders, who live in the extreme

In Finnish Lapland, children often wear traditional, brilliantly colored garments.

north of Scandinavia. They number about 45,000, scattered across Norway, Finland, Sweden, and Russia, and their origins date back perhaps 30,000 years.

The Laplanders traditionally raise reindeer. This occupation, which obliges them to follow the seasonal migration of the animals, made them a nomadic people, moving with the herds and sheltering under skin tents. Some Laplanders have remained nomadic, but many have today settled into stable communities where they practice animal husbandry, farming, and fishing. The culture of the Lapps is unique and finds expression in the highly colorful traditional clothing that they still wear today. There is a strong oral tradition, which developed out of their traditional nomadic way of life, and includes the stories and legends of the Great North.

Are the world's highest mountains inhabited?

The highest mountains in the world are found in the Himalayan range, which extends more than 1,500 miles (2,500 kilometers) across South Asia. Many of its peaks surpass 23,000 feet (7,000 meters) in altitude. Mount Everest, the highest of these mountains, reaches an altitude of 29,130 feet (8,880 meters). Twenty million people live difficult and impoverished lives in this mountain region.

Many narrow valleys are cut deeply between the mountains of the Himalayas, called the "roof of the world." In these valleys live the varied populations of the Himalayas. Many distinct cultures have evolved in Tibet, Nepal, Sikkim, and Bhutan, the four countries crossed by the mountain range. The best known of these people are the Sherpas of Nepal, who live at altitudes of 10,000 feet (3,000 meters). Famous for their hardiness and for their remarkable skills as climbers, they are indispensable to visitors to this region as guides, porters, and companions to mountaineers.

Nepalese houses are built on two levels; the first story is used as a stable and to store wood, while the inhabitants live and sleep on the upper level. Despite the intense cold, people are often barefoot.

How do the people of the Himalayas make a living?

These mountain peoples have adapted their mode of life to their environment. In general, they raise animals and run small farms as well as working as guides and porters.

The people of the Himalayas raise sheep, goats, yaks, and cattle. In the high mountain altitudes, the animals have only a meager food supply because vegetation is relatively sparse. Grains such as wheat and barley, vegetables such as potatoes, and some fruit trees are cultivated here. Trade in the markets is for the most part by barter – people exchange food and craft goods, such as blankets and clothing, for goods such as tea, spices, utensils, and tools.

How do the people of the Himalayas build their houses?

Stone, which is easily found in the mountains, is the principal building material for houses. These are built with few doors and windows, to conserve heat inside.

Although quite small, these houses generally have two stories. The first level is set aside for animals, whose body heat

In Tibet and Nepal the yak is very common. Its thick wool protects it from the intense Himalayan cold. Its strength and its docility have made it an effective pack animal.

generates warmth, and for the storage of tools and wood. The family lives in the upper story. It is here that everyone eats and sleeps, in a single room that is often filled with smoke from the hearth, as the houses do not have chimneys. This story also serves as storage for hay and food supplies.

The roofs of the houses are often weighted with stones that prevent the strong winds common at these high altitudes from tearing the roofs away.

What do the people of the Himalayas eat?

Families eat the food that they grow and the meat of their animals. Grains, potatoes, and meat are the basis of the Himalayan diet.

Cereals (barley and wheat) are generally eaten in the form of small cakes made of ground and toasted grain. The meat of sheep and goats is commonly eaten, either freshly cooked or dried. Yak meat is considered a great delicacy. Tea is seasoned with salt and yak butter.

How do people travel in the high mountains?

On foot, since the geographic and physical conditions of the mountains

make the construction of roads practically impossible.

There are very few roads in the Himalayas, and people travel on foot, sometimes over great distances. The trails are often very steep and dangerous, winding along precipitous slopes and crossing tumultuous rivers. When snowfall is heavy, many of these routes become impassable.

raised for its milk, its wool, and its meat. It is also used as a pack animal.

The yak, with its great horns, looks a little like a buffalo. Its thick coat of fur protects it from the cold. A very hardy animal, it can carry heavy loads and sometimes also serves as a mode of transport. The people of the Himalayas drink its milk, from which they also

What peoples inhabit the Cordillera of the Andes Mountains?

After the Himalayas, the Cordillera of the Andes is the world's highest chain of mountains. It is also the longest, extending 4,660 miles (7,500 kilometers) along the western coast of South America. It crosses four countries: Peru, Equador, Bolivia, and Chile. The mountain chain is principally inhabited by peoples indigenous to this region.

The native tribes of Lake Titicaca often organize festivals on floating islands made of matted reeds. Everyone wears the famous bowler hat.

What is a yak?

It is a mammal of the bovine race that lives in regions as high as 20,000 feet (6,000 meters) in altitude. The domestic yak, smaller than the wild yak, is

make butter and cheese. Only when a yak is very old is it slaughtered. Its meat is then eaten, very often in dried form. The women weave blankets and clothing from the long wool of the yak. Boots are made of its skin and musical instruments from its horns.

These Native Americans are descended from a number of different peoples and cultures. Their languages, physical characteristics, their way of life, their dress, and their customs vary from tribe to tribe and from one country to another. They are the oldest inhabitants of the South American continent, descendants of peoples such as the Inca and the Aymara. The Cordillera of the Andes is also inhabited by peoples descended from Spanish colonists and other European and African settlers.

How do these peoples live?

Often extremely poor, the peoples of these countries live mainly from small-scale farming. They raise sheep, llamas, alpacas, and vicuna, from whose wool they make garments.

The people of the Andes live in relative isolation. They farm small plots of land, sometimes at very high altitudes, with only the most basic tools and in the traditional manner of their ancestors. Corn is the principal crop. Llamas, which look like small camels, but without a hump, are raised as beasts of burden and to provide milk, meat, and wool. Some people also raise poultry, especially turkeys. The native peoples of Lake Titicaca (Peru, Bolivia) and those of the Pacific coast are also fishermen.

Where is the the Amazon basin?

The Amazon basin is an enormous territory located in the north of South America. It is covered with a vast forest that spreads out from the banks of the Amazon and its tributaries, from the Cordillera of the Andes to the Atlantic coast.

The Amazon basin extends across Peru, Columbia, Brazil, and Venezuela. Many of the tribes that originally inhabited this region disappeared at the time of the Spanish conquest. They were either captured and enslaved or killed, or driven from their traditional territories to take refuge deep in the forest. Primitive tribes remain, however, of which the most famous are the Tupi-Guarani of Brazil. Some tribes live an isolated existence in the depths of the forest. Today they are again threatened by the construction of the trans-Amazonian highway and the advance of civilization, which has brought with it the destruction of their habitat.

How do Amazonian tribes survive?

Hunters, fishers, and farmers, the Amazonian people have adapted to life in a setting that would seem very hostile to us.

Certain Amazonian tribes wear no clothes. Here is a group of women net fishing in the river.

Inhabitants of the Amazon basin cultivate sweet potatoes, corn, and cassava root. They gather nuts and fruits in the forest, and the river provides them with many varieties of fish. In the forest brush they hunt monkey, tortoise, wild pig, and the armadillo. They sometimes raise poultry. They may suck stalks of sugarcane to quench their thirst. Contact with settlers has introduced them to other foods.

How do the people of this region dress?

Many of the native inhabitants of the Amazon wear little or no clothing, for the climate is hot and humid.

They may wear only a loincloth held around the waist by a plaited belt. They often wear jewelry, adorning themselves with bracelets, necklaces, earrings, and headdresses made of glass beads, shells, colorful plumes, or the claws and horn of animals. During ceremonies and festivals they cover their bodies in geometric designs, painting themselves with dyes extracted from forest plants.

Do the people of native tribes become ill?

The natives of the Amazonian basin are generally very hardy. When they are struck with illness, many still believe that this is because an evil spirit has invaded their bodies. They then consult a shaman or a sorcerer to expel the malign spirit.

As in many other regions of the world, shamanistic practices are still in use in the Amazonian basin. The shaman carries out ceremonies designed to exorcise evil spirits, but he also prescribes herbal preparations. Today, doctors go from village to village, along the river banks, to provide medical assistance to those who need it.

Are there many Native Americans in North America?

Today, there are fewer Native Americans in North America than there used to

In the United States, Native Americans, even those living on reservations, dress in the same way as everyone else. But their sense of tradition and festival remains very strong, as this Zuni-Pueblo parade shows.

be. **Many tribes were decimated during the European conquest. Some tribes have entirely disappeared, while others have suffered greatly from the arrival of settlers. Today, many Native Americans live on reservations.**

The native peoples of America are the descendants of peoples who migrated from East Asia more than 35,000 years ago, crossing a narrow band of earth that once spanned the Bering Strait. Numerous tribes settled in scattered territories, and each developed their own customs and way of life. These people practiced neither farming nor animal husbandry, but were hunters and fishermen. With the arrival of European settlers they were driven farther and farther from their ancestral territories, leading to the break-up and destruction of the tribes. Today, around 2,000,000 Native Americans live in the United States, and almost 500,000 Native Canadians live in Canada. Half of them live on reservations.

In India, festivals are a major part of the cultural tradition, as this scene of young Indian women shows.

Why do reservations exist?

The reservations are territories set aside for the native populations by the government. There are approximately 500 of these in the United States and 2,200 in Canada.

Native Americans are not obliged to live on reservations, but those who do, do not have to pay taxes. A few Native Americans on the reservations have turned to farming and animal husbandry. Others practice crafts, making fabrics, pottery, and jewelry inspired by traditional customs, and selling their work to tourists. Life on the reservations is generally difficult, and many natives have tried to seek work elsewhere. However, they often remain very much on the margins of society.

Caravans are a common sight in the Sahara. Here is one led by a nomad (a Tuareg) of the desert.

Why were Native Americans once called Indians?

The name "Indian" was given to the inhabitants of the Americas by Christopher Columbus, who thought he had reached the Indies when he landed in America.

The name "Indians" is still sometimes used, but some find it offensive, and the terms Native Americans or American Indians are preferred.

Can people live in the desert?

We call the driest regions of the Earth, where it never rains, deserts. A desert can be of sand or of rock, but its most important characteristic is that very little water is found there. In spite of this, some people have been able to survive in these inhospitable regions.

The world's largest desert is the Sahara, which is located in North Africa. Daytime temperatures in the Sahara can rise to 122°F (50°C), although the nights there are cold. Even so, many species of wildlife are found in the Sahara, as well as several forms of vegetation that have adapted to the dry conditions. Three peoples with distinct languages and customs inhabit the Sahara: the Moors to the west, the Tuareg in the central region, and the Tubu to the east.

Is there water in the desert?

There are underground tables of water, and these have made possible the development of islands of vegetation called oases.

Oases are a source of life for the human and animal populations of the desert. The water rises up in springs and brooks, although wells must sometimes be dug to reach it.

How do nomads live?

Nomads are peoples who have no fixed homes and

are constantly on the move. Nomads of the desert are driven on to find food and water for their herds.

The sparse vegetation of the desert is quickly eaten by sheep,

Who are the Tuareg?

They are a nomadic people who inhabit the Central Sahara. They live in tents,

camelback. The camel is a ruminative mammal with a fatty hump on its back and is well adapted to life in the desert. Its long legs make it a remarkable and hardy runner, and its large hoofs prevent it from sinking into the sand. A camel can go for several

An encampment in Niger. The nomads of today still use primitive methods to prepare fires.

goats, and camels. The nomads must move from one pasturage to another every few weeks. They move on camelback and must always have adequate provisions of food and water for crossings, which can last several days. Some nomads are merchants. When they gather together, they form what is called a "caravan."

speak Berber, and are Muslim. They wear dark turbans around their heads, leaving only their eyes visible, to protect themselves from the blazing sun of the Sahara.

Like the other nomads of the desert, the Tuareg travel on

days without water because it has water reserves stored in its body. A camel may be used to carry passengers or transport goods. The camel does not destroy vegetation in the same way as herds of goats do. Goats are the principal cause of the expansion of the desert into the Sahel region to the south of the Sahara.

Who are the Berbers?

The Berbers are a group of peoples who lived in North Africa well before the Arabs invaded the region in the 8th century.

Mainly inhabiting the Atlas Mountains, the Rif and the Aurès in Morocco, and the Kabylie in Algeria, the Berbers are Muslims and speak Berber. Over the centuries, they have often come into conflict with the Arabs of the region. The Berbers of Kabylie are a sedentary people.

What do people eat in the desert?

The peoples of the desert typically eat boiled meat (mutton, lamb, chicken) and ground semolina (couscous) with vegetables.

Their dishes are generally very spicy. Roasted mutton and lamb are eaten at feasts. Milk from camels is drunk, and is also used to make cheese. A substance referred to as "butter," extracted from the fat of the hump of the

The people of the desert often drink mint tea. A degree of ceremony accompanies teatime, whether enjoyed alone or within the family.

camel, is used to season certain delicacies. Tea, served hot with sugar, is drunk in these arid lands.

What is the principal natural resource of the Sahara?

Petroleum, a combustible natural mineral oil, is plentiful beneath the surface of the Sahara. Found concentrated in oil fields, petroleum is the world's principal energy source.

The major oil fields of the Sahara are found in Libya and Algeria. The depth of an oil field can vary from several feet to several hundred feet. The petroleum is pumped to the surface and then transported through pipelines to the major ports of North Africa. From here it is carried in oil tankers to cities throughout the world. Once it has been refined, it is used for fuel and as a raw material in the manufacture of a broad range of goods.

What people inhabit the Kalahari Desert?

The Kalahari Desert covers the territory of Botswana, located in southern Africa between the Zambezi and Orange river basins. The Bushmen live here.

The Pygmies are the smallest race of humans. They live in the rain forests of equatorial Africa. The group shown above has just taken part in a successful elephant hunt.

The Bushmen inhabit one of the most desolate regions of southern Africa. Very little water and vegetation are found here. However, this region provides a refuge for the nomadic people, who have been driven from their former home in southern Africa. The Bushmen live by hunting antelope and small game and by gathering roots and berries. They are extremely skilled in locating the desert's rare underground sources of water. They gather water with a sponge of vegetable fibers attached to the end of a stick.

A gentle and peaceful people, the Bushmen were immortalized in the film The Gods Must Be Crazy.

Where do Pygmies live?

The Pygmies inhabit the most isolated regions of the equatorial forest in Gabon, Cameroon, and the Democratic Republic of Congo. Here they have found refuge from persecution.

The Pygmies are characteristically quite short (less than 5 feet on average). They live in huts made of branches and wear only loincloths attached around their waists. They fish and hunt and gather fruits, berries, and roots in the forest. They make pottery, weapons, and instruments of wood and bone. The Pygmies are nomads who move through their territory as their needs dictate. Their numbers are rapidly dwindling.

Who are the Zulu?

The Zulu live in the territory of Zululand in the Natal province of South Africa. The Zulu speak one of the Bantu languages common to this part of Africa.

The Zulu were once a powerful tribe that set out in the beginning of the 19th century to conquer neighboring peoples. The Zulu warriors were armed with spears called assegai. They were defeated after South Africa became part of the British Empire. Today more than five million Zulu live in *kraals* (villages), and their principal occupations are animal husbandry and farming.

How do the Masai live?

The Masai are shepherds who live in the east of southern Africa, in Kenya and Tanzania, on the banks of Lake Victoria.

In contrast to the Pygmies, the Masai are characteristically very tall and thin. Until the age of 30, the men live in separate communities as warriors responsible for the protection of the herds of cattle and the flocks of sheep. Armed with lances and shields, they maintain watch. Once they reach the age of 30, Masai men take wives and settle in villages with their families. The Masai eat millet, corn, and the meat of their sheep. Masai warriors also take nourishment from the blood of their cattle. They draw blood from cattle by cutting a vein in the neck of the animal, then leave the wound to heal naturally. Nowadays the Masai are responsible for the protection of the wild animals in the reserves of Kenya.

Characteristically tall and thin, the Masai live in Kenya and in Tanzania. They are responsible for the protection of the regional wildlife.

Where do the Mongols live?

The Mongols live in Asia between the north of China and the Russian frontier.

The Mongols were formerly a powerful conquering people who came from Manchuria and the northeast of China. They invaded many lands, especially in the 13th century, when they were ruled by the emperor Genghis Khan. Today the Mongols are confined to the vast territory of Mongolia, a wild and arid region where the winters are long and harsh. A nomadic people of traders and camel raisers, they live in *yurts*, circular tents made of cloth and skins stretched over wooden frames.

How is rice grown?

Rice needs a hot and humid climate in order to grow. This is why the crop is well suited to Asia where it is cultivated in constantly flooded fields called rice paddies.

Work is generally done manually. The farmers who work the paddies typically use water buffalo to pull their plows. The rice seeds are sown in the furrows plowed into the mud. When the grain is ripe, the rice is harvested by cutting the germinated stalks. Spread out upon the ground, the stalks are then trampled by the water buffalo in order to separate the grain from the stems.

Why is rice often cultivated on terraces?

When rice paddies are located on mountainsides, rice farmers have to construct terraces on different levels to stop the water from draining away and to keep their fields flooded.

To flood the fields, irrigation canals are dug to carry water from nearby rivers. Dikes are then constructed to keep the water in. The abundant rains that fall in this region of the globe make it possible to keep the rice paddies while the crop grows.

How do the aborigines of Australia live?

The aborigines of Australia are the earliest known human inhabitants of that continent. Their ancestors are thought to have first arrived in Australia from Southeast Asia 30,000 years ago.

In mountainous regions terraced rice culture has become an art. In China this common landscape is still much admired by tourists.

Originally nomadic, the aborigines of Australia moved across the country, living by fishing and hunting (which they often still practice using boomerangs) and gathering food. Their way of life may appear primitive, but their customs, their arts (music, song, and painting), and their beliefs are very highly developed. The aborigines of Australia suffered enormously from the arrival of the British colonists on their territory. Many were killed, and the aboriginal population fell from 300,000 to 100,000 inhabitants. Many aborigines still suffer from their contact with other civilizations, especially from the ravages of alcoholism.

The aborigines were the first inhabitants of Australia. They live today in the same manner as their ancestors, who arrived more than 30,000 years ago.

Is there a white race of Asiatic origins?

Yes, they are the Ainu, who live on islands in the northwestern Pacific.

The Ainu are the descendants of a white population that once lived in Asia. Some Ainu live on the Kurile Islands and on the island of Sakhaline, which belongs to Russia. Others live on the Japanese island of Hokkaido. Their physical traits, their way of life, and their civilization have revealed them to be more closely related to peoples of European origin. Out of a population of 4,000 there remain very few Ainu of pure race. The Ainu, moreover, have tended increasingly to abandon their customs so they can integrate better with neighboring Russian and Japanese populations, whose cultures they have adopted.

Where do the Polynesians live?

The Polynesians live in Oceania, also known as the Pacific Islands, the many thousands of islands that lie to the east of Australia in the South Pacific. Groups of islands such as these are called archipelagos.

The Basque dance is part of a very rich and ancient folklore. The origin of the Basque people is not precisely known. Their language and blood grouping are highly distinctive.

and bodies are partly a means of tribal identification.

The application of tattoos is a rite of passage for both men and women. The tattoo identifies a person as a member of a certain group or tribe and can also indicate the rank or function of an individual in the society. It thus varies from tribe to tribe, and from one individual to another, according to whether the person who bears it is chief, fisherman, merchant, wife, or unmarried. Tattooing allows the initiated individual immediately to recognize the origin of another person.

Where did the Basques originally come from?

The Basques inhabit the two slopes of the western Pyrenees, which form the border of France and Spain. The origins of the Basque people are unclear.

The ancestry of the Basques remains difficult to determine because their unique language bears no relation to the Indo-European languages of

The principal Polynesian archipelagos are French Polynesia, New Zealand, the Samoan Islands, and Hawaii, the fiftieth state of the United States. With the exception of the New Zealanders, Polynesians live from the cultivation of the coconut palm, from fishing, and from tourism. It is believed that the peoples of Polynesia came originally from southern China.

What do Maori tattoos signify?

The Maori are Polynesian inhabitants of New Zealand, and were the first to discover these islands several centuries ago. The tattoos that they draw in spiral forms on their face

neighboring countries. In addition to this, their unique blood group sets them apart. The Basques have a unique culture that has enabled them to retain their special identity.

Who are the

Gypsies?

They are a European nomadic people who probably originated in the north of India.

The Gypsies, also referred to as "bohemians," "Romanies," or "travelers," have always been migratory. Their arrival in western Europe dates back 600 years. They spread across Europe as far as France and the British Isles in the Middle Ages, although their culture flourished for the most part in Russia, Central Europe, and Spain. All speak the same language of Indo-European origin. The Gypsies were never conquerors, nor were they nomadic shepherds. Living in caravans, they were mainly merchants, musicians, and blacksmiths. The horse-drawn, handpainted wagons in which they once traveled are rarely seen today. These vehicles have largely been replaced by trailers and motor homes.

Are the Iranians

Arabs?

No. Iran is a Middle Eastern country whose Persian-speaking inhabitants are not of Semitic origin, but are descendants of an Asian people known as Aryans.

The origin of Iran, ancient Persia, goes back to the 1st millennium B.C. when tribes of Aryans, who spoke an Indo-European language, arrived there from the plains of central Asia. In the 7th century B.C. the Medes laid down the foundations of Persian power, which developed into what became the famous Persian Empire under Cyrus II (the Great, c. 600–529 B.C.). The great majority of Iranians are Muslim. Persians, the largest ethnic group of Aryan origin, make up about 60 percent of the population.

Young Iranian women at Isfahan.

Methods of Transportation

Who invented the wheel?

We do not know precisely who invented the wheel. It first appeared in Asia more than 6,000 years ago. The first wheels were solid disks of wood. They were fragile and very heavy.

The first chariots had only two wheels fixed to an axle of wood attached directly to the body of the vehicle. The Egyptians were the first to develop wheels with spokes of wood that radiated from the hub of the wheel to its rim. The Romans later developed wheels of iron, which were more solid but very heavy. It was not until the 16th century that the idea of attaching iron rims to wheels of wood was put into practice. Modern wheels are much lighter. They are surrounded by air-inflated tires that absorb much of the shock of impact. Originally, chariots were pulled by people. They were later drawn by animals, although travel by road remained difficult for a long time.

How were goods transported before the invention of the wheel?

Before the invention of the wheel, goods were carried by animals or by people.

Draft animals were also used, such as horses and cattle, and camels, and llamas among the Incas, even dogs among the indigenous people of North America. Sleds were also employed. These were simple boards sometimes mounted on wooden runners. Travois, vehicles made of material stretched over two poles, were harnessed to draft animals, the ends of their poles simply dragging along the ground. Heavy loads were rolled over logs of wood. It is believed that this technique was used by the Egyptians to move the stones with which they built the pyramids. It is difficult to believe that such sophisticated civilizations as those of the Maya and Inca never knew the wheel, but they did use tree trunks over which they rolled enormous stones for their vast building projects.

The airplane is by far the fastest and safest mode of transportation.

What was the first use of the wheel?

Soldiers were the first to use the wheel. They developed two-wheeled, horse-drawn chariots that could accommodate two men, a driver and a soldier, usually an archer.

Above: The pulley. The colors represent the effort that must be expended (red) in relation to the length of the rope (brown) to raise a bucket (yellow). From left to right: a fixed pulley, a movable pulley, and a tackle pulley.

The chariot made it possible to move troops very quickly from point to point on the field of battle. An archer could also aim arrows much more accurately from the platform of a chariot than from the back of a horse. Ancient Egyptian bas-reliefs exist that show the pharaoh poised on his chariot, aiming arrows at his enemies. Chariots were later used for the transportation of goods. However, whereas the light chariots designed for military use could cross a wide range of terrain, the heavier chariots used for the transportation of merchandise required good roads, so for many years trade was still conducted by caravans or over water routes.

It was soldiers who first understood the advantages of the wheel. Here is a depiction of the Egyptian chariot owned by pharaoh Amenhotep II. The wheels were simple bands of iron joined to the axle by four spokes.

What else are wheels used for?

In addition to transportation, the wheel has many other applications: the pulley, the toothed wheel, the reel or spool, and the paddlewheel.

The pulley makes it possible for people to lift objects not only by the force of their muscles, but also with their own weight. Indented wheels are used in the gear mechanisms of bicycles, thus permitting a cyclist to adjust effort in relation to incline. The same

The first automotive vehicle was perfected by Fardier de Cugnot in 1770. It was steam-powered, but it had no braking system and was forgotten.

principle is applied in the hand drill, where turning the crank of a larger wheel rotates the smaller wheels that finally drive the rotation of the drill bit. Indented wheels are also used in the workings of clocks and watches. Thanks to paddlewheels, the power of a river can be harnessed to run machinery. Reels and spools, another use of the wheel, are used to store thread and wire.

What was a stagecoach?

A stagecoach was a horse-drawn carriage that carried mail and passengers. There were places for six to eight persons. Before the stage-coach, only the nobility possessed carriages, and ordinary people had to travel on horseback or by foot. During the 17th century, however, regular stagecoach services were established for public use.

Stagecoaches were very uncomfortable. They were not equipped with spring suspensions until the 18th century, and they had to travel over rough roads, in constant danger of robbers. However, they made long distance travel possible throughout North America and Europe during this period. The most famous of the stagecoach companies in the United States was Wells Fargo, which connected the eastern and western states.

Until when were horse-drawn carriages used?

The rise of the railroads in the 19th century brought an end to stagecoaches, but individuals continued to use carriages privately until World War I. After the war, carriages were rapidly replaced by automobiles.

The 19th century was the golden age of the horse-drawn carriage. Carriage-makers competed vigorously for the business of their clientele, producing a variety of models from small cabs to spacious carriages, which were ever more elegant, rapid, and comfortable. These vehicles were often constructed from precious woods and fine leathers, and used the best available steel in their suspensions.

When did the first automobiles appear?

It was not until the 1880s that gas-driven "modern"

The first true automobiles only appeared at the end of the 19th century. Here is a Renault Model C that dates from 1900.

The first gas-driven automobiles were constructed in the mid-1880s. They used motors of four fixed cylinders, which had been perfected around 1875. At the end of the 19th century, the automobile was still regarded as something so extraordinary that British law required that they be preceded on the road by a man on foot waving a red flag. Little by little, engine performance and suspension systems were improved. By the mid-1920s the use of hydraulic brakes had become common, and synchronized gears were widely in use by 1930.

automobiles first made their appearance.

Progress made both in metallurgy and in mechanics, together with a taste for speed and a fascination for machines, encouraged engineers, sportspeople, and the rich to join in the construction of automobiles. Steam cars had been built as early as 1820, and an electric car was built in 1891, but it was the more consistent, powerful, and reliable gas-driven internal combustion engine that carried the day. By 1900 the automobile was no longer the preserve of a few enthusiasts – it had become a symbol of social rank and success. The making of automobiles, which at first had been a craft industry, soon became a full-scale industrial enterprise for which Henry Ford developed assembly-line production in the United States.

Who invented the first gas-powered cars?

Two German engineers, Gottlieb Daimler and Karl Benz, each independently invented the gas-driven internal combustion engine that is still used today.

When did motor-racing begin?

Racing plays a fundamental role in the development of faster and more reliable models. The first race, between Paris and Rouen (77 miles/125 kilometers), was organized in July 1894.

Only 17 of the 21 participants completed the race, and the winners achieved average speeds of 12 miles per hour (19 kilometers per hour). In the following years, a Paris–Bordeaux–Paris race of 732 miles (1,178 kilometers) was held, and in 1899 the Belgian Camille Jenatzy set the first speed record, 65 miles per hour (105 kilometers per hour). The first international race, between Paris and Berlin, took place in 1901. The early automobiles had neither protective cockpits nor windshields, and drivers dressed accordingly in rubber coats, leather helmets, and protective visors. The roads were dangerous, and there were many sharp turns. The vehicles were fragile and there were many accidents. In 1901 Renault publicized the fact that all five Renault cars that had been entered in the race had arrived at the finish line – obviously no mean achievement!

Why do automobiles have tires?

The cover of the Petit Parisien *of June 5, 1904, was devoted to the new sporting event: motor racing.*

Tires play an important role in the suspension of motor vehicles. They absorb shock and help the car maintain a good grip on the road. The tire protects an airtight rubber tube that is inflated with pressurized air through an airtight valve. Tires without inner tubes, however, are increasingly common.

The body of the tire is composed of synthetic or steel fibers, which are layered in highly resistant crisscross patterns and sealed in latex. The surface of the tire that comes into contact with the ground is thicker and is hardened with lampblack. It is stamped with tread patterns designed to grip the road surface and to expel water to the side on wet roads. The rim on the side of the tire encloses a rod of steel that supports it. Tires should be inflated enough to avoid the risk of their rupturing, and they should be changed when the treads become worn.

How did the first cars work?

The first steam-powered motor vehicles were built on the model of locomotives.

Water brought to boil in a boiler produced steam whose pressure drove a piston. The back-and-forth motion of the piston was transformed by a crankshaft into the rotary movement that turned the wheels.

Steam cars very quickly became competitive with coaches. Some steamers traveled at speeds of almost 30 miles per hour (50 kilometers per hour), but they were too heavy and too expensive to become private vehicles. Very powerful, but noisy, dangerous, and frightening, they spat burning cinders of coal into the air. Nevertheless, in the United States in 1906 the Stanley brothers produced a steamer that surpassed 125 miles per hour (200 kilometers per hour). However, the future belonged to the internal combustion engine.

What is an internal combustion engine?

This engine exploits the principle that certain substances explode when they are mixed with oxygen and exposed to a spark. The energy of this explosion is used to drive a piston whose force is transmitted to turn the wheels.

The mixture passes through valves to enter a cylinder that houses a piston. The fuel is sucked

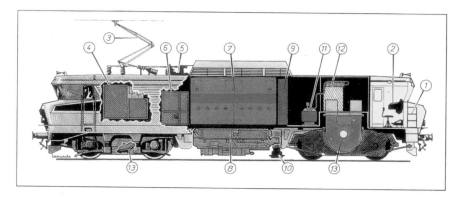

The principal components of a classic electric locomotive. (1) Protective shield. (2) Engineer's cabin. (3) Pantograph. (4) Batteries. (5) Circuit-breaker. (6) Protective housing. (7) Electrical equipment and rectifiers. (8) Transformer. (9) Electrical control box. (10) Signal box. (11) Compressor. (12) Pneumatic box. (13) Traction motor.

into the cylinder by the vacuum created when the piston descends. The valves close, and the mixture is compressed when the piston again rises. Ignited by a spark produced by a spark plug, the mixture explodes. The explosion drives the piston back down. This movement is transmitted through a crankshaft to the axle that joins the wheels, causing them to make a complete turn. The force of the explosion spent, the piston rises and expels the burned fuel through escape valves. Another charge of mixed air and fuel enters the cylinder

and the cycle starts again. Several pistons are usually fitted to the crankshaft, one acting after the other. A motor can turn between 10 and 6,000 revolutions per minute (rpm).

How does a diesel engine function?

The diesel engine (named after its inventor, Rudolf Diesel), is also an internal combustion engine. The difference rests in the fact that the explosion of the mixture of fuel and air is not caused by a spark from a spark plug but by the compression of air.

The compression of a gas raises its

temperature. When the air in a diesel engine is sufficiently compressed, temperatures of more than 900°F (500°C) are reached inside the cylinder. Pulverized fuel oil is then injected into the cylinder and ignites spontaneously, expelling gases that violently drive back the piston. Because the fuel is injected into the cylinder, the motor is referred to as a fuel-injected engine. Diesel engines use fuel oil, a less-refined fuel than gasoline. Larger and more powerful than classic internal combustion engines, diesel motors are often used in trucks.

For what else are diesel motors used?

The diesel motor is highly efficient and powerful. Unlike the electric motor, it does not depend on high-tension power lines. This is why it is used in large vehicles that consume a lot of energy, such as trucks, tractors, and cranes.

Because of this advantage, diesel engines are chosen to equip certain locomotives, especially those that require a lot of power to haul trains at fast speeds. These are called diesel electric engines. The diesel engine does not directly provide the power to turn the wheels of a train. It provides the power that turns a small turbine which generates the electricity for several electric drive motors that run the train. Diesels are also used as emergency power generators in case of power failures. These provide back-up electricity to hospitals and other vitally important institutions.

How does an electric locomotive work?

Unlike diesel locomotives, an electric locomotive does not carry its source of energy with it. A device called a pantograph is mounted on top of the locomotive. To power the motor of the locomotive, this pantograph collects and transmits energy from an electric cable suspended over the tracks.

The electric motor has given locomotives a flexibility and regularity unknown in early steam locomotives. An electric locomotive does not have to warm up, but is ready to go immediately. In addition, the engineer can adjust the electric current collected and transmitted by the pantograph to suit the power requirements of whatever maneuver needs to be made at any given moment: starting up or reversing the train, or adjusting its speed. Finally, like all electric motors, those of electric locomotives can also serve as generators and produce an electric current, restoring to the cable by means of the pantograph the energy produced in braking the train.

France's high speed train, the TGV (Train à Grande Vitesse), has a cruising speed of 190 miles (300 kilometers) per hour and a maximum speed of 320 miles (515 kilometers) per hour. It is the world's fastest train.

What is the difference between a catenary system and a pantograph?

The catenary system is the electric power cable and the supporting structure by which the cable is suspended over the tracks. The pantograph is the device mounted on the locomotive that collects and transmits the electric current that powers the train.

The subway is a system of public transportation that facilitates the movement of millions of commuters and passengers throughout the world.

To avoid any interruption in the transmission of electric current, the pantograph has a jointed attachment that gives it a degree of flexibility, allowing it to adjust to differences in level and above all to maintain a consistent pressure. This means the pantograph is kept in firm contact with the power cable at all times. Vertical wires called pendulums extend from the power cable to the catenary suspension structure, so the cable is maintained in a stable position parallel to the tracks. Suspension insulators prevent loss of current, and counterweights adjust the tension of the cable when changes in temperature cause it to vary. The catenary system makes it possible for electric locomotives to attain speeds beyond the capacities of diesel locomotives.

Why are there few electric automobiles?

The idea of an electric automobile is not new. Some were constructed in 1890 at the beginning of the automobile era. But they were abandoned because of their low power and lack of autonomy. Today ecological concerns have brought them back into fashion.

Electric automobiles are quiet and they do not pollute, but problems remain with their batteries. Research is currently being conducted into new batteries – nickel-iron, sodium-sulfur, and zinc-air – which may increase the autonomy of these vehicles. The policies of many governments that impose production quotas on nonpolluting vehicles have given the electric car a second chance, and the major vehicle manu-facturers are producing electric vehicles designed for city use. Some of these models have an autonomous range of 60 miles (100 kilometers) and can reach speeds of 55 to 60 miles per hour (90 to 100 kilometers per hour).

How will the trains of the future run?

Will magnetic suspension or air suspension "rail" systems replace electrically powered trains, just as the latter replaced the steam trains of yesterday? France, Japan, and Germany have all developed such trains, but none has yet been entered into commercial service.

Magnetic suspension trains all require superconductors at ambient temperatures. These have not yet been perfected. At present, a train powered by gravitational pull is being studied. Pulled by gravity, this train descends through a vacuum tunnel at speeds of up to 600 miles per hour (1000 kilometers per hour) to a mid-point from which, powered by the buildup of energy it has collected in its descent, it climbs an ascending

slope at the same speed. This is an idea for the distant future and it may never be realized.

Are there subway systems in every city?

There are approximately 70 underground systems operating in the world today. These systems of intersecting lines allow people to move freely throughout cities with an ease and speed that would otherwise be impossible.

Subway systems are very expensive to build and operate. They are economically feasible only in very large cities. Subway systems take up little surface space and may provide daily transportation for millions of people. New York's subway is the world's busiest system, carrying some two billion passengers per year. London has the world's oldest subway. Opened in 1863, it became so filthy and foul-smelling that Londoners referred to it as the "sewer." The world's most luxurious subway system is in Moscow, whose hundred stations are clad in marble. The most

crowded is in Tokyo, where stewards in white gloves push passengers into the cars to make sure the doors can close.

Entirely automatic railroad systems, such as this airport shuttle system near Paris, France, are becoming increasingly common.

What is a tram?

A tram car is a surface passenger transportation vehicle that circulates on rails in large cities. In the past, the cars were pulled by horses, the rails enabling them to pull heavier loads than would otherwise be possible, and to climb steeper inclines with the

Since World War II, trams have largely been abandoned. Now, however, some tramway systems are being revived. In some cities, entirely new lines have even been built.

harnessing of an additional horse. Modern trams are electrically powered.

Trams tap electricity by means of a trolley pole and wheel that glides along a conducting cable suspended above the middle of the street with insulating lines attached to the sides of buildings. The rails make it possible for the vehicle to circulate smoothly and to use energy efficiently. Electricity is a flexible power source, well adapted to city traffic where stops are frequent. The electric motor also recovers energy during braking and is silent. In cities where there are many steep inclines, the tram cars are pulled by a continuous steel cable installed in a slit in the tram. The cable-cars of San Francisco are the most famous example of this.

What is the advantage of a trolley bus?

The rails of a tram can interfere with the circulation of traffic. The trolley bus is more mobile, circulating much like a regular bus on open streets.

The trolley bus taps electricity from conducting cables by means of a system much like that used for trams: two poles fitted with wheels at the end glide along two parallel lines. The poles are long and can pivot, giving the trolley bus great freedom to maneuver in traffic. This is why trolley buses are increasingly replacing trams. More powerful and economical to use than buses and much cheaper than subway systems, trolleys offer a practical solution to public transport problems in modern cities.

How do ships float?

Any body submerged in water is buoyant if its weight is less than the weight of the volume of

water that is displaced. **If the density of the solid is less than the density of the water, the water will support the weight of the solid and it floats. If the density of the solid is greater than that of the water, it will sink.**

A steel-hulled ship floats because it contains a great volume of air and its overall density is less than that of water. The depth of a ship's hull is calculated to allow it to take on a certain volume of freight. If the ship makes a crossing empty, ballast has to be added to make it settle deep enough into the water. A ship sinks when a rupture in its hull allows water to replace air in the shell, adding weight to the ship until the density within the hull is greater than that of the water supporting it.

The French steamship Normandie *was one of the world's most luxurious ocean liners. It measured 1,026 feet (313 meters) in length and could carry 1,972 passengers. It burned in the port of New York in 1942.*

What kind of ships transport oil and liquified gas?

They are called tankers. Some of these have capacities of hundreds of thousands of tons and are called supertankers.

These enormous ships have their own specially equipped ports, which are fitted with facilities that pump dangerous residual gas from the storage tanks of the ships. As they approach coastlines, tankers must follow special routes called navigation channels in order to avoid running aground. When a tanker arrives at port, it discharges its cargo through pipelines that carry it to refineries. These enormous ships can cause serious pollution if they wash out their tanks at sea. Some have been damaged or have sunk when they have deviated from the designated navigation channels to save time.

How is an oil tanker constructed?

The pursuit of profits has led to the construction of ever-larger vessels. Some of these are more than 1,300 feet (400 meters) in length and 200 feet (60 meters) wide. Entirely automated, they have very small crews.

The storage tanks are integrated into the very structure of the ship. Because oil is lighter than water, it can fill almost the entire volume of the ship. The hold of the ship is divided by bulkheads which prevent the movement of the ship – lifting, listing, or rolling – from shifting the entire mass of its liquid freight, which could cause the ship to capsize and sink. Computerized controls keep the cargo balanced, shifting it from the central tank by the automatic opening and closing of safety valves. Fireproof bulkheads separate the cargo from the diesel motors, which are installed in the aft of the ship. The crew use bicycles to move across the ship's vast deck. The rear superstructure houses the bridge and the quarters of the crew.

How is a large ship steered?

Traditionally sailors have used instruments such as the compass and the sextant to navigate. They also make use of marine charts. Modern ships use radio navigation.

Large ships are now entirely automated. Computers control the power and speed of the motors in relation to sea conditions. Before departure, the navigator lays out the best course to follow and indicates the course on a marine chart. Guided by the ship's various instruments, the commander of the vessel follows the route laid out by the navigator. When entering a port, a ship is guided by radio signals emitted from onshore. If the passage is especially difficult, a pilot comes on board to steer the ship.

How does a sailor find his way?

In antiquity sailors close to the shore navigated by sight. In open waters they navigated by the stars. The compass and the astrolabe were developed toward the end of the Middle Ages, but in the 17th century precise clocks and sextants were

All airports now have radar. Thanks to this technology, thousands of planes safely take off and land each day throughout the world.

invented. Today, navigation relies on radar and satellite.

Radio signals and satellites provide information with which a computer calculates the position of the ship. With due attention to sea conditions, weather reports, and ocean currents, the computer then indicates the course to be followed. Modern ships are equipped with magnetic compasses that indicate the angle of the ship's course in relation to the magnetic north, and the sextant is still used to determine the position of the ship in relation to the position of the stars.

How does radar work?

Radar is a system that can detect objects. It works on the principle of the echo. If you shout in front of a cliff face, the sound is reflected off the wall of the cliff and back to its source. Measure the time elapsed and multiply the number of seconds by the speed of sound (1,115 feet per second). Divide this figure by two to give the distance separating the source of the sound and the reflecting object.

Radar uses microwaves, which are very short and are reflected like light. An antenna emits short bursts of microwave beams toward an object. These beams are reflected back and are captured by a receiver. A computer calculates the time between emitting the beams and receiving the return signals, thus determining the distance and the position of the object. This information is then displayed on a screen where it appears as a small spot representing the object. If the object is moving, its speed can also be calculated.

What is the difference between a hydrofoil and a hovercraft?

A hovercraft floats on a cushion of air. A hydrofoil

The hydrofoil, top, navigates with its hull fully out of the water and is supported on underwater skis. The hovercraft, bottom, does not touch the water. It is supported on a cushion of air that is trapped beneath its skirts. This makes it possible for the craft to move across land as well as water.

advances on a ski-frame that is fixed beneath the hull and keeps the boat a certain distance from the water.

The pressure of the water under the skis lifts them to the surface when the hydrofoil reaches a certain speed. The hull is thus raised out of the water and offers much less resistance to the boat's forward movement. The hovercraft, also called an airfoil, works on a different principle. Its hull is surrounded by a floating skirt made of synthetic rubber, under which air is blown by motors fitted with large propellers that drive the craft forward, raising it above the water or ground (the hovercraft is amphibious). The airfoil uses less energy to counteract water resistance and moves at greater speeds than classic boats. However, hovercrafts are not suitable for use in choppy waters, and need a relatively smooth sea to function well.

What is an icebreaker?

An icebreaker is a ship equipped to open routes for other ships through waters that have frozen
over. Its reinforced prow is specially designed to rise over the ice sheet and break it.

An icebreaker uses its prow as a ram and is equipped with ballast from front to rear. When the impact of its prow is not enough to break the ice, ballast is moved from the front to the rear. The ship then rises over the ice and comes down on it to break it. Lateral ballast is shifted in the same manner when the ship is required to break ice along its flanks. An icebreaker's engines are extremely powerful, so it can attack ice barriers 30 feet (10 meters) thick and push icebergs of several million tons.

A crew lives and works in very confined quarters aboard a submarine.

How does a submarine move underwater?

To move vertically in water, a submarine makes use of water ballast. The tanks of a submarine are filled with water to make it descend and are emptied to allow it to rise to the surface.

Pumps expel the ballast from the tanks, replacing the water with compressed air. When the tanks are empty, the submarine floats. When its ballast tanks are full and the submarine dives underwater, steel diving fins are angled toward the bottom to make the submarine descend, and are turned upward to return it to the surface. The classic submarine is propelled by electric motors powered by storage batteries, but military submarines use atomic energy.

What is a periscope used for?

A periscope is an optical device equipped with lenses and reflecting prisms that

makes it possible to see around or above an obstacle. A simple periscope can be made by setting two mirrors at 45° angles into a cardboard tube. One can see over the heads of a crowd with such a device. Submarine periscopes are, of course, much more sophisticated.

When the submarine is slowly cruising underwater at a depth of less than 25 feet (8 meters), the surface can be scanned by means of a periscope. The periscope is composed of two tubes, one fitted into the other. At the top of the periscope behind protective glass, a movable prism can be oriented to observe the surface of the sea and all points of the horizon. This prism reflects the light down to another prism that transmits it to an eyepiece. This eyepiece is fitted with lenses that focus and enlarge the images.

How does one

breathe in

a submarine?

At one time, the only air available was that which a submarine carried with it when it descended, limiting the time underwater to only a few minutes. **With a snorkel, a tube that draws air from the surface, an unlimited amount of time**

Life on board a nuclear submarine is very difficult. The crew impatiently anticipates shore leave, sometimes after six months of isolation at sea.

can be spent underwater, but the submarine must remain near the surface.

However, during wartime, the limitations of the snorkel soon became apparent. When a submarine is near the surface, it can easily be seen by airplanes. To avoid depth charges, the submarine must dive deeply. It is then no longer possible to use a snorkel. Modern submarines produce for themselves the oxygen necessary to support the crew. This makes it possible for submarines to remain submerged at great depths for months on end.

What is sonar?

Sonar functions on the same principle as radar. It emits sound waves and receives their echoes, thus determining the position of underwater objects.

Because electromagnetic waves cannot pass through water, sonar emits ultrasound waves. To determine the nature of the object that the ultrasound waves reflects, different measures can be taken, just as with radar. Surveying ships use sonar to map the ocean floor, and fishermen can use it to detect schools of fish. Here, nature has once again anticipated humans: dolphins use a sonar system to orient themselves, emitting ultrasound waves whose echoes they can perceive.

What is a bathyscaph used for?

The bathyscaph is used to explore the depths of the oceans that are inaccessible to submarines. It functions in the water in the same manner as a balloon in air. Equipped with projectors and cameras, it films submarine life, and its remotely controlled arms collect marine specimens.

The bathyscaph houses a spherical steel cabin 6 feet (2 meters) in diameter. This is fitted with a porthole, through which the spotlight-illuminated ocean depths can be viewed. When it descends, contact is maintained with the surface ship by means of buoys and ultrasound radio and television.

What purpose does the Argos beacon serve?

The Argos beacon is a device carried on board a boat that makes it possible to determine its position at sea. Thanks to this beacon, many lives have been saved. It is also useful in transatlantic races, making it possible to know the positions of all the contestants.

But the Argos beacon is more than an instrument of navigation – it serves above all to inform people on land of the position of a boat. To broadcast that position, the beacon installed on board emits signals to a satellite. The speed and position of the satellite in relation to the position of the ship distorts these signals: the frequency is higher when the satellite approaches and lower when it becomes more distant. This is called the Doppler effect and makes it possible to determine the position of the boat.

Perfected in 1948, the bathyscaph was a kind of underwater balloon developed for the exploration of the ocean depths. The descendants of the original bathyscaph look more like submarines.

How does a hot-air balloon float in the air?

When a gas is heated, it expands and becomes lighter and less dense, thus rising in colder and denser atmospheres. If this hot gas is enclosed in an airtight envelope of plastic or waxed cloth, it rises in the air with its carriage and passengers.

The balloonists maintain the heat of the air in the balloon by means of compressed air and a burner. To make the balloon rise, ballast is thrown overboard. To descend, a valve installed on top of the balloon is opened, permitting the escape of hot air. Such a balloon cannot be steered, and the wind determines its speed and direction. Modern balloons, such those used by meteorologists, are filled with gases lighter than air, such as helium.

Why are there no more airships?

Hot-air balloons are no longer used for long-distance travel, except as a sport. For a time they were replaced by airships, which were in their turn abandoned. When inflated with hydrogen, they were too dangerous, and it was too expensive to fill them with helium.

An airship has a long oval shape, like that of a fat cigar, which enhances its stability. Its framework is of metal. Airships have stabilizing wings and a rudder at the rear of the craft. A motor-driven propeller pushes it forward. The best-known airships were the zeppelins. They were used during World War I for reconnaissance, and later in a transatlantic company that carried tens of thousands of passengers. But in 1937, the *Hindenberg,* the largest airship ever constructed, caught fire while it was landing. Dozens of passengers were killed, and the age of airships came to an end.

What prevents an airplane from falling to the ground?

An airship is not a hot-air balloon. It has a framework, usually made of metal.

In order to take off, an airplane must first attain a certain speed, from around 45 miles per hour (70 kilometers per hour) for smaller craft and up to more than 125 miles per hour (200 kilometers per hour) for larger planes. At that moment, the supporting force of air passing under the wings of the plane balances the pull of gravity and pushes the plane upward.

To achieve take-off speed, the motors must generate enough power to counteract the drag effect created as the airplane moves through the air. When the lift force has canceled out the force of gravity and when the plane's velocity cancels out the drag on the plane, the aircraft takes off and achieves stable flight. The higher a plane climbs, the weaker is the force of gravity, and the speed of the plane increases. But beyond a certain altitude, the air becomes too thin to support the plane.

How is a glider

able to fly?

A glider is a motorless airplane that soars through the air, supported by atmospheric currents. The aircraft weighs little more than its pilot and has a large airfoil. A glider requires an external source of energy to take off, usually provided by a motorized airplane that pulls the glider in its wake. It can also be launched by a large catapult called a bungee cord.

What is a

hang glider?

A kind of large kite. It takes the form of a triangular sail attached to a metal frame to which the pilot is secured by means of a harness. Descending the slope of a hill or racing into the wind

To pilot a glider, one must know how to use air currents in the atmosphere.

The pilot climbs into the sky on hot air currents rising from heated flat terrain, or winds. An experienced pilot can use the complex circulation of the air generated by clouds, storms, and topography to remain in the air for hours at a time. The gliders are equipped with runners, which make it possible to land them in open country.

off the edge of a cliff, the pilot of the hang glider takes off into the sky.

By shifting his weight, the pilot uses the bar of the triangular structure on which he is suspended to determine the speed and direction of his flight. A beginner can quickly learn to fly for several minutes at a distance of 15 feet (5 meters) above the ground. More experienced pilots can fly at much higher altitudes for much longer periods. The principal danger of hang gliders is that they can plunge to the ground if the wind suddenly shifts. If the pilot does not react immediately, he risks a serious crash. Hang gliders have now been developed with stabilizing flaps, but purists find these safer models less elegant.

How does a propeller airplane function?

As the blades of the propeller turn, they press against the air. The air is sucked into the motor and pushed out toward the rear, exercising a pulling effect on the motor housing and thus on the plane itself.

If the propeller is mounted in the front, the aircraft is pulled through the air, but if it is positioned at the rear, the plane is thrust forward. The speed of a propeller airplane depends on the number and size of its engines. A single-engine plane designed to carry five or six passengers can normally reach

According to legend, Icarus had wings of feathers held together with wax, which melted in the sun. This modern-day Icarus pilots a hang glider, a kind of giant kite.

speeds of 190 miles per hour (300 kilometers per hour).

How does an airplane slow down?

To reduce speed the pilot uses airbrakes, which increase the wind resistance of the airplane.

Small adjustable flaps are installed along the edges of the wings. To reduce speed, the pilot opens these flaps against the wind by means of flap controls. When landing modern jet aircraft, pilots reverse their engines (causing the jet reactors to push air in front of the plane) to reduce ground speed before applying disk brakes, which are designed with large surfaces to dissipate the heat generated during braking. The large, highly resistant tires of these planes absorb a great deal of energy through friction. This wears the tires down rapidly.

What is a jet engine?

At velocities of more than 450 miles per hour (700 kilometers per hour), the internal combustion engine becomes inefficient. Jet engines, based on the principle of reaction, are more suited to high speeds. Reaction is the same principle that can be observed when a deflating balloon spins around in the air.

A turbine pulls air into the reactor. This highly compressed air ignites kerosene fuel, which is injected into the reactor under very high pressure. The burning fuel gives off extremely hot gases that create enormous pressure within the reactor and then escape toward the rear through an afterburner. As the gases escape, they push the plane forward, and they power the turbine that drives the air compressor. This kind of motor is called a turbo reactor. The turbine sometimes also powers a propeller, called a turboprop. Another kind of jet engine, called a ramjet, has no moving parts. It is a kind of flying tube. When a certain speed is reached, the very velocity of the aircraft compresses air into the

The difficulty in maneuvering a helicopter is in making its blades move in a cyclical manner. It is an extremely ingenious mechanism: (1) rotary axle, (2) movable plate, (3) stationary plate.

central part of the tube. This serves as the combustion chamber where fuel is injected and ignites, producing gases so hot that they are ejected to the rear faster than the air enters, thus producing a powerful forward thrust.

What is a supersonic airplane?

This is an aircraft which flies faster than the speed of sound – that is, at around 1,200 miles per hour, or more than 340 meters per second.

Certain military aircraft can attain speeds of 2,000 miles per hour (3,500 kilometers per hour). A supersonic aircraft in flight produces shock waves, which when they reach the ground give off a loud noise, the famous supersonic "boom."

How does a helicopter stay in the air?

Above the cockpit of a helicopter is a rotor, made up of a hub around which turn three long, narrow wings or blades. When the engine is started, these blades, turning at great speeds around their vertical axis, describe a large circle. The air churned by the blades exerts a powerful upward thrust on them, which raises the helicopter into the air.

If the helicopter had only one propeller, it would tend to turn on itself. This is why a small, vertical, stabilizing propeller is added. To move forward, the helicopter is inclined in a forward direction. To turn, the craft is tilted in the chosen direction. An automatic system constantly adjusts the angle of each blade in order to maintain speed. Adjustment of the variable pitch of the blades modifies the lift of the helicopter, causing the helicopter to rise or to fall. For stationary flight, the blades are kept in a horizontal position.

Why can't we travel to the Moon in airplanes?

At the Kennedy Space Center in Florida, the departure of a space shuttle is always an unforgettable spectacle. Pictured is a lift-off of the Columbia.

The upward thrust of air on an airplane's airfoil structures (its wings) cancels the effect of gravity and supports it in flight.

In addition, engines need not only fuel but also oxygen to burn their fuel. And at altitudes above 3,000 feet (5,000 meters) the Earth's atmosphere begins to thin to the point that the cabin has to be pressurized. Above 9 miles (15 kilometers) from the Earth's surface the atmosphere begins to thin rapidly until it completely disappears at an altitude of 310 miles (500 kilometers). Without air to support the craft and without oxygen with which to burn its fuel, there still remain 219,461 miles (353,180 kilometers) before it reaches the Moon!

How does a rocket engine work?

The fuel in a rocket engine is burned in a combustion chamber and hot gases are pushed downward. The great downward pressure of the escaping gases provokes a strong counter-reaction that thrusts the rocket up.

For a rocket to escape the force of the Earth's gravity, its speed must reach 7,000 miles per hour (11,200 kilometers per hour). As the rocket rises higher, the pressure of the atmosphere decreases, eventually disappearing, and the force of gravity diminishes. In interplanetary space, the force of gravity pulls only faintly on the rocket, which continues at the same speed with no need to expend much energy except to modify the trajectory of its orbit.

What is a multiple-stage rocket?

The higher a rocket rises, the less energy it needs to expend, since the forces it must counteract become weaker. On the other hand, **the oxygen and the fuel it must carry are heavy. Because of this, the required fuel is divided into separate compartments that can be released one after the other as the fuel they contain is expended.**

The first fuel tank is the most important because the engine of the first stage must lift the entire rocket and counteract gravity at its strongest force nearest to the surface of the Earth. Once empty, the first stage is jettisoned, reducing the weight of the rocket and igniting the second stage. The lift of the second stage does not need to be nearly as strong as the first stage. Not only is it thrusting less weight, but air resistance and the force of gravity are also much weaker. Once its fuel has been used it too falls away, igniting the third stage, which places the satellite or space capsule into orbit.

Why are space capsules so small?

Each pound sent into orbit requires the launching of a rocket 20 to 30 times its weight, so the heavier the capsule, the heavier, more complex and more expensive the launch vehicle.

The largest rocket ever built, the Saturn V, could lift 100 tons into orbit and was used to launch the Apollo moon missions. But, since the cost of a launch is determined by the weight destined for orbit, such launch vehicles are extremely expensive, especially as they can be used only once. Therefore designers of space vehicles do everything possible to reduce the weight of the capsule and make full use of the available interior space. This is the reason that another means of transport, the space shuttle, has been designed.

After a perfect flight, the space shuttle Columbia *prepares to land, escorted by a T38 airforce jet.*

For what purposes is the space shuttle used?

The space shuttle is designed to replace rockets as the means of getting astronauts and satellites into orbit. It is less expensive because it can be reused.

This "space bus" has the characteristics of both a rocket and an airplane: launched like a rocket, it lands like an airplane. It is composed of three elements: a huge tank containing fuel for the main engine, two solid fuel launch rockets that can be recovered and reused after they are jettisoned, and finally the shuttle itself. In space the shuttle can be maneuvered by means of small rockets placed at the front and rear. Returning to Earth, the shuttle can be landed like an airplane. The shuttle makes it possible to transport components of space stations into space where they can be assembled. It can also recover satellites and return them to Earth where they can then be repaired. The shuttle also makes it possible to transport into space scientists who are not themselves experienced astronauts.

What is an artificial satellite?

This is a man-made device that is launched into space by means of a spacecraft. Satellites are especially useful for the observation of the Earth, providing valuable information for meteorology and the prospecting of mineral resources. They provide means by which ships can locate their positions and also transmit radio and television signals.

When satellites are in orbit, they are still within the sphere of gravitational pull. But when a satellite is launched into orbit at a certain speed, the centrifugal force of its orbit counteracts the force of gravity. To place a satellite into orbit at a given altitude, the speed that it must attain to maintain a stable orbit has to be calculated.

Why does a bicycle wheel turn so easily?

A ball-bearing joint is installed at the hub of the wheel. The bearings, which are housed in one or two rings between the axle and the wheel, reduce friction.

The Russian MIR space station is an assembly of various modules, of which the first elements were launched in 1986.

These two exterior elevators were constructed for the Sofitel hotel near the Versailles gateway to Paris.

The friction is effectively minimized because, instead of acting on the entire surface of contact between the wheel and the axle, it is limited to the bearings, which roll against each other. This way, almost all the energy expended by the cyclist is used to turn the wheel rather than in overcoming friction. The friction is further reduced by lubricating the mechanism. The lubricants are in essence composed of small platelets that slide over each other. Finally, the wheel itself is a very light construction of specially alloyed, high-strength metals, whose weight poses little resistance to the efforts of the cyclist.

Can bicycles be motorized?

The idea of equipping bicycles with motors was realized as soon as very small, lightweight motors became available. Because the bicycle itself weighs little, the motor does not have to be very powerful. Simple, compact motors are used, fueled with a mixture of gasoline and oil.

A permit is now required for a motorbike whose motor has an interior cylinder of less than 50 cubic centimeters. Anything greater than this is considered to be a motorcycle, and must therefore have a stronger frame and larger tires to withstand faster speeds. Beyond the fact that they have two wheels, powerful motorcycles hardly resemble bicycles.

What makes an elevator rise?

An elevator is equipped with an electric motor at the top of the shaft. This motor turns a winch driving a cable system, to which the cabin of the elevator is attached.

At the other end of the cable is a counterweight that balances the weight of the cabin. When the cabin ascends, the counterweight descends, and vice versa. This means that the motor only has to lift the weight of the load carried in the cabin. Within the shaft, the lifter and the counterweight move on rails. The cable rotates through a groove in the drum winch that drives it. The lift is equipped with speed controls and brakes that regulate its stops precisely. These are activated when passengers choose the levels at which they want to disembark.

How does an escalator work?

All the steps of an escalator are connected by a continuous chain that rotates through the notches of a drum driven by a motor. The drum and motor are located in a space beneath the landing of each escalator.

Each step is equipped with two small wheels that roll on two looped rails installed beneath the escalator. The reverse sides of the

A cable car in Austria. These cabins, suspended from cables, can cross great distances.

steps are rounded so each step fits precisely into the step immediately preceding it as it reaches the upper landing. Here, the steps follow the movement of the chain and disappear from view. They then begin a descent in the reverse direction, their position inverted and parallel to their visible trajectory. When the steps complete their rotation and arrive at the bottom landing, they again turn and resume their original position to begin another ascent.

What is the difference between a ski lift and a cable car?

A ski lift is a simple cable from which are suspended poles, each equipped with a basic horizontal bar. Skiers wrap their legs around these horizontal bars and, grasping the poles, are then pulled on their skis to the top of a slope. In a cable-car system, a cabin suspended in midair from a supporting cable is pulled by a cable, making it possible to traverse steep slopes.

Pylons set at regularly spaced intervals support the suspension and cables. The cable rotates through a pulley at the bottom.

The Way Things Work

How does a dynamo produce electricity?

A dynamo is a machine that generates electricity by transforming mechanical energy into electrical energy through the rotation of a coil of metal wires between a set of magnets.

All magnets produce magnetic fields. When a copper wire moves through a magnetic field, an electric current is induced in the wire. A dynamo consists of an "armature," composed a coil of wire wrapped around an iron bar, placed between the poles of magnets. The armature is connected to an axle that is turned by a mechanical force such as the pedaling of a bicycle or the rotation of the turbine in a hydroelectric power station. In its rotation the coil crosses the fields of the magnets and an electrical current is induced in the coil. Very large generators designed to supply electrical power to cities are equipped with highly powerful electromagnets. In small dynamos – such as those used to power bicycle lights, for instance – a permanent magnet, the rotor, is used, and it is this that turns inside the coil.

Technology is becoming increasingly sophisticated. Here a robot plays a synthesizer. A profuse array of microprocessors and mechanical devices are used to achieve this prodigy of invention.

Where are electric motors found?

Electric motors have a wide variety of applications from the very small motors found in electric razors to the very powerful ones that propel nuclear submarines.

Electric motors are powerful, reliable, and silent, and they do not produce exhausts of toxic gases. One of their greatest virtues is that they directly generate rotational motion. There is no need for the complex and fragile transmission systems required by internal combustion and steam engines to transform linear movement into circular motion. Because they expend no energy for such transformations, they are also more efficient. Electric motors are also more flexible, since their power can almost instantly be adjusted. The principal disadvantage of electric motors is that they must be constantly connected to a power grid because electric batteries are heavy, expensive, and not very powerful. This is why there are few electric cars.

Why does an electric device emit heat?

An electric current is the flow of electrons through a

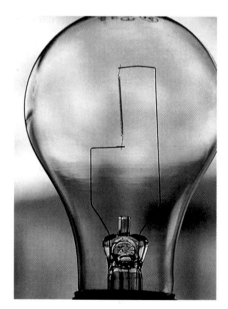

The coiled filament in an electric light bulb is heated to 5,500°F (3,000°C) by the current, emitting a very bright light.

material. When a device such as an electric radiator is connected to a supply of electricity, electrons flow through the coils of wire in the radiator. The flow of the electrons through the wire is impeded by the atoms in the wire, with which the electrons collide. The energy lost by the electrons in these collisions is converted into heat and light.

This resistance to the flow of current is dependent on the length and width of the wire. A long, thin coil of wire produces more resistance and therefore more heat. Once the wire, or filament, of radiator reaches a certain temperature, it glows red. By convection, the hot filament heats the surrounding air, which becomes less dense, rises, and circulates through the room. A fan may be added to the radiator to accelerate this transfer of heat. To achieve a steadier output of heat, a liquid, such as water or oil, is used instead of air.

How does an electric bulb emit light?

It operates on the same

principle as the radiator in that an electric current is passed though a wire, which becomes hot and glows. But in a bulb, the wire is extremely fine and the temperature is much higher. The wire glows first red and then white and emits a bright light.

The temperature in an electric light bulb reaches 4,500–5,500°F (2,500–3,000°C). If the filament was in contact with the air (and therefore in contact with oxygen), it would burst into flame. This is why the filament is contained in an evacuated bulb filled with an inert gas, such as nitrogen. The filament is made from tungsten, an extremely strong metal with a high melting point, which can be shaped into fine coils of wire. However, little by little, oxygen seeps into the bulb, and the wire burns in parts. It becomes thinner and finally breaks, interrupting the circuit and cutting off the supply.

Why do we need transformers?

Electricity is transmitted over long distances at very high voltages. However, before it is supplied to

Inside the big cupboard stamped with a skull, you will find colorful wires that only a specialist can recognize.

houses and other con-sumers, it is converted to very low voltages, which are less dangerous and better adapted to domestic appli-ances. The voltage is con-verted by transformers.

Transformers consist of two coils of wire. One coil, known as the primary winding, carries the voltage that needs to be changed, and the other coil, the secondary winding, supplies the output voltage. Both coils are wound around a hollow core made of soft iron and shaped into a square or ring. The two coils are not connected. Transformers operate on the principle of electromagnetic induction. The voltage applied to the primary winding produces an alternating current in the coil. This sets up a varying magnetic field. When this varying magnetic field passes through the secondary winding, it induces an alternating voltage in the coil, which flows through any circuit connected to the coil. The ratio between the input and output voltages is related to the ratio between the number of turns in the primary and secondary windings. There-fore, if the secondary winding has half the number of turns of the primary, the output voltage will be half the size as the input.

What is a fuse for?

A fuse is an element with a very low melting point. Installed in an electrical circuit, the fuse melts and thereby cuts the current if the circuitry overheats.

In the case of a light bulb or a radiator, intense heat is desirable. But a fire can break out if an electrical circuit becomes hot. To avoid this, a fuse, a wire made of an alloy of lead, is installed between the power supply and the equipment. The fuse can then stop the electrical circuitry and the equipment from overheating. In modern electrical installations, all the fuses (one per electrical outlet) are grouped together in a fuse box. The lead alloy filaments are enclosed in small porcelain cylinders. Fuses are easy to change, as they can easily be put in or taken out. Larger fuses govern the flow of electricity to entire apartments and houses. Electricity companies can cut or reestablish electrical current by means of these.

How are infrared rays useful?

Infrared rays are invisible because they transmit heat instead of light. These rays, among others, transmit the energy of the Sun across the emptiness of inter-planetary space to Earth.

Infrared rays travel through air without dissipating – that is, they do not heat the air through which they pass.

It is this property that is used to heat and roast foods. Infrared rays are also used in heaters, such as those used for outdoor tables of restaurants and in open-air markets where the rays pass through the cold air to provide warmth for the standholders and their customers. But infrared radiation has many other uses. People and objects emit infrared radiation as heat. By examining these emissions, one can determine the size and shape of the emitting body and its temperature. This is the principle behind infrared

Embers heat the air by emitting infrared radiation. They also give off carbon dioxide, which is damaging to health.

photography. Alarm systems also work by the detection of moving sources of infrared radiation. Infrared rays can also be used to transmit information to receivers. This is how the remote controls for televisions, stereos, etc. operate.

How do automatic doors open?

A photoelectric cell is installed in front of the door; this produces an electric current when it is exposed to light. This makes it possible for it to activate a switch that triggers the opening or the closing of a door.

When a person crosses the ray of light beaming into the cell, this causes a change in the intensity of light that acts on a circuit breaker. One of the main uses of photoelectric cells, also known as electric eyes, is in alarm systems. They are also used to turn on street lights or house lights when it becomes dark. Photoelectric cells are currently used in modern cameras to automatically adjust lighting in relation to the surrounding light and distance.

What is the advantage of the transistor?

Transistors are tiny electronic components that control the flow of current in an electric circuit. Their small size makes it possible to integrate into a single system the many connections required to make an electrical device function.

Radio and television use electromagnetic waves to transmit signals. To amplify these signals, electronic valves were used. These valves were the basis of the development of electronics. During the 1940s it was discovered that certain types of materials conducted electrical currents only partially. By implanting electrodes on portions of semiconductors such as silicon, it became possible to create miniature components, called transistors, that acted in the same way as electronic valves. With this began the race to miniaturize. It was then possible to build computers with miniature transistors instead of valves that heated and constantly burned out. Electronics emerged from its infancy.

How does a tape recorder work?

A tape recorder records and plays back sound, thanks to a magnetic tape.

Using a battery, a recording head alters the state of the magnetic tape, recording the sound waves captured by a microphone. The playing head is charged with a modulating electric current and reads the sounds recorded on the magnetic tape. A third tape head erases tapes. This is charged with a high-frequency alternating current that erases all signals recorded on a tape. The running speed of the tape is important. The faster the tape runs, the more faithful is the reproduction of sound recorded on it. Professional equipment has a running speed of 30 inches (76 centimeters) per second, which allows the reproduction of the full range of sounds.

In what way is the laser disk superior to cassettes or vinyl records?

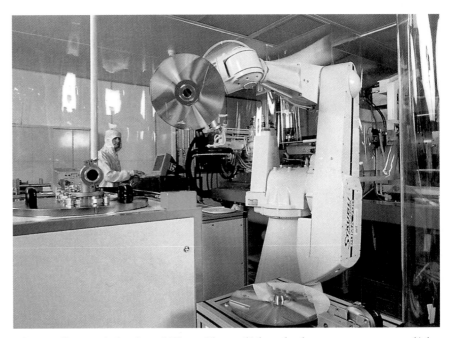

The quality and the durability of laser disks, also known as compact disks, are incomparable.

As is the case with vinyl records, sound waves are transformed into electrical impulses, but instead of being engraved in a groove they are presented as a series of bumps and hollows on the surface of the laser disk.

To read these signs, a laser beam differentiates the bumps and hollows as it passes over them. A converter translates this information into electric signals that cause, just as a classic record player does, the membrane of a loudspeaker to vibrate and the sound to be reproduced. The laser beam is a ray of light. It does not come into friction with the disk and thus has no harmful effect on it. The disk is protected by a transparent film and does not scratch easily. They sound better than cassettes or vinyl records because laser disks carry almost no background noise or distortion.

What is stereophonic sound?

This is a recording process that captures the depth of sound and makes it possible

to distinguish sounds from the left or the right. Recording is carried out with two series of microphones that are arranged at each end of the source of sound. Two tracks are separately recorded.

On a stereophonic record, the two recordings are read together, but sent to their respective speakers. Each one then reproduces a part of the recording that the ear will combine. This system gives depth to the sound, which seems more natural because it appears to come from different sources.

How does one program a video recorder?

Until recently, video recorders were programmed by using a remote control to choose the desired television channel and the times to begin and end recording. Today, however, recording methods are much more advanced.

Some video recorders are now equipped with barcode readers similar to those used at cash registers. For each scheduled broadcast, program guides give a barcode that indicates the channel, time, and date of the broadcast. When this barcoded information is transmitted to the machine, it is registered in the memory system that controls the programming of the video recorder, whose digital clock then triggers the recording at the time and date indicated. Some other systems work simply by entering the numbers of the programs selected. The video recorder then automatically programs itself.

The video recorder is already self-programming, thanks to a special television remote control that can be used with almost all video recorders. The number of a program (printed in television listings) must be entered using a keyboard, and the device placed in front of the video recorder. It's as simple as that!

Why do we no longer see amateur motion picture cameras?

Amateur cameras have been replaced by video cameras. These cameras record film on cassettes that can be played on video recorders and watched on television screens.

The amateur Super-8 cameras used film that was very expensive to develop. A projector and a screen were needed to view the film. Also, editing the film was complicated and difficult. On the other hand, video cassettes can be viewed immediately on a television screen, they can be edited easily with simple equipment, and text and special effects can be added. Video cameras also record sound and automatically self-adjust for light and distance. They are very light, and microchips automatically stabilize the images. The quality of their images, which also depends on that of the television receiver, is inferior, however, to that of the amateur film cameras, which often rival those of film professionals.

When will high-definition television become available?

The technology has already been developed, although it can still be improved (the receivers are still too large). But the equipment is very expensive at present, and high-definition broadcasting is rare. Professionals still do not know which system will prevail, and until this becomes clear, they are reluctant to make the important investments in the new equipment that will be needed.

When high-definition television finally comes into being, it will not only be necessary to change all television receivers, but also all studio cameras and broadcast and transmission equipment. Great events such as the Olympic Games have been filmed in the 16/9 format (16/9 indicates that the width of the screen is equal to 16/9ths of its height, proportions approximately equal to those of panoramic cinema), but there is presently in the U.S. only

Everyone will soon be equipped with new televisions that have panoramic screens in the 16/9 format, in which high-definition broadcasts are filmed.

experimental and infrequent broadcast programming in this format. High-definition television does at present offer high fidelity stereo sound, and it has access to satellites. While we await the arrival of this new television standard, broadcasts take place under an intermediate norm that makes it possible to receive traditional 625-line images in the 16/9 format.

Will everyone have cable television?

Cable systems make possible the reception of broadcast stations whose signals are too distant or are blocked by geographic configurations. Cable systems presently make dozens and dozens of stations available at the same time. You only have to be connected to the cable!

Cable systems are easily installed in urban areas where entire apartment buildings can be quickly wired, but for isolated small communities and homes it is necessary to lay down a special cable that is sometimes very long. The cost of installation can be very expensive for only a few subscribers. To recover their investments in installations and programming, cable operators have to find paying subscribers while competing with hertz-wave broadcasters whose transmissions

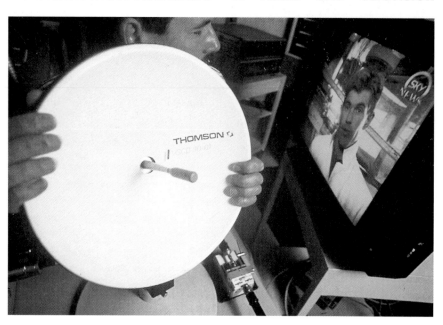

If you do not have cable television, you must buy a satellite dish to receive all the channels relayed by geostationary satellites.

are available without charge. In spite of these problems, the number of cable-subscribing households is growing each year. The advantages of cable include a better quality of sound and image, the elimination of interference due to variations in atmospheric conditions, a wider choice of programming, the possibility of credit-card pay-for-view, inter-active television, and so forth.

Why are satellite antennae round?

The big round antenna of a satellite is called a para-bolic dish. A large number of radio and television

channels are relayed by geostationary satellites, whose signals are trans-mitted or received by the antennae. The antennae vary in size: the smaller ones are for domestic use.

Radio signals travel in straight lines, and so, because the Earth is round, there is a limited distance

at which they can be broadcast along the Earth's surface. They are therefore beamed to a geo-stationary satellite. This orbits at the same speed as which the Earth turns, and so in effect remains stationary above the same point on the surface of the Earth. The satellite amplifies the signal and resends it to a different antenna. In fact, the satellite does not remain entirely stationary, so the dish must be able to track the motion and remain aligned to the satellite. A parabolic dish antenna consists of a metal bowl that collects the radiation and reflects it to a central receiver. The radio signals, which travel at the speed of light, are decoded and sent to your television receptor. To receive channels from more than one country, more dishes are required, each one pointing to a different satellite.

What developments have been made possible by computers?

One of the first and most spectacular was the de-velopment of the atomic

There are many types of computer systems, each designed with a specialist function. In France, a system known as Minitel allows you to book hotels or theater seats from the comfort of your own home, using the telephone.

bomb. The first computers were developed in the U.S. to cope with the enormous and complex calculations that its design required. But since then, the computer has made possible other, less destructive advances.

Among other things, computers have enabled people to land on the Moon, have made weather forecasting more reliable, and have led to the development of extremely realistic interactive video games. They control airplanes and calculate their routes, manage the production of oil refineries, organize movements of capital and goods, provide surveillance of nuclear power stations, and interpret the images of scanners and aerial photographs. In fact, there is practically no aspect of modern life in which computers do not play an important supporting role, sometimes completely replacing humans.

Is a calculator

a computer?

A basic calculator is essentially a small computer, but one that handles only numbers. All computers are in fact highly developed calculators.

It is both the formidable speed with which electronic calculators calculate, and their constantly enhanced miniaturization that have made it possible for calculators to treat not only numbers but also any sign that can be signified by a series of 0 and 1, and can thereby be represented as a number. To accomplish this, ever-more complex circuits are constantly being conceived, created with microchips that are more and more powerful. Some of these microchips can store several million bytes of information. Super calculators used by meteorologists and physicians can perform up to 10 billion operations per second!

How does a

camera work?

A camera functions like an eye: the lens corresponds to the crystalline lens of the eye; the diaphragm that regulates the exposure to light, to the iris; the film on which the images are imprinted, to the retina; and even the shutter of the camera, to the eyelid.

Light is concentrated in the black box of the camera through a skillfully designed system of lenses. A shutter composed of two blades is installed behind the lens and controls the duration of exposure to light. The diaphragm defines the shape of the light beam and makes it possible to focus the camera. With all the adjustments made, the beam of light passes through the lens and makes an impression on photosensitive film that is loaded in the camera's black box. The film is enclosed in a spool to protect it from light when loading and unloading the camera. Either a mechanical or an automatic system advances the film shot after shot. In the interior of the camera, an inclined mirror reflects the light captured by its lens into the camera's viewfinder, which allows the photographer to frame the pictures.

In spite of its technical complexity, the use of the computer has been so simplified that today a child is capable of using one, often with more skill than an adult.

What is an electronic flash?

The success of a photo depends on light. When studio equipment, such as light projectors, sun lamps, etc., is not available, the photographer uses a flash, which produces a burst of light that is synchronized with the shooting of a camera.

Many years ago photographers spread magnesium powder on boards which they held above their heads and ignited to create bright flashes. But this created as much smoke as brightness and it was dangerous. Then came the idea of enclosing the magnesium in an incandescent light bulb furnished with a stem that could be attached to the camera. An electric spark ignited the magnesium, creating the flash. The burned bulb could not be reused and was thrown away. The electronic flash can be used many times over. It comprises a small glass tube that contains xenon. gas. The gas becomes extremely bright when it receives a discharge from a capacitor. Because one can obtain flashes at very short intervals (1/500th of a second), fleeting movements such as the twirling of a dancer can be captured.

How is a house heated?

Rather than heating each room individually, a central heating system can be used that diffuses its heat by circulating hot water through pipes to radiators in each room of the house, or blows warmed air through a series of vents.

Water is heated in a coiled pipe by a hot-water heater whose flame is fueled by gas or oil. The water then rises by convection in the system of pipes and passes through cast-iron radiators that diffuse the heat into the rooms. Cooled water redescends to the water heater where the cycle begins anew. The difference in the density of hot and cold water makes the hot water (which is less dense) rise. Pumps can accelerate the circulation of water. When they pass through areas that are not heated, the pipes are insulated to prevent the water from cooling. There is a reservoir at the top of the building that serves to contain overflows.

There are different models of electronic flashes. Flash equipment now exists that suppresses the "red-eye" effect, thanks to two bursts of light, the first of which causes the pupil to contract.

Why is air-conditioning installed?

During the hot summer months, air-conditioning systems cool houses and buildings. The atmosphere is cooled by ventilating air from refrigerator systems.

Thanks to the air conditioner, the temperature of air can be controlled as well as its humidity. Stale and impure air can also be filtered. Air conditioning is used in countries where temperatures vary widely. It is also used in structures such as high-rise apartment buildings and skyscrapers where natural ventilation is difficult, as well as in such places as meeting rooms and theaters, where the temperature rises sharply when large groups of people gather. Air-conditioning makes it possible to maintain good working conditions where excessive heat would otherwise slow activity. The system is, however, very costly in energy consumption and, because of the contrasts between interior and exterior conditions, it can also provoke colds, and nose and throat ailments.

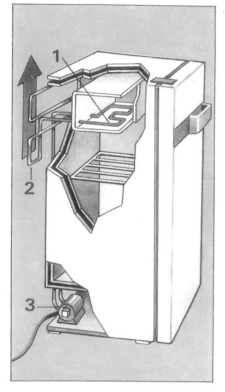

Principal elements of a typical refrigerator: (1) evaporator, (2) condenser, (3) pump.

What makes a refrigerator cold?

The principle that a liquefied gas chills when it evaporates is applied to create a cold environment. A refrigerated gas is circulated around a refrigerator to lower its temperature.

A gas such as ammonia is condensed into a liquid state and is then compressed and transferred to an evaporator where it becomes colder as it evaporates. The cold gas then circulates through pipes in the refrigerator and lowers its temperature. This gas is then returned to the condenser where it returns to liquid form, to become compressed and evaporated again. The cycle is thus renewed indefinitely.

What purpose does a thermostat serve?

Many devices are used today that raise or lower the temperature. It would not be practical to measure the temperature constantly with a thermometer and then to stop or restart these devices to assure that the desired temperature is maintained. A thermostat does this work for us automatically, measuring the temperature and regulating heaters and appliances to make sure they remain at the desired settings.

A thermostat is an automatic circuit breaker, activated by two contiguous blades of metal installed in an electrical circuit. Above a given temperature setting, they change position and interrupt or reestablish the electric current. Thermostats have also been installed in appliances such as ovens where they help to control cooking, and in central-heating systems and the radiators connected to them, making it possible to regulate the temperature of rooms and to save energy. They are also used as safety devices in gas appliances.

Where does petroleum come from?

Oil is a natural substance, a mixture of carbons and hydrogen. Like coal, it was formed out of the decomposition of animal organisms and vegetable matter that has accumulated over hundreds of millions of years.

Oil deposits are contained in gigantic "sponges" of soft and porous rock. To find these deposits, it is often necessary to drill through

When oil is located, it may be pumped to the surface by giant oil wells.

layers of rock that cover them. To do this, huge drill bits are lowered on steel cables into the depths of wells, where they are rotated and cut into the rock. When a pocket of oil is discovered, tubes are installed in the hollowed wells through which the oil is brought to the surface. If the pressure of the gas located beneath the oil pocket is not high enough, the precious liquid is pumped to the surface. Solar energy is released when oil is burned. This solar energy was originally captured and transformed through the photosynthesis of plants that lived millions upon millions of years ago. This energy is neither inexhaustible nor renewable.

How is gasoline made?

Oil wells supply crude oil, but this oil has to be refined and "cracked" before it can be used as fuel. These operations are carried out in oil refineries. Gasoline is extracted from the most volatile part of petroleum.

Tankers and pipelines carry the oil to refineries, where it is pumped into an oven. Here it is heated and circulated through coiled pipes. Once it has been vaporized, it is introduced into the bottom of a cracking tower. The vaporized oil is partially condensed there. Its heaviest elements settle in the bottom of the tower and are used for asphalt road-surfacing, lubricating oils for tools and motors, kerosene, and the heavy fuels used by boats. As the lighter elements rise in the tower, the more volatile elements are progressively deposited on trays.

Gasoline is collected at the top of the tower. By a special refining process called cracking, the larger molecules of the heavy refined product are broken down to obtain liquefied high-octane anti-knock fuels that preserve the life of engines.

What kinds of engines run on gasoline?

Gasoline, in the strict sense of the term, is used to fuel motor vehicles and machines equipped with small engines. The larger engines of more powerful machines use other fuels. Cars, motorcycles, outboard engines, lawn mowers, and chainsaws all use gasoline as fuel. Gasoline is also used in lamps and lighters.

Gasoline is also used to fuel generators in remote regions where there is no electric power grid and electricity has to be generated locally to provide power for such appliances as refrigerators. Many other engines are fueled with oil-derived products that are less volatile than gasoline. Airplanes use kerosene, a fuel very similar to

This oil refinery in Algeria devours huge quantities of crude oil. Here the "black gold" is transformed into a wide variety of products, such as asphalt, gasoline, and oils.

gasoline. Tractors and trucks use diesel oil, as do assault tanks, some of which can run on any kind of fuel. Light oils fuel hot-water heaters. Heavy oils are used to fuel power stations. Many other

products are produced from oil: solvents, cleaning agents (kerosene is used in dry cleaning), as well as a seemingly infinite variety of plastics.

Why do we no longer use oil lamps?

When electric lighting became widespread, oil lamps became obsolete, as did candle and gas lighting. These are only used today when there are power failures.

Besides, oil lamps were extremely dangerous and had been the cause of many fires. In addition, they had an unpleasant odor, were difficult to use, and did not give as powerful a light as electric illumination. Because they had to be refueled, itself an unpleasant task that could be dangerous, they could not be used continuously.

Is natural gas less dangerous than coal gas?

Coal gas is an industrially produced extract of coal. Natural gas, like petroleum, is produced by the fermentation of organic matter. It is not toxic like coal gas.

Natural gas is distributed to homes through networks of pipes. It is extracted from deposits of porous rock that are sealed in layers of impermeable earth and stone. Principally composed of methane gas (up to more than 95 percent), it is a "dry" gas (a gas that does not condense at normal temperatures). It is not dangerous, but because it is heavier than air, it can stagnate. Gas can expand and replace air in an unventilated space. Anyone confined in such a space will be suffocated, not by the gas but by the absence of air. To avoid such incidents, natural gas is treated to eliminate sulfuric hydrogen, which corrodes pipes and causes leaks. Because natural gas is odorless, a product is added to give it a characteristic smell, making any leaks readily detectable. Coal gas, formerly used for lighting, is a humid gas that condenses readily. It is very similar to fire-damp or pit gas and is therefore very dangerous, since such gases mixed with air form highly volatile mixtures. Coal gas is very rarely used today.

Where does paper come from?

Paper is made from all kinds of vegetable matter, which is reduced to pulp in water. This pulp is then placed on moving belts of very fine cloth that carry it to heated drums that press and dry it. The pulp emerges in long ribbons of paper that are rolled on spools.

Wasteful sources of pollution, gas flares such as these are being replaced by installations that will collect the gas that is now burned off.

Invented in China in the 1st century, the process of paper-making remained practically unchanged until the innovation of wood-pulping in the 20th century. Until that time only "rag" papers made out of linen and cotton were available. These were prepared first by soaking the old rags in water and grinding them into pulp by the action of mill-powered hammers. The pulp was placed in strainers, filtered and drained, and then was placed between felt plates, which were put under pressure in a wood press. The resulting sheets of paper were then set aside to dry. Paper has played a fundamental role in the conservation and distribution of knowledge, making it more possible to record what is in effect the memory of humanity.

How does a vacuum cleaner suck dust up?

An electric motor powers a suction fan that pulls air from a reservoir. This creates a vacuum into which air is drawn, carrying with it particles of dust and small objects.

The body of a vacuum cleaner is divided into two parts. The motor and the fan are installed in the first part. The second part, separated from the first by a filter, houses a paper sack that collects dust and small objects. Extending out from the sack is a tube to which a flexible hose is attached. At the end of the hose is a suction broom. Air passes through the sack and the motor compartment, and is expelled at the rear of the machine, with dust and small objects remaining in the sack. To protect the motor and fan from dust, the joints of the panel that separates the two compartments are sealed tightly and fitted with a replaceable filter with a very fine weave, which prevents even microscopic particles of dust from passing to the motor compartment.

How does a sewing machine work?

A seamstress sews with a single thread that is passed through the eye of a needle. A sewing machine uses two threads, and the eye of its needle is located in its point.

In the base of the machine is installed a case, in the interior of which is found a bobbin of thread.

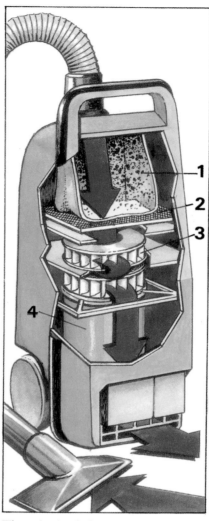

The principal elements of a vacuum cleaner: (1) the sack, (2) the filter, (3) the fan, (4) the motor.

A spool of thread is placed on the top of the sewing machine. This thread is drawn through the eye of a needle, which descends from above and passes through the cloth, drawing the thread after it. A hook attached to the bobbin catches the thread from above, curls it, and ties it around the thread of the bobbin. It remains only to tighten the stitch thus constituted. This is done when the needle rises, pulling the thread tight after it while the prongs beneath which the material is guided hold the cloth in position. The spool and the needle return to their original positions, and the cycle can begin anew.

How does a washing machine work?

Dirty clothes are washed by soaking and churning them in soapy water for a period of time.

The upper part of the machine is a vat, within which is a drum perforated with holes. This contains the dirty washing. Electrically heated water is mixed with soap and fills the vat. The drum is alternately rotated by an electric motor, first in one direction and then in another, churning the soiled items in the drum. Subtle electrical phenomena result from this. The dirt particles washed from the material by the soapy water, having the same electrical charge as the clothes, are repelled from them and remain suspended in the water. A pump then drains all the dirty water from the machine. Clean water is introduced for rinsing. The drum then turns at top speed to dry the laundry, the centrifugal force of the spinning drum expelling water through its perforated sides and into the bottom of vat, from which it is pumped and drained away. Electronic commands control the wash cycles and the temperature of the water.

How does a dishwasher work?

Dirty dishes are arranged on wide-mesh wire racks through which water can freely circulate. Rotating sprinklers installed above and below the racks vigorously spray jets of hot water onto the dishes.

A dishwasher works very much like a laundry machine. The dishes are washed by the action of soapy water. The dirty water is then drained from the machine. The dishes are rinsed with clean water that is introduced into the machine and then also drained. A thermostat raises the temperature inside the machine and heat condenses the remaining water, sterilizing the dishes at the same time and leaving them clean and dry.

Arranging each glass and dish as rationally as possible in a dishwasher assures an impeccable result. The correct detergent should always be used.

How does a lawn mower cut grass?

A lawn mower is equipped with an electric or gasoline-fueled motor that turns a horizontal blade to cut grass at the desired height.

A lawn mower easily cuts grass that has been trampled flat because the blade, turning like a fan, draws air upward and makes

the grass stand erect. The air drawn up into the lawn mower is vented through an opening to its side. The uniform cut gives a lawn a finish like that of a carpet. The cut grass is either expelled with the air to the side of the machine, or can be collected in a basket or sack that is attached to the lawn mower. Most lawn mowers are now equipped in this way, eliminating the need to rake the cuttings from the lawn afterward. A lawn mower also acts as a kind of vacuum cleaner and collects papers, dead leaves, and twigs in its sack.

How are matches made?

Matches have to meet strict standards of safety and reliability. They should light only when struck on an abrasive surface and should otherwise remain inert, and their inflammable tips must be non-toxic.

Safety matches only light when they are struck on an abrasive surface. The inflammable tip is composed of six different non-toxic substances, among which are potassium chlorate, gelatin as a bonding substance, and powdered glass. The striking surface has a phosphorus base. Matchsticks are made of wood cut into smooth cylinders, from which a blade then shaves sheets one-tenth of an inch thick. These sheets are then sliced into small squared matchsticks. Their tips are coated using a kind of carpet brush, and then they pass head-down into basins where they are soaked in paraffin and with an inflammable mixture. They are then dried and put into boxes.

How is rubber produced?

Two kinds of rubber exist: latex, or natural rubber, and synthetic rubbers. Latex is a secretion of the hevea, a tree native to the Amazon basin that grows in the tropics. Synthetic rubbers are products distilled from extracted hydrocarbons.

Initially, rubber was obtained by cutting incisions into the trunks or the creepers of wild, latex-producing hevea trees of the Amazonian forest. The latex was collected in small cups attached to the trunks. At the end of the 19th and the first years of the 20th

centuries, workers known as seringueros would tap the latex from trees growing wild throughout the forest. The seringueros

Latex, the basic raw material used in the production of rubber, comes from the hevea, a tree native to Brazil. Here, the sap is harvested.

would coagulate the latex, dry it, and roll it into balls, which they sent to Manaus, a city in the north of Brazil. The rubber was then processed and vulcanized (heated to a temperature of 285°F / 140°C with sulfur) which toughened it, made it waterproof, and enhanced its elasticity. In the 1920s the British successfully cultivated the hevea in Malaysia, where they

established huge plantations. In the 1930s chemists perfected synthetic rubbers, which today account for 60 percent of world consumption. But for certain uses latex remains irreplaceable.

What is a tire made from?

A tire is an envelope of reinforced synthetic rubber that surrounds an inner tube, itself made of rubber, in which is hermetically sealed an air chamber. But tubeless tires without inner tubes are coming into more frequent use.

The tire is much more complex than the inner tube. A reinforcing structure composed of layers of woven steel wires gives it its form and its relative rigidity. Because it is exposed to major sources of friction, it is much thicker and its rubber is hardened with doses of carbon or of chalk. Racing cars use special, very large tires which actually melt under the intense action of the forces of friction. The surface layer of the tire softens and literally sticks to the road, considerably improving the racing car's traction on the speedway.

What is glass made of?

Glass has been known since antiquity. It is made by melting silica (60 percent), lime, and potassium in a crucible at a temperature of 2,700°F (1,500°C). Special glasses can be manufactured by adding various ingredients.

Borax, for example, is added to manufacture optical glass. Lead is used in the manufacture of crystal, arsenic in the manufacture of enamels. Traditional methods of making glass could not produce transparent glass or perfectly flat sheets. With a hollow tube of metal, a ball of melted glass compound was taken and spun to give it a regular form. The glassmaker blew through the tube as if he were blowing a soap bubble. The globe of glass was detached with a knife, and was cleaved lengthwise and flattened to make panes of glass. Bubbles of air, however, remained trapped inside the sheets of glass made by this method. Today, to obtain a perfect result, the technology of flotation is used. Molten glass is poured into a basin of molten tin, over which it spreads perfectly without creating bubbles of air. Great care is taken in cooling the glass to ensure its quality. Glass is used to make many pieces of scientific apparatus, such as mirrors, lenses, prisms, retorts, and test tubes.

How are bottles manufactured?

In former times, bottles were made by glassblowers. This long, difficult, and dangerous technique – glassblowers had short life expectancies – is now used only for specially crafted pieces. Bottles are now made by machines that can produce thousands of vessels per hour.

The quantity of molten glass needed to produce a bottle is deposited into a first mold. The rough casting is then introduced into a definitive mold, which is divided into two parts. This mold is then sealed shut, and a powerful blast of compressed air pushes the glass compound to the sides of the mold, which is then cooled and opened.

There are many other methods of working with glass. It can be cast, molded, polished, diamond-engraved, hot-forged,

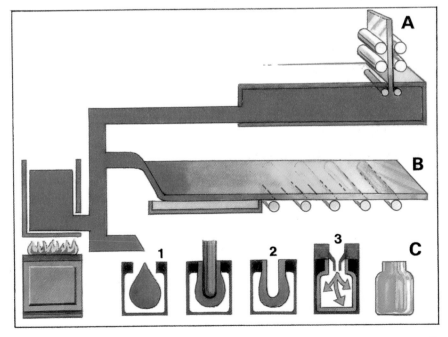

Three techniques are used to produce glass: (A) the water-cooled rolling mill; (B) flotation, in which molten glass is poured into a basin of melted tin; and (C) bottle-making. (1) molten glass, (2) intermediate stage, (3) air blower.

carved and even spun. Despite competition from the many types of plastic materials, glass still has a bright future.

Why does one see oneself in a mirror?

A mirror is made of a perfectly flat, unblemished plate of glass, the back of which is coated with a layer of very shiny metal, silver, or aluminum. Light passing through the glass is reflected by the layer of metal.

Glass can be worked in many different ways. Here, two glass tubes are joined.

In the days before it was known how to produce perfect, transparent sheets of glass, plates of polished metal were used. These surfaces were often dented, however, and they deformed images. They also oxidized and became tarnished. A mirror is made from a sheet of plate glass whose edges are then beveled. The sheet of glass is then polished with fine abrasives, and its back is coated with a thin layer of silver salt that is then sheathed with copper to protect it from oxidization. The mirror is finally protected with a coating of varnish. A flat mirror laterally inverts the image seen in it, so that the image is reversed from left to right. This defect can be corrected by using a second mirror. The image in a flat mirror is the same size as the object it reflects and appears to be behind the mirror.

How do glasses help us see better?

Glasses have two functions: protecting the eyes and correcting vision by compensating for deformations in the lenses of the eyes by appropriate corrective forms in the lenses of the glasses. Sunglasses and the protective goggles of welders filter blinding light. Glasses correct defective vision.

The eye resembles the black box of a camera. In order to see an object well, its image must be focused on the retina. Deformation of the crystalline lens of the eye moves the image away from the eye for those with myopia, or nearsightedness, and moves the image toward the eye for those with hypertropia, or farsightedness. Glasses with lenses specifically designed to compensate for these faults correct the vision. There are two principal kinds of corrective lenses. Divergent lenses, whose edges are thicker than their centers, correct myopia. Convergent lenses, whose centers are thicker than their edges, correct hypermetropia.

How does a microscope work?

A microscope uses a

system of convergent lenses. The first lens, the objective, located at the base of the tube, gives a real, enlarged image of the object placed on the stage of the microscope. The second lens, the ocular, located at the eyepiece, enlarges that enlarged objective image even more. Thus, if the objective has a power of enlargement of 15 and the ocular lens has a power of 20, the enlargement power of the microscope at this particular setting is 15 x 20, or 300.

In order to correct irritating colorations, supplementary lenses can be used. The microscope can be focused by adjusting the length of its tube. This is done by means of an adjustment rack that is moved by turning a calibrated screw. An object to be studied is sliced into a fine cross-section through which light can pass and is placed between two strips of glass, making a slide beneath which a source of bright light is placed. This makes it possible to see and study the object properly. When an object is enlarged 300 times, the fraction observed through a microscope receives 300 times less light than the object as a whole.

This is one of the last professional astronomical refracting telescopes, that of the observatory of Marseilles, France. Astronomers today use reflecting telescopes, which are much more powerful.

What is the difference between a refracting and a reflecting telescope?

The first optical device used to look into the distance was a refracting telescope, composed of a system of lenses. The modern telescope uses a parabolic (concave) mirror that captures light and focuses it on a second, flat mirror that is inclined at 45°, or on a hyperbolic mirror. The light is then transmitted to the eyepiece.

Galileo's refracting telescope combined a convergent lens as the objective lens and a divergent lens as the eyepiece. However weak it may have been, it did make important discoveries possible. The principle on which it was based is still applied today in opera glasses, which combine two small refracting telescopes of the kind used by Galileo. More powerful astronomical telescopes can be obtained by using two convex lenses. This yields an inverted image, which poses little problem for astronomical observation, but is a defect that is corrected in other telescopes by a third convex lens or by prisms. All astronomers now use reflecting telescopes, which are more powerful and less cumbersome.

Index

Index

Acknowledgments

1, 3, 4, 15, 17, 18, 21, 23, 24, 31 Shu Chi Nan/ Newton Publishing; 5, 6, 8–10, 12–14, 19, 20, 22, 25–30, 32–39 Zdenek Burian; 40 Le Moigne/Jacana; 42 Mammifrance/Jacana; 43, 46, 71, 74, 78, 82, 428 J.P. Varin/Jacana; 44, 52 J.M. Labat/Jacana; 45 M. Luquet/Jacana; 46, 77, 182 Rouxaime/Jacana; 47, 48, 76, 150, 170, 172, 183, 401 DR; 49 Mero/ Jacana; 47 T. Dressler/Jacana; 50, 55, 70, 91, 190, 274, 278 Jacana; 51 W. Layer/Jacana; 53, 54, 62, 175, 211, 223 S. Cordier/Jacana; 58 J. Robert/Jacana; 59, 207 R.Konig/Jacana; 59, 230, 273, 280 Frédéric/Jacana; 60 E. Dragesco/Jacana; 61, 263, 437 Y. Arthus-Bertrand/ Jacana; 63, 66, 174, 241, 242, 249 F. Gohier/Jacana; 67, 244 T. Walker/Jacana; 68 J. Blanc/Jacana; 69 J.L. Duibois/Jacana; 72 J. Cancalosi/Jacana; 73 Robertson/Jacana; 75 Hellio-Vaningen/Jacana; 77 H. Chaumaton/Jacana; 83 D. Cauchoix/Jacana; 84 K. Amsler/Jacana; 85 Vala/Jacana; 86 Soury/Jacana; 87 Mc Hugh/Jacana; 88 Kerban/Jacana; 89, 436 De Wilde/Jacana; 90 A. Kerneis-Dragesco/Jacana; 92, 198 Carrara/Jacana; 93 A. Lariviere/Jacana; 94, 97, 169, 185, 186, 187 T. da Cunha; 95, 214 C.M. Moitton/Jacana; 96, 215 J.P. Champroux/Jacana; 98 Axel/Jacana; 100, 394 T. Borredon/Explorer; 105, 157 Sipa-Press; 107 Voccon-Gibod/Sipa-Press; 109, 110 Explorer; 113 Rouquet/Explorer; 116 Tchaen/ Explorer; 117, 270 Sipa-lmage; 118 H. Royer/Explorer; 122, 130 STSCI-D. Berryl/Ciel et Espace; 120, 123, 124, 126, 134, 135, 136, 139, 143, 192–194, 201, 213, 218, 219, 376, 379, 381, 383, 384, 387 Editions Auzou; 127, 129 A. Fujii/Ciel et Espace; 127, 128, 133 J.M. Joly/Ciel et Espace; 147, 153 S. Brunier; 149 E. Seigoud; 158 Biron/Jacana; 161, 257 Kraft/ Explorer; 162 Claye/Jacana; 163, 166, 259 Ifremer; 165 A. and C. da Cunha; 171 Xavier/Jacana; 173, 431, 443, 455, 481, J.P. Thomas/Jacana; 176, 247 J.P. Nacivet/Explorer; 177 S. Kraseman/Jacana; 178 D. Huot/Jacana; 181 P. Plisson/Explorer; 184 F. Wirener/Jacana; 185, 186, 187, 188, 189 H. Nègre/ Explorer; 197 H. Berthoule/Jacana; 199, 212 C. Nardin/Jacana; 200, 226 P. Pilou/Jacana; 202 F. Lieutier/Jacana; 203 J.P. Soulier/Jacana; 204 P. Lome/Jacana; 205, 208 C. Favardin/Jacana; 206 Vasserot/Jacana; 209 C. Carré/Jacana; 210 M. Viard/ Jacana; 216 M. Le Roy/Jacana; 217 H. Miller/Jacana; 220–222 J. Brun/Jacana; 224 Rouan/Jacana; 225 R. Dulhoste/Jacana; 228, 240 G. Carde/Jacana; 229 Roguemant/Jacana; 232 K. Russel/Explorer; 232 T. Laird/Explorer; 237 C. Delu/Explorer; 238 Le Toquin/Jacana; 243 T. Dressier/Jacana; 245 N. Thibaut/Explorer; 246 Gludea/Explorer; 248 M. Cambazard/Explorer; 251 P. Petit/Jacana; 252 G. Sommer/Explorer; 233, 326, 374, 391 Ph. Roy/Explorer; 253, 266, 316 Barbey/Magnum; 254 S. Cordier; 258 R. Hernandez/Jacana; 260, 389 J.L. Bohin/Explorer; 261 Totopoulos/Explorer; 262, 436 G. Philippart de Foy/Explorer; 264 P. Wild/ Explorer; 265 M. Kraene/Explorer; 267 A. Le Toquin/ Explorer; 268 Rex/Sipa-Press; 271 P. Montbazet/ Explorer; 272, 452, 454, 457 Shone/Explorer/Gamma; 275 J.P. Ferrero/Explorer; 276 J.P. Varin/Jacana; 277 Le Toquin/Jacana; 282–285, 289, 290, 292–307, 309–314, 318, 346–349, 353, 355, 359, 360, 363–371, 445, 447, 451, 453 Kharbine-Tapabor; 286, 308, 338, 341, 354, 375, 380 Dagli Orti; 287 D. Clément/ Explorer; 291, 339, 340, 384, 392 Explorer; 320 Documentation Française/H. Stierlin; 323, 329, 331, 335 RMN; 321 Pratta/lconos/Explorer; 324 Monuments Historiques; 325 Varin/Explorer; 327, 422 Holton/Explorer; 328 Hernst/Magnum; 330 Lewandowski/RMN; 332–334 Lessing/Magnum; 336 BN; 337 Lenars/Explorer; 342 Le Floc'h/Explorer; 343 W. Peter/Explorer; 344, 352 J.L. Charmet/ Explorer; 351 J.L. Nou/Explorer; 357 Musée de Clermont-Ferrand/Coll. Roger-Viollet; 361 Keene/ Explorer; 362 BN Manuscrits Orientaux/Explorer; 315 FPG/Explorer; 372 Wysocki/Explorer; 376 Sioen/ Cedri; 377 D. Dorval/Explorer; 378, 379, 393 G. Boutin/Explorer; 382 P. Merchez/Explorer; 383 Viard/Explorer; 386 C. Cluny/Explorer; 387 A. Audano/Explorer; 388 J. Dupont/Explorer; 390 Ph. Leroux/Explorer; 395 Ribieras/Explorer; 396 H. Massumoto/Explorer; 397 A. Wolf/Explorer; 399 A. Autenzio/Explorer; 424 J.M. Gauthier/Cedri; 425 Mauger/Explorer; 426, 439, 441. Lenars/Explorer; 427 P. Weisbecker/Explorer; 429 R. Mattes/Explorer; 430 G. Sioen/Cedri; 432 Niou/Explorer; 433 H. Fouque/Explorer; 434 Ascani/Hoaqui; 435 Verbeek/Explorer; 438, 480 Layma/Explorer; 440 F.Jalain/Explorer; 444 P.Tetrel/Explorer; 442 Kord Russel/Explorer; 446 F. Delabarre; 448, 462, 479 Editions Auzou; 447, 450 Mouraret/Explorer; 451 J.P. Porcher/Explorer; 452 Plassart/Explorer; 455 Plisson/Explorer; 456 Wysocki/Explorer; 457 Gellie-Denize/Gamma; 458 Gladu/Explorer; 459 Benali/ Gamma; 460 J.P. Raynal/Explorer; 461 Gunther/ Explorer; 463 Starlight/Cosmos; 465 CNES; 466, 481 J.L. Bohin/Explorer; 468 Dannenbe/Cosmos; 470 W. Mullins/Explorer; 471 A.Wolf/Explorer; 472 Westlight/Cosmos; 473, 476 P.Gontier/Explorer; 474 JVC; 475 SicPTT; 478 V.Hazat/Explorer; 477 D.R.; 485, 489 D.P.A./Explorer; 484 A. Le Bot; 486 C. Boisvieux/Explorer; 488 G. Vanderelst/Explorer; 489 D.P.A.E./Explorer.